The QuickBASIC System

(For details, see Workshop II, Section 4.5, and Appendix 5)

Using the QuickBASIC Menus

Key	Action
Alt + <letter(s)>	Activates menu or menu option
arrow keys (↑, ↓)	Moves through options in a menu
Tab	Moves through fields of dialog box
Esc	Cancels current menu or dialog box
Enter	Executes selected menu option

Editing Programs

Key	Action
arrow keys (↑, ↓, →, ←)	Moves up, down, right, left in text
Home, End	Moves to beginning/end of line
Ctrl-Home, Ctrl-End	Moves to beginning/end of program
Page Up, Page Down	Moves up/down one screen
Tab, Shift-Tab	Indents/outdents line (or marked block)
Delete	Deletes highlighted character (or marked block)
Backspace	Deletes character preceding cursor
Insert	Toggles Insert/Overtype modes
Shift + <direction keys>	Marks a block of text
Shift-Delete	Cuts marked block (deletes and saves in clipboard)
Shift-Insert	Pastes text from clipboard at position indicated by cursor

Meanings of Function Keys

Key	Action
F1	Displays Help window for term at cursor location
Shift-F1	Displays Help on Help window
F2	Displays SUBs Dialog box
Shift-F2	Cycles through subprograms, functions, and main program
F3	Repeats last Find operation (option from Search menu)
F4	Toggles between output screen and editing window
F5	Executes program from line where it was halted
Shift-F5	Executes program from beginning
F6	Cycles between Editing window, Immediate window, and Help window (if active)
F7	Executes program up to cursor position
F8	Executes one line of program
F9	Toggles breakpoint at cursor position
Shift-F9	Selects Instant Watch of variable at cursor position
F10	Executes one line of program, with immediate execution of all subprograms and user-defined functions

Common-Sense

BASIC

Structured Programming with Microsoft® QuickBASIC

Common-Sense

BASIC

Structured Programming with Microsoft® QuickBASIC

Alice M. Dean/Gove W. Effinger
Skidmore College

Harcourt Brace Jovanovich, Publishers
and its subsidiary, Academic Press
San Diego New York Chicago Austin Washington, D.C.
London Sydney Tokyo Toronto

Apple Macintosh is a registered trademark of Apple Computer Corporation.

Commodore Amiga is a registered trademark of Commodore Business Machines Corporation.

IBM Personal Computer, IBM Personal System 2, IBM OS2, and IBM PC DOS are registered trademarks of International Business Machines Corporation.

Flight Simulator, Microsoft, the Microsoft logo, Microsoft® QuickBASIC, and Microsoft® QB Express are registered trademarks of Microsoft Corporation.

Monopoly is a registered trademark of Parker Brothers Corporation.

PacMan is a registered trademark of Midway Manufacturing Corporation: A Bally Company.

Some of the product names mentioned in this textbook are used for identification purposes only and may be trademarks of their respective companies.

ISBN: 0-15-512297-5
Library of Congress Catalog Card Number: 90-82764
Printed in the United States of America

For Laura and Sean, who,
by going off to kindergarten,
gave us time to write this book.

PREFACE

Common-Sense BASIC is an introduction to structured programming using Microsoft QuickBASIC on an IBM or compatible microcomputer. It is intended for use in a one-semester course for students who have little or no experience with computers, particularly those apprehensive about their ability in science and math. The book could also be used as a textbook by individuals who have purchased QuickBASIC for personal use.

The programming language presented here is *Full BASIC,* an extension of the original BASIC language approved by the American National Standards Institute in 1987. Because Full BASIC is a *structured* language, we refer to it as *Structured BASIC.* Structured BASIC retains the simplicity of the original BASIC language but incorporates—and improves upon—many features of such structured languages as Pascal. For example, every control structure has beginning and ending clauses, and the conditional looping structure, the DO...LOOP, is more flexible and natural than Pascal's comparable structures. After several years of teaching Structured BASIC, we have found that if a student designs a "common-sense" algorithm for a problem and refines it in a natural way, then Structured BASIC makes it easy to translate the algorithm into a program. This is why we have included "Common-Sense" in our title.

Just as Structured BASIC provides the language elements that make writing a program easy and natural, the Microsoft QuickBASIC programming system makes implementation and testing of programs simple and enjoyable. The QuickBASIC system provides an easy-to-use, menu-driven programming environment; its *Smart Editor* catches typing errors; and its incredibly fast compiler encourages students to test their programs thoroughly. In addition, there is an extensive on-line *Help system* that permits students to get information on the language and programming system. We focus on Microsoft QuickBASIC, Version 4.5, for IBM and compatible microcomputers, but we include additional instructions for Version 4.0 when it differs from Version 4.5. Our goal was to provide students with a text from which they can learn the full program design process, both the theory of structured programming and the practicality of producing a thoroughly tested program.

The text comprises two parts: two workshops followed by ten chapters. The workshops provide step-by-step tutorial introductions to the use of computers and the DOS operating system (Workshop I) and to the use of the QuickBASIC system (Workshop II). (More advanced features of DOS and the QuickBASIC system are covered in Appendices IV and V.) While some schools may have their systems set up in special ways, these workshops should bring most students quickly to the point where they feel comfortable using IBM microcomputers and the QuickBASIC system.

The core material of the book is contained in the first seven chapters. The fundamental principles of structured programming are introduced in these chapters, along with the major Structured BASIC control structures. Throughout the book, we emphasize top-down design, modularity, good program style, and thorough testing. And, after covering the main control structures, we introduce the use of subprograms and user-defined functions, tools central to the design of larger programs. We then cover arrays and provide a brief introduction to searching and sorting.

The last three chapters, 8 to 10, contain more advanced topics that may be suited to a particular course. Chapter 8 covers sequential data files and random-access data files. Both the text and exercises are presented so that an instructor who wishes to cover only sequential files can easily do so. Chapter 9 covers output design techniques, including text graphics and menus. And Chapter 10 covers graphics and sound, including a brief introduction to animation.

A typical one-semester course would probably begin with an introduction to using the system, referring the student to Workshops I and II as needed, and go on to cover most or all of the material in Chapters 1 to 7. In our course, we also cover sequential files (Sections 8.1 to 8.4) and Chapters 9 and 10 on graphics and sound. The material on graphics is certainly less central, and many instructors may choose to omit some or all of it. However, we have found that even our least motivated students often turn in beautiful programs incorporating animation and sound.

Most sections of this book conclude with a set of *practice exercises.* We have purposely kept them brief so that students will be encouraged to do *all* of them, as part of their reading, to confirm their understanding of the material. Each chapter concludes with a set of *review questions* and an extensive list of *programming problems.* Again, students should be encouraged to do *all* the review questions to reinforce what they have learned. Finally, the instructor should regularly assign a reasonable number of programming problems to ensure that students gain hands-on experience.

This book is accompanied by a *SAMPLES disk,* containing more than eighty sample programs corresponding primarily to examples presented in the text. These programs are an integral part of the text, and we encourage students to look at them as they read the book. They provide concrete examples of good program design; the QuickBASIC system makes it easy to try them out and experiment with modifications. Further information about the Samples Disk and the Instructor's Manual are available from your local Harcourt Brace Jovanovich representative.

Acknowledgments

We would like to thank all those whose encouragement and hard work have helped bring this book into existence: production editor Richard Lynch, who steered the book through a demanding production schedule; copy editor Candace Demeduc for her careful proof-reading of the manuscript and for her many helpful suggestions; and most of all, acquisitions editor Richard Bonacci, for his consistent support and help from beginning to end of the project.

We would also like to thank those reviewers whose careful reading and comments helped us produce the best manuscript we could: William J. Beaver, City College of San Francisco; Michael Berman, Glassboro State College; Jan W. Buzydlowski, Community College of Philadelphia; Mary U. Carlson, Valparaiso University; Barbara A. Gentry, Parkland College; Joe H. Jones, University of Arkansas; Lewis D. Miller, Cañada College; Jesse H. Ruder, Jr., Austin Community College.

Finally, we would like to thank our colleagues at Skidmore College for their continuing support. Many thanks to Bob DeSieno for encouraging us to take on this challenging project; to Mark Huibregtse, Pierre von Kaenel, and Bohdan Szanc, who used preliminary versions of the manuscript, for their helpful suggestions; and to Anita Miczek, our department secretary, for her many cheerfully offered hours of assistance, and for her consistent encouragement.

Alice M. Dean
Gove W. Effinger
Saratoga Springs, New York

CONTENTS

WORKSHOP

I

FUNDAMENTAL CONCEPTS OF COMPUTERS AND DOS

WORKSHOP PREVIEW

In this workshop, we'll get our first look at *microcomputers,* including terminology and a discussion of how they're used to solve a variety of problems; we'll introduce the idea of a *programming language* and discuss *structured programming* as a technique for solving problems; finally, we'll devote the bulk of this workshop to a step-by-step introductory session using *DOS*, the *IBM Disk Operating System.*

WS1.1 Introduction

If you know nothing at all about computers and programming but are eager to learn, this book is written for you. However, it's likely that you have already made use of a computer, even if you've never written a program—perhaps you've written term papers using a word processor, used a computer to study data from scientific experiments, or played video games from time to time. After you've worked your way through this book, you should have a better understanding of how software like this is designed; for instance, you should be able to *create* your own video games as well as many other programs. Our goal is to help you learn how to use the computer as a general purpose *tool* to solve a wide range of problems and to perform a variety of interesting and important functions.

There are three things we will need to accomplish this goal: first, a *computer*; second, a *programming language* that allows us to use the computer to carry out our instructions; third, and most important, an organized, common-sense approach to problem solving that allows us to take even very complex tasks, break them down into a collection of simpler problems to be solved, and then reassemble them for a complete solution. This technique is called **modular design**. **Structured programming** refers to a way of writing programs that reflects the modular design approach and that yields programs that are easy to understand and modify. In this workshop and in Workshop 2, we'll focus on the fundamental ideas and terminology of computers and programming languages; the rest of the text will be devoted to problem solving through modular design and structured programming.

WS1.2 Fundamental Ideas and Terminology of Computers

What is a computer—what distinguishes a computer from your digital watch or your electronic calculator? As technology advances, it becomes harder and harder to differentiate between these three objects, but there are at least two important characteristics that make a computer different from a calculator or a watch.

First, the functions performed by the latter two are *fixed*—for instance, some watches have a stopwatch function and some don't. A computer, on the other hand, can read and execute *any* properly written set of instructions—it will act like a stopwatch if we tell it to. A set of instructions written in a language understandable by the computer is called a **program**.

The second difference is the ability of a computer to deal with an arbitrarily large amount of data. Your calculator may have one or two "store" buttons, which allow you to enter a couple of numbers, which are then stored in the calculator's memory. But what if you want to store payroll data showing the number of hours worked each day in a given month by each of 50 employees—not many calculators can hold 1,500 numbers at one time, but computers have *unlimited storage capacity*. This property may not seem as crucial as the first difference, but without it our programs would be useless!

You can think of these two properties as the defining characteristics of a computer:

> **Computer** A machine that can read and execute sequences of instructions, called *programs*, and that has *unlimited storage capacity*.

The computers that we'll refer to throughout this text are the *IBM PC* and the *IBM PS2* (there are also many computers made by other companies that are *compatible* with these, i.e., they operate in exactly the same way; sometimes they're called *clones*). Pictures of these IBM computers are shown in Figure WS1.1.

The IBM PC and PS2 are examples of **microcomputers**—computers designed to be used by a single person (*PC* stands for "Personal Computer" and *PS2* stands for "Personal System 2"). Examples of other microcomputers that are not compatible with the IBM PC include the Apple Macintosh and the Commodore Amiga. Your school may also have a **minicomputer** or **mainframe**—these are larger, more powerful machines that are shared by many users at the same time (a minicomputer has more memory and speed of operation than a microcomputer but less than a mainframe). The most powerful computers available today are called **supercomputers**; they have vast amounts of memory and perform operations at rates that are thousands of times faster than a microcomputer. Despite the differences in computers, all have many similarities in their basic structure.

Hardware, the collection of physical items that make up a computer, consists of five main parts:

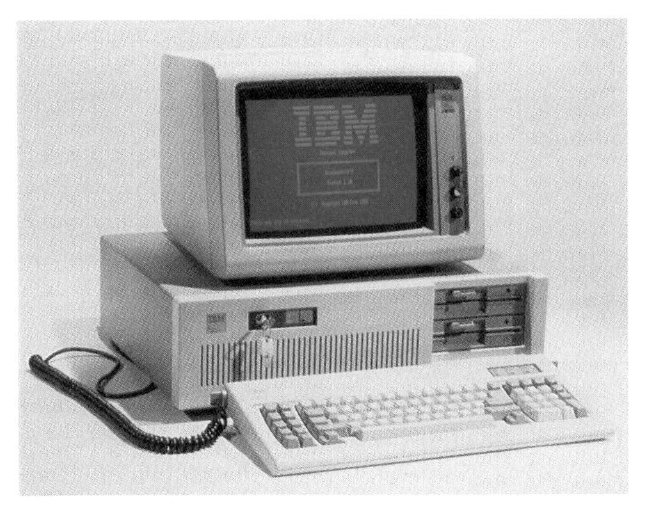

FIGURE WS1.1

IBM PC and PS2 Computers

1. **Central processing unit (CPU)**: The CPU is the circuitry that constitutes the physical "brains" of the computer. In the IBM PC and PS2, the CPU is housed in a rectangular metal box.
2. **Internal memory**: Every computer contains some circuitry that electronically stores the programs currently being executed and some or all of the data being used. The IBM PC, for example, can have up to about *640,000 bytes* of memory. A *byte* is a unit of memory; the simplest form of text storage requires 1 byte per letter. We sometimes say *640K bytes* or *640KB* instead of 640,000 bytes. The letter *K* is short for "kilo," which means 1000 (technically, one kilobyte equals 1024 or 2^{10} bytes, but that number is frequently rounded to 1000 for simplicity). The internal (or "main") memory of the IBM is housed in the box with the CPU.
3. **Input devices**: These machines allow you to enter ("input") data or instructions into the computer's memory. Our main input device will be the *keyboard*; other input devices include the *mouse* and the *light pen*.
4. **Output devices**: In contrast to input devices, output devices permit the computer to give information back to the user. The two main output devices we'll use are the computer's *monitor* (a video screen on which information is displayed); and a *printer*, which prints the information on paper.
5. **External storage devices**: In addition to its internal memory, a computer always contains one or more devices that allow you to store programs and data that can then be entered (or "read") into the computer's internal memory at another time. These devices are usually *disk drives* of some sort: machines that magnetically record ("write") and read data on a *floppy disk*, *hard disk*, or sometimes even a *compact disk* like those on which music is recorded. Note that a disk drive is really both an

input *and* an output device. The computer you use will probably have two *built-in* disk drives (i.e., they will be contained in the same housing as the CPU and the main memory) and might also have additional disk drives connected to it.

Don't be intimidated by all the terminology—it will become natural as you progress through the book. (See Figure WS1.2 for some photographs of computer hardware.)

WS1.3 Software and Programming Languages

In the last section, we observed that one of the important differences between a computer and a calculator is that the computer can read and execute *programs* written in an appropriate language. Another word for a computer program is **software**. In contrast to hardware (the physical circuitry of the machine), software is *not* built into the computer. A program can be stored on a disk and read into the computer—thus, a computer has access to an unlimited number of programs. Here are some examples of the kinds of programs that are used by computers:

Word processors: These programs allow the user to write and edit documents such as term papers, novels, letters, and so on. This textbook was written using a word processing program.

FIGURE WS1.2

Several Types of Computer Hardware

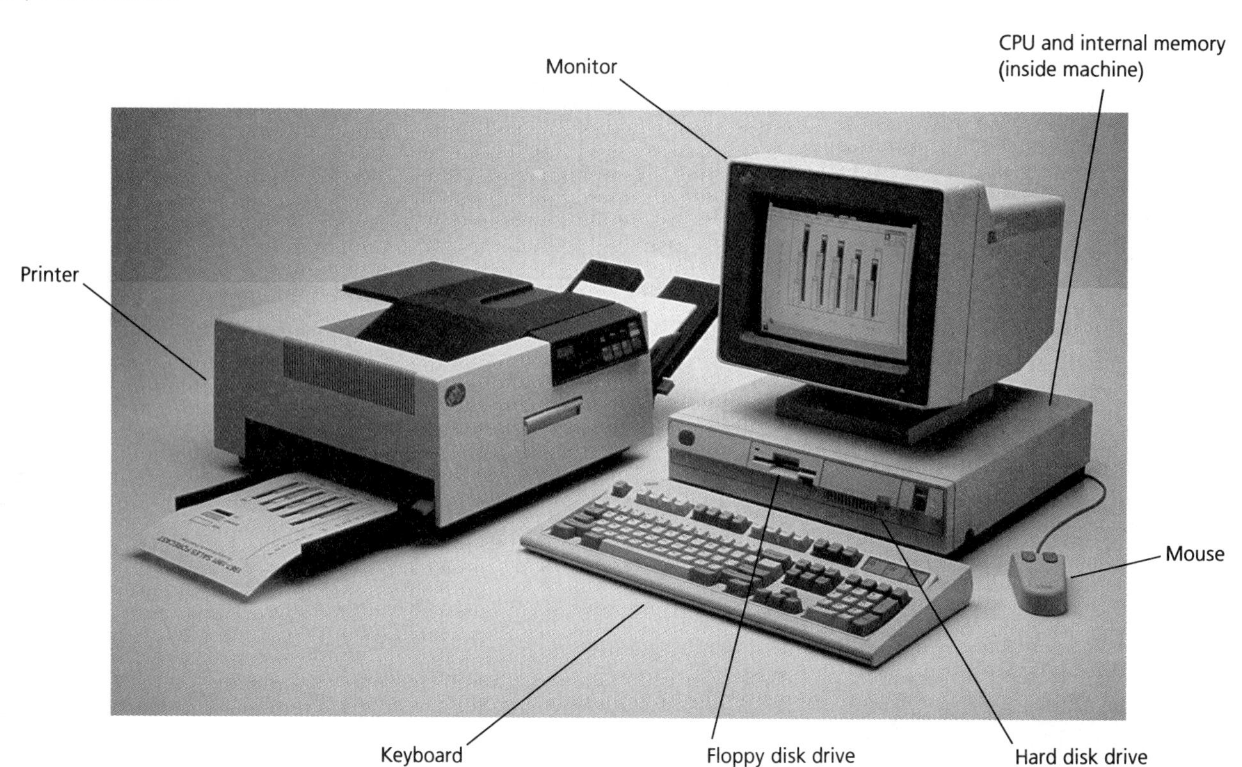

Spreadsheets: A spreadsheet program provides the user with a worksheet consisting of rows and columns into which numerical or textual data can be entered (e.g., a teacher's grade book). It also makes it easy for the user to perform a variety of operations on the data, such as sorting it, finding averages, and so on.

Games: There are programs that allow you to play almost any game imaginable, from traditional board games (Chess, Monopoly, Backgammon) to games that could not exist without modern computer graphics techniques (Flight Simulator, PacMan).

Operating systems: An operating system[1] is a collection of programs that help you coordinate the various functions of your computer. Its instructions let you read and write on disks, execute programs, activate the printer, and so on.

Programming language systems: These programs provide an environment in which you can write and execute computer programs in a wide variety of computer languages, such as BASIC, Fortran, Pascal, C, Prolog, Lisp, Cobol, and others.

For every computer, there is one language understandable by its CPU, called **machine language**. The "alphabet" for machine language usually consists of two symbols: the *binary numbers* 0 and 1. The reason for this is that all modern computers operate by using a complex system of electronic *switches*, which are either *off* (position 0) or *on* (position 1). Each such switch is called a *bit*, and it represents the smallest possible unit of information. More complex information (e.g., numbers bigger than 1 or letters and other characters) is stored in *memory locations* comprised of several bits. For example, the most common way to store letters requires a memory location consisting of 8 bits, called a *byte*.

Each *word* in machine language is a string of 0s and 1s and represents a single *instruction* (some instructions require two or three words). These instructions are very primitive: a typical machine language instruction might be to add 1 to a memory location or to set a memory location to 0; it might take quite a few machine language instructions (say 10 or so) to perform the more complex task of printing the word *hello* on the monitor screen.

Because of its very simple alphabet and primitive instructions, machine language is called a **low-level language**: easily understood by the machine, but not by the humans who write the programs. Most of the computer languages you may have heard of are **high-level languages**: these are very close to *natural languages*, such as English. In this text, we will learn to program in the high-level language called *QuickBASIC*. For example, the following instruction in QuickBASIC makes the computer print the word *hello* on the screen:

```
PRINT "hello"
```

[1] In the context of software, the word *system* usually refers to a *collection of programs* that perform a set of related tasks.

Many modern high-level languages, including QuickBASIC, adhere to the principles of *modular design* and *structured programming* that we mentioned earlier. We'll explore these notions in detail as we proceed, but, roughly speaking, they refer to a natural, common-sense approach to problem solving: given some relatively complex problem, we break it down into a sequence of simpler subproblems; we then write program segments (or ''modules'') to solve each of the subproblems; finally, we put these modules together to form a complete program.

QuickBASIC makes it easy to design a program built out of modules; it also provides instructions that correspond very closely to the instructions that would occur to us naturally—these natural instructions are called **BASIC statements**. We'll learn more about these ideas in Chapter 1; the remainder of this workshop and Workshop 2 are devoted to getting you to *use* a microcomputer and the QuickBASIC system.

WS1.4 Using IBM PCs, PS2s, and DOS

The best way to learn to solve problems using a computer is ''hands-on''; right from the start, the computer should be a tool for exploring ideas and testing solutions. In this section, we'll take you through an introductory session at the computer. Remember, though, that what a computer does is read and execute programs—without a program, it might as well be turned off!

In the last section, we introduced the term *operating system*, a collection of programs that coordinate the various functions of your computer. In a sense, an operating system is an *administrative program* that supplies you with the commands you need to tell the computer to examine the contents of a disk, output data to a disk or a printer, execute a special-purpose program (e.g., a word processor, a game, QuickBASIC), and so on. For this reason, you must always invoke the operating system when you first start the machine.

Operating systems are designed specially for each type of computer—for example, the IBM PC will have a different operating system than the Apple Macintosh. The operating system designed to work for both the IBM PC and PS2 is called **DOS**, short for **Disk Operating System.**[2] In the remainder of this section, we'll show you how to get started on your IBM PC or PS2 using DOS. *Note*: It's possible that your school has its computers set up in some special way that will not correspond exactly to our descriptions. If your machine doesn't behave the way we say it should, talk to your teacher, a computer assistant, or anyone who has some experience. Try not to

---

[2] There is another operating system, *OS2* (short for *Operating System 2*) designed especially for the IBM PS2, but in this text we will always assume you are using DOS.

IBM PC
Two floppy drives

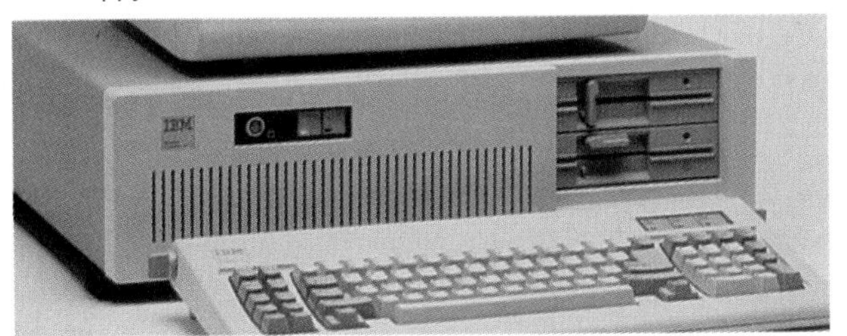

IBM PC
Floppy drive and hard drive

IBM PS2
Two floppy drives

IBM PS2
Floppy drive and hard drive

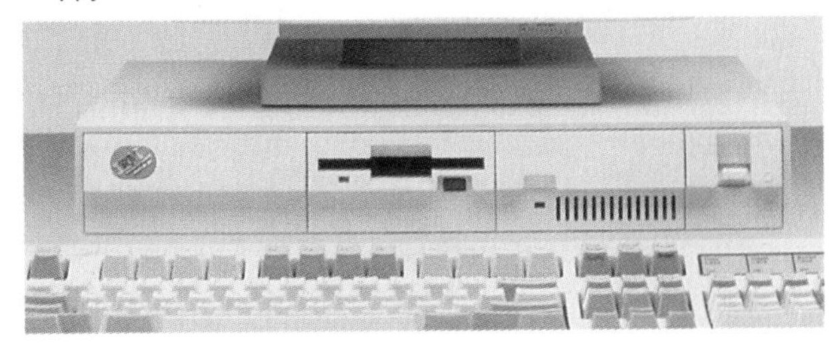

FIGURE WS1.3

Disk Drives

get too frustrated; the ideas we're about to discuss will soon be second nature, but it's always confusing when you are just beginning.

To get started, you will need a computer and one or more disks. To know what kind of disks you'll need, you must first examine the computer you're going to use. As we said earlier, most machines have two built-in disk drives: either two *floppy-disk drives* or one floppy drive and one *hard-disk drive*. (Even if your machine has two floppy drives, it may also have a hard drive—don't hesitate to *ask* someone!) A floppy drive appears as a narrow opening on the front of the computer, while a hard drive appears as a closed rectangular area; both will have small LEDs (light-emitting diodes) that light when they are in use. The hard disk itself is permanently installed *inside* the machine (for this reason it is sometimes called a *fixed disk*), while a floppy disk is *removable*.

See Figure WS1.3 for photographs of machines with two floppy drives and machines with one floppy and one hard drive for both the IBM PC and the IBM PS2. (If you're using a compatible machine made by another company, it should look similar to one of the photos in the figure.)

Now, examine the width of the opening on the floppy drive: is it more or less than 4 inches wide? There are two common sizes of floppy disks: 3½ inch and 5¼ inch. The more modern 3½-inch disks are actually quite rigid, but we'll call both kinds "floppy" disks (see Figure WS1.4).

For the purposes of this section, you'll need up to *four disks*. The number of disks you'll need and the instructions you'll follow for the

FIGURE WS1.4

Floppy Disks

remainder of this section will depend on whether or not your machine has a hard drive.

> ***Important: Determine whether the machine you'll be using has a hard drive (ask a teacher or assistant if necessary). For the rest of this section, follow the instructions that apply to your machine.***

MACHINES WITH HARD DISKS

The SAMPLES disk: This text is accompanied by a floppy disk containing sample programs and other examples; the examples on the SAMPLES disk are referred to throughout the book. Ask your teacher for a copy of this disk.

Two data disks: You'll need a disk on which to *save* the work that you do; in addition, you should always have a *backup disk* on which to make a second copy of your work in case one disk gets damaged. Thus, you'll need two blank floppy disks (either 3½ inches or 5¼ inches wide).

MACHINES WITHOUT HARD DISKS

A DOS disk: This means a disk that has DOS (Disk Operating System—remember?) on it. When we turn on the machine and start DOS, we say we are *booting up*; for this reason, a disk with DOS on it is also called a *boot disk*. Ask your teacher or a computer assistant for a copy of this disk.

The SAMPLES disk: This text is accompanied by a floppy disk containing sample programs and other examples; the examples on the SAMPLES disk are referred to throughout the book. Ask your teacher for a copy of this disk.

It's almost certain that your machine's hard disk has DOS (Disk Operating System—remember?) stored on it, so you will not need a separate floppy disk for it.

Two data disks: You'll need a disk on which to *save* the work that you do; in addition, you should always have a *backup disk* on which to make a second copy of your work in case one disk gets damaged. Thus, you'll need two blank floppy disks (either 3½ inches or 5¼ inches wide).

Once you've obtained the disks you need, you're ready to get started.

The rest of this section should be read while working at a computer with the necessary disks as described above. Check off each step as you complete it.

Step 1 (identifying the drives). After you've obtained the disks you need, sit down at a computer. Before you turn it on, you first need to learn how to refer to the disk drives, which are named using a single letter followed by a colon (*A:*, *B:*, *C:*, etc.). The following naming conventions usually hold:

Name	Type	Description
A:	Floppy	The left-hand slot on the machine (the upper slot on some machines)
B:	Floppy	The right-hand slot on the machine (the lower slot on some machines)
C:	Hard	The built-in hard drive

If your machine has two floppy drives, they are called *A:* and *B:*. If your machine has a hard drive, it is called *C:*, and the single floppy drive is called *A:*. We also refer to these drives as the **A-drive**, **B-drive**, and so on.

Step 2 (inserting the DOS disk). See below for instructions pertaining to the type of machine you have.

MACHINES WITH HARD DISKS

Omit Step 2; skip to Step 3.

MACHINES WITHOUT HARD DISKS

If you have a machine with two floppy drives, it's time to put the DOS disk in the machine. Follow the instructions below and refer to Figure WS1.4.

If you have a 5¼-inch disk, insert it in the *A-drive* so that the label is facing up and the oval segment of exposed disk goes in first; when it's all the way in, close the door of the disk drive.

If you have a 3½-inch disk, insert it in the *A-drive* so that the metal label is facing up and goes in first; you should hear a click when it's all the way in.

Step 3 (booting up). You're now ready to boot up your machine. Both the computer and the monitor have on-off switches: *turn both switches on*. You should hear the whirring noise of the fan in the computer; then, after anywhere from a few seconds to a minute, you should see the disk drive lights come on as the computer looks for the DOS system.

After the start-up program has been executed, the monitor should display a message indicating the date and another message "prompting" you to change it if you wish. Find and press the key labelled ←┘ or **←┘ Enter**; it is in the middle of the right side of the keyboard, just to the right of the letter keys. Whenever we want to refer to this key, we'll use the notation <Enter>. You'll see a similar message concerning the time: Again, press **<Enter>**. (If you wish to change the date or time, go ahead and try it out, copying the format used by the machine.)

You should now see a copyright message followed by the **DOS prompt**, which starts with a letter and ends with a greater-than symbol (>) and a dash flashing on and off (called the **cursor**). The DOS prompt probably looks like one of the following:

MACHINES WITH HARD DISKS	MACHINES WITHOUT HARD DISKS
C> *or* **C:\>**	**A>** *or* **A:\>**

The letter (*A* or *C*) tells you which disk drive is currently being used; we call this the **default drive**. The computer will assume that any instructions you enter refer to this drive (unless you specify a different disk drive, as we'll learn to do later). After you first boot up, the initial default drive is the one containing the DOS operating system.

Step 4 (files and file names). All the programs and other data that you save on a disk are organized into **files**, which you can create, read, copy, delete, print, and so on. Every file has its own name. In the next several steps, we will experiment with commands for manipulating the files on a disk, but first we must learn how files are *named*.

A file name consists of three parts. *First*, the name of the disk drive where the file is to be found; *second*, the main part of the name, which can have up to eight characters; *third*, a "suffix," consisting of a period followed by up to three characters. Although some characters are not permitted in file names, letters and numbers are allowed. The first and third parts of the file name are optional—if you omit the drive name, the computer assumes you mean the default drive. This seems confusing, but it becomes simple after a little practice. Some examples will help:

1. A:MOMLETT.TXT	A file on the disk in the A-drive
2. C:MOMLETT.TXT	A file on the hard drive (1 and 2 are two different names)
3. B:ASSIGN7.BAS	A file on the disk in the B-drive
4. B:ASSIGN7	*Another* file on the B-drive (3 and 4 are two different names)
5. SURVEY.DOC	A file on the default drive (look at the DOS prompt to see which drive is the default)

The optional suffixes are usually used to help indicate what *kind* of file we are naming. For example, for files that contain a document with regular text, like a letter to Mom or a term paper, we might use the suffix *.TXT* or *.DOC* to remind us. For files that contain programs, we might use suffixes that tell us which programming language is being used, for instance, *.BAS* for BASIC, *.FOR* for Fortran, and so on. Note that the computer does not distinguish between upper and lowercase in file names. Each of the following refers to the same file: A:JUNK.TXT, a:junk.txt, A:jUnK.TxT.

Now, let's use the SAMPLES disk to try out some commands that let us manipulate files.

Step 5 (inserting the SAMPLES disk). See below for instructions pertaining to the type of machine you have.

MACHINES WITH HARD DISKS

At this point, the A-drive on a hard-disk machine should be empty. Following the directions in Figure WS1.4, insert the SAMPLES disk into the A-drive; be sure to close the drive door if there is one.

MACHINES WITHOUT HARD DISKS

At this point, your DOS disk should be in the A-drive, and your B-drive should be empty. Following the directions in Figure WS1.4, insert the SAMPLES disk in the B-drive; be sure to close the drive door if there is one.

Step 6 (the DIR command). The DIR command lets you see a list of the files on any specified drive (DIR is short for "directory"). Let's first get a list of the files on your DOS disk. At the DOS arrow prompt, type the following (as with files, the computer will not distinguish between upper and lowercase letters for DOS commands):

MACHINES WITH HARD DISKS	MACHINES WITHOUT HARD DISKS
`> DIR C:`	`> DIR A:`

The computer should respond by giving you a list of all the files on the specified drive (if the list is very long, the beginning may have gone off the screen; we'll learn a way to prevent this shortly). The directory listing you obtained should look similar to that in Figure WS1.5 (although the specific information will be different, of course).

Each line in the list gives information about a single file. First comes the main part of the file name, then its suffix (note that everything is aligned in columns to make it easy for you to scan the list when searching for a particular name or suffix). Next comes the number of bytes the file occupies on the disk, and finally the date and time when that file was written on the disk. At the bottom of the list appears the number of unused bytes that remain on the disk.

Note that the last line in the list looks different; instead of a number of bytes, it shows "<DIR>." That is because BOOK is not a file but rather a **subdirectory**: a collection of several files all gathered under the group name BOOK. As you accumulate files, you may find subdirectories useful for organizing your files and making them easy to locate. To learn about subdirectories, see Appendix 4.

Now, let's see a directory listing of the SAMPLES disk. Simply type **DIR** and then the name of the drive that the disk is in; that is, type one of the following:

MACHINES WITH HARD DISKS	MACHINES WITHOUT HARD DISKS
`> DIR A:`	`> DIR B:`

Notice that we have tried to name the files on the SAMPLES disk so that you can tell *where* in the text the file is discussed and what *type* of file it is (i.e., a program or a text file). For instance, there are two files with the following names: W01ST07.TXT and C03EX09.BAS. The first file name (W01ST07.TXT) indicates that the file is discussed in Workshop 1, Step 7 and contains *text*; the second file name (C03EX09.BAS) indicates that the file is discussed in Chapter 3, Example 9 and contains a BASIC program.

It is always good practice to choose* descriptive file names *that give you information about what the file contains.

Now, type the following (note that no drive is specified):

```
> DIR
```

When you don't specify a drive, the computer assumes you want the default drive and shows you that drive's directory; so you should see a listing of the files on the "boot drive" (the drive from which the computer read DOS during boot-up).

```
A>dir a:

 Volume in drive A has no label
 Directory of  A:\

COMMAND  COM     25307   3-17-87  12:00p
NOTES    TXT      4256   6-12-90  10:47a
NOTES              916   6-19-90  10:46a
GRADES   TXT      1536   6-13-90   1:59p
DRAW     BAS      1536   3-01-90   2:49p
BOOK         <DIR>       7-12-90  12:37p
        6 File(s)    693248 bytes free

A>_
```

FIGURE WS1.5

Directory Listing

For the last part of this step, let's learn how to make a long directory listing *pause* so that you can read the beginning before it goes off the screen. Look on the left-hand side of your keyboard for a gray key labelled **Ctrl** (short for "control"). This key is used like the Shift keys to allow other keys to have multiple meanings. For example, the S key pressed all by itself prints a lowercase *s* on the screen, whereas pressing **Shift-S** (i.e., pressing **S** while holding down the **Shift** key) prints uppercase *S* on the screen. Pressing **Ctrl-S** has yet another meaning: if characters on the screen are "scrolling" by, as in a long directory listing, pressing **Crtl-S** causes scrolling to pause. Try it by doing a **DIR** command and then pressing **Ctrl-S.** When you want scrolling *to resume*, press **Ctrl-S** again: the Ctrl-S key combination "toggles" the screen between scrolling and pausing.

An alternative version of the DIR command will make the scrolling pause when the screen fills up. Type the following (P is for "pause"):

```
> DIR /P
```

Note that the Ctrl-S toggle can be used to stop and start screen scrolling in a variety of situations other than with the DIR command (for example, the TYPE command, described in Step 7 below).

Step 7 (the TYPE command). We've seen that both the DOS disk and the SAMPLES disks contain quite a few files. The next logical step is to *view the contents* of these files. The DOS command that lets you view the contents of a file on your monitor is the TYPE command. Let's see the contents of the file W01ST07.TXT on the SAMPLES disk.

MACHINES WITH HARD DISKS

The SAMPLES disk should be in the A-drive. Thus, you should enter:

```
> TYPE A:W01ST07.TXT
```

MACHINES WITHOUT HARD DISKS

The SAMPLES disk should be in the B-drive. Thus, you should enter:

```
> TYPE B:W01ST07.TXT
```

The contents of W01ST07.TXT should appear on the screen. As with the DIR command, you can use Ctrl-S to make the screen stop and start scrolling.

The only files that will be displayed properly by the TYPE command are *ASCII files,*[3] which are files that contain ordinary text characters. This means that the TYPE command will have limited usefulness for us, because BASIC programs created using the QuickBASIC programming system are not usually stored as ASCII files. To see what we mean, try using the TYPE command as you did above, but this time use the file W01ST07A.BAS; although there may be some recognizable words, there will also be a lot of bizarre symbols and maybe a beep or two!

To view BASIC programs, we'll use commands supplied by the QuickBASIC programming system. Nonetheless, we'll need the TYPE command from time to time to print or view files containing *data* that we'll use with our programs.

Intermission: In this long section, the many new terms may seem confusing—but they'll seem simple in a week or so. Check off the steps as you complete them and take a break if you need one; we still have a few more DOS commands to learn. You may find it useful to refer to the *summary* at the end of this workshop—and you may find it refreshing to simply turn off the machine and come back to it a little later!

Step 8 (formatting the data disks): This step concerns a command that you don't use very often, but which you'll need whenever you wish to begin using a *new* floppy disk, such as the new data disks you just obtained. The **FORMAT** command prepares a new floppy disk for reading and writing by initializing it in a way that makes it usable with the DOS operating system. (Each computer's operating system formats disks specifically for use on that computer; therefore, a disk formatted by DOS for use on an IBM PC or PS2 could not be used on an Apple computer, whose operating system formats disks to its own specifications.) You'll need to use the FORMAT command twice in this session, once for each floppy data disk.

---

[3] ASCII is an acronym for American Standard Code for Information Interchange, which is a standard system for representing characters on a computer.

Important: The FORMAT command* erases everything on the disk; *thus, you should use this command* only once *for each floppy disk. If you use FORMAT after you have data on your disk, all your data will be erased!

MACHINES WITH HARD DISKS

Remove the SAMPLES disk from the A-drive. Insert one of your new data disks and enter the following command:

```
C> FORMAT A:
```

MACHINES WITHOUT HARD DISKS

Remove the SAMPLES disk from the B-drive. Insert one of your new data disks and enter the following command:

```
A> FORMAT B:
```

Follow the instructions that appear on the screen; the machine will then take a minute or so to format your disk. (If the message "Bad command or file name" is displayed, it probably means that your DOS disk does not contain the FORMAT command; ask someone for help in obtaining the correct DOS disk.)

If you have a second floppy data disk, remove the first disk and repeat the FORMAT process for the second disk.

If you haven't yet done so, write your name on disk labels and stick them onto your data disks for identification (be careful about writing directly on the disks; the pressure of a pen can dent the magnetic material inside and destroy the disk!). Figure WS1.4 shows where the labels should be positioned on the disks.

Step 9 (the COPY command). Use the DIR command (Step 6) to see a directory listing for one of your newly formatted data disks; you should see the message "File not found," because your disk doesn't yet have any files on it. In this step, we'll use the COPY command to copy some files from the SAMPLES disk to your data disk.

To use the COPY command, you must first indicate which file you want to copy and then where you want to copy it to. In other words, the COPY command has the following form:

>COPY <name of file to copy> <location to copy it to>

Each of the three words in the COPY command is separated by a space. In order to illustrate the COPY command, suppose we have a disk in the A-drive that contains files named INFO.TXT and FIRST.BAS. Here are some examples:

`>COPY A:INFO.TXT B:`	Makes a copy of INFO.TXT from the A-drive onto the B-drive (the copy's name is B:INFO.TXT)
`>COPY A:FIRST.BAS C:JUNK`	Makes a copy of FIRST.BAS from the A-drive onto the C-drive with the name JUNK

`>COPY FIRST.BAS B:NUM1.BAS`	Makes a copy of FIRST.BAS from the *default drive* (no drive name was included in the file name of the file to be copied) to B-drive with the name B:NUM1.BAS
`>COPY A:INFO.TXT MOREINFO`	Makes a copy of INFO.TXT from the A-drive onto the default drive with the name MOREINFO

Note: Do not make copies of the files on your DOS disk without permission from the company that produced it—these files are the copyrighted property of that company (e.g., IBM or Microsoft; the company's name should be displayed when you boot up).

Remove your data disk from the machine and insert the SAMPLES disk, so that we can practice the COPY command by making several copies of the file W01ST07.TXT. Using the style of the examples above, make the following copies of W01ST07.TXT:

MACHINES WITH HARD DISKS

1. A copy on the hard disk. With the SAMPLES disk in the A-drive, you could type:

   `>COPY A:W01ST07.TXT C:`

   or

   `>COPY A:W01ST07.TXT C:W01ST07.TXT`

   Use the **DIR** command to check that the file has been copied.

2. A copy with the same name on one of your data disks. Remove the SAMPLES disk from the disk drive and replace it with one of the data disks; we'll copy the file *from* the hard disk *to* the data disk. Before reading the commands given below, look at the general format of the COPY command above and write down what you think is a correct command.

MACHINES WITHOUT HARD DISKS

1. A copy with the same name on the DOS disk. For example, if the SAMPLES disk is in the B-drive and your DOS disk is in the A-drive, you could type:

   `>COPY B:W01ST07.TXT A:`

   or

   `>COPY B:W01ST07.TXT A:W01ST07.TXT`

   Use the **DIR** command to check that the file has been copied.

2. A copy with the same name on one of your data disks. Remove the SAMPLES disk from the disk drive and replace it with one of the data disks; we'll copy the file *from* the DOS disk *to* the data disk. Before reading the commands given below, look at the general format of the COPY command above and write down what you think is a correct command.

On a hard-drive machine, with the data disk in the A-drive, you could type:

```
>COPY C:W01ST07.TXT A:
```

or

```
>COPY C:W01ST07.TXT A:W01ST07.TXT
```

Again, use the **DIR** command to check that the file has been copied.

In general, copying from one floppy disk to another on a hard-drive machine is a *two-step* process as above: first, we copy *from* the SAMPLES disk in the A-drive to the C-drive; then, we replace the SAMPLES disk with the data disk and copy *from* the C-drive *to* the A-drive.

3. A *backup copy* of the file on your other data disk. Remember that the purpose of having two data disks is to *duplicate* files so that if one disk is damaged, you'll still have a copy of the file on the other disk. To make the backup copy, simply repeat the procedure described above, using your second data disk for the copy.

4. Yet *another* copy (this is the last one—we promise!) of the file on the disk in the default drive (that should be the hard disk), but with the name MOREINFO. Remember that if you omit the drive name the computer assumes you mean the default drive, so you can type:

```
>COPY W01ST07.TXT MOREINFO
```

On a two-floppy machine, with your data disk in the B-drive and your DOS disk in the A-drive, you could type:

```
>COPY A:W01ST07.TXT B:
```

or

```
>COPY A:W01ST07.TXT B:W01ST07.TXT
```

Again, use the **DIR** command to check that the file has been copied.

Note that on a two-floppy machine, an alternative way to copy from the SAMPLES disk to a data disk would be to remove the DOS disk and place both data disks in the machine; then you could copy from A: to B: or vice versa.

3. A *backup copy* of the file on your other data disk. Remember that the purpose of having two data disks is to *duplicate* files so that if one disk is damaged, you'll still have a copy of the file on the other disk. To make the backup copy, simply repeat the procedure described above, using your second data disk for the copy.

4. Yet *another* copy (this is the last one—we promise!) of the file on the disk in the default drive (that should be the hard disk), but with the name MOREINFO. Remember that if you omit the drive name the computer assumes you mean the default drive, so you can type:

```
>COPY W01ST07.TXT MOREINFO
```

After using the COPY command, you should always use the DIR command to confirm that the file has been copied as you intended.

Step 10 (printing text). In Step 7, we learned how to use the TYPE command to view the contents of a text file on the screen. Now, we'll learn two methods for printing text on the *printer* rather than on the screen. The first method uses the COPY command.

There are several words that have special meaning when used in place of file names in DOS commands. One of these words is **PRN**, which is short for "Printer"; when you copy a file to PRN, that means you *print the file*! Try printing out the file W01ST07.TXT (a copy of which should be on the A-drive at this point) by typing:

```
>COPY A:W01ST07.TXT PRN
```

If your computer is connected to a printer that is turned on, the contents of the file W01ST07.TXT should be printed out in a minute or two. (Note: The first time you use the printer, it's a good idea to find someone to help you with its controls.)

As with the TYPE command, this method of printing files will have limited usefulness for us because BASIC programs created using QuickBASIC are not stored as ASCII files. However, the COPY command itself will still be useful for making backup copies of files.

There is another method of printing that we'll find useful when we want to print the **output** of BASIC programs, that is, the text that appears on the screen when we execute the program, as opposed to the program itself. This method uses a special key on the keyboard labelled either **Print Screen** or **PrtSc**, depending upon the particular keyboard you're using. In either case, it should be somewhere on the right-hand side of the keyboard; stop and find it now.

This key does just what it says: it prints out whatever currently appears on the screen. To use it, you hold the Shift key while pressing the PrtSc key: try it now by pressing **Shift-PrtSc**. If your machine is connected to a printer, the printer should then print out the current contents of the computer monitor.

Step 11 (the DEL command). The **DEL** command (short for "delete") lets you delete files from a disk. In Step 9, you should have created two files, on your DOS disk or hard disk, named W01ST07.TXT and MOREINFO. Use the DIR command (Step 6) to get a directory listing for your default drive, then confirm that these two files are listed—if they're not, repeat Step 9. Now, delete the MOREINFO file by typing the following command:

MACHINES WITH HARD DISKS	MACHINES WITHOUT HARD DISKS
`>DEL C:MOREINFO`	`>DEL A:MOREINFO`

Now, get another directory listing for your default drive; the file MOREINFO should no longer be there. There are two things worth noting. First, remember that once you delete a file it's *gone forever*! So be careful to delete only the files that you are sure you don't want. Second, it's a good idea to include the drive prefix in the file name (e.g., C: or A: in the above example), so that you'll be sure of deleting the correct file (if you don't use the drive name, the computer will look for the file on the default drive).

Now, delete the other file you created on your default drive by following the above procedure, using the file name W01ST07.TXT instead of MOREINFO. Get yet another directory listing to confirm that this file is gone.

To complete this step, check the directories of each of your data disks to see if they have W01ST07.TXT on them (if you've followed all our directions, they should); delete these files (being sure to use the appropriate drive prefix), and then do a final directory check to verify that they are gone.

Step 12 (changing the default drive). When you first boot up your machine, the default drive is the A-drive on a two-floppy machine and the C-drive on a hard-drive machine. Most machines have two (or more) drives, and sometimes you'll find that most of the files you want are on the second drive; in this case, you may wish to *change the default drive*. The command to do this is simply the name of the drive.

MACHINES WITH HARD DISKS	MACHINES WITHOUT HARD DISKS
With your data disk in the A-drive, type:	With your data disk in the B-drive, type:
`>A:`	`>B:`

Look at the DOS input prompt; it should have changed to indicate the new default drive.

To change back to the first drive, simply type its name:

MACHINES WITH HARD DISKS	MACHINES WITHOUT HARD DISKS
`>C:`	`>A:`

Again, notice that the input prompt has changed to indicate the new default drive. Also note: If you wish to change to one of the floppy drives, you *must* have a disk in that drive.

Step 13 (ending the session). That's all for now. When you are done, remove your data disks and turn off both the computer *and* the monitor. Congratulations on hanging in there through this last step!

Workshop Summary

In this workshop, we've learned some fundamental ideas about computers and programming. A *computer* is basically a machine with unlimited storage capacity that can read and execute *programs*, which are sets of instructions written in a computer language. In this text, we are using a microcomputer, and all references pertain to the *IBM PC* and the *IBM PS2*.

The physical objects that make up a computer system are called *hardware*. The five main types of computer hardware are: the *CPU*, the circuitry that controls the operation of the machine; the *main memory*, where the computer stores the programs and data that it is currently using; *input devices*, such as a keyboard or mouse; *output devices*, such as a monitor or printer; and *external storage devices* (i.e., *disk drives*).

The programs executed by a computer are also called *software*, and they are written in a variety of computer languages. The most primitive computer language, understood by the computer but difficult for humans to understand, is *machine language*, which is a *low-level language*. *Higher-level languages*, such as BASIC, Pascal, or Fortran, are close to natural languages like English. We will study the high-level language called *QuickBASIC*; this language facilitates the use of *structured programming* to write programs based on a commonsense approach to problem solving called *modular design*.

When a computer is first turned on or "booted up," it executes a program called the *(disk) operating system (DOS)*, which contains commands that allow you to manipulate files on your disks or execute other programs such as QuickBASIC. You know you are in the operating system if you see the *DOS prompt*, which consists of a letter indicating the default drive and the greater-than symbol (>), that is, something similar to this:

```
A>
```

We learned several *DOS commands* that allow us to manipulate the files on our disks in a variety of ways. These commands are:

DIR <drive name>: Lists all the files on the disk in the specified disk drive; if no drive name is given, the files on the disk in the *default drive* are listed. To make the screen pause during a long directory listing (or anytime output goes off the screen), press **Ctrl-S**; to resume screen scrolling, press **Ctrl-S** again. An alternative for pausing in the DIR command is to type **DIR /P**.

TYPE <file name>: Displays the contents of the specified file *on the monitor screen*; this works properly only for ASCII files.

FORMAT <drive name>: "Formats" the floppy disk in the specified disk drive, that is, prepares the disk for reading and writing files. Anything that was previously on the disk is *erased*.

COPY <file to copy> <location to copy it to>: Makes a copy of the indicated file in the indicated location. If the location is a file name, that will be the name of the copied file; if the location is simply a drive name, the copy will be made on that drive with the same name as the original file. The special name *PRN*, which stands for "printer," can be used in place of file names. The command *COPY <filename> PRN* will *print* the indicated file (this works properly only for *ASCII files*, which are files containing text characters).

The contents of the monitor *screen*, as opposed to the contents of a file, can be printed by pressing **Shift-PrtSc**.

DEL <file name>: Deletes the indicated file from the disk (as usual, if no drive name is given, the computer assumes you're referring to a file on the *default drive*).

<Drive name>: Typing a drive name all by itself (e.g., **A:**, **B:**, or **C:**) causes the computer to make that the *default drive*.

Review Questions 

1. Explain each of the following terms:

   (a) computer
   (b) program
   (c) microcomputer
   (d) minicomputer
   (e) mainframe
   (f) supercomputer
   (g) hardware
   (h) CPU
   (i) internal memory
   (j) input device
   (k) output device
   (l) disk drive
   (m) software
   (n) machine language
   (o) low-level language
   (p) high-level language
   (q) operating system
   (r) DOS

2. Explain briefly the different kinds of disk drives a microcomputer can have (floppy and hard, 3½ inch and 5¼ inch) and explain how to refer to disk drives using letters.

3. Explain how files are named on the IBM PC and PS2 machines.

4. Explain carefully what each of the following DOS commands does:

   (a) FORMAT B:
   (b) DIR A:
   (c) DIR
   (d) TYPE SECRET.CIA
   (e) COPY A:JUNK.ABC B:
   (f) COPY CHEECH CHONG
   (g) COPY CHONG C:ECHO.TXT
   (h) COPY B:BOOK PRN
   (i) DEL A:JUNK.CBA
   (j) A:

Computer Exercises

The following exercises should be done at a computer using the same disks that were used in Section WS1.4. Before beginning the exercises, you should boot up the machine.

1. (a) Put the SAMPLES disk in the machine and get a directory listing for it in two different ways:

(i) Type **DIR <drive name>** (with the appropriate drive name) without changing the default drive (see Step 6).

(ii) Type **DIR** with *no* drive name, after changing the default drive to the one that contains the SAMPLES disk (see Steps 12 and 6).

(b) Look in the list of files for a file named W01PB01.TXT (remember that you can press **Ctrl-S** to stop and start scrolling if you need to, or alternatively, type **DIR /P**). How many bytes does this file have? When was it created?

2. (a) Make a copy on one of your data disks, named PROBLEM2.TXT, of the file you found in Exercise 1b (see Step 9). Use the **DIR** command (Step 6) to confirm that the file has been created.

(b) Use the **TYPE** command (see Step 7) to display the contents of the file named PROBLEM2.TXT on the screen.

(c) Print a copy of this file (see Step 10).

(d) Make a *backup copy* of PROBLEM2.TXT on your second data disk; again, use the **DIR** command to confirm that the backup file has been created.

(e) *Delete* all the copies you made in 2a and 2b. Use the **DIR** command to check that they have been deleted.

3. When you finish the exercises, remove your disks and turn off the machine *and* the monitor.

WORKSHOP

II

USING THE QuickBASIC SYSTEM

WORKSHOP PREVIEW

In this workshop, we'll learn how to use the QuickBASIC programming system, including the *QuickBASIC menus*, to perform tasks such as loading, running, and saving programs; we'll also learn how to use the extensive *QuickBASIC Help system*.

WS2.1 Introduction

In Workshop 1, we learned how to use the DOS operating system to perform such tasks as booting up the system, listing directories and the contents of individual files, and copying and printing files. Another important task that we can perform using DOS is to *start up a special-purpose program* such as a word processor, a game, or, most important for us, a *programming system.*

Microsoft QuickBASIC is a multipurpose programming system for the new *Structured BASIC* programming language.[1] The QuickBASIC system is fun and easy to use, and it provides everything you need for programming from start to finish—from typing in the initial version of your program, to testing and editing it and subsequent versions, to producing a polished final product. In addition, you'll find that the Structured BASIC programming language is very close to English; it provides natural statements that make it easy to translate a sensible solution to a problem into a sensible BASIC program. This workshop is another "computer session" showing you how to get started using the QuickBASIC system; in Chapter 1, we'll begin our study of the Structured BASIC programming language as a tool for problem solving.

[1] You may have some experience with one of the earlier versions of BASIC, which used line numbers and the GOTO statement. If you give the new Structured BASIC a chance, we think you'll find that it's better and easier in every way!

WS2.2 Using the QB Express Tutorial

Before you continue with this workshop, you may wish to use a *tutorial program* that Microsoft provides with the QuickBASIC system. Called **QB Express**, it's fun and easy to use—and it takes only ten minutes or so to complete. If that program is not available, or if you wish instead to proceed with Section WS2.3, skip over the instructions that follow. Remember, though, that *whenever* you wish to use a computer, you need a *DOS disk* in order to boot up (of course, a hard-disk machine usually has DOS on its hard disk).

INSTRUCTIONS FOR USING THE QB EXPRESS TUTORIAL DISK

1. Obtain a floppy disk containing the QB Express program (and a DOS disk if you need one).
2. Boot up the computer (don't insert the QB Express disk yet).
3. *After* you receive the DOS prompt, put the QB Express disk in a floppy disk drive.
4. Make that floppy drive the default drive (by typing **A:** or **B:** at the DOS prompt; see Step 12 of Workshop I).
5. To start the QB Express program, type the following (in upper or lowercase letters):

```
> LEARN
```

6. Now, follow the tutorial's instructions to learn a little about using QuickBASIC; when you're finished, continue with the rest of this workshop.

WS2.3 Introduction to the QuickBASIC System

The DOS system that we learned about in Workshop I is **command driven**; this means that it performs its various jobs based on commands typed in by you, the user. We've learned some of these commands (COPY, DEL, TYPE, etc.), but there are many more. In fact, one of the difficulties of using a command-driven system is that it's hard to learn and remember all the commands. The QuickBASIC system, on the other hand, is **menu driven**. This means that the system provides you with a list (or "menu") of the jobs it can perform, and you simply pick what you want from the list. This makes menu-driven software much more **user-friendly**, that is, easy to use. Now, let's see how the QuickBASIC system works.

Because of its many functions and extensive Help facilities, the QuickBASIC system is a large program occupying many bytes on a disk. For this reason, we recommend that you use a hard-disk machine (with QuickBASIC on the hard disk). If a hard-disk machine is unavailable, choose a machine with a 3½-inch floppy-disk drive over one with a 5¼-inch drive, because 3½-inch disks hold about twice as much data as 5¼-inch disks. Don't worry too much about these choices: most machines—even those with 5¼-inch disk drives—will work fine.

As in any session at the computer, you first need to obtain the appropriate disks. For this session, you'll need:

MACHINES WITH HARD DISKS

- Your two data disks
- The SAMPLES disk
- Both DOS and the QuickBASIC system on the hard disk

MACHINES WITHOUT HARD DISKS

- Your two data disks
- The SAMPLES disk
- A DOS disk
- The QuickBASIC system disk (you may need *additional* QuickBASIC disks if you wish to have the complete Help system; see Section WS2.4)

Once you've obtained the disks described above, you're ready to go to the computer and start exploring the QuickBASIC system.

Step 1 (starting QuickBASIC). The first step in any computer session is always the same: *boot up the machine* (see Steps 2 and 3 of Workshop I). What you do next depends on whether you have a hard-disk or a two-floppy machine:

MACHINES WITH HARD DISKS

The QuickBASIC system has probably been installed in a *subdirectory* of the hard disk; ask someone to help you change to the QuickBASIC subdirectory. If no one is around to help, try typing the following at the DOS prompt (with C: as the default drive):

```
> CD C:\QB45
```

If you don't get an error message, you're all set; otherwise, you'll have to find someone to help you.

MACHINES WITHOUT HARD DISKS

Remove the DOS disk from the A-drive and insert the QuickBASIC system disk. If you just turned on the machine, your default drive should be A:; if it isn't, change your default drive to A: (see Step 12 in Workshop I).

Once you've followed the instructions above, your machine should be able to find the QuickBASIC system on the default drive (A: or C:). If you wish, type **DIR** for a directory listing; the QuickBASIC system is contained in a file named QB.EXE.[2] To start the QuickBASIC system, type the following command at the DOS prompt:

[2] The suffix *EXE* is short for "executable"; a file with the *EXE* suffix can be *executed* (i.e., *run*) by typing the main part of its name as a DOS command.

```
> QB
```

After you type the QB command, the computer will take a minute or so to *load the program*, that is, to transfer all the information it needs from the disk to the computer's main memory. You should then see the **QuickBASIC screen** with a welcome message in a box called a **dialog box**. (If there is no box with a welcome message, don't worry; someone has set up your QuickBASIC system without it, but it shouldn't cause any problems for you.)

Step 2 (the QuickBASIC screen). *Press the* ***Esc*** *key* (short for "escape"; a gray key at the upper left-hand corner of your keyboard) to make the dialog box go away. The screen should now look like the one in Figure WS2.1.

Starting at the top, examine the screen. The top line is called a **Menu Bar**, and each word in the bar (*File*, *Edit*, *View*, etc.) represents a particular **menu**, or list, of QuickBASIC commands; you'll see how to use the menus in Step 3. The large empty area where the cursor is located is called the **View Window**; this is where you write, read, and edit the text of your BASIC programs. The title of the current program you're working on is centered at the top of the View Window (right now it should say "Untitled"). The narrow rectangular area below the View Window is called the **Immediate Window** (we'll talk more about

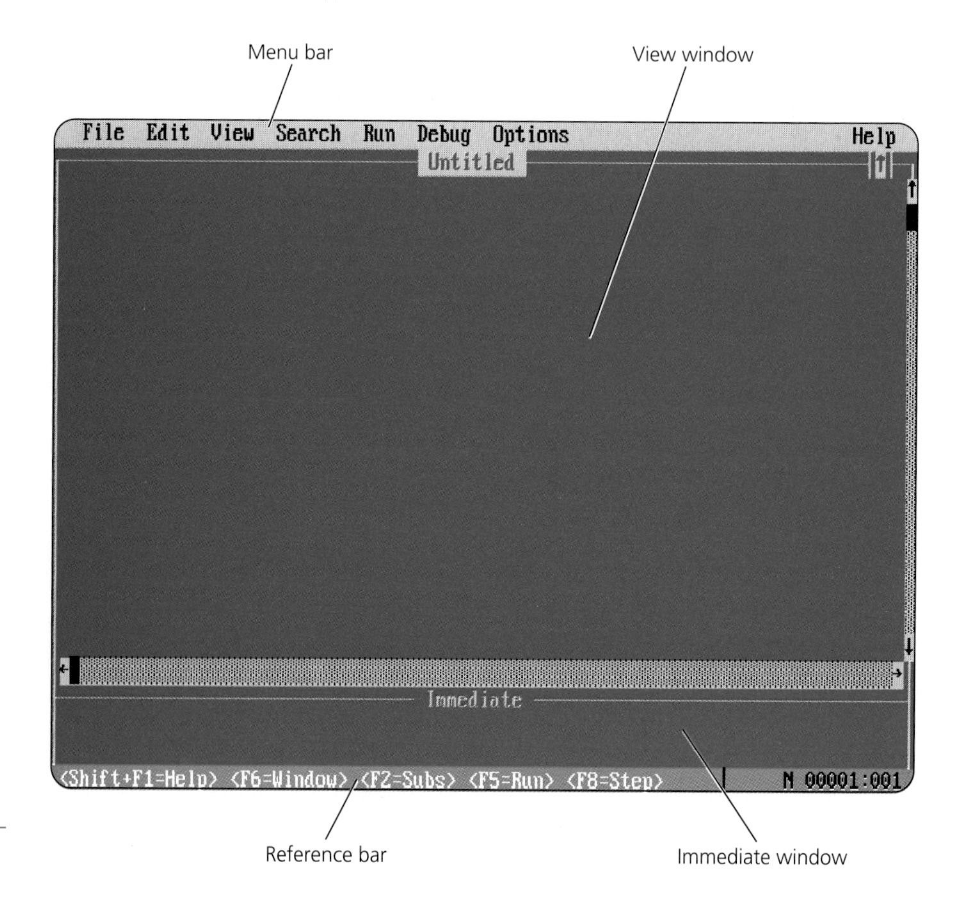

FIGURE WS2.1

The QuickBASIC Screen

it in Chapter 4). Finally, the bar along the bottom of the screen is called the **Reference Bar**; its contents change depending on what you're doing with the QuickBASIC system, but generally it contains reminders of particular commands that might be useful.

Step 3 (using the menus). There are two keys important to the menu system. The first is the **Alt** key (short for "alternate"), a gray key located at the bottom of the keyboard near the space bar. The second is the **Esc** key, which you used at the beginning of Step 2. Basically, the Alt key helps you *start* using the menus and the Esc key helps you *cancel* them (when you decide to not use a QuickBASIC command that you've already selected).

Press the **Alt** key: Notice that both the Reference Bar and the Menu Bar have changed. The Reference Bar now contains information to help you use the menus. In the Menu Bar, the first letter of each word is highlighted; in addition, the entire word *File* is highlighted. If you now press one of the highlighted letters, that particular menu will be displayed. Alternatively, you can use the left and right **arrow keys** (see Figure WS2.2) to highlight the word you want, then press **<Enter>** to choose that menu.

Press the **F** key *to select the File Menu:* A box containing a list of QuickBASIC commands should appear (see Figure WS2.3). These commands all have to do with accessing *files*; the other menus (Edit, View, etc.) contain commands that are similarly grouped. Notice that each command contains a highlighted letter and that one of the commands is also highlighted.

Use the **arrow keys** *to explore the menu options*: The **<Up>** and **<Down>** arrows highlight the options in the current menu; the **<Left>** and **<Right>** arrows move you from one menu to another. Notice also that the Reference Bar is always giving you information about the highlighted option. Don't let the large number of options intimidate you; you'll be using only two or three of the menus for quite a while. When you're done with this step, press **Esc** to *cancel* the Menu Bar.

FIGURE WS2.2

Direction Keys

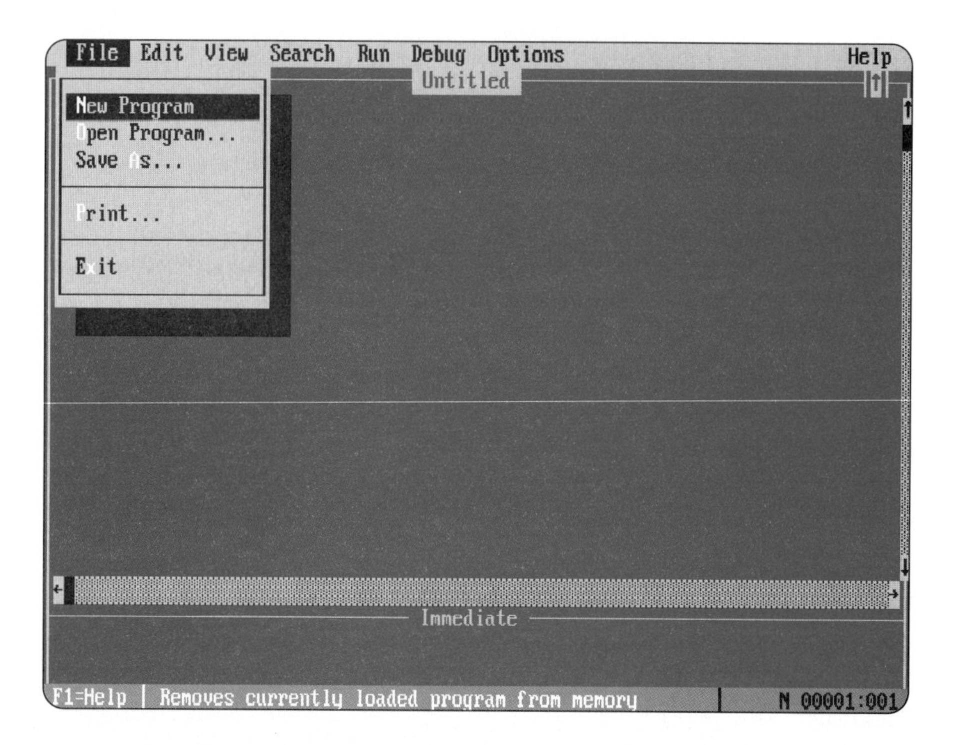

FIGURE WS2.3

The *File* Menu

Step 4 (opening a program). Let's use the File Menu to look at one of the programs on the SAMPLES disk. *Insert the SAMPLES disk* into the empty floppy-disk drive. Since we want to access a file from that disk, we need the File Menu: Press **Alt** and then **F**. The Open Program option lets us select a file from the disk and bring it into the View Window for editing and other actions. *Choose the Open Program option* by either pressing the **O** key or by using the **arrow keys** and then pressing **<Enter>**.

The File Menu should be replaced with a box, called a **dialog box**, that gives you a number of options for choosing a file (see Figure WS2.4). This dialog box, like most others, contains several different regions or **fields**. At the top is a field in which you can type the name of a file (the figure shows the file name *.BAS). Note that below this field and at the far left, the name of the current disk drive is displayed. Below that and on the left is a field containing a list of all files on the current drive having the suffix *BAS*; on the lower right is another field, which lists possible alternative drives and subdirectories; finally, the narrow region at the bottom lists three commands, one of which is highlighted. We need to move to the Dirs/Drives box to change the drive from which files are chosen.

> ***To move from one field to another in a dialog box, use the* Tab *key (a gray key with two arrows on it, just to the left of the Q key).***

Use the **Tab** key *to move to the Dirs/Drives field*. We now need to select the letter corresponding to the drive containing the SAMPLES disk, that is, [-A-] for the A-drive, and so on.

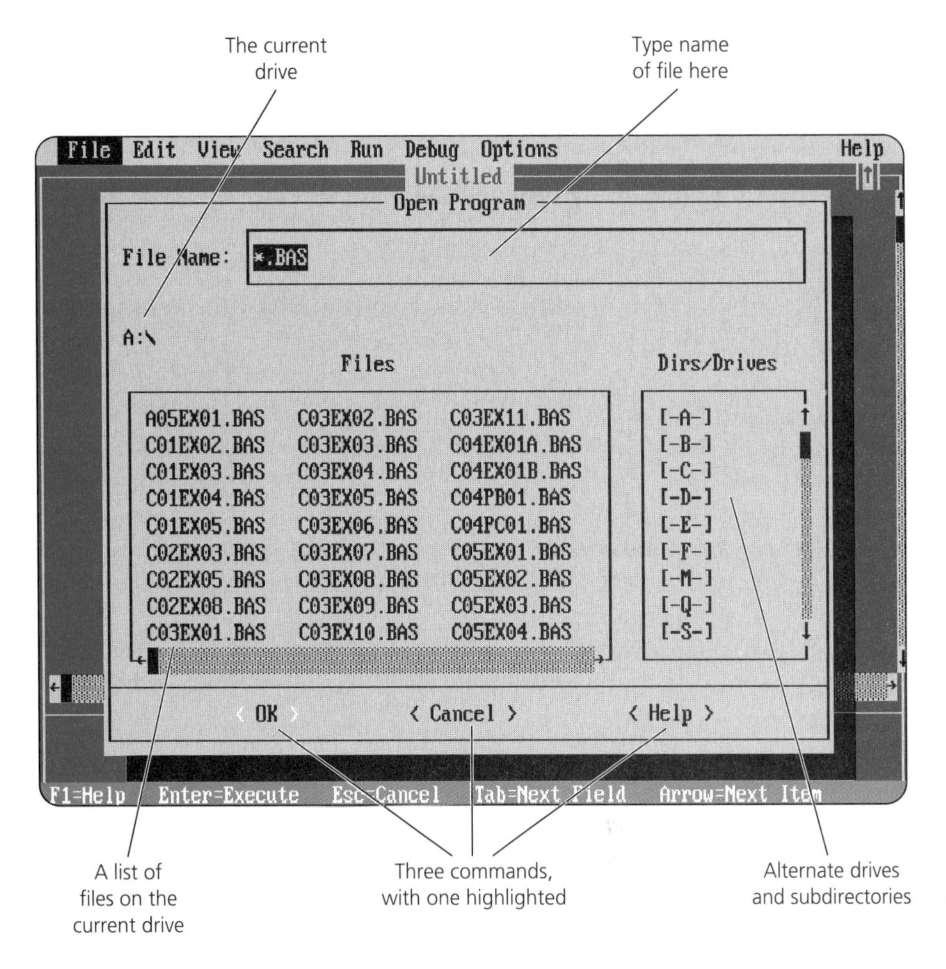

FIGURE WS2.4

The *Open Program* Dialog Box

To highlight an entry from a list in a particular field, use the <Up> and <Down> arrow keys.

Use the **<Up>** and **<Down>** arrow keys *to highlight the drive containing the SAMPLES disk* (notice how the name in the top field changes as you move down the list).

To execute the menu with the choice you've made, press <Enter>.

Press **<Enter>** *to change the disk drive*. The Open Program menu doesn't go away because we still haven't chosen a *file*, but it now displays the files that are available on the new disk drive; if you've correctly chosen the drive containing the SAMPLES disk, the list in the Files box should be pretty long.

Let's open the program titled W02ST04.BAS. There are two ways to choose this file: you can either type the name of the file in the top box (you don't need to type the suffix *BAS*) or you can use **Tab** and then the **direction** keys to highlight it in the Files box. Looking back at Figure WS2.2, you'll see that in addition to the arrow keys, there are keys labelled **PgDn** (or **Page Down**) and **PgUp** (or **Page Up**). You can use these direction keys to find the screen that contains the name W02ST04.BAS (the SAMPLES disk contains many files, so W02ST04.BAS will probably not appear on the first screen), and then use the arrows to highlight that file. Using either method, *select the file W02ST04.BAS* and press **<Enter>** *to execute the command.*[3]

> ***Don't let all this new terminology and all these new commands bowl you over; with practice (just a little!), they'll become natural. And remember to look at the Reference Bar for reminders.***

You should now see the program W02ST04.BAS in the View Window (finally!). This process of bringing a copy of a file from a disk into memory for use in the QuickBASIC system is called **opening**, or **loading**, a program. Any changes we make to this copy do *not* affect the original file on the disk; later, we can *save* the copy on the disk if we want to.

Step 5 (the File Menu options; printing a file). Although we'll want to study the program W02ST04.BAS, let's first summarize the options available on the File Menu. "Pull down" the File Menu by pressing **ALT-F** to get a list showing each of the options with brief descriptions. (Note: If your File Menu shows more options than those listed below, don't worry—just ignore the other options for now! Your Quick-BASIC system has been set up a little differently to show more advanced options, which we'll discuss in Chapter 6.)

SUMMARY OF OPTIONS IN FILE MENU

New Program: Clears the current program in the View Window (if any) from memory; choose this to start writing a new program when you're done with a previous one. (Note: When you first start QuickBASIC, you can start a new program if you wish.)

Open Program: Lets you select a program from your disk and load a copy of it into memory.

Save As: Lets you save a copy of the program currently in memory onto your disk.

Print: Prints out a copy of the program currently in memory.

Exit: Terminates the QuickBASIC system and returns you to DOS.

Let's use the File Menu to print a copy of the program named W02ST04.BAS. Select the **Print** option from the File Menu by pressing **P** or using the **arrow keys** and **<Enter>**. You should now see a dialog box like the one shown in Figure WS2.5, giving you three printing options. The default option, *Current Module,* is the one we'll use most often in this book. Press **<Enter>** to select this option and print the

---

[3] Actually, there's yet *another* way to select this file—by tabbing to the Files box and typing the *first letter* of the file's name, instead of using arrow keys. QuickBASIC usually provides a variety of ways to perform a given task. We'll cover the ones we think you'll find most convenient and try not to overwhelm you with *too* many options.

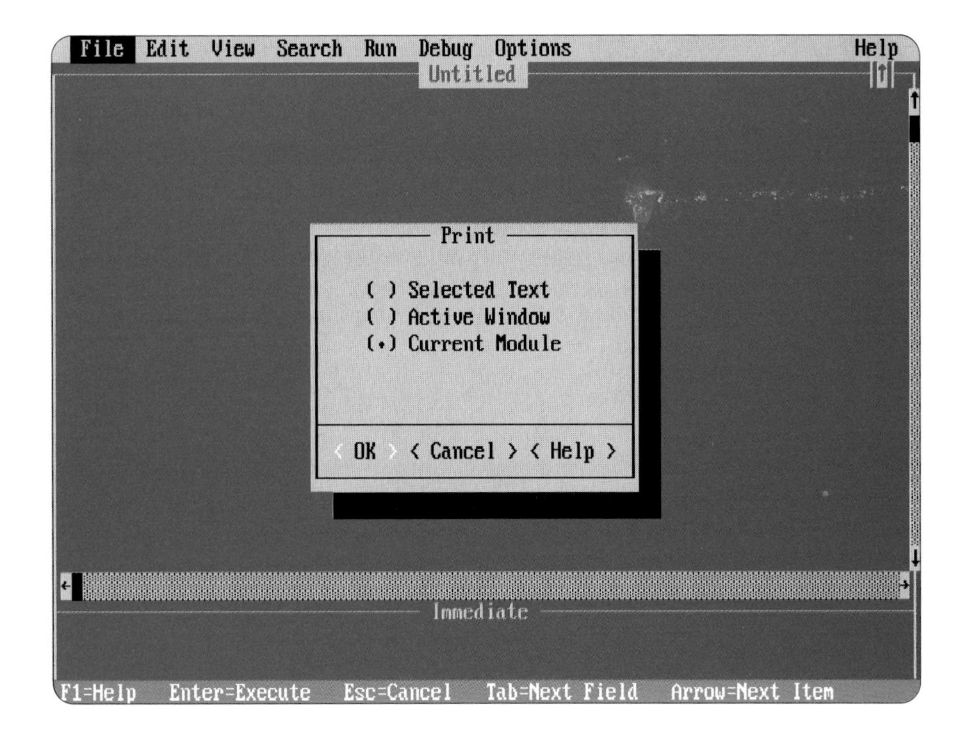

FIGURE WS2.5

The *Print* Dialog Box

program. (Recall from Workshop I that we are generally unable to view or print files containing QuickBASIC programs using DOS commands; now, we can see them on the screen and print them out by using QuickBASIC.

Step 6 (using the editing keys). Once the file has printed, the dialog box should disappear and you should be back to the View Window containing the program W02ST04.BAS. Now, we'll see how easy it is to move around the text of the program and make changes.

The four *arrow keys* let you move the cursor anywhere you like in the program. Using them, *move the cursor* to the right-hand end of the line that names the author of the program.

The other *direction keys* can also be used for moving around in the program. These keys—**Home**, **End**, **PgDn**, and **PgUp**—are described below (also see Figure WS2.2). Try them out as you read their descriptions.

Home:	Moves cursor to beginning of current line
End:	Moves cursor to end of current line
PgDn:	Moves cursor down one screen in program
PgUp:	Moves cursor up one screen in program

Once you've moved the cursor to where you want it, you can erase the words that are there and/or add new words. *Move the cursor* to the Author line and edit it so that there are two authors, Bob Basic and Pat Programmer. Now give Bob and Pat the titles "Mr." and "Ms.," respectively. To do this, you simply move the cursor to the correct place and start typing: the QuickBASIC system will move the other letters over to make room.

To *erase* text, you can use either the **Delete** key (also labelled **Del** on some machines) or the **Backspace** key (sometimes labelled with a large arrow pointing to the left). The Delete key erases the character where the cursor is; the Backspace key erases the character to the left of the cursor. Using the **arrow keys** and the **Delete** or **Backspace** keys, *erase* the names "Bob" and "Pat" and *replace* them with "Robert" and "Patricia."

Step 7 (executing a program; printing output). Let's remember now that a BASIC program is really a set of instructions designed to be carried out by a computer. But instructions written in the BASIC language, which is a *high-level* language, must first be translated to low-level *machine language* (see Workshop I, Section WS1.3); only then can we ask the machine to read and carry out the instructions.

The QuickBASIC system provides a special program, called a **compiler**, that takes a BASIC program and translates it into machine language. We can then **run** (i.e., execute) the translated BASIC program immediately, or we can store it in a separate file with the suffix *EXE*, to be executed any time we wish from DOS without having to start QuickBASIC. The process of translating a program written in a high-level language such as BASIC to machine language is called **compilation**. (Earlier versions of BASIC usually used an *interpreter* rather than a compiler; an interpreter simultaneously translates *and* executes a program one line at a time.)

To use the QuickBASIC compiler, pull down the **Run** Menu; do this now by typing **ALT-R**. You'll see that the Run Menu has four options (see Figure WS2.6), but for the time being, we'll need only the first, **Start**. The Start option causes the current program to be compiled (i.e., translated) and then automatically executes the resulting machine language version. The machine language version is stored in the computer's main memory rather than on a disk; if we wanted to save the executable version on a disk, we would choose the last option, **Make EXE File**—but for now we'll simply run our programs from the computer's memory.

Compile and run the program W02ST04.BAS now by choosing the Start option from the Run Menu (i.e., type **S** or press **<Enter>**). The compilation process for this (and for most of the programs we'll write in this book) is so quick that the execution will happen almost instantly. You should now see the **output screen**, which should look like the one in Figure WS2.7.

Look at the printout you made of the program and see if you can understand why executing it produced this output (don't worry if you have questions—they'll be answered by the end of Chapter 1). By the way, the line at the bottom of the screen, "Press any key to continue," is *not* part of the program's output; it's a message from the QuickBASIC system indicating that the program is done executing. Follow its direction now and **press any key**; you should be returned to the View

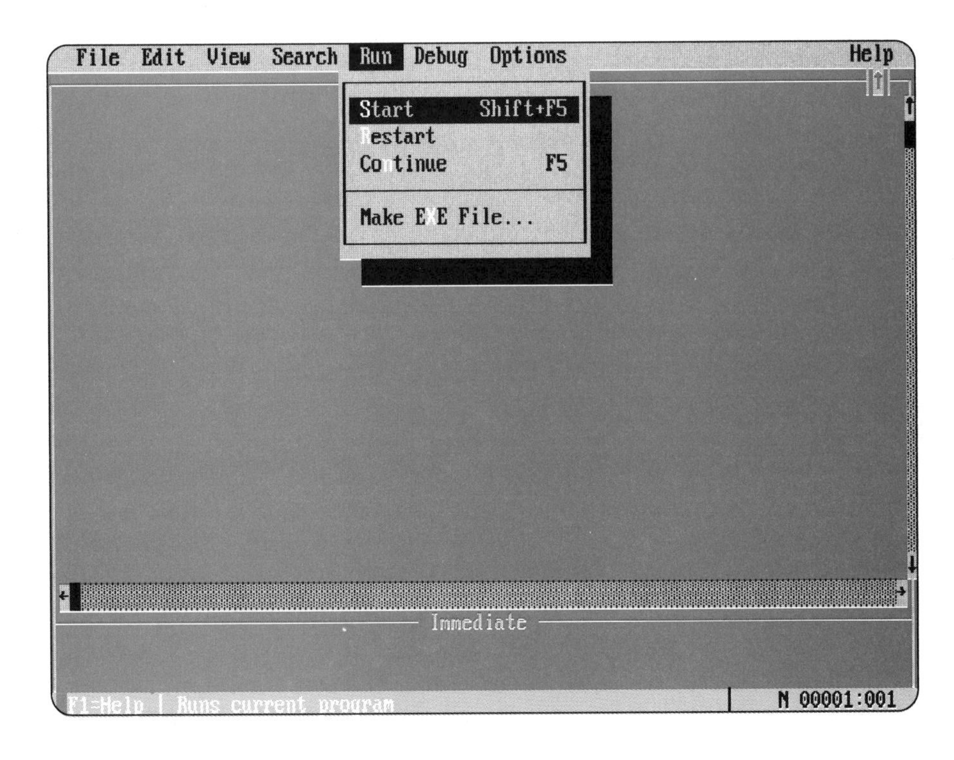

FIGURE WS2.6

The *Run* Menu

```
Hello there, and welcome to QuickBASIC.


Well, it's been nice talking to you. Farewell for now.

Press any key to continue
```

FIGURE WS2.7

An Output Screen

Window. If you wish to see the output again, you can simply repeat Step 7 and execute the program a second time. (In Chapter 4, we'll learn how to switch back and forth between the output screen and the View Window *without* reexecuting the program.)

Now, make one more change to the program. Move the cursor to the line that says:

```
PRINT "Hello there, and welcome to QuickBASIC."
```

Replace the word *there* with your first name and run the program again for a *personalized* welcome message!

Now that we have learned how to use the File Menu to print the program itself, how do we print the *output*? Well, we can use the method we learned in Workshop I, Step 10 for printing the contents of the screen. With your program's output showing on the screen, press **Shift-PrtSc** to print the screen. (To use this method to print output that is more than one screen long, you'll need to use **Ctrl-S** to make the output pause, and then print it one screen at a time.)

Step 8 (saving a program). Everything we've done so far with the program W02ST04.BAS has taken place in the computer's memory; the file on disk remains unchanged. If we wish to save our new version of this program on disk, we'll need the File Menu (makes sense, right?).

To save this version of the program on your data disks, remove the SAMPLES disk from the disk drive and replace it with one of your data disks. After returning to the View Window, pull down the File Menu (**Alt-F**) and choose the **Save As** option. You'll see another dialog box (Figure WS2.8) that lets you decide what file name and what disk drive to use and whether to make the file a text or a QuickBASIC file. If you press **<Enter>** now, you'll get a copy of this program, in a file named W02ST04.BAS, on your data disk. You can make a backup copy by repeating Step 8 with your other data disk.

If you wish, you can type in a different file name (for example, GREETING.BAS), but remember that it's good practice to use *descriptive* file names so that you'll be able to easily find the file you want (and

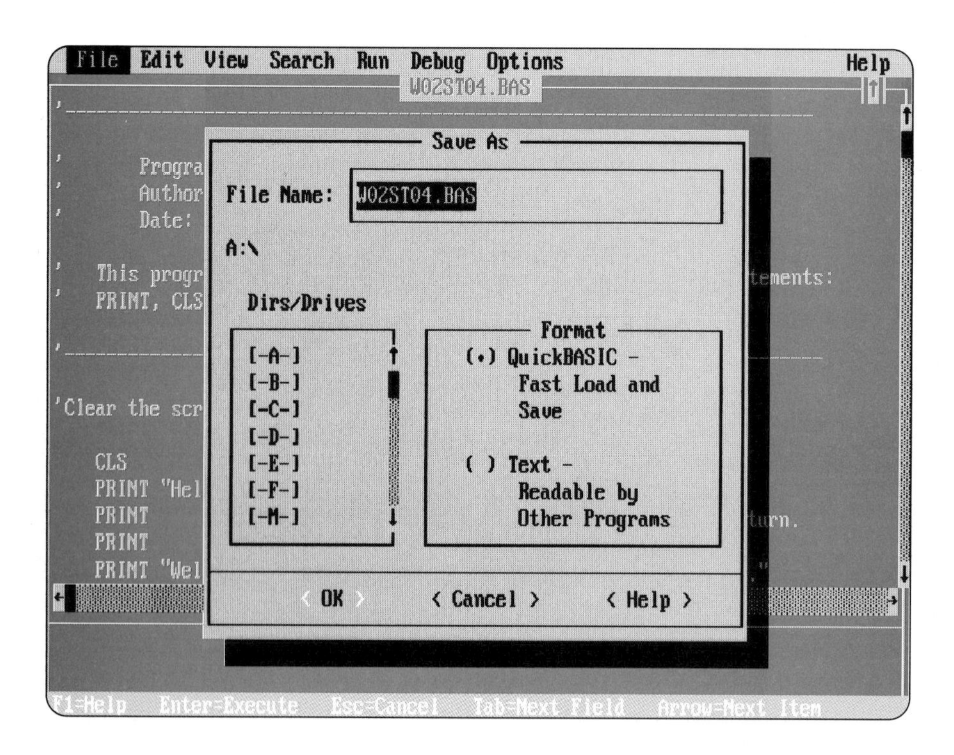

FIGURE WS2.8

The *Save As* Dialog Box

as you continue to write more and more programs, creating more and more files, this will become increasingly helpful).

Step 9 (creating a new program). To create a *new* program, we first need to clear the old program, W02ST04.BAS, from the View Window. Do this now by opening the **File Menu** and choosing the **New Program** option. You should get an empty View Window; in fact, this is what you get when you first start QuickBASIC. (If you haven't saved the previous program and you try to start a new one, QuickBASIC will warn you by asking if you want to save the old program on disk before it's removed from the View Window.)

Type in the short program shown below. If you make any typographical errors, you'll probably discover that QuickBASIC has what is called a **Smart Editor**, which examines the lines of your program as you type them in and performs several other functions. First, it *checks for syntax errors,* that is, spelling or grammatical errors in the use of the BASIC language. Second, it *formats* the line to make it easier to read (for example, it puts all BASIC words into capital letters). Third, it does whatever *preliminary compiling* it can, to speed things up later when you run the program. See why it's called a "Smart Editor"? If you get any dialog boxes containing error messages, press **Esc** or **<Enter>** to make the box go away; then try to find and correct the error (make sure that what you type *exactly* matches the following lines).

```
CLS
PRINT "Here is the output from my first program!"
PRINT
PRINT
PRINT "Not bad, huh?"
END
```

Now, *compile and run* your program by choosing **Start** from the **Run Menu**. After running your program, **press a key** to get the View Window back, then erase the word *CLS*; run the program again. Can you guess what the word *CLS* means? Put the word back and run the program again.

Save this little program on your data disk under the name FIRST.BAS. To do this, select the **Save As** option from the **File Menu**, with your data disk in one of the floppy drives. To make sure that you save the file on the correct drive, use the correct *drive prefix* when typing the file name. For example, if your disk is in the B-drive, type **B:FIRST.BAS**. (Alternatively, you could **Tab** to the Dirs/Drives box, change the drive, and **Tab** back. Note also that you can omit the *BAS* suffix, e.g., type B:FIRST, since QuickBASIC *assumes* you want that suffix unless you say otherwise.) The program should now be copied onto your data disk; to make a backup, simply repeat this process using your other data disk.

Step 10 (ending a QuickBASIC session). The final thing we'll do is *end* the QuickBASIC session, that is, terminate the QuickBASIC program and return to DOS. To do this, simply pull down the **File Menu** and select the **Exit** option. Doing this should return you to the DOS prompt (unless you haven't saved your program, in which case QuickBASIC will warn you first). Before removing your disks and turning off the machine and monitor, use the **DIR** command to check that the programs you saved in Steps 8 and 9 appear on your data disks (W02ST04.BAS from Step 8 and FIRST.BAS from Step 9).

WS2.4 The QuickBASIC Help System

The QuickBASIC programming system has been designed to make writing and testing your programs as easy as possible. In addition to such helpful features as the menus and the Smart Editor, QuickBASIC has an extensive Help facility that supplies answers to most questions you may have about using QuickBASIC or the Structured BASIC language. In this section, we'll "help" you learn to use the Help system. (It's not absolutely necessary to use Help, but it can be very useful, so we suggest that you work through this section at some point, either now or later.)

To try out the Help system, you'll need to start QuickBASIC again (see the beginning of Section WS2.3). You'll also need to have a program in the View Window (to illustrate how you can get help with the words in your programs), so *load the program FIRST.BAS* from one of your data disks (this is the program you created in Step 9 of Section WS2.3; if you've forgotten the procedure for loading a program, review Step 4 of Section WS2.3).

The QuickBASIC Help system is essentially a built-in reference manual, organized so that it's a breeze to find what you're looking for. To access the Help system, you can use either the menus or the *function keys*. We'll look at both ways, beginning with the function-key approach.

IBM keyboards provide either 10 or 12 **function keys** (see Figure WS2.9), which have special meanings that depend on the software being used. Several of these keys are used in QuickBASIC as shortcut alternatives to using the menus and for other purposes. The function key **F1** is the "Help" key in QuickBASIC. If you press the **F1** key, QuickBASIC will display information about the item highlighted by the cursor; you can use this technique to get detailed information about words in the BASIC language or about the QuickBASIC system itself.

At this point, the program FIRST.BAS should be in the View Window. Move the cursor to any of the letters in the word *CLS* (the top line of the program); now press the function key **F1**. You should see a **Help Window** that explains the word *CLS* (see Figure WS2.10). To remove the Help Window, press the **Esc** key.

Warning: QuickBASIC's Help system is contained in several large files. If your QuickBASIC system is on a hard disk, the entire HELP system should be there. However, if your QuickBASIC system is on

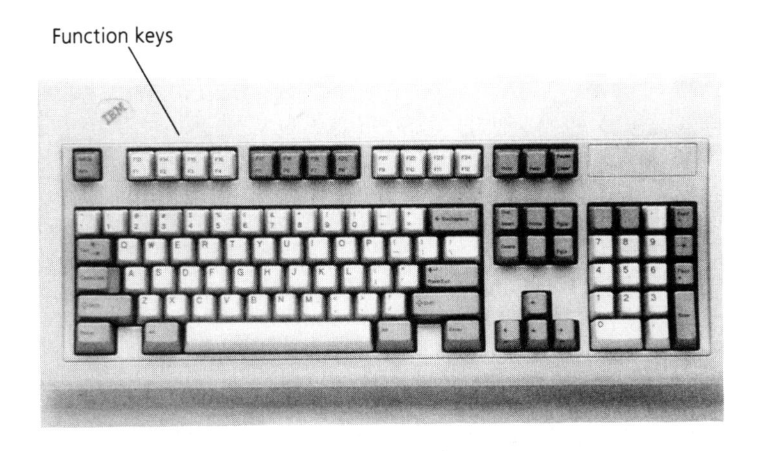

FIGURE WS2.9

Function Keys

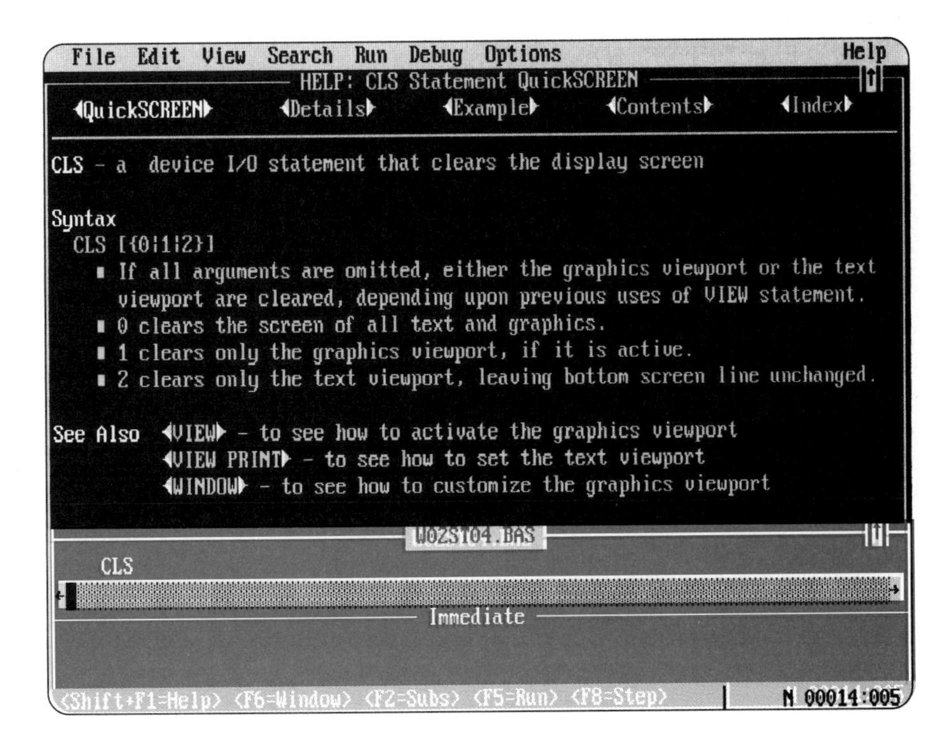

FIGURE WS2.10

The *CLS* Help Window

floppy disks, there isn't enough room on one disk to store both the QuickBASIC programming system and the complete Help system. The Program disk will contain help on all the words in the BASIC language (such as CLS *above), but some of the topics illustrated below will require you to remove the* Program *disk and insert either the* Utilities 2 *disk (5¼ inch and 3½ inch) or the* QB Advisor *disk (5¼ inch only).*

If you're using QuickBASIC on a floppy disk, the easiest strategy may be to use only the Program *disk and simply press* Esc *if you get a "File not found" message while using the Help system. Whether or not you obtain additional disks, continue now with the rest of this section.*

After clearing the Help Window, press **ALT-F** to pull down the **File Menu**; use the **<Down>** arrow to highlight the **Open Program** option (but don't press <Enter> yet). Now press the Help key, **F1**, again. You should see a Help Window explaining the Open Program option. After you've read it, press **Esc** to make it go away; then press **Esc** again to remove the File Menu.

As you can see, the F1 key brings up help on whatever item the cursor points to. In some cases, you can get additional details or examples as well. Move the cursor to the word *PRINT* in the second line of your program and press the **F1** key (see Figure WS2.11). Below the Help Window, notice that the View Window still appears (reduced to one line) and that, in fact, the Immediate Window appears below that. The cursor is still where you positioned it in the View Window. We'll need to first move the cursor into the Help Window to find out how to get additional help.

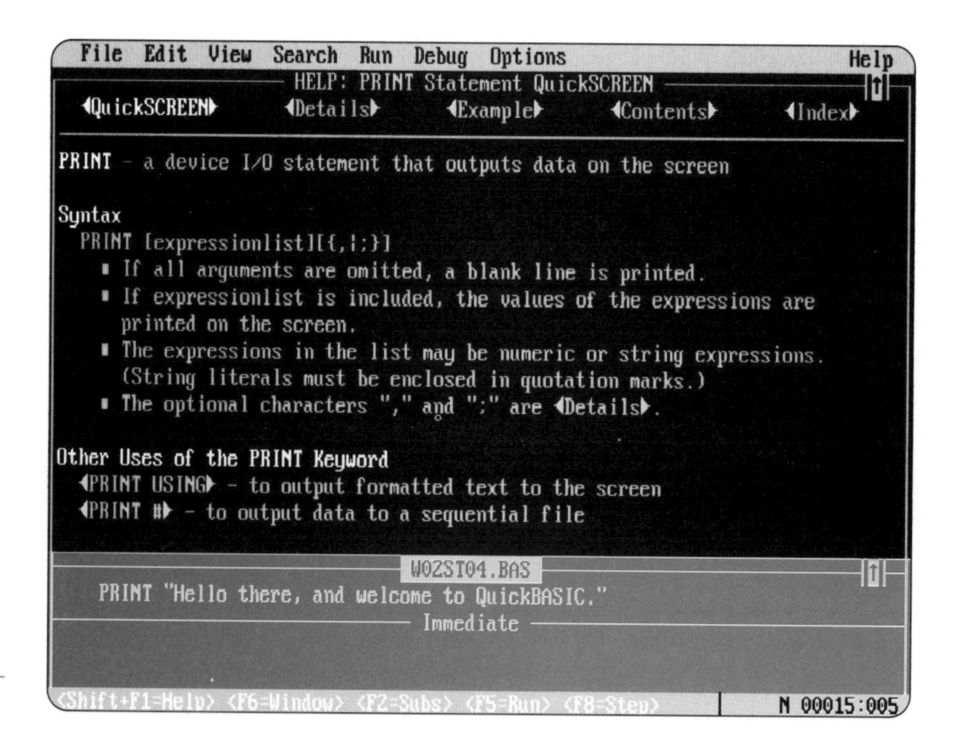

FIGURE WS2.11

The *PRINT* Help Window

It is the job of another function key, **F6**, to move the cursor from one window to the next. Press **F6** twice to move the cursor into the Help Window. Notice that some of the words in the window are surrounded by odd *triangular brackets;* these bracketed words are called **hyperlinks**. When a word or phrase is bracketed as a hyperlink, it means that the Help system has more information available on it. The hyperlink *QuickSCREEN* is highlighted because you're currently looking at the "PRINT Statement QuickSCREEN." These hyperlinks provide examples, details, and cross-references on everything having to do with QuickBASIC.

To display the information for a particular hyperlink, you move the cursor *inside* the brackets and then press either **F1** or **<Enter>**. To move the cursor around the Help Window, you can use either the usual **direction** keys (the arrow keys, Home, End, PgUp, PgDn) or the **Tab** key. Move the cursor to the hyperlink <Example> and press **F1** or **<Enter>** to display the information for that hyperlink. To erase the Help Window, press **Esc**.

Sometimes you may want to find Help on a topic for which you don't know the BASIC word. Like a traditional textbook or reference manual, the QuickBASIC HELP system has both a *Table of Contents* and an *Index*. To bring up a general-purpose *Help on Help* Window, press **Shift-F1** (i.e., press **F1** while holding down the **Shift** key). Do that now to bring up the Help on Help Window (see Figure WS2.12).

Notice that among the hyperlinks are <Contents> and <Index>. With the cursor inside the <Contents> hyperlink, press **F1** or **<Enter>**. The Table of Contents (see Figure WS2.13) is organized into two main sections, "Using QuickBASIC" and "BASIC Programming

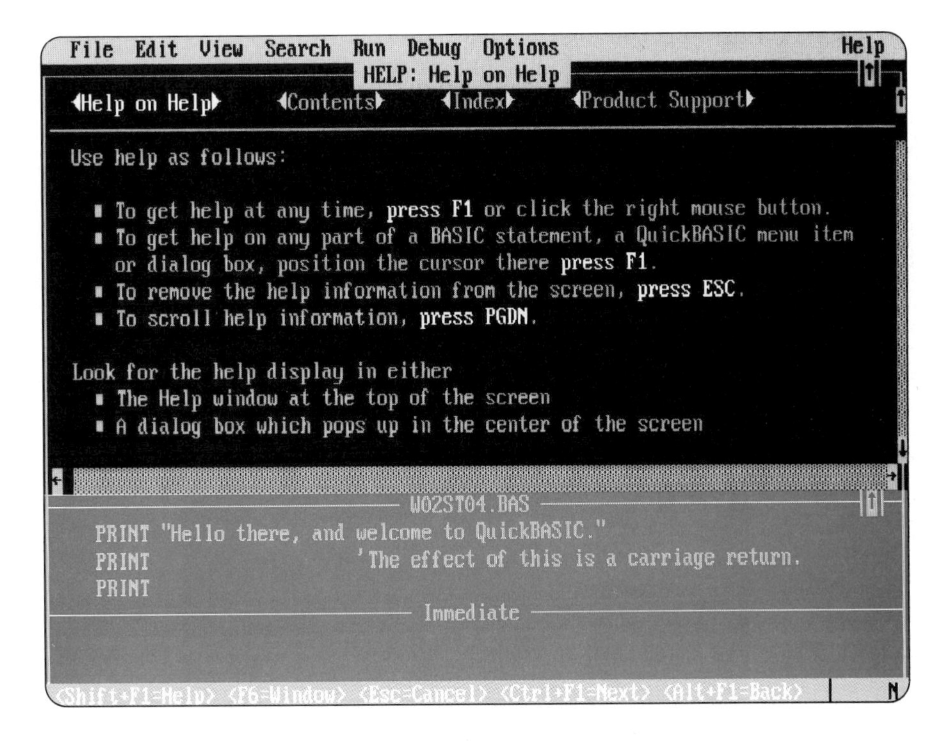

FIGURE WS2.12

The *Help on Help* Window

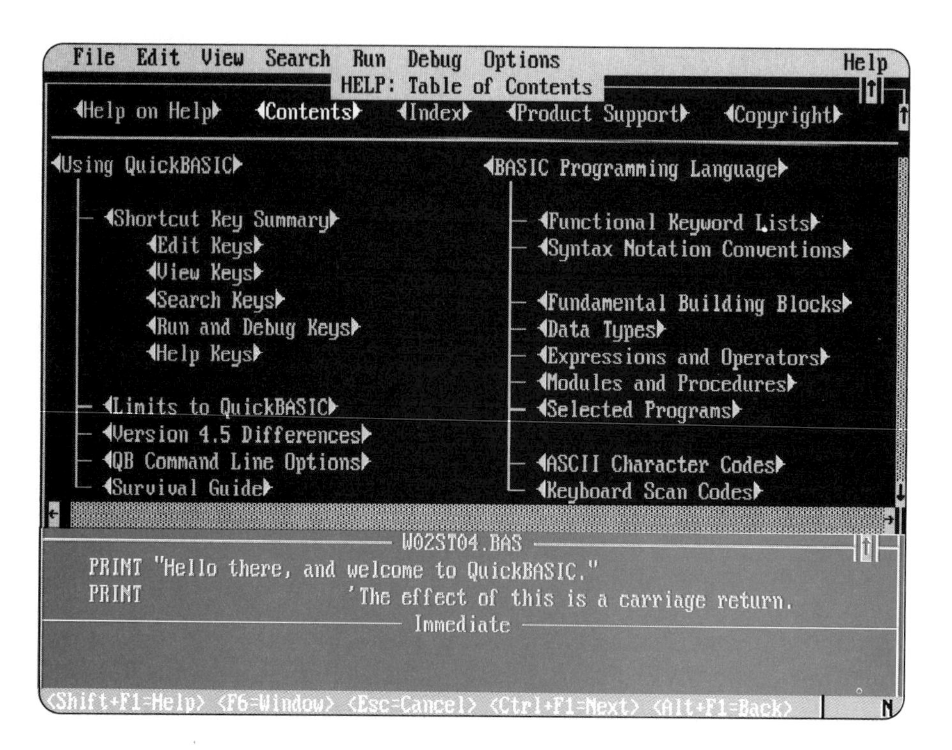

FIGURE WS2.13

The Help System *Table of Contents*

Language." Notice that each topic is a hyperlink, so you can move the cursor to the one you want and press **F1** or **<Enter>**.

If you look at the hyperlink <Index>, you'll see an alphabetical list of all the words in the BASIC programming language, and you can get information on them the same way you do for hyperlinks. For now, though, let's clear the Help Window by pressing **Esc**.

We're almost done—but there are two more things to say about the Help system. First, as we mentioned earlier, you can use the menus to access Help. No doubt you've noticed the word *Help* on the far right-hand side of the Menu Bar. Press **ALT-H** to pull down the Help Menu (see Figure WS2.14). You can now select from the four options listed, which let you see the Index or Table of Contents, get help on the BASIC word pointed to by the cursor, or access Help on Help. Notice the reminders about using the function keys in the last two options. Select the last option, Help on Help (i.e., press **H**).

The last thing we'll say about the Help system is that you can *print* the Help Window in the same way you print a program. With the Help on Help Window showing, pull down the **File Menu** and select the **Print** option. Press **<Enter>**, and the whole Help on Help Window will be printed out. You can do this for any Help Window of which you'd like to have a printed copy.

When you're done exploring the Help system, you can exit QuickBASIC, remove your disks, and turn off the machine and monitor (see Step 10 of Section WS2.3).

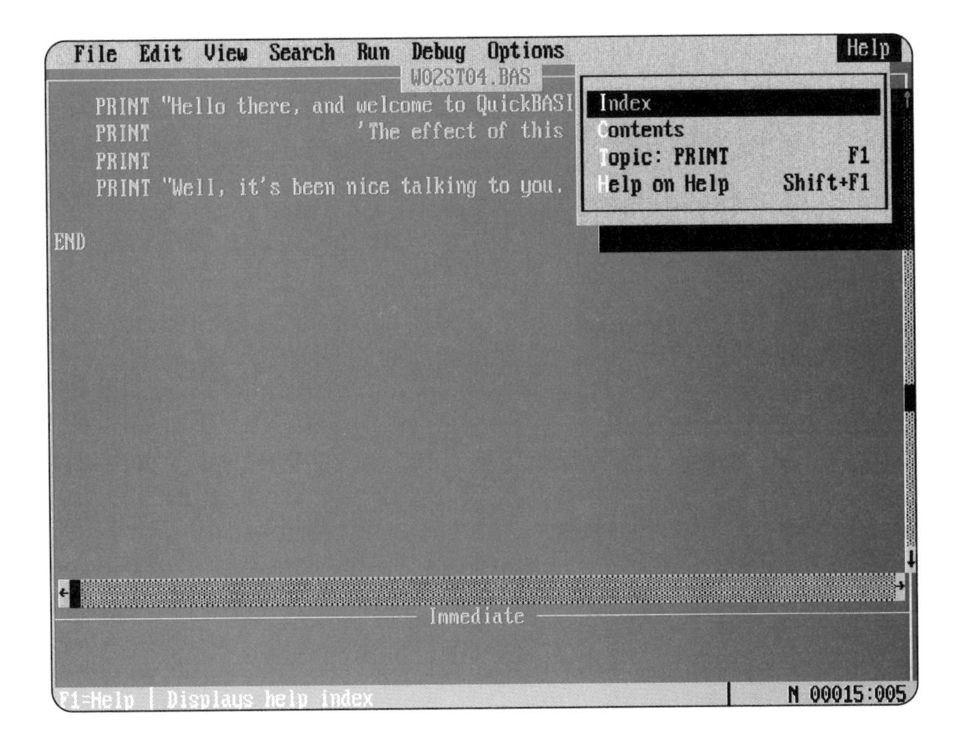

FIGURE WS2.14

The *Help* Menu

Workshop Summary 

In this workshop, we've learned a lot about using the QuickBASIC programming system. Unlike DOS, which is a *command-driven* system, QuickBASIC is *menu driven,* which means that you pick commands from lists of options.

QuickBASIC is started by typing **QB** at the DOS prompt. The QuickBASIC screen consists mainly of a *View Window*, where you can read, write, and edit your programs; in addition, there is a *Menu Bar* at the top of the screen, a smaller window called the *Immediate Window* (see Chapter 4), and a *Reference Bar* at the bottom of the screen.

To "pull down" one of the menus listed in the Menu Bar, you press the **Alt** key and then the highlighted letter of the menu you want; to choose an option from a menu, you press its highlighted letter (or use **arrow keys** and press **<Enter>**). To cancel the menus at any time, press **Esc**.

Choosing an option from a menu is often followed by the appearance of a *dialog box*, which requests further information from you. To move from one *field* of a dialog box to another, use the **Tab** key; to choose among a list of options in a single field, use the **arrow** keys. Once you've filled in the options that you want, press **<Enter>** to carry out the command. The three menus that we'll use most are *File*, *Run*, and *Help*.

The *File Menu* provides commands for loading and saving programs, creating new programs, printing programs, and exiting QuickBASIC. The *Print* option can also be used to print Help screens. It cannot be used, however, to print the *output* of a program (one way to do this is to use **Shift-PrtSc**).

The *Run* Menu provides commands for *compiling* and *executing* programs. *Compilation* is the process of translating a program written in BASIC into machine language. We can then have the machine execute, or *run*, the machine language version. The option *Start* on the Run Menu compiles a BASIC program and then executes the machine language version.

Finally, the *Help Menu* is one way to access the excellent QuickBASIC Help system; it's probably the easiest method if you want to see the *Table of Contents* or *Index*. If you want information about a menu option or a particular word in the BASIC language, simply position the cursor on that item and press the function key **F1**; to get a general-purpose HELP screen, press **Shift-F1**. Most Help screens provide additional information through *hyperlinks*. Hyperlinks are words or phrases enclosed in *triangular brackets*; to display the information they refer to, move the cursor inside the brackets (using **Tab** or **arrow** keys), and then press **F1** or **<Enter>**. If your QuickBASIC system is on a floppy disk, you may not have access to the complete Help system, but information on words in the BASIC language will still be available.

Review Questions

1. Explain the difference between a *command-driven* and a *menu-driven* system.

2. Explain the following terms having to do with QuickBASIC:

(a) Menu Bar	(d) compilation
(b) View Window	(e) output screen
(c) dialog box	(f) hyperlink

3. Describe briefly the steps you would take to carry out the following tasks (in each, assume that the previous steps have already been carried out):

(a) start the QuickBASIC system

(b) open a program contained on a disk in the B-drive

(c) obtain a Help Window for the word *END* in a BASIC program

(d) compile and run the program currently being edited (i.e., the program currently in the View Window)

(e) print a program *and* its output

Computer Exercises

Before doing the following exercises, obtain the disks appropriate to your machine as described at the beginning of Section WS2.3 (immediately before Step 1); then start the QuickBASIC system as described in Step 1.

1. (a) Using the program shown on page 35 as a guide, write a new program that clears the screen and then uses several PRINT statements to print your name and address in a box. For example, if George Bush did this exercise, the output from his program might look like this:

```
******************************
*                            *
*    Pres. George Bush       *
*    1600 Pennsylvania Ave.  *
*    Washington, D.C. 20500  *
*                            *
******************************
```

(b) Run your program several times, editing it, if necessary, to get the output looking just right.

(c) Print the final version of the program *and* its output.

(d) Save the program on your data disk using a descriptive file name, such as W02PB01.BAS or ADDRESS.BAS; make a backup (as usual) on your backup disk.

2. (a) The SAMPLES disk contains a program named W02PB02.BAS. Put the SAMPLES disk in a floppy drive and open the program W02PB02.BAS, that is, load it into memory from the disk. This program contains several additional BASIC words that we will learn more about in Chapter 1.

(b) Read over the program carefully before running it, trying to guess in advance what it will do; use the Help system to get Help screens explaining the BASIC words *INPUT* and *LET*.

(c) Run the program. Notice that you are requested to enter a Fahrenheit temperature; enter the number 72 and press **<Enter>**. Run the program several more times, entering different numbers each time; use trial and error to discover the Fahrenheit temperature that corresponds to a Centigrade temperature of 15 (note that this would be trivial if we had a program to convert *from* Centigrade *to* Fahrenheit).

(d) Print the program *and* a sample of its output.

C H A P T E R

1

AN INTRODUCTION TO STRUCTURED BASIC

CHAPTER PREVIEW

In this chapter, we'll begin to learn about designing programs in Structured BASIC to solve a variety of problems. We'll introduce several of the most fundamental *BASIC statements*; we'll learn about numeric and string *variables*, including two ways to give values to variables; we'll learn how to combine variables to form *expressions*, using numeric and string *operators* and *built-in functions*; finally, we'll summarize the steps involved in *designing and testing* a BASIC program to perform a specified task.

1.1 First Concepts of BASIC Programs

Now that you've learned something about using a computer and the QuickBASIC system, you're ready to proceed with the central purpose of this book: learning to use Structured BASIC as a tool to solve problems. In this chapter, you'll build up your vocabulary in the BASIC language, and you'll begin to get a sense of the fundamentals of good programming design.

Let's start by taking a closer look at the program you used in Workshop II to practice using the QuickBASIC system. The text of the program W02ST04.BAS is shown below.

```
'------------------------------------------------------------------

'       Program title:  W02ST04.BAS
'       Author:         Bob Basic
'       Date:           1/25/91

'   This program illustrates the use of our first four BASIC
'   statements: PRINT, CLS, ' (single quote), and END.

'------------------------------------------------------------------

'Clear the screen and print a greeting.

    CLS
    PRINT "Hello there, and welcome to QuickBASIC."
    PRINT                   'The effect of this is a carriage return.
    PRINT
    PRINT "Well, it's been nice talking to you. Farewell for now."

END
```

This simple program illustrates some important features of the Structured BASIC language. First, a BASIC program consists of a sequence of instructions called **statements**. As in this program, there is one statement per line.[1] When the program is executed, the statements are carried out one at a time, *in order*; for this reason, we say that a BASIC program obeys the rule of **sequential execution**. The *output* of W02ST04.BAS is shown below.

[1] *Blank lines* and the *indentation* of lines have no meaning in the BASIC language; we use these and other techniques to make the program more readable to *us*, as we'll discuss in Section 2.7.

```
Hello there, and welcome to QuickBASIC.


Well, it's been nice talking to you. Farewell for now.
```

The program W02ST04.BAS uses four fundamental BASIC statements that will appear in practically every program you write. Their descriptions follow.

CLS

CLS is short for "clear screen"; its effect is to clear, that is, *erase*, the output screen, leaving the cursor in the upper left-hand corner. If the CLS statement is not used, output simply begins directly below the output of previously run programs, making it difficult to distinguish one output from the other. It's a good idea to have a CLS statement near the beginning of every QuickBASIC program.

PRINT

PRINT causes a single line of output to be printed. The PRINT statement has several variants. If nothing follows the word *PRINT*, a *blank line* is printed (thus, its effect is a "carriage return"). If *PRINT* is followed by a **string constant**, that is, characters enclosed in quotation marks, then those characters are printed, followed by a carriage return. We can also follow *PRINT* with *expressions* or *variables* (which we'll study in the next section), in which case their *values* are printed.

END

The END statement signals the end of the program; when the END statement is reached, program execution ceases. It's good practice to have an END statement as the last statement of every program.

' (Single Quote)

The appearance of a single quote indicates that any characters following it on that line should be *ignored by the compiler*; this allows us to include explanatory *remarks* or comments that help the reader but don't affect the execution of the program. An alternative to the single quote is the word **REM**, which was used in older versions of BASIC; however, we'll use the single quote exclusively.

The PRINT statement is a little more complex than the other three because the user can choose among several options to follow the word *PRINT*. Example 1 illustrates these options.

EXAMPLE 1

Below, we show several PRINT statements and their corresponding output lines.

PRINT STATEMENT	OUTPUT LINE
`PRINT "*** Far Out!! ***"`	`*** Far Out!! ***`
`PRINT`	
`PRINT "6 + 2 - 3"`	`6 + 2 - 3`
`PRINT 6 + 2 - 3`	`5`
`PRINT "total"`	`total`
`PRINT total`	(prints the value of the variable *total*; see Section 1.2)

If the word *PRINT* is followed by characters enclosed in quotation marks (i.e., a string constant), these characters are simply reproduced exactly as they appear; if they're *not* enclosed in quotes, the program assumes they represent an expression and tries to compute and print the resulting value.

PRACTICE 1.1

1. What is the output of each of the following program segments?

(a)
```
CLS
PRINT "abracadabra"
CLS
```

(b)
```
CLS
PRINT "1 + 2 + 3 + 4 = "
PRINT
PRINT 1 + 2 + 3 + 4
```

(c)
```
PRINT "ALABAMA"
'PRINT "ALASKA"
PRINT "ARIZONA"
'PRINT "ARKANSAS"
```

(d)
```
PRINT "CALIFORNIA"
PRINT "COLORADO"
END
PRINT "CONNECTICUT"
```

2. Write a BASIC program segment that prints the titles of your three favorite movies, one title per line; use each of the four BASIC statements described in Section 1.1.

1.2 Variables and Data Types

As fundamental as the four statements described in Section 1.1 are, our programs won't be able to solve any interesting problems unless they are able to get data from the person running the program. Some people say that the basic design of any computer program is:

1. Get data from user
2. Do calculations on data
3. Output results

Most programming languages, including BASIC, use variables to store data. A **variable** is simply a *memory location* that can hold data of some kind. Think of a memory location as a *box* that holds a single piece of data. This data can be of two basic kinds: *numeric* or *string*. A **numeric variable** can have as its value any *number*, positive or negative, whole number or fraction. A **string variable** has as its value any finite sequence of *characters* (up to 32,767 characters in length for the QuickBASIC system). The particular values taken on by variables are sometimes called **constants**; a number is called a **numeric constant**, and a character string is called a **string constant**.

We refer to each variable by giving it a **name**, which can be any string of letters and/or digits subject to the following three rules:

1. Variable names must *start* with a letter.
2. A variable name may not be a word that's part of the BASIC language, such as *PRINT* or *END* (these words are called *BASIC reserved words*; see Appendix 1).
3. A *string* variable name must end in the dollar symbol ($), and *only* string variable names may do so.

Thus, a variable has associated with it *two* pieces of information: its *name*, which is a label on the memory location, and its *value*, which is the data stored *in* that memory location at any given time. For example, we might have a numeric variable named *score1* whose value is 83; if we think of a memory location as a box, then this box is named *score1* and the box contains the number 83. If we have another variable named *student$*, then it must be a *string* variable; its value could be any string of characters, such as "Tina" (see Figure 1.1).

We can use PRINT statements to print the values of variables by naming the variables without quotation marks. The following examples assume that the variables *score1* and *student$* have the values 83 and Tina, respectively:

PRINT STATEMENT	OUTPUT LINE
`PRINT score1`	`83`
`PRINT student$`	`Tina`
`PRINT student$; "'s score:"; score1`	`Tina's score: 83`

In the third PRINT statement, notice that we printed three different items: two variables and a string constant. If the items are

```
 83                    Tina

score1                 student$
```

FIGURE 1.1

Numeric and String Variables

separated by a *semicolon*, they print right next to each other;[2] if we separate them with a *comma*, they are printed in columns, with five columns to a line.

Semicolons and commas can also be used at the *end* of PRINT statements, in which case the output of the next PRINT statement will begin right after the output of the first PRINT statement. Here's an example, which assumes that the variables *score1* and *student$* have the same values as above:

PRINT STATEMENTS	OUTPUT
`PRINT student$;`	`Tina's score: 83`
`PRINT "'s score:",`	`That's all`
`PRINT score1`	
`PRINT "That's all"`	

Giving Values to Variables

The big question right now is how do we *put* the value 83 in the variable *score1*? One way to give a value to a variable is the **INPUT** statement. Its simplest form is:

INPUT <variable name>

When this statement is executed, the program prints a question mark (the "input prompt") and then *waits* for the user to type in a value at the keyboard; that value is then stored in the memory location whose name is specified in the INPUT statement. For example, if the statement

```
INPUT score1
```

is executed, the program prints a question mark and waits for a number to be typed in at the keyboard; if 83 is typed in, then 83 is stored in the memory location labelled *score1*.

We can input more than one variable in an INPUT statement if we separate their names by commas. For example, if the statement

```
INPUT name$, hoursWorked, hourlyWage
```

is executed, the program prints the question mark input prompt and then waits for *three* items to be typed in: a string constant and two numbers. The user is expected to enter the three values on one line, in the correct order, separated by commas. (Note: You *don't* need quotes when you input string constants.) The following is an output screen for this INPUT statement (user input is shown in regular type):

? Ike, 38, 6.43

The question mark prompt doesn't help us know what we're supposed to enter. To remedy this, we *could* precede the INPUT

---

[2] You may have noticed an extra space in front of the number 83 in the third output; a space is always reserved in front of a number for a *minus sign*.

statement with a PRINT statement that explains what input is expected. Alternatively—and better—we could replace the question mark with our own input prompt. For example, the statement

```
INPUT "Enter your name, please:", name$
```

causes this output, after which it waits for input from the user:

```
Enter your name, please:
```

Note that in the INPUT statement, the input prompt is enclosed by quotes and separated from the first variable by a comma.

Once we've used INPUT to get data from the user, we'll probably want to do some calculations and then print out the results. Variables are also used to store the results of the calculations. We can use the **LET** statement (also called the **assignment statement**) to do this. Its form is:

LET <variable name> = <expression>

When the LET statement is executed, the value of the expression on the right-hand side of the equal sign is evaluated and then its value is stored in the variable specified on the left-hand side of the equal sign. For example, suppose that the variables *hoursWorked* and *hourlyWage* have the values 38 and 6.43, respectively. We could compute their product and store the resulting value in the variable *grossPay* as follows (the asterisk character [*] represents a multiplication sign):

```
LET grossPay = hoursWorked * hourlyWage
```

When this line is executed, the variable *grossPay* will be given the value 244.34 (i.e., the product of 38 and 6.43). Notice that the LET statement does not produce any output; if we want the value of the variable *grossPay* to appear in the output, we'll need to use a PRINT statement.

EXAMPLE 2

Let's design a program that lets drivers enter the number of miles they've driven and the number of hours it took and then prints out their average speed. To do this, we must first outline our **algorithm**, that is, the basic steps our program must take to solve this problem:

1. Input number of miles and hours
2. Compute average speed
3. Print results

The average speed is equal to the number of miles divided by the number of hours. We should also add (to every program!) a Step 0: *Introduce* the program to the user, *explaining* what it will do. Now that we have planned our program, we can choose names for our variables, and then we're ready to go. The following program does the job:

```
'------------------------------------------------------------
'    PROGRAM TITLE:   C01EX02.BAS
'    AUTHOR:          Ralph Nader
'    DATE:            2/14/91

'This program inputs a number of miles driven and the number
'of hours it took, and prints the average speed.
'------------------------------------------------------------

'Introduce program and get numbers of miles and hours

    CLS
    PRINT "This program computes your average driving speed."
    PRINT
    INPUT "How many miles did you drive? ", numMiles
    PRINT
    INPUT "And how many hours did that take? ", numHours
    PRINT
    PRINT

'Calculate and print results

    LET speed = numMiles / numHours
    PRINT "Your average speed was"; speed; "miles per hour."

END
```

Sample output follows.

```
This program computes your average driving speed.

How many miles did you drive? 132

And how many hours did that take? 2.5


Your average speed was 52.8 miles per hour.
```

Notice that we've made both the program and its output easy to read; it's important to develop these good habits *now* while you're writing simple programs, so that they'll be second nature by the time you're writing more complex programs. By the way, you should also notice the single space on either side of the number 52.8 in the last output line; these spaces are part of the way QuickBASIC printed the number, *not* part of our quoted strings. When you write a program, first make sure it's producing correct results; then fine-tune it to make your output look just right.

PRACTICE 1.2

1. For each of the following words, indicate whether it is a legal variable name; if it's not, indicate why not; if it is, identify it as a *numeric* or *string* variable:

   (a) `money` (e) `CLS`
   (b) `moreMoney` (f) `xyz123$`
   (c) `2Sheds` (g) `print`
   (d) `HAROLD$` (h) `5thExam`

2. For *every line* of the following BASIC program segment, write down the *exact output*; in a separate area, keep track of the values of variables, assuming that the person running the program enters the following values (in the order they appear): Quayle, Dan, 60, 50, 40. (Keeping track of what a program does line by line is called *hand-tracing the program*; in a sense, you're pretending to be the computer.)

```
CLS
PRINT "This program computes your exam average."
PRINT
INPUT "Enter your last name: ", last$
INPUT "Enter your first name: ", first$
PRINT
PRINT "Enter three exam grades, separated by commas."
INPUT exam1, exam2, exam3
LET average = (exam1 + exam2 + exam3) / 3
PRINT
PRINT "NAME: "; first$; " "; last$
PRINT "AVERAGE: "; average
```

1.3 Operators and Precedence

We have already seen how we can use symbols like +, *, and / to form **arithmetic expressions**, that is, expressions that yield numbers when evaluated. These symbols are called **arithmetic operators**, because they "operate" on one or more numbers to produce a new value. Table 1.1 summarizes the most commonly used arithmetic operators.

TABLE 1.1 **Arithmetic Operators**

Name	Symbol	Example
Exponentiation	^	`2 ^ 3 = 8`
Negation	−	`-(-3) = 3`
[Multiplication	*	`5 * 7 = 35`
[Division	/	`14 / 5 = 2.8`
Integer division	\	`14 \ 5 = 2`
Modulo arithmetic (i.e., remainder)	**MOD**	`14 MOD 5 = 4`
[Addition	+	`6 + 5 = 11`
[Subtraction	−	`13 - 4 = 9`

EXAMPLE 3

Two of the arithmetic operations, *integer division* and *modulo arithmetic,* may seem unfamiliar, but they are simply the *quotient* and the *remainder* (remember those terms from *long division*?). The following program segment illustrates their use (it also shows the use of *commas* in PRINT statements for printing data in *columns;* the full program can be found in the file C01EX03.BAS):

```
'Introduce program and get dividend and divisor

    CLS
    PRINT "This program does LONG DIVISION for you!"
    PRINT
    INPUT "Enter DIVIDEND (number to be divided): ", dividend
    INPUT "Enter DIVISOR: ", divisor

'Compute quotient and divisor

    LET quotient = dividend \ divisor
    LET remainder = dividend MOD divisor

'Print results

    PRINT
    PRINT
    PRINT "DIVIDEND", "DIVISOR", "QUOTIENT", "REMAINDER"
    PRINT "--------", "-------", "--------", "---------"
    PRINT dividend, divisor, quotient, remainder
```

Sample output follows:

```
This program does LONG DIVISION for you!

Enter DIVIDEND (number to be divided): 90
Enter DIVISOR: 11


DIVIDEND      DIVISOR       QUOTIENT      REMAINDER
--------      -------       --------      ---------
 90            11            8             2
```

While some special problems have associated formulas that require integer division and modulo arithmetic, most of the time we'll use the four basic operations of addition, subtraction, multiplication, and (exact) division, whose symbols are +, −, *, and /.

An important question concerning operators is how to evaluate expressions that use more than one operator. For example, consider the following expression:

$$4 + 3 * 2$$

Does the value of this expression equal 14 (= (4 + 3) * 2) or does it equal 10 (= 4 + (3 * 2))? We need to know which answer the QuickBASIC system will choose. Well, QuickBASIC evaluates arithmetic operators in a certain fixed order, called the **order of precedence**. To say one operator has *precedence* over another means that if both appear in the same expression, the one with higher precedence will be evaluated first. In Table 1.1, we listed the operators *in order of precedence*, with bracketed operators having equal precedence. For example, multiplication and division have equal precedence, and they both have precedence over addition and subtraction, which themselves have equal precedence. Thus, since multiplication has precedence over addition, the following is true:

$$4 + 3 * 2 = 4 + 6 = 10$$

If we want to do the addition first in this example, we must use *parentheses*:

$$(4 + 3) * 2 = 7 * 2 = 14$$

If two or more operators with equal precedence appear in an expression, they are evaluated *from left to right*, as follows:

$$2 + 3 - 4 + 5 = 5 - 4 + 5 = 1 + 5 = 6$$

and

$$6 + 7 * 8 - 9 = 6 + 56 - 9 = 62 - 9 = 53$$

If you have a complex expression in a program and want to be especially sure of how it will be evaluated, *use parentheses*!

In addition to the arithmetic operators described above, there is also one **string operator**, called **concatenation**, whose symbol is the plus sign (+). The concatenation of two strings is the new string that results when the two strings are joined into one. For example,

```
LET firstName$ = "Oscar"
LET lastName$ = "Meyer"
LET wholeName$ = firstName$ + " " + lastName$
PRINT wholeName$
```

will produce the output

```
Oscar Meyer
```

PRACTICE 1.3

Using the values shown for the variables listed below, evaluate the expressions that follow (remember to consider the rules of precedence if more than one operator is present).

first	*second*	*third*	*good$*	*bad$*
4	28.2	−9	Happy	Sad

(a) `second - 10 * 2`
(b) `-third`
(c) `good$ + bad$`
(d) `second / 2 + third`
(e) `8 * (20 \ 8) + 20 MOD 8`
(f) `9 - 2 ^ 3 + 4 * 5 MOD 6`
(g) `bad$ + " and " + good$`

Note: In Sections 1.4 and 1.5, we will introduce the wide variety of built-in numeric and string functions that are available in QuickBASIC. The goal of your first reading of this material should be to get a general idea of what functions there are and how to use them. Later, you can refer back to these sections to remind yourself about particular functions.

1.4 Numeric Functions in QuickBASIC

The arithmetic operators described in Table 1.1 let us form many of the arithmetic expressions we'll need—but what if we need the *square root* of a number (used to compute the standard deviation in statistics) or a *trigonometric function* such as sine or cosine (used in geometric formulas)? These kinds of quantities can be calculated using

TABLE 1.2 Built-in Numeric Functions

Function Name	Description
ABS(*x*)	Absolute value of x
CINT(*x*)	Value of x rounded to the nearest integer
INT(*x*)	Largest integer not greater than x
FIX(*x*)	The integer obtained by removing the fractional part of x
LOG(*x*)	Natural logarithm of x
EXP(*x*)	Natural exponential function
SGN(*x*)	If x is positive, SGN(x) = 1 If x is zero, SGN(x) = 0 If x is negative, SGN(x) = −1
SQR(*x*)	The (nonnegative) square root of x
SIN(*x*)	Sine of x radians
COS(*x*)	Cosine of x radians
TAN(*x*)	Tangent of x radians
ATN(*x*)	Arctangent of x (result in radians)
TIMER	Number of seconds past midnight on computer's internal clock
RND	Pseudorandom number (0 <= RND < 1)

numeric functions provided by QuickBASIC. For example, if x is some number, then the BASIC expression for its square root is **SQR(x)** and its sine is **SIN(x)**. Table 1.2 shows a list of *built-in* numeric functions provided by QuickBASIC (in Chapter 6, we'll learn how to design our own *user-defined* functions to augment those supplied by QuickBASIC). In the table, x represents either a numeric variable or an arithmetic expression.

Since Table 1.2 contains a lot of information, let's look at some of the numeric functions in more detail.

ABS(x)

The **absolute value** of a number is its *magnitude* or *positive part*, that is, what you get if you "erase the minus sign." So, for example,

$$ABS(-5.43) = ABS(5.43) = 5.43, \ ABS(0) = 0$$

and

$$ABS(4 * 5 - 6 * 7) = ABS(20 - 42) = ABS(-22) = 22$$

The quantity inside the parentheses of a function, such as *−5.43* or *4 * 5 − 6 * 7* in the above examples, is called the **argument** of the function; in other words, the argument of a function is the quantity that we "plug in" to the function.

One use of the ABS function is to compute the *distance* between two numbers, which is simply the absolute value of their *difference*. For instance, the distance between the numbers −5 and 7 is ABS(−5 − 7) = ABS(−12) = 12.

The Rounding Functions CINT(x) and INT(x)

Both these functions round off numbers with fractional parts to whole numbers. **CINT(*x*)** rounds x to the *nearest* whole number; **INT(*x*)** rounds x *down*, that is, to the closest whole number not larger than x. Depending on the value of x, these two rounded values can agree or disagree. Table 1.3 illustrates this.

QuickBASIC provides these two varieties (and a third, FIX(x), which we won't discuss) to meet most of the rounding needs you might have in a program. For instance, if you wrote a program to simulate a cash register, you'd probably want to round to the nearest penny, so CINT might be useful (also see Example 4 below); however, if you wrote a program that calculated how much of your salary to withhold for taxes, you'd probably want to round down, so you'd use INT.

TABLE 1.3 Some Results of Rounding Functions

Value of x:	9.5	6	2.1	−2.1	−6	−9.5
CINT(x):	10	6	2	−2	−6	−10
INT(x):	9	6	2	−3	−6	−10

EXAMPLE 4

Let's write a program that allows a shopper to enter prices and weights of two grocery items, measured in dollars and ounces; the program should then print the *unit prices* of the two items, rounded to the nearest penny. For instance, if 12 ounces of True Grit cereal costs $1.79, its unit price is obtained by dividing 1.79 by 12 to get .1491667 or $.15 per ounce to the nearest penny. The division is easy, but how do we use our rounding functions (probably CINT) to round to *two decimal places* instead of to the nearest whole number? The trick is to move the decimal over two places, do the rounding, and then move it back. The way to move decimals is to multiply or divide by powers of 10, so we could do the following:

Multiply by 100:	.1491667	→	14.91667
Use CINT to round off:	14.91667	→	15
Divide by 100:	15	→	.15

Get the idea? Let's write an algorithm for the problem:

1. Introduce program and get prices and weights
2. Compute unit prices
3. Round off unit prices
4. Print results

At this point, the program is fairly straightforward, as follows:

```
'-------------------------------------------------------------
'        PROGRAM NAME:    C01EX04.BAS
'        AUTHOR:          J. M. Keynes
'        DATE:            JULY 21, 1992
'This program inputs prices and weights for two grocery items,
'and then prints the corresponding unit prices.
'-------------------------------------------------------------

'Introduce program and get prices and weights.

    CLS
    PRINT "$$$$$$$$$$$$$$$$$$$$$$$$$$$$$$$$$$$$$$$$$$$$$$$$$$$$$"
    PRINT "$$$                                          $$$"
    PRINT "$$$       CONSUMER'S COMPARISON              $$$"
    PRINT "$$$              CORNER                      $$$"
    PRINT "$$$                                          $$$"
    PRINT "$$$$$$$$$$$$$$$$$$$$$$$$$$$$$$$$$$$$$$$$$$$$$$$$$$$$$"
    PRINT
    PRINT
    PRINT "Why pay more? We help you choose"
    PRINT "the less expensive of two items!"
    PRINT
    PRINT
    INPUT "Enter price of first item ($): ", price1
    INPUT "Enter weight of first item (oz.): ", weight1
    PRINT
```

```
    INPUT "Enter price of second item ($): ", price2
    INPUT "Enter weight of second item (oz.): ", weight2

'Compute unit prices

    LET unit1 = price1 / weight1
    LET unit2 = price2 / weight2

'Round unit prices off to nearest penny

    LET unit1 = CINT(unit1 * 100) / 100
    LET unit2 = CINT(unit2 * 100) / 100

'Print results

    CLS
    PRINT "PRICE", "WEIGHT", "UNIT PRICE"
    PRINT "-----", "------", "----------"
    PRINT
    PRINT "$"; price1, weight1; "oz.", "  $"; unit1
    PRINT "$"; price2, weight2; "oz.", "  $"; unit2

END
```

Sample output follows.

```
$$$$$$$$$$$$$$$$$$$$$$$$$$$$$$$$$$$$$$$$$$
$$$                                    $$$
$$$      CONSUMER'S COMPARISON         $$$
$$$             CORNER                 $$$
$$$                                    $$$
$$$$$$$$$$$$$$$$$$$$$$$$$$$$$$$$$$$$$$$$$$


Why pay more? We help you choose
the less expensive of two items!


Enter price of first item ($): 1.79
Enter weight of first item (oz.): 12

Enter price of second item ($): 2.29
Enter weight of second item (oz.): 14.6
```

(new screen)

```
    PRICE         WEIGHT        UNIT PRICE
    -----         ------        ----------

    $ 1.79         12 oz          $ .15
    $ 2.29         14.6 oz        $ .16
```

Be sure to look carefully at the lines where we do the rounding to the nearest penny, for example,

```
LET unit1 = CINT(unit1 * 100) / 100
```

If you work *outward* from the variable *unit1* in parentheses, you see that we multiply by 100, *then* use the CINT function, *then* divide that result by 100; if you prefer, these three operations can be done on three separate lines (the power of 10 that we use corresponds to the number of decimal places we want, e.g., for two decimal places we use $10^2 = 100$). Also notice that we stored the final result back in the same place, namely, the variable *unit1*; this is perfectly legal, but again, if you prefer, you could use another variable to store the rounded price.

SQR(*x*)

This function computes the (nonnegative) *square root* of the number x, that is, the nonnegative number whose square is x. For example,

$$SQR(9) = 3 \qquad SQR(35) = 5.91608 \qquad SQR(0) = 0$$

Of course, negative numbers don't have square roots; if your program contains the SQR function with a *negative argument*, when you *run* the program you'll get the error message "Illegal function call."

PRACTICE 1.4

1. Calculate the value of each of the following expressions:

   (a) `ABS(-11.48)`
   (b) `CINT(7.661)`
   (c) `INT(7.661)`
   (d) `CINT(-9.2)`
   (e) `INT(-9.2)`
   (f) `SQR(81)`
   (g) `SQR(0)`
   (h) `INT(SQR(9) / 2)`
   (i) `CINT(123.456 * 10) / 10`

2. The formula below performs yet another kind of rounding not provided by the two functions CINT and INT. Calculate its result for the following values of the variable x and then describe in words what kind of rounding is being done:

   Values of x: 3.2, 3.9, 3, 2.001, −2, −2.4, −2.99

   Rounding formula: −INT(−x)

1.5 String Functions in QuickBASIC

In Section 1.4, we saw that, in addition to arithmetic operators, QuickBASIC provides a large selection of built-in *numeric functions* that allow us to form many different arithmetic expressions. In the same way, just as QuickBASIC provides the *string* operator + (i.e., concatenation), it also provides a wide variety of *built-in string functions*.

Table 1.4 below lists some of the most frequently used built-in

TABLE 1.4 **Built-in String Functions**

Function Name	Description
LEFT$(*x$*,*n*)	Returns a string consisting of the *first n* letters of x$
RIGHT$(*x$*,*n*)	Returns a string consisting of the *last n* letters of x$
MID$(*x$*,*start*,*n*)	Returns a string consisting of *n* letters from x$ starting with position *start*
LCASE$(*x$*)	Returns the string that results from changing all uppercase letters (A–Z) in x$ to *lowercase* (a–z)
UCASE$(*x$*)	Returns the string that results from changing all lowercase letters (a–z) in x$ to *uppercase* (A–Z)
SPACE$(*n*)	Returns a string consisting of *n blank spaces*
STRING$(*n*,*x$*)	Returns a string consisting of the *first character* of x$ repeated *n* times
LEN(*x$*)	Returns a number equal to the *length* of x$
ASC(*x$*)	Returns a number equal to the *ASCII code* of x$
CHR$(*n*)	Returns a string consisting of the *character* whose *ASCII code* is *n*

string functions. As you read this table, notice several things. First, some of the functions have *more than one argument*, that is, they require more than one quantity to be plugged in. In addition, sometimes the arguments are strings and sometimes they are numbers; we have used the symbol **x$** to stand for a string variable or expression and the symbols **n** and **start** to stand for numeric variables or expressions. Second, the *result produced by the function* is sometimes a string and sometimes a number; you can tell which it is by looking for a **$** in the function name. For example, the name of the first function, LEFT$, includes the dollar symbol, indicating that its result is a string, while the name of the next-to-last function, ASC, without the symbol, indicates that its result is a number.

Let's look at some of these functions in more detail now.

LEFT$(*x$*,*n*), RIGHT$(*x$*,*n*), and MID$(*x$*,*start*,*n*)

All three of these functions return *parts* of the string specified in the arguments; a *left*-hand piece, a *right*-hand piece, or a piece taken from the *middle* of the string. The numeric arguments are used to specify exactly which pieces. For example, if

x$ = "Bruce Springsteen"

then

LEFT$(x$,3) = "Bru"

RIGHT$(x$,3) = "een"

MID$(x$,5,3) = "e S"

LCASE$(*x$*) and UCASE$(*x$*)

These functions return the strings that result from changing all the letters in the specified string to all *lowercase* or all *uppercase*:

LCASE$("10 Downing St.") = "10 downing st."

UCASE$("10 Downing St.") = "10 DOWNING ST."

EXAMPLE 5

Let's write a program that inputs a five-letter word and then prints it out diagonally in capital letters. For instance, if the user enters "Howdy," the output is:

```
H
 O
  W
   D
    Y
```

The algorithm is:

1. Introduce program and input word
2. Print out the diagonal word, one line at a time:
   a. Print capitalized first letter, then carriage return
   b. Print one space, then capitalized second letter, then carriage return
   c. Print two spaces, then capitalized third letter, then carriage return
   d. Print three spaces, then capitalized fourth letter, then carriage return
   e. Print four spaces, then capitalized fifth letter, then carriage return

To produce a "capitalized" *n*th letter in Steps 2a–2e, we'll need the MID$ function to get the letter, followed by the UCASE$ function to capitalize it. Although this can take two steps, we can actually achieve it in one. If we use the variable name *word$* for the variable that stores the inputted five-letter word, the following expression returns the capitalized *n*th letter (we'll actually use the numbers 1 to 5 in place of *n*). Study it to make sure you understand it.

```
UCASE$(MID$(word$, n, 1))
```

The program appears below (also, see the file C01EX05.BAS on the SAMPLES disk).

```
'------------------------------------------------------------

'      PROGRAM NAME:   C01EX05.BAS
'      AUTHOR:         J. Gutenberg
'      DATE:           July 26, 1992

'This program inputs a 5-letter word and prints it out
'diagonally with the letters capitalized.
'------------------------------------------------------------
```

```
'Program intro and get word

    CLS
    PRINT "This program prints a word on the slant!"
    PRINT
    INPUT "Enter a 5-letter word -->", word$

'Print word on diagonal, one line at a time

    CLS
    PRINT UCASE$(MID$(word$, 1, 1))
    PRINT " "; UCASE$(MID$(word$, 2, 1))
    PRINT "  "; UCASE$(MID$(word$, 3, 1))
    PRINT "   "; UCASE$(MID$(word$, 4, 1))
    PRINT "    "; UCASE$(MID$(word$, 5, 1))

END
```

Note that we used string constants to insert the spaces we needed for Steps 2b–2e; an alternative would have been to use the SPACE$ function described in Table 1.4. If you like, try modifying this program yourself to use that function.

What do you think happens if the user enters a word with more than five letters? A more difficult question is what if the user enters a word with *fewer* than five letters; in that case, one or more of our MID$ functions will look for characters that aren't there! In this case, the MID$ function returns what's called the **null character**: this character really means the *absence* of a character (not the same as a blank space, which *is* an actual character). If we were to write the null character as a string constant, it would be two consecutive quotes with *nothing* in between (because the null character *is* nothing), that is, "", whereas the string constant representing a blank space is " ".

In Chapter 2, we'll introduce the notion of a *looping structure*, which could be used to improve this program. With a loop, we'll be able to print diagonal words of *arbitrary length*, rather than deciding in advance how many letters to handle (see Chapter 2, Programming Problem 4).

PRACTICE 1.5

1. Calculate the value of each of the expressions below and identify it as a *number* or a *string*. Assume that the variables used have the following values: *name1$* = "Captain Kirk", *name2$* = "Mr. Spock", *num1* = 4, *num2* = 10.
   (a) `LEFT$("Goodbye", 3)`
   (b) `RIGHT$(name1$, num1)`
   (c) `MID$("Goodbye" + name2$, 6, 3)`
   (d) `LCASE$("A1b2C3d4")`
2. Write a program segment that inputs a word and then prints

the capitalized first letter. Thus, the output for any of the following words should be "Y": YES, Yes, yes, yeah, YO, yellow-bellied sapsucker.

1.6 Designing and Testing Programs

We have already learned a lot about the BASIC language in this chapter. Now, we'd like to focus on some of the techniques of algorithm design we've used and also say a few words about testing programs once they're written. Program writing can be viewed as a *three-stage process*:

Stage 1: Design an algorithm and refine it as needed

Stage 2: Translate the algorithm into a computer program

Stage 3: Test and debug the program

We'll discuss this process briefly now and study it in more detail in subsequent chapters (especially Chapter 4).

When you're given any problem you want to solve or task you want to perform using a BASIC program, the first step is to take the time to make sure that you *understand the problem*. Once you know what your goal is, you can proceed with *Stage 1* of its solution: *outline an algorithm* to solve the problem. At this point we should say precisely what we mean by the word *algorithm*.

> **Algorithm** The careful specification of a *finite* sequence of steps that, when carried out, will always result in a correct solution to a problem (a cookbook *recipe* is an excellent example of an algorithm).

The algorithm outlines that we've designed in this chapter have been relatively simple, in the sense that it has been fairly easy to go from an "English language algorithm" to a "BASIC language algorithm," that is, a program. In subsequent chapters, as our problems become a bit more complicated, we'll need to design our algorithms in *phases*. In other words, we'll start with a rough outline of the *major steps* and then *refine those steps* little by little until we're able to translate our design into a program. As you become more comfortable with the BASIC language, you'll often find that you write your algorithms in a mixture of English and BASIC words; this "mixed language" is called **pseudocode**.

The process of designing an algorithm in phases and refining the steps little by little is sometimes called **top-down design**: you start at the "top" (i.e., with the problem statement) and work your way "down" into the specific steps of the final algorithm. This idea can be displayed graphically by the use of **top-down diagrams** (also called **hierarchy charts**). Figure 1.2 shows a possible top-down diagram for Example 4 in Section 1.4.

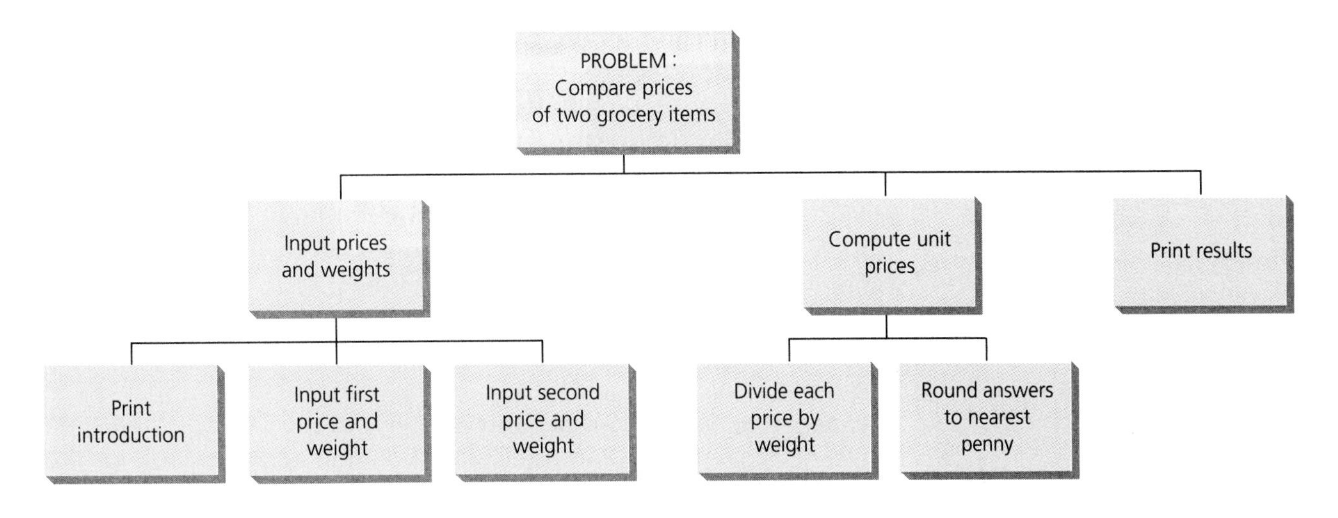

FIGURE 1.2

A Top-Down Diagram

After you design an algorithm, you translate it into a BASIC program in *Stage 2*. As we indicated above, this is a gradual process; as you refine your algorithm, spelling it out in more and more detail, you're usually simultaneously writing the skeleton of your final program. As you begin the program-writing process, keep the term structured programming in mind.

Structured programming A technique of writing programs so that the physical setup of the program (i.e., its spacing, indentation, comments, variable names, etc.) clearly reflects the main steps of the corresponding algorithm design.

Look back now at some of the programming examples in this chapter (e.g., Examples 2, 4, and 5) to see what we mean. In every case, we have used *comments, spacing,* and *indentation* to "set off" the program segments that correspond to each of the main steps in our algorithm. We've used *meaningful variable names* so that our BASIC statements reflect the associated English language steps in the algorithm. We've begun each program with a *heading* composed of comments that describe what the program does. As you write your own programs, you should try to adhere to this style; if you concentrate on it now, it will be natural by the time you write more complex programs.

Remember: You* will *develop* some *programming style; now is the time to make sure you develop a* good *programming style!

In Section 2.7, we'll return to the subject of programming style, spelling out in detail specific techniques that we use—and that we want *you* to use—when writing programs. For now, though, you should try to mimic the programming style used in the examples in the text and on the SAMPLES disk. In particular, notice our use of comments, spacing, indentation, and meaningful variable names.

We do need to say a few words about indentation in QuickBASIC. The QuickBASIC system makes it easy to indent: once you use tabs or spaces to indent a line, all subsequent lines are indented that same amount; if you want to "outdent" a subsequent line, that is, indent it less, you can use the *Backspace* key to move to the previous indentation level. We use tab settings of equal size, *four spaces each*—and we strongly recommend that you do the same. Unfortunately, the default setting for QuickBASIC is tab settings of eight spaces each. Happily, it's easy to find out what tab settings your system has and to change them if necessary.

To change the QuickBASIC tab settings. From the *Options Menu*, select the *Display* option.[3] In the Dialog Box that appears, look for the field called *Tab Stops;* if the number in that field is *4*, you can use the Esc key to cancel the menu; otherwise, use the Tab key to move to the *Tab Stops* field; enter the number **4** and press **<Return>** to change the tab stops. You should only have to do this *once;* the tab settings should remain changed the next time you start QuickBASIC.

Once you've written a "first draft" of a program, it's time to *test and debug* it, which is *Stage 3* of the program-writing process. This means typing it into the QuickBASIC system and running it several times to check for errors. There are two kinds of errors (also known as **bugs**) that your program can have. First, there are **syntax errors**, which are grammatical or spelling errors in the use of the BASIC language (e.g., "PWINT" instead of "PRINT"); these errors usually prevent your program from compiling. Second, there are **logical errors** (also called **semantic errors**), that prevent your program from correctly performing the jobs it was designed to do. For instance, the following BASIC program, which is supposed to input two numbers and compute their average, is *syntactically correct* but gives *incorrect answers* (the reason is that there should be parentheses around the quantity "num1 + num2"):

```
INPUT "Enter two numbers: ", num1, num2
LET average = num1 + num2 / 2
PRINT average
```

To test for logical errors, you have to design a set of **test data**, that is, data on which to run the program; in gathering this data, you should try to think of all the possible kinds of data that the program might encounter. Then, you must run the program on each piece of test data and *carefully read the output to determine whether it gives correct results.* Remember, too, that if you change your program to correct one bug, you should run it on *all* the test data again, because you may have introduced another, different bug!

The process of finding and correcting bugs in your programs can sometimes be difficult. We'll look informally at some debugging tech-

---

[3] If you're using QuickBASIC Version 4.0 rather than 4.5, use the *View Menu* and select *Options*.

niques in the examples in the next two chapters; then we'll devote all of Chapter 4 to a study of techniques of algorithm design and program testing. As your programs get larger, this process will take place on *pieces* of your program, which you can then merge into a complete program; this is the essence of *modular design*. First, though, we must learn about Structured BASIC *control structures*, needed for writing programs to carry out algorithms, which we'll introduce in the next chapter.

Chapter Summary 

In this chapter, we've begun the process of learning to design BASIC programs to perform specified tasks. A BASIC program consists of a sequence of instructions called *statements*. When we run a BASIC program, it obeys the rule of *sequential execution*: each statement is executed one at a time, in order.

The first four statements that we learned were *CLS*, *PRINT*, *END*, and ' (single quote). CLS clears the output screen; PRINT, followed by variables and/or string constants, prints the specified quantities on the output screen; END indicates the end of the program, and ' signals a *comment*, that is, characters that should be ignored by the compiler.

BASIC programs use *variables*, which represent memory locations, to store data. A *numeric variable* can be any kind of number (whole number or fraction, positive or negative); a *string variable* can be any finite sequence of characters (any particular sequence of characters is called a *string constant*, just as any particular number is a *numeric constant*). *Variable names* may be any sequence of characters that do not form a BASIC reserved word, provided they start with a letter and, for string variables only, end with the dollar sign, $.

We learned two ways to give values to variables. The *INPUT* statement allows users to enter values while the program is running; the *LET* statement (also called the *assignment statement*) allows users to do calculations within the program and store the results in variables.

We can combine variables and constants in numeric or string *expressions* to produce new values. BASIC provides both *operators* and *built-in functions* for use in forming expressions. The *arithmetic (or numeric) operators* we saw, ^, −, *, /, \, MOD, +, and −, represent, respectively, the operations of *exponentiation*, *negation*, *multiplication*, *division*, *integer division*, *modulo arithmetic*, *addition*, and *subtraction*. They are listed in *order of precedence*, for example, all multiplications in an expression will be performed before any additions are performed. We also saw a single *string operator*, +, representing the operation of *concatenation*.

QuickBASIC provides a large number of *built-in functions*. We discussed *numeric functions* (see Table 1.2 in Section 1.4) for rounding fractions and calculating square roots, and other functions such as the logarithmic and trigonometric functions.

In addition to numeric functions, QuickBASIC has various *built-in string functions*, which allow us to do such things as calculate *parts* of strings, change all letters in a string to upper or lowercase, and compute the *length* of a string.

Finally, we outlined the *three-stage program design process. Stage 1* is the design and refinement of an *algorithm* to solve the given problem; this begins with carefully reading and *understanding* what is being asked. *Stage 2* is the translation of the algorithm into a computer program; if the algorithm is clearly spelled out, this is the easiest of the three stages. *Stage 3* is the testing and debugging of the program to remove all *syntax errors* and *logical errors.*

When writing the program that corresponds to the algorithm, it is important to use techniques of *good programming style* to produce a *structured program*, that is, an easy-to-read program whose physical setup reflects the main steps of the algorithm. This can be done by the use of spacing, comments, indentation, and meaningful variable names, as our examples illustrate.

? Review Questions

1. Explain each of the following ideas briefly:

(a) sequential execution
(b) variable
(c) numeric variable
(d) string variable
(e) INPUT statement
(f) assignment (LET) statement
(g) arithmetic expression
(h) arithmetic operator
(i) precedence
(j) string operator
(k) built-in function
(l) algorithm
(m) pseudocode
(n) structured programming
(o) syntax error
(p) logical error

2. Explain exactly what happens when each of the following BASIC statements is executed, both in the computer's memory and on the output screen:

(a) `CLS`
(b) `PRINT "ABC"; "XYZ"`
(c) `PRINT "ABC", "XYZ"`
(d) `END`
(e) `'Introduce program`
(f) `INPUT num`
(g) `INPUT "Please enter a number: ", number`
(h) `INPUT name$, height, weight`
(i) `LET sum = 111 + 93 - 100 * 5 + 63 / 2`
(j) `LET result = first + second + third`
(k) `LET answer = CINT(answer)`
(l) `LET num = INT(num * 10) / 10`
(m) `LET init$ = LEFT$(firstName$, 1) + LEFT$(secondName$, 1)`
(n) `LET x$ = UCASE$(x$)`
(o) `PRINT$ MID$("Goodbye", 5, 3)`

Programming Problems

While designing and writing the following programs, be sure to use the three-stage process of program design discussed in Section 1.6. When writing your programs, mimic the style used in the examples and on the SAMPLES disk. The goal is a program that is easy to understand and that clearly reflects your algorithm design.

1. Write a program that clears the screen and then uses several PRINT statements to draw a box with a message of your choice inside.

2. Write a program that inputs a Centigrade temperature and outputs the equivalent temperature in degrees Fahrenheit and degrees Kelvin. To convert from Centigrade to Fahrenheit, you multiply by 9/5 and then add 32; to convert from Centigrade to Kelvin, you add 273.16. For instance, a Centigrade temperature of 20° corresponds to 68° Fahrenheit and 293.16° Kelvin. (You may also wish to compare this program to W02PB02.BAS on the SAMPLES disk.)

3. Write a program that asks users to input their last, first, and middle names. The program should then print the full name, with all letters capitalized, in the form "FirstName MiddleInit. LastName." For example, if the input strings are Newman, Alfred, and Edward, then the output string is as follows (notice the period after the middle initial):

```
ALFRED E. NEWMAN
```

4. (a) There are two different units of measure for *angles*: degrees and radians. To convert an angle from degree measure to radian measure, you multiply by the number *pi* (pronounced "pie" and also denoted by the Greek symbol π), which is approximately equal to 3.141593, and divide by 180. For example, a right angle has degree measure 90° and radian measure 90 * 3.141593 / 180 = 1.570796. Write a program that inputs the degree measure of an angle and computes and prints the equivalent radian measure.
   (b) The *built-in trigonometric functions,* SIN, COS, and TAN, all require that their arguments be *angles in radian measure*. Modify the program you wrote in part (a) so that after the user inputs an angle in degree measure, the program prints the sine, cosine, and tangent of the angle; do *not* print the radian measure of the angle (although you'll have to *compute* the radian measure in order to evaluate the three trigonometric functions).

5. Gasoline at the Cost Cutter Gas Mart costs 115.9¢ (= $1.159) per gallon. Write a program that lets users enter the number of gallons they bought, computes the total cost, and prints it in dollars, rounded *up* to the nearest penny (see Practice 1.4, Exercise 2). Be sure to check your program's output for correctness! While testing, you might want to print both the exact cost and the rounded cost, to see that they're being calculated correctly—but your final output should show only the rounded cost.

6. (a) Write a program that displays a table showing the squares and square roots of the integers from 1 to 5. Make the table easy to read (i.e., neat and clearly labelled).

(b) Modify the program in part (a) so that it lets the user choose the starting point and then prints a table showing the squares and square roots of the integers from the starting point to the starting point plus 4. What happens if the user enters a negative starting point?

(c) Modify the program in part (b) so that it prints the square roots rounded to three decimal places.

7. Design a simplified automatic bank teller that inputs the user's last and first name, account number, and bank balance. It should then ask for the amount of money to be deposited and the amount to be withdrawn. Last, it should clear the screen and print a display showing name, account number, old balance, and new balance.

8. The Mall 24 Cinema has the following pricing policy: children $2, adults $5, and senior citizens $3. Write a program that simulates an automatic cashier at the Mall 24 Cinema. It should ask how many children, how many adults, and how many senior citizens. It should then print the total cost and ask for payment. Finally, it should print the change due.

9. Write a program that asks users their first name, then the current year, then their age. The program then tells them (a) in what year they were born, and (b) what age they will turn in the year 2000. The output should contain the user's name at least once. The following is a sample of how the output might look:

```
Please type in your first name. Bob

What is the current year? 1992

How old are you, Bob? 38

Well, Bob, if you have already had your birthday this year,
then you were born in 1954 and you will turn 46 in the
year 2000.

Otherwise, you were born in 1953 and you will turn 47 in
the year 2000.

See you later, Bob.
```

10. Write programs, each of which inputs a five-letter word and then uses string functions to print it out in the following "decorative" ways (output is shown for the word *Hello*):

(a)
```
     O
    L
   L
  E
 H
```

(b)
```
H
EE
LLL
LLLL
OOOOO
```

CHAPTER

2

INTRODUCTION TO CONTROL STRUCTURES: THE FOR...NEXT LOOP

CHAPTER PREVIEW In this chapter, we'll learn how to write programs to do more complex tasks by using *control structures*; we'll study in detail the *FOR...NEXT* structure, which lets us *repeat* a specified set of statements; we'll introduce the *READ* and *DATA* statements, which, together with the FOR...NEXT structure, let us process large sets of data conveniently; finally, we'll discuss the use of *good programming style* to help make our increasingly complex programs easier to understand.

2.1 Control Structures

In Chapter 1, we learned how to write simple programs using the BASIC statements CLS, END, PRINT, INPUT, and LET. We also learned the rule of *sequential execution*: the statements in a BASIC program are executed *one by one in order from first to last*. For example, program segment 1 below makes sense, but program segment 2 does not.

1. ```
   INPUT price, quantity
   LET unitPrice = price / quantity
   PRINT unitPrice
   ```
2. ```
   LET unitPrice = price / quantity
   INPUT price, quantity
   PRINT unitPrice
   ```

This important rule of sequential execution is natural, but there are many circumstances in which we might want more flexibility about the order in which statements are executed. In the unit pricing example above, for instance, we may want to *repeat* the lines in segment 1 several times to compute the unit prices of several different items; or, after computing a single unit price, we may want to make a *decision* based on its value about whether to print "expensive" or "cheap."

QuickBASIC provides several special statements called **control structures** that allow the programmer to *alter the order* in which statements are executed. There are two fundamental types of control structures.

Looping structure Allows the program to *repeat* a group of statements over and over. We will study two QuickBASIC looping structures, FOR...NEXT and DO...LOOP.

Decision structure Allows the program to *decide* between two or more alternative groups of statements to execute, depending on what conditions happen to hold. We will learn about two QuickBASIC decision structures, IF...END IF and SELECT...END SELECT.

The rest of this chapter will focus on the FOR...NEXT looping structure.

2.2 The FOR...NEXT Structure

The **FOR...NEXT** looping structure permits a program to *repeat* a particular set of statements a specified number of times. Let's begin with a very simple example; try to guess what the program below does before reading on.

EXAMPLE 1

```
FOR num = 1 TO 5
    PRINT num, num * num
    PRINT "-----------------"
NEXT num
```

The program segment above causes the two PRINT statements to be executed five times, with the value of the variable *num* starting at 1 and finishing at 5. The two PRINT statements in this example are called the **body of the loop**, that is, the set of statements being repeated; the variable *num* is called the **loop counter**, because its value corresponds to the number of times that the body of the loop has been executed (also called the number of **iterations**). The output of the program segment in Example 1 is shown below.

```
 1             1
-----------------
 2             4
-----------------
 3             9
-----------------
 4            16
-----------------
 5            25
-----------------
```

The syntax of the FOR...NEXT structure is shown below. Be sure to compare the general format with Example 1 above.

FOR <counter> = <start> **TO** <finish>

⋮

body of loop

⋮

NEXT <counter>

The counter must be a *numeric variable* and the start and finish values each may be any *numeric expression* (i.e., a constant value, a numeric variable, or an algebraic expression). The counter variable on the last line of the loop must be identical to the counter variable on the first line of the loop.

The FOR...NEXT loop operates as follows:

1. The loop counter is automatically assigned the start value when the loop begins.
2. The loop counter is automatically increased whenever the NEXT statement is reached.
3. The loop is terminated when the loop counter gets beyond the finish value.

PRACTICE 2.2

1. What is the output of each of these program segments?

(a)
```
FOR i = 1 TO 4
   PRINT "Hello"
NEXT i
```

(b)
```
FOR i = 1 TO 4
   PRINT "Hello"
NEXT i
```

(c)
```
FOR num = 0 TO 5
   LET ans = 2 * num
   PRINT ans
NEXT num
```

2. Write down FOR...NEXT loops that produce these outputs:

(a)
```
3
4
5
6
7
```

(b)
```
Fun!
Fun!
Fun!
```

(c)
```
5 10 15 20 25 30
```

2.3 Changing the Step Size

QuickBASIC provides the option of incrementing the loop counter by amounts other than +1. The syntax of the opening line becomes

FOR <counter> = <start> **TO** <finish> **STEP** <step size>

where "step size" is any numeric expression. Indeed, the step size can be a whole number or a fraction, and it can be positive or negative. In any case, the loop counter is still initially given the start value, the loop counter is increased or decreased by the appropriate amount when the NEXT statement is reached, and the loop terminates when the value of the loop counter passes the finish value.

EXAMPLE 2

In each row shown below, the first column gives the opening line of a FOR...NEXT loop, and the second column gives the sequence of values taken on by the loop counter *i* as the loop is repeated.

FIRST LINE OF LOOP	VALUES OF LOOP COUNTER
`FOR i = 1 TO 5 STEP 2`	1, 3, 5
`FOR i = 5 TO 1 STEP -1`	5, 4, 3, 2, 1

`FOR i = 1 TO 5 STEP 1.5`	1, 2.5, 4
`FOR i = 5 TO 1 STEP -3`	5, 2
`FOR i = 1 TO 5 STEP -2`	none
`FOR i = 5 TO 1`	none

Notice that in the last two lines the loop counter takes on *no values*! This is because, in both cases, the start value is already *past* the finish value, so the statements in the body of the loop will never be executed at all.

PRACTICE 2.3

1. As in Example 2 above, fill in the values of the loop counter *i* that go with the given FOR line.

FIRST LINE OF THE LOOP	VALUES OF THE LOOP COUNTER
`FOR i = 6 TO 10`	
`FOR i = 1 TO 12 STEP 2`	
`FOR i = 4 TO 0`	
`FOR i = 4 TO 0 STEP -1`	
`FOR i = .2 TO 1.5 STEP .3`	

2. What is the output of each of the following program segments?

(a)
```
FOR num = 0 TO 8 STEP 2
     PRINT num * num
NEXT num
```
(b)
```
FOR k = 1 TO 4 STEP .7
     PRINT CINT(k);
NEXT k
```

2.4 Accumulating Totals

One of the most important uses of loops is the accumulation of various kinds of totals, for example, keeping running sums or products, or keeping counts of quantities under consideration.

EXAMPLE 3

Suppose we wish to write a program segment that allows consumer reporters to enter a number of gasoline prices they have recorded during a tour of local service stations; it then prints the average price. To do this, we need to know *how many* prices were recorded; we need to compute the *sum* of all the prices; and, finally, we must divide the sum by the number of prices to compute the average. An algorithm for a solution to this problem would be:

1. Take in the number of prices and initialize the sum
2. For each price:
   a. Take in the price
   b. Add that price into the accumulating sum
3. Compute the average = sum / number of prices

Here is a QuickBASIC program that does that, printing the average to the nearest tenth of a cent:

```
'---------------------------------------------------------------
'     Program title: C02EX03.BAS
'     Author:        J. P. GETTY
'     Date:          Sept. 23, 1991

'This program computes the average gasoline price per gallon of
'regular gas among all the service stations in town.
'---------------------------------------------------------------

'Find out how many prices there are.

     CLS
     INPUT "How many prices do you have? ", howMany

     LET sum = 0

'Find out the prices and accumulate the sum.

     PRINT
     PRINT "Enter the prices (in cents):"
     FOR counter = 1 TO howMany
            INPUT price
            LET sum = sum + price
     NEXT counter

'Compute, round off (to the nearest tenth), and print out
'the average.

     LET average = sum / howMany
     LET average = CINT(10 * average) / 10
     PRINT
     PRINT "The average price is"; average; "cents."

END
```

The variable *sum* keeps a running sum of the prices as they are entered. Suppose a reporter has five prices: 99.5, 101.2, 100.9, 102.9, and 99.7. The variable *sum* is initially set to 0 and then, as each price is input, the line "LET sum = sum + price" *adds* the current price to the sum. Thus, if this program segment is executed with the five prices listed above, *sum* will take on the following values, in the order they're listed:

sum: 0 99.5 200.7 301.6 404.5 504.2

The average is then computed from the final value of the variable *sum*, namely, *average* = 504.2 / 5 = 100.84. Here's the output of the program for this set of prices:

```
How many prices do you have? 5

Enter the prices (in cents):
? 99.5
? 101.2
? 100.9
? 102.9
? 99.7

The average price is 100.8 cents.
```

In the line "LET sum = sum + price," we say we are **updating** the variable *sum*. This actually corresponds very closely to the way you might keep a running sum with paper and pencil. It is important that we *initialize* the variable sum to 0 before we start the loop; otherwise, the line "LET sum = sum + price" will not make sense the first time it is executed.

Actually, if you forget to initialize *sum* in this example, you'll get away with it because QuickBASIC automatically sets all uninitialized numeric variables equal to 0. However, if you use some other programming system you might not be so lucky. Also, as the next example shows, 0 is not always the correct initial value. So, we remind you:

Always* initialize *variables before they are used; in particular, any variables that will be updated* inside *a loop must be initialized properly* before *the loop.

EXAMPLE 4

If n is a positive integer, then "*n factorial*" (usually denoted "$n!$") means the product of all the integers from 1 to n. Thus, for example, 4 factorial = 1 * 2 * 3 * 4 = 24. The following program segment inputs a positive integer n and uses a FOR...NEXT loop to compute n factorial. The variable *product* is used to accumulate the product of the integers from 1 to n.

```
INPUT "Enter a positive integer: ", n

LET product = 1
FOR num = 2 TO n
   LET product = product * num
NEXT num

PRINT
PRINT n; "factorial equals: "; product
```

Notice that we initialize *product* to 1 rather than 0. What would happen if we initialized it to 0 (or equivalently, if we forgot to initialize it)?

PRACTICE 2.4

1. What is the output of each of these program segments?

(a)
```
LET total = 0
FOR j = 1 TO 5
   LET total = total + 4
NEXT j
PRINT total
```

(b)
```
LET total = 50
FOR count = 1 TO 5
   LET total = total - count
NEXT count
PRINT total
```

(c)
```
LET answer = 1
FOR k = 1 TO 4
   LET answer = answer * 3
NEXT k
PRINT answer
```

2. Write a program segment with a FOR...NEXT loop that computes the sum of all the whole numbers from 1 to 100.

2.5 Nested Loops

In the course of designing an algorithm for a particular problem, you may find that the resulting program contains a **nested loop**, that is, a loop that lies within another loop. This is perfectly acceptable; the body of a loop may contain *any* legal BASIC statements, including other loops.

EXAMPLE 5

Suppose the reporters in Example 3 actually checked gasoline prices in *several* area towns and wanted a program that prints the averages for each town. An algorithm for such a program would be:

1. Determine the number of towns
2. For each town:
   a. Determine how many prices were recorded
   b. Input the prices, keeping track of the sum
   c. Compute and print the average

The point here is that we will need a loop to process the information for all the towns, and, as part of the process for each town, we'll need another loop to handle the list of prices for that town: therefore, this program will have *nested* loops. Below is a modification of the program in Example 3 that corresponds to this new algorithm. Basically (if you'll pardon the expression), we simply put that entire program inside a FOR...NEXT loop that causes it to be executed one time for each town.

```
'---------------------------------------------------------------
'    Program title: C02EX05.BAS
'    Author:        J. P. Getty
'    Date:          Sept. 24, 1991

'This program finds the average price per gallon of regular
'gasoline among various towns.
'---------------------------------------------------------------

'Find out how many towns.

     CLS
     INPUT "How many towns did you visit? ", numTowns
     PRINT

'For each town:

     FOR townCount = 1 TO numTowns
          CLS
          PRINT "TOWN #"; townCount
          PRINT

          'get the number of prices,
          INPUT "How many prices do you have? ", howMany
          LET sum = 0

          'get each price and add into the sum,
          PRINT
          PRINT "Enter the prices (in cents):"
          FOR count = 1 TO howMany
               INPUT price
               LET sum = sum + price
          NEXT count

          'and compute the average for that town.
          LET average = sum / howMany
          LET average = CINT(10 * average) / 10
          PRINT
          PRINT "For town #"; townCount; ", the ";
          PRINT "average price is"; average; "cents."
          PRINT
     NEXT townCount

END
```

Try out this program (C02EX05.BAS on the SAMPLES disk). It is the first of many in this text that require nested loops. Another occurs in the next example.

EXAMPLE 6

The program segment below draws a rectangle of stars with dimensions *numRows* by *numCols* (which we assume have been given values earlier in the program). The algorithm used is:

1. For each row, from 1 to *numRows*:
   a. Print the correct number of stars
   b. Print a return (to get to the next line)

The corresponding program segment is:

```
FOR row = 1 TO numRows
    FOR col = 1 TO numCols
        PRINT "*";
    NEXT col
    PRINT
NEXT row
```

For example, if *numRows* is set to 3 and *numCols* to 10, then the output would be:

```
**********
**********
**********
```

Notice that the "inner" loop (with loop counter *col*) must be completely executed *for every iteration* of the "outer" loop (with loop counter *row*). By the way, there is a way to write this program segment without nested loops. (Hint: Use the STRING$ function defined in Section 1.5, Table 1.4.)

PRACTICE 2.5

1. What is the output of each of these program segments?

(a)
```
FOR i = 1 TO 4
    FOR j = 1 TO 3
        PRINT i,
    NEXT j
    PRINT
NEXT i
```

(b)
```
FOR i = 1 TO 4
    FOR j = 1 TO i
        PRINT i,
    NEXT j
    PRINT
NEXT i
```

(c)
```
FOR x = 0 TO 2
   FOR y = 0 TO 3
      PRINT x * y,
   NEXT y
   PRINT
NEXT x
```

2. Write program segments that use nested FOR...NEXT loops to produce these outputs:

(a)
```
##########
##########
##########
##########
```

(b)
```
*
**
***
****
```

(c)
```
********
******
****
**
```

2.6 The READ and DATA Statements

One of the many important features of looping structures is that they permit us to process large sets of data—larger than we could possibly have handled if we had to type in a separate LET or INPUT statement every time we wanted to assign a value to a variable. In Example 3, for instance, the program segment can process *any* number of gasoline prices. Although there is only a single INPUT statement to input all the gasoline prices, because it is inside a FOR...NEXT loop we can execute it as many times as we wish, each time giving a new value to the variable *price*.

On the other hand, while the program segment of Example 3 *can* handle any number of gasoline prices, it is not the *ideal* program to use if that number actually is large. Suppose that we ran that program segment inputting 35 gasoline prices; suppose further that while inputting the 34th price we made a typing error—AAARGHH!! We would have to start the whole program over and reenter every price!

QuickBASIC provides two ways to handle large amounts of data more easily. One is to use *data files*, which we'll study in Chapter 8. With this method, data used by the program is stored in a separate file (hence the name "data file") and is input using a special variation of the INPUT statement. This allows the user to type in all the data and check it for correctness *before* running the program. Similarly, if we have large amounts of data to output, a variation of the PRINT statement prints output to a data file rather than to the screen.

Another way to handle large sets of input data is to use the two statements **READ** and **DATA**. Example 7 uses READ and DATA to compute the average of a list of 35 grades. Study it and see if you can figure out how it works.

EXAMPLE 7

The following program segment reads a set of 35 grades from DATA statements and computes their average:

```
    READ howMany

    LET sum = 0
    FOR count = 1 TO howMany
           READ grade
           LET sum = sum + grade
    NEXT count

    LET average = sum / howMany
    PRINT average

'------------------------------------------------------------
'DATA SECTION: The first data item is the number of grades;
'the remaining data items are the grades themselves.
    DATA 35
    DATA 81, 61, 60, 81, 95, 66, 68, 90, 60, 94
    DATA 83, 81, 85, 65, 88, 75, 86, 98, 91, 58
    DATA 88, 72, 90, 87, 73, 69, 81, 64, 80, 64
    DATA 96, 84, 85, 82, 89
```

This program segment is similar to Example 3 in that they both use a FOR...NEXT loop to accumulate a sum. The main difference is that in Example 3 we used an INPUT statement to obtain from the user the values to be added *while the program was being run*; in this program segment, we used a READ statement to get the values from the DATA statements at the end of the program—this data was entered *into the program itself*, allowing the programmer/user to check that the data was complete and correct *before* running the program.

When a FOR...NEXT loop is being used to read and process data contained in DATA lines, the *first* piece of data (for example, the 35 in Example 7 above) is most often the *number* of data items to be processed. This item is called the **header** for the data. In Chapter 5, when we learn how to process data with a different type of loop (the DO...LOOP), we shall instead use a "trailer," at the *end* of the data.

The syntax of the READ and DATA statements is quite straightforward:

READ <variable 1>, <variable 2>, <variable 3>, . . .
DATA <value 1>, <value 2>, <value 3>, . . .

The READ and DATA statements work together. When a READ statement is encountered as the program is run, the program will look for the first "unused" piece of data in a DATA statement and will assign it to the variable being read. The next time a READ statement is encountered, the *next* unused data item will be read. The program processes DATA statements in the order they appear. Hence, the number 35 will be the first data item read in Example 7, 60 will be the fourth, and 94 will be the eleventh.

The advantage of READ/DATA over INPUT for large amounts of data is that you have the opportunity to enter all your data and check it for errors before you run the program. READ/DATA also provides a convenient way to do several LET statements in one fell swoop. For example, the following two statements set ticket prices for an automated movie cashier:

```
DATA 5.00, 3.00, 2.50, 2.00
READ adult, senior, student, child
```

READ/DATA can be used for string values, too. String data items are listed, separated by commas; *quotation marks are not required,* although they are permitted (you *do* need quotes around any string that begins with one or more blank spaces—can you see why?). Furthermore, a single DATA statement can contain both numeric and string data items.

EXAMPLE 8

The following program reads a list of data statements containing the names and birth years of several famous people. It then prints their names and ages in the form of a table.

```
'-------------------------------------------------------------
'    Program title:      C02EX08.BAS
'    Author:             Poor Richard
'    Date:               November 22, 1988

'This program inputs the current year and then prints a table
'showing the names and ages of several famous people. The names
'and birth years are contained in DATA statements at the
'beginning of the program - see that section to add or delete
'names.
'-------------------------------------------------------------

'Data section: First line contains number of data lines to
'follow; subsequent lines contain last name, first name, middle
'name, year of birth.
```

```
    DATA 5
    DATA Pauling, Linus, Carl, 1901
    DATA King, Coretta, Scott, 1927
    DATA Robinson, Ray, Charles, 1930
    DATA Oates, Joyce, Carol, 1938
    DATA Chase, Cornelius, Crane, 1943

'------------------------------------------------------------------

'Program intro and input current year

    CLS
    PRINT "This program tells you the ages of several famous ";
    PRINT "people."
    PRINT
    INPUT "What is the current year? ", thisYear

'Clear screen and print table heading

    CLS
    PRINT " NAME", , "AGE IN"; thisYear
    PRINT " ----", , "-----------"

'Read and print info from each data line

    READ numPeople
    FOR person = 1 TO numPeople
        READ last$, first$, middle$, birthYear
        LET f$ = LEFT$(first$, 1)           'first initial
        LET m$ = LEFT$(middle$, 1)          'middle initial
        LET age = thisYear - birthYear
        PRINT f$; "."; m$; ". "; last$, , age
    NEXT person

END
```

Sample output follows.

```
This program tells you the ages of several famous people.

What is the current year? 1991
```

(new screen)

```
 NAME                          AGE IN 1991
 ----                          -----------
L. C. Pauling                   90
C. S. King                      64
R. C. Robinson                  61
J. C. Oates                     53
C. C. Chase                     48
```

There are some precautions that must be taken when using READ/DATA. First, you must make sure that the *variable type* always matches the *data type* (i.e., both numeric or both string). This means that you must clearly understand the *order* in which the data items will be read and organize them accordingly. Second, you must make sure that when a READ statement is executed, there is data left to be read. Again, this is accomplished by carefully organizing the data and carefully planning the corresponding READ statements.

One last precaution: do not put comments at the end of DATA statements because the compiler cannot distinguish them from the *data* itself! In Example 8, it might be tempting to add a comment to the last data line:

```
DATA Chase, Cornelius, Crane, 1943     'Chevy Chase
```

Unfortunately, the READ statement would simply interpret the comment as part of the last data item on that line, so that the program would encounter a *run-time error* (i.e., an error that occurs while the program is running) trying to assign the following *string* value to the *numeric* variable *birthYear*:

```
"1943     'Chevy Chase"
```

Let's end this section with one additional QuickBASIC statement that is sometimes useful when using READ/DATA. As explained earlier in this section, any READ statement will look for the first data item *that has not yet been read*. Thus, unless we direct the computer otherwise, no data item can ever be read more than once. If you *do* need to start over and read from the beginning of the data, QuickBASIC provides the RESTORE statement. **RESTORE** simply directs the computer to reset back to the first item of data; therefore, the first READ after a RESTORE will read the first data item again. For example, the output of

```
READ a, b, c
PRINT a, b, c
RESTORE
READ x, y, z
PRINT x, y, z

DATA 5,3,8,7,4,9
```

would be

```
5       3       8
5       3       8
```

PRACTICE 2.6

1. What is the output of each of these program segments?

   (a)
```
READ amount
FOR j = 1 TO amount
   READ k
   PRINT k
NEXT j

DATA 4,7,3,-1,2
```

(b)
```
FOR count = 1 TO 5
    READ word$
    PRINT LEFT$(word$, 1);
NEXT count

DATA Beginner's,All-Purpose,Symbolic
DATA Instruction,Code
```

(c)
```
DATA 3,5,2,6

READ howMany
LET answer = 1
FOR k = 1 TO howMany
   READ num
   LET answer = answer * num
NEXT k
PRINT answer
```

2. Write a program segment with a FOR...NEXT loop that reads a DATA line like the one below (where the first data item is a header), and then prints the words that follow as a sentence ending with a period.

```
DATA 6,Programming,in,QuickBASIC,seems,like,fun
```

2.7 Programming Style

The program in Example 8 uses techniques of *good programming style* to make it more readable, to make it easy to correct and modify, and to make the *structure,* that is, the underlying algorithm design, as clear as possible. The following techniques are used in this and all the sample programs in this book.

Comments

Comments are used liberally throughout the program, wherever they can clarify what is going on. There are three main uses for comments:

1. A *program heading,* consisting of several comment lines, gives the title, author, date, and a brief description of what the program does (*not how* it does it!) and any special instructions needed for using the program.
2. *Segment descriptions* are used, one before each program segment, to describe what the segment does.
3. *In-line comments* are appended to the end of any statements that require additional clarification (except for DATA lines, as mentioned).

Blank Lines

One or more blank lines separate each program segment to aid readability. Don't overdo—if you leave a blank line after every statement, it's as bad as having no blank lines at all.

Indentation

Indentation is used to aid readability by displaying the flow of execution of program statements. You should indent your programs as follows (remember that we recommend tab settings that are four spaces apart; see Section 1.6):

1. The program heading, the segment descriptions, and the END statement all are aligned on the left, so that the reader can scan from beginning to end, one section at a time, for an overview of the design of the program.
2. The statements in each segment are also aligned, *one tab setting in*. So long as the lines contain simple statements executed sequentially, they should be aligned to indicate that fact.
3. The *only* additional indentation is for the *body of a control structure*, such as FOR...NEXT (for instance, see the FOR...NEXT loop in the last section of Example 8). This use of indentation accomplishes two things: first, it lets you clearly see where the structure begins and ends; second, it lets you clearly see what actions are taken inside the structure.

Meaningful Variable Names

Choose variable names that indicate what the variables represent (e.g., *numPeople, last$, birthYear*, etc.; not *a, b, x, y, twizzledorp*, etc.). Since QuickBASIC always capitalizes BASIC reserved words, use lowercase letters whenever possible, saving capitals to indicate two-word variable names (e.g., *taxRate, highGrade*, etc.).

Readable Output

Remember that a program has *two* audiences: the person who reads the program itself and the person who *runs* the program and reads its output. Both audiences deserve to see something that is as easy as possible to read and understand. Your output should contain good explanatory headings and user prompts, and you should use spacing to help readability.

If these guidelines seem extremely specific and even picky, it's because they are! The point is that you will develop *some* programming style as you start writing more and more programs. The goal is to form good habits so that you don't have to break bad habits later.

PRACTICE 2.7

Read carefully through the program in Example 8, noting uses of each of the four style techniques described in this section.

Chapter Summary

In this chapter, we've begun to learn about the two kinds of *control structures*: *looping* and *decision*. Looping structures allow program segments to be repeated; decision structures allow a choice between two or more alternative actions.

The *FOR...NEXT* looping structure lets us repeat a set of statements a specified number of times. More complicated repetitions may involve *nested* loops, that is, one loop that contains another as one of its statements.

An important use of loops is the *accumulation* of totals such as sums and products. Any variable that is used to accumulate totals in a loop must be properly *initialized* before the loop begins (more generally, *any* variable must be initialized before it is used).

READ and *DATA* statements provide a convenient way to supply large amounts of data to a program. They are frequently used together with looping structures to read and process large data sets.

The introduction of control structures makes it crucial that we use *good programming style* to make our programs easier to understand. The use of *comments, blank lines, indentation,* and *meaningful variable names* are four ways to make our programs more readable.

? Review Questions

1. Explain each of these ideas briefly and give an example:

(a) control structure
(b) looping structure
(c) loop counter
(d) accumulating a total
(e) nested loops

2. (a) We now have three distinct ways to put the value 7 into the memory location labelled *number*. What are they? Specifically, write down the QuickBASIC statements.

(b) Discuss more generally in what circumstances we use each of these three statements.

3. Consider the following QuickBASIC program segment:

```
CLS
READ numRows, numCols
FOR i = 1 TO numRows
    LET rowSum = 0
    FOR j = 1 TO numCols
        READ number
        LET rowSum = rowSum + number
    NEXT j
    LET rowAv = rowSum / numCols
    PRINT rowAv
NEXT i

DATA 3,4
DATA 7,2,8,9
DATA 12,5,3,8
DATA 4,8,2,5
```

(a) What is the output of this program?

(b) What, in general, does this program accomplish? That is, what does the program do, regardless of the particular data?

(c) is program would malfunction if the initialization statement "LET rowSum = 0" were omitted. Explain why.

Programming Problems 

While designing and writing the following programs, be sure to use the techniques of algorithm design explained in Section 1.6 and to follow the style guidelines described in Section 2.7.

1. Write a program that prints out the following table, which shows the squares and square roots of all the whole numbers from 1 to 20:

Number	Square	Square Root
1	1	1
2	4	1.41
3	9	1.73
.	.	.
.	.	.
20	400	4.47

2. Write a program that asks the user for two whole numbers (the second larger than the first) and then prints out every third whole number between them (for example, an input of 4, 15 would result in an output of 4 7 10 13).

3. Write a program that asks the user to input a positive whole number; it then outputs the sum of all the numbers from 1 up to that number. For example, if the user types in 5, the computer responds with 15 $(=1+2+3+4+5)$.

4. Write a program that inputs an arbitrary string and then prints it out diagonally (this problem modifies Example 5 in Section 1.5).

5. Write a temperature conversion program that prints out a table containing a column of the Fahrenheit temperatures 0, 10, 20, . . . , 100 and a column of the corresponding Centigrade temperatures. The formula for converting Fahrenheit to Centigrade is:

$$C = 5 / 9 * (F - 32)$$

6. (a) When their baby Jenny was born, Bob and Carol put $5000 in a savings account that earns 9.5% interest compounded annually. They hope that this will help toward their daughter's college education. Figure out how much will be in the account 18 years from now by printing out a table showing the years from 0 to 18 and the balance after that many years.
   (b) Bob and Carol's friends Ted and Alice also put $5000 in an account that earns 9.5% interest, but their interest is compounded quarterly. Print the same table for Ted and Alice's account, showing values for years 0 to 18.

7. Write a triangle-drawing program as follows: the user types in a character with which to build the triangle and indicates the size of the widest part;

the program then draws a triangle like the one below. For example, if the user types in **$** and **4**, the output is:

```
$                                      $
$$                                     $ $
$$$                                    $ $ $
$$$$       or, if you prefer           $ $ $ $
$$$                                    $ $ $
$$                                     $ $
$                                      $
```

Note: Do not use *width* as a variable name, because it is a reserved word in QuickBASIC.

8. Outline a rectangle. The user types in a character, length, and height, and the program outputs a rectangle using those attributes. For example, an input of *, **20**, **5** results in:

```
********************
*                  *
*                  *
*                  *
********************
```

9. Write a name-reversal program, that is, a program that accepts a person's name as input and returns the name backwards. For example, the output might be:

```
Type in your name --> Bruce Stringsteen
Your name backwards is neetsgnirtS ecurB.
```

Hint: You will need two of the string functions introduced in Section 1.5.

10. The Acme Department Store is having a storewide 25%-off sale. Write a program for the store's advertising that reads from DATA lines the number of items advertised, followed by the name and regular price of each item, and then prints out a table showing item name, regular price, and discounted price. Use the following data:

```
DATA 6
DATA Television,350,Dishwasher,270,Stereo,210
DATA Snow Blower,425,VCR,325,Electronic Keyboard,130
```

11. In 1988, the city of Yonkers, New York, was found in contempt of court in a case concerning housing discrimination. The judge in the case fined the city $100 for the first day, with the fine doubling every day thereafter. Write a program that outputs a table showing the accumulating fine over the first 25 days that the city does not comply with the court order. Given that the entire annual budget for Yonkers is about $337 million, how long would it take for the city to go broke?

12. For your Sociology of Sport class, you have a project that involves finding out the average height (in inches) of the starting men's basketball team from each of 12 nearby colleges. Write a program that reads the 60 (5 times 12) heights from DATA and prints out the 12 averages in a table.

13. Computing standard deviation: Given a list of numbers, the standard deviation is (roughly) the average distance of the data items from the

mean (mean = average). If we denote the mean of the list by *xBar*, then the standard deviation is computed by:

1. Adding up all the numbers (item − *xBar*)^2
2. Dividing the sum by the number of data items − 1
3. Taking the square root

Write a program that reads a list of numbers from DATA lines, computes and prints out their mean, restores the data (using the RESTORE statement), and computes the standard deviation.

CHAPTER

3

DECISION STRUCTURES

CHAPTER PREVIEW

In this chapter, we'll learn how to write programs in which different courses of action can be taken depending on certain *conditions*. To do this, we'll use QuickBASIC's two *decision control structures*: *IF...END IF* and *SELECT...END SELECT*. We'll also learn about *compound conditions* and *computer simulation*, which makes use of all the control structures introduced in Chapters 2 and 3 together with the *RND* function (which is used to generate random numbers).

3.1 Decision Making in QuickBASIC

From Section 2.1, you'll recall that there are two types of *control structures* in QuickBASIC: *looping structures,* which allow you to repeat a task over and over, and *decision structures,* which allow you to choose between two or more courses of action. Chapter 2 concentrated on the FOR...NEXT looping structure; now, it's time to learn how to make *decisions* in our QuickBASIC programs. Let's start by looking at an example.

EXAMPLE 1

Suppose we want to write a program that takes in the score you got on your latest math test and compliments you if you got 90 or better. In outline form, the algorithm would be:

1. Put in the score
2. If the score is 90 or better
   Print out "Wow! Great job!"

It's easy to implement this program in QuickBASIC; it ends up looking almost exactly like the algorithm above:

```
INPUT "What was your score? ", score

IF score >= 90 THEN
    PRINT "Wow! Great job!"
END IF
```

What will happen when you run it? *It depends*! Suppose you got a 93 on the test—the output is:

```
What was your score? 93
Wow! Great job!
```

But if you got an 86, the computer makes no comment at all:

```
What was your score? 86
```

This program produces different results depending on the value of the input variable *score*; a *decision* is made depending on what *score* is. The IF...END IF section of the program is a **decision structure**, the first of many we shall see throughout the remainder of this book.

Continuing with the math score example, you might want the computer to say *something* to you no matter what your score was, perhaps congratulations for a high score and encouragement otherwise. This, too, is easy to do in QuickBASIC:

```
INPUT "What was your score? ", score

IF score >= 90 THEN
    PRINT "Wow! Great job!"
ELSE
    PRINT "Keep at it! You'll make the 90's next time."
END IF
```

Take a good look at this new form of the IF...END IF decision structure. The output of this program segment is exactly what you would expect; the program takes one of two courses of action depending on the value of *score*.

You don't need to limit yourself to two choices; in fact, you can have as many as you like. For instance, here's a way to have the computer give you a more careful assessment of your latest math performance:

```
INPUT "What was your score? ", score

IF score >= 90 THEN
    PRINT "Wow! Great job!"
ELSEIF score >= 80 THEN
    PRINT "Honors work, but room for improvement."
ELSEIF score >= 70 THEN
    PRINT "Mathematically, I'm afraid you're just"
    PRINT "an average Josephine."
ELSE
    PRINT "Have you considered dropping math?"
END IF
```

A sample output would be:

```
What was your score? 56
Have you considered dropping math?
```

Here, *four* outputs are possible, depending on the value of *score* —but, again, what you should appreciate is that the output is exactly what anyone would expect from reading this segment. The different versions of the IF...END IF decision structure are all easy and natural; they do exactly what it looks like they should do. Be sure to try out the program segment above—it's on your SAMPLES disk under the name C03EX01.BAS. (Remember that most of the examples in this book are on the SAMPLES disk and that you will learn the ideas in the book more easily—and have more fun!—if you use the disk while you read the text.)

Let's finish this section with an example that uses both decision making *and* looping.

EXAMPLE 2

Suppose that in DATA lines you have the names and math test scores for your whole math class; you want to write a program that will print out only the names of those whose scores were 90 or above. An algorithm for this would be:

1. Print out a heading
2. Read how many students are in the class
3. For each student:
   a. Read the name and test score
   b. If the score is greater than or equal to 90
      Print out the name and score

The program is easy to write, so let's go ahead (and try out the file C03EX02.BAS on the SAMPLES disk).

```
'-----------------------------------------------------------------
'     Program title: C03EX02.BAS
'     Author:        B. Pascal
'     Date:          10/23/90

'   Prints out the students with scores of 90% and over
'   on the latest math test.
'-----------------------------------------------------------------

'Print table heading

      CLS
      PRINT "Top Scores on Math Test"
      PRINT "-----------------------"
      PRINT

'Get number who took test

      READ classSize

'Find and print out the high scores

      FOR student = 1 TO classSize
             READ name$, score
             IF score >= 90 THEN
                   PRINT name$, score
             END IF
      NEXT student

'Data Section: the first line contains the number of students
'who took the test. Following that is each student name and
'score.

      DATA 16
      DATA A. Aardvark, 76, B. Brown, 83, C. Clemens, 99
      DATA D. Duck, 56, E. Eucalyptus, 91, F. Friendly, 72
      DATA G. Gobel, 85, H. Hughes, 43, I. Ives, 95
      DATA J. Jones, 68, K. Klutz, 74, L. Luster, 96
      DATA M. Monroe, 88, N. Nohead, 34, O. Otter, 92
      DATA P. Prentiss, 76

END
```

Based on the above DATA lines, the output of this program is:

```
Top Scores on Math Test
-----------------------

C. Clemens      99
E. Eucalyptus   91
I. Ives         95
L. Luster       96
O. Otter        92
```

Again, all you have to do is carefully read this program once to see that it does exactly what you wanted it to do.

PRACTICE 3.1

1. What is the output of each of these program segments?

(a)
```
LET num = 6
IF num <= 5 THEN
   PRINT "low"
ELSE
   PRINT "high"
END IF
```

(b)
```
READ x, y
IF x < y THEN
   LET z = -1
ELSEIF x = y THEN
   LET z = 0
ELSE
   LET z = 1
END IF
PRINT z
DATA 7, 4
```

(c)
```
FOR k = 1 TO 19
   IF k <= 10 THEN
      PRINT k;
   ELSE
      PRINT 20 - k;
   END IF
NEXT k
```

2. Write a QuickBASIC program that takes in a number from the keyboard and prints out one of the following correct messages: "Your number is positive"; "Your number is negative"; or "Your number is zero."

3.2 Conditions and the IF...END IF Structure

Example 1 in Section 3.1 contains the line "IF score>=90 THEN." The section "score>=90" of that line is called a **condition** (also sometimes called a *boolean expression*), which is an expression that is *either true or false*. In our example, *score* is a variable (i.e., a memory location) that at any given time has a particular value. If the value is less than 90, then the condition *score>=90* is *false*; but if that value is 90 or greater, then the condition is *true*. Here are some other examples of conditions:

```
price < 21.00        name$ = "Fred"        40 >= 50
```

Notice that the "truth value" of the third condition is obvious (it's false!) but that the first two can have different truth values depending on what is stored in the variables *price* and *name$*. Notice also that the second condition illustrates that you can have conditions involving *strings* as well as numbers. For example, if "Wilma" is currently stored in the variable *name$*, then the condition is false. We'll say more about comparing strings in Example 4 below.

Every condition in QuickBASIC must contain a **relational operator**, which is a fancy name for "is equal to," "is greater than," and so on. There are only six relational operators, as shown in Table 3.1.

Notice that the last three relational operators require *two* characters each, necessary because the keyboard does not contain the more familiar characters ≤, ≥, and ≠.

You should also observe that the equal symbol (=) gets used in two completely different ways in QuickBASIC: in the LET statement between the variable's name and its assigned value; and as a relational operator in conditions. Look at the following two lines and convince yourself that the equal symbol is being used for different purposes:

```
LET number = 8

IF number = 8 THEN
```

To avoid confusion, some people read the upper line as "let *number* **get** the value 8," or simply "let *number* **get** 8," to emphasize that when this statement executes, a new value is placed in the memory location labelled *number*. When the IF line executes, on the other hand, the computer finds out what value is in location *number* and then labels true or false the condition *number* = *8*, depending on

TABLE 3.1 Relational Operators in QuickBASIC

Operator	Meaning
=	is equal to
<	is less than
>	is greater than
<=	is less than or equal to
>=	is greater than or equal to
<>	is not equal to

whether that value is or is not 8 (and the value in location *number* is *not* changed).

We are now ready to discuss the general syntax of the IF...END IF structure, which has various forms depending on the number of alternatives desired. First, if one course of action is or is not supposed to execute depending on the truth value of a condition, the syntax is:

IF <condition> **THEN**
⋮
block of statements
⋮
END IF

Next, if we still have only one condition but want alternate actions depending on whether that condition is true or false, we use the ELSE clause for the alternate action:

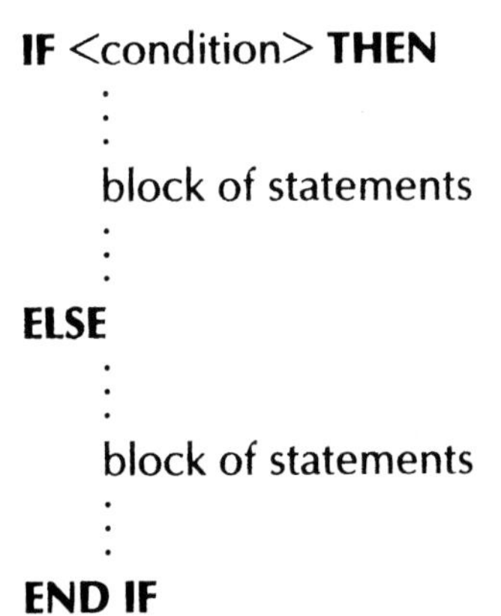

IF <condition> **THEN**
⋮
block of statements
⋮
ELSE
⋮
block of statements
⋮
END IF

Finally, we can use one or more ELSEIF clauses if we want to check additional conditions. Below are two sets of actions depending on two conditions in the column on the left, and three sets of actions depending on two conditions in the column on the right.

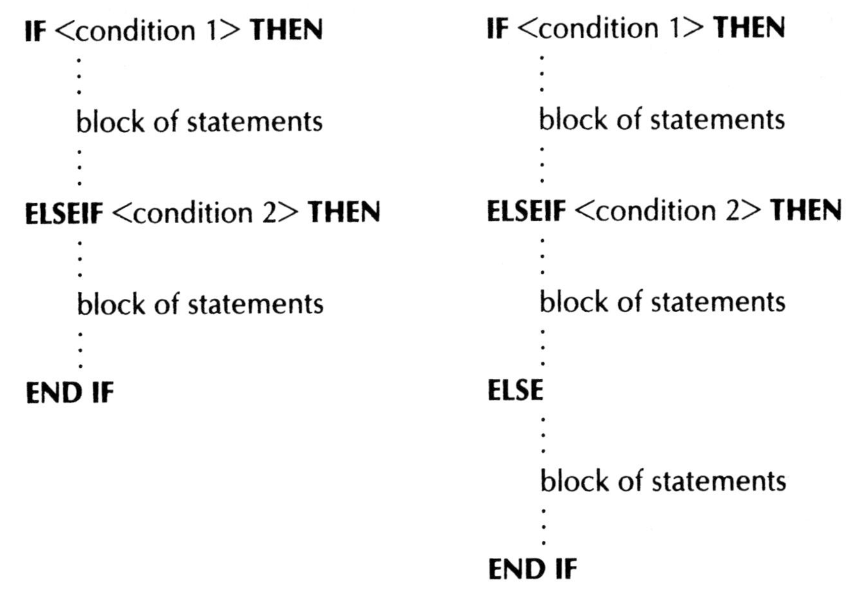

IF <condition 1> **THEN**
⋮
block of statements
⋮
ELSEIF <condition 2> **THEN**
⋮
block of statements
⋮
END IF

IF <condition 1> **THEN**
⋮
block of statements
⋮
ELSEIF <condition 2> **THEN**
⋮
block of statements
⋮
ELSE
⋮
block of statements
⋮
END IF

Obviously, we could go on like this indefinitely, but let's stop here. Don't be concerned about the number of variations of the IF...END IF structure; you'll see as we go on that the structure you need will arise *naturally* as part of the problem-solving process.

Before we begin looking at examples, let's summarize the operation of the IF...END IF control structure.

- The condition in the IF line is tested.
- If the condition is *true*, the block of statements that follows is executed; the program then continues at the first line following the END IF.
- If the condition is *false*, and if there are no ELSEIF or ELSE clauses below, the program then moves immediately to the first line after END IF. (The use of ELSEIF and ELSE is optional—but if ELSE is used, it must come last.) If the condition is false and the next block is an ELSEIF clause, then the new condition is tested and the process begins again. Finally, if the condition is false and the next block is an ELSE clause, that block always executes and the process ends.

Notice the way this structure operates: *at most, one block will execute* on any given run; if an ELSE line is present, then *exactly one block will execute.*

If you find this discussion of syntax and operation somewhat difficult, go back, slow down, and read it carefully once more. Remember also that this IF...END IF structure, like every control structure in QuickBASIC, is really quite easy and natural once you work with it for a while.

Let's end this section with two examples, the first from retailing.

EXAMPLE 3

Clyde's Clothes Closet is having a post-Christmas clearance sale. Items with a ticket price of less than $20.00 are discounted 10%, items with tickets between $20.00 and $49.99 are discounted 20%, and all items $50.00 and over are 30% off. Let's write a program for Clyde's that, given an item's ticket price, calculates the discount price, the 7% state sales tax, and the total price the customer must pay.

Here's an outline of an algorithm for this program:

1. Find out the old ticket price
2. Compute the new discounted price
3. Compute the tax
4. Compute the total price
5. Print out the new price, the tax, and the total price

The outline suggests the following variable names: *oldPrice*, *newPrice*, *tax*, and *total*. Although Steps 1, 3, and 5 are fairly straightforward, we need to describe Step 2 in more detail:

2. Compute the new discounted price:
   a. If *oldPrice* is less than $20, then *newPrice* is 10% off *oldPrice*
   b. Otherwise, if *oldPrice* is less than $50, then *newPrice* is 20% off *oldPrice*
   c. Otherwise, *newPrice* is 30% off *oldPrice*

To calculate, say, "10% off *oldPrice*," we compute the value of the expression "*oldPrice* − (.1 * *oldPrice*)." The parentheses in this expression are not really needed but help readability; note also that an equivalent form of that expression is ".9 * *oldPrice*." Similar expressions can be used in Steps 2b and 2c.

We've now spelled out the individual steps clearly enough to translate them into a QuickBASIC program.

```
'---------------------------------------------------------------
'      Program title: C03EX03.BAS
'      Author:        J. C. Penney
'      Date:          January 2, 1989

'Computes the sale price, tax, and total price for items
'in the Clyde's Clothes Closet Clearance.
'---------------------------------------------------------------

'Get the ticket price

      CLS
      INPUT "What is the ticket price? $", oldPrice

'Compute the discount price

      IF oldPrice < 20 THEN
             LET newPrice = .9 * oldPrice
      ELSEIF oldprice < 50 THEN
             LET newPrice = .8 * oldPrice
      ELSE
             LET newPrice = .7 * oldPrice
      END IF
      LET newPrice = CINT(100 * newPrice) / 100 'Round off!

'Compute the tax

      LET tax = .07 * newPrice
      LET tax = CINT(100 * tax) / 100 'Round off!

'Compute total price

      LET total = newPrice + tax
```

```
'Print out results

        PRINT "Your discounted price is $"; newPrice
        PRINT "Your tax is $"; tax
        PRINT "You must pay $"; total

END
```

Sample output is below.

```
What is the ticket price? $24.99
Your discounted price is $ 19.99
Your tax is $ 1.39
You must pay $ 21.38
```

A word about *programming style* is appropriate here. As discussed in Section 2.7, you should indent the *body* of any control structure. For IF...END IF, this means that all the *key words* IF, ELSEIF, ELSE, and END IF should be *aligned* with each other, whereas each block of *statements* should be *indented*. Looking at each example that we've had so far in this chapter, observe how easy it is to see the logic of the program when this style is used.

The last example in this section shows you another use of the IF...END IF structure.

EXAMPLE 4

In addition to numbers, you can compare *strings* in QuickBASIC. The comparison is "lexicographic," that is, *alphabetical*. So, for example, the following conditions are true:

```
"apple" < "zoo"    "NOW" > "HOW"    "table" < "tables".
```

QuickBASIC's method (i.e., its algorithm) for determining these conditions is quite simple: it compares the leftmost characters in each string. If one comes before another, that settles it. Otherwise (if they are identical, that is), QuickBASIC looks at the next two characters, and so on. What, in fact, gets compared is the *ASCII codes* for these characters, rather than the characters themselves (see Appendix 2); whichever character's code has the lesser value comes first. This leads to one slightly troublesome point: since uppercase letters have smaller codes than lowercase letters, all uppercase come before any lowercase. For example, both the conditions

`"Zoo" < "apple"` and `"MacMurphy" < "Mack"`

are true! However, as long as the letters all have the same *case* (upper or lower), the ordering is completely natural.

But now for our example. Let's write a program that simply takes in two words and alphabetizes them. Given what we've said, this shouldn't be too hard. One possible algorithm is:

1. Take in the two words
2. Compare them; if they are in the wrong order, switch them
3. Print them out

Steps 1 and 3 are easy, but Step 2 needs refining; we'll also introduce the variable names *word1$* and *word2$* for the two words to be alphabetized.

2. Compare them:
   If *word1$* > *word2$*
   a. Give *word1$* the value of *word2$*
   b. Give *word2$* the value of *word1$*

It's tempting (but wrong!) to translate this step into QuickBASIC code as follows:

```
IF word1$ > word2$ THEN
   LET word1$ = word2$
   LET word2$ = word1$
END IF
```

Try *tracing* the above program segment, assuming that *word1$* and *word2$* start out with the values "BBB" and "AAA," respectively. The first LET statement gives *word1$* the value "AAA" (so far so good); but then we have *lost* its original value "BBB," so the second LET statement does not change *word2$* the way we want. We must *save* the original value of *word1$* before we wipe it out with the first LET statement. To do this, we need a *third* memory location in which we temporarily save the value of *word1$*. See how the following code does this (you can find the complete program in C03EX04.BAS on your SAMPLES disk).

```
'If words are out of order then switch them

 IF word1$ > word2$ THEN
     LET temp$ = word1$    'save value of word1$ in temp$
     LET word1$ = word2$   'give word1$ value of word2$
     LET word2$ = temp$    'give word2$ old value of word1$
 END IF
```

That'll do it. Note that comparing strings is only one of two important ideas in this example. The other is: how do you *switch the contents* of two memory locations? As we've seen, what you need is a third, *temporary* location. Take a good look at the above example, for you will see this idea often in programming.

From now on, you will hardly ever write or read a program that does not contain at least one decision structure. The fact that we can get the computer to make decisions and follow different courses of action, based on data we give it, is one of the great powers of computer programming.

PRACTICE 3.2

1. What is the output of the program segment below if the input is (a) 5, (b) 10, (c) 1, or (d) 2?

```
LET message$ = "no info"
INPUT x
IF x > 8 THEN
    LET message$ = "yes"
ELSEIF x <= 1.5 THEN
    LET message$ = "no"
ELSEIF x >= 3.7 THEN
    LET message$ = "maybe so"
END IF
PRINT message$
```

2. Write a QuickBASIC program that takes in a client's adjusted gross income and returns the amount of federal income tax he or she owes. The tax brackets are:

Adjusted Gross Income	Tax Rate
$0 to $10000	0%
$10001 to $25000	15%
$25001 and up	24%

3.3 Logical Operators and Compound Conditions

All the conditions we have seen so far are called **simple conditions**, meaning that they involve only one relational operator (=, >, etc.). Sometimes, however, we find that we need to use more than one simple condition to get the result we want in an IF...END IF or another control structure. An example will illustrate this.

EXAMPLE 5

Look back at the program C03EX02.BAS (Example 2 in Section 3.1), which reads a list of student names and math test scores and prints out only those names and scores for which the score was 90 or better. A useful modification of this program would allow the user to input lower and upper ends of a *range* of scores; the program then prints out the names and scores that lie in that range. So, the new parts of this program (C03EX05.BAS on your SAMPLES disk) would begin with lines like the following:

```
PRINT "Type in the range of scores you want."
INPUT "Lower limit: ", lower
INPUT "Upper limit: ", upper
```

Then the IF...END IF section would be:

```
IF (score >= lower) AND (score <= upper) THEN
    PRINT name$, score
END IF
```

Look at the IF line. The key word AND is called a **logical operator** (since it "operates" on two simple conditions the way the arithmetic operator "+" operates on two numbers); the two simple conditions together with the logical operator are called a **compound condition**. When is this compound condition true? As usual, it's true exactly when you think it should be; in this case, because the operator is AND, it's true precisely when *both* of the simple conditions are true. So, for example, suppose that *lower* is 70 and *upper* is 80. If *score* is 76, then both simple conditions are true; the compound condition is true; and the name and score are printed out. But if *score* is 83, then, although condition *score >= lower* is true, condition *score <= upper* is false—so the compound condition is false and nothing is printed.

This may seem complicated, but it's not. If you take a minute to think about it, it all makes sense.

We might also have occasion to need an IF...END IF (or another control structure) that looks like the following:

```
IF (answer$ = "Y") OR (answer$ = "y") THEN
```

Because the logical operator is now OR, *this* compound condition is true if *either or both* of the simple conditions are true.[1] As time goes on, we will write conditions like this one frequently.

There are three logical operators in QuickBASIC: AND, OR, and NOT. We have seen examples using AND and OR already; they are both used a great deal. We repeat:

> ***A compound condition with AND is true if and only if* both *simple conditions are true. A compound condition with OR is true if* either or both *of the simple conditions are true.***

NOT is less commonly used than the others but comes in handy on occasion. It does not stand between two simple conditions; rather, it stands in front of a *single* simple condition and simply reverses that condition's truth value. For example, if *amount >= 25* is true, then *NOT (amount >= 25)* is false.

We need to say a few more things about compound conditions. First, a matter of *style*. The parentheses we've put around the simple conditions in our various examples in this section are not strictly necessary, but we strongly advise you to use them to aid readability.

---

[1] The operator OR in structured BASIC is what's called the "inclusive or," since it's true when *either or both* separate conditions are true. In everyday English, on the other hand, we tend to use the "exclusive or," meaning that *exactly one* of the conditions is true ("I'll have a date with Bob *or* Joe Saturday night").

```
IF (answer$ = "Y") OR (answer$ = "y") THEN
```

is just plain easier to read than

```
IF answer$ = "Y" OR answer$ = "y" THEN
```

Second, though they are not commonly needed, compound conditions can contain three or more simple conditions. In these cases, it's important to know that logical operators, like arithmetic operators, obey *rules of precedence*: NOT has highest precedence, AND next highest, and OR lowest. As with arithmetic expressions, you can use *parentheses* to assure that a compound condition will be evaluated the way you intend it to be. For example, you might write something like

```
IF ((a$ = "Y") OR (a$ = "y")) AND (number < 100) THEN
```

in which the condition is true provided there's a "y" (upper or lowercase) in location *a$*, *and* the value in location *number* is less than 100 (notice that the parentheses separating the first two conditions from the third are necessary in this case). Such compound conditions should be handled with care; they can get somewhat confusing.

PRACTICE 3.3

1. Suppose that the current values of *num* and *word$* are 8 and "hi," respectively. Assess the truth value of each of the compound conditions below:

```
(a) (num > 5) AND (num < 10)
(b) (num >= 8) OR (word$ = "hi")
(c) (num > 5) AND (num > 10)
(d) (num >= 8) AND (word$ = "hi")
(e) (num > 5) OR (num > 10)
(f) NOT (num <> 8)
(g) ((num < 12) AND (word$ = "Bye")) OR (NOT (word$ = "low"))
```

2. Write a QuickBASIC program that finds the sum of 12 numbers typed in at the keyboard but does not include in the sum any inputted numbers below 0 or above 100.
3. Write a QuickBASIC program asking users to type in their favorite flavor of ice cream. If the response is "chocolate" or "strawberry," the computer says, "I love that, too!" Otherwise, it says, "I'm not crazy about that."

3.4 The SELECT...END SELECT Decision Structure

The IF...END IF decision structure gets the most use, since it corresponds so nicely to the way in which we articulate decisions in English. However, SELECT...END SELECT, another QuickBASIC decision structure, is sometimes more natural to use. Specifically, this new structure may be easier to use in either of the following situations:

1. The alternative actions at hand fall naturally into "cases" (e.g., first case, second case, third case)
2. There are a large number of alternative actions

Suppose, for example, that you have a program involving a different action for each (uppercase) letter of the alphabet. If the current letter is contained in a variable called *letter$*, we might have a program segment that looks like the following:

```
SELECT CASE letter$
    CASE "A"
    .
    .
    .
    CASE "B"
    .
    .
    .
    CASE "C"
    .
    .
    .
    CASE "Z"
    .
    .
    .
END SELECT
```

In fact, we will be concerned with a program like this in Example 8 of Section 6.10 and in Programming Problem 1 at the end of Chapter 6. The point here is that, in a situation like this, the use of cases is more natural than the use of IF...THEN.

The syntax of the SELECT...END SELECT structure is as follows:

SELECT CASE <variable name or expression>
    CASE <list of values, or condition>
        .
        .
        .
        block of statements
        .
        .
        .
    CASE <list of values, or condition>
        .
        .
        .
        block of statements
        .
        .
        .
    .
    .
    .
    CASE ELSE
        .
        .
        .
        block of statements
        .
        .
        .
END SELECT

As is often the case, an example shows that what may seem complicated is not really so bad. Here's a sample SELECT...END SELECT structure that shows all the possibilities:

```
SELECT CASE points
    CASE 0
        PRINT "Nothing"
    CASE 1 TO 10
        PRINT "Not much"
    CASE 11, 12, 13, 14
        PRINT "A lot"
    CASE IS > 14
        PRINT "Plenty"
    CASE ELSE
        PRINT "Invalid value"
END SELECT
```

We need to make four remarks about this segment.

1. *All* the cases refer to the variable or expression in the top line; in this example, it is the variable *points.*
2. The first three cases involve a *list* of values; note that these can be separated by commas, or the word *TO* can be used for a *range* of values.
3. The fourth case involves a *condition* on the value in *points;* note that the word *IS* must precede the relational operator.
4. The CASE ELSE is optional.

Just as with IF...END IF, on any given run, *at most one* block of statements will execute; if the CASE ELSE is present, *exactly one* block will execute. That block is, of course, the first block for which one of the given values matches the value in the variable *points* or for which the given condition is true (or, if all else fails, it is the CASE ELSE block). In fact, it is true that the IF...END IF and SELECT...END SELECT structures are "logically equivalent," that is, whenever you can use one, you can also use the other. Given this, you should use the one that seems easiest and most natural under any given circumstance.

As to *programming style* for SELECT...END SELECT, it is best to "double indent," that is, indent both the CASE lines and each block of statements within those lines. The word *SELECT* on the first line aligns with the words *END SELECT* on the last line, so that it's easy to see where the control structure begins and ends; and because all the CASE lines are aligned, it is easy to see what the different cases are. Example 6 should illustrate that this scheme produces a very readable program.

EXAMPLE 6

At State University, incoming freshmen must take a quantitative placement exam consisting of 25 questions. The rules say that if students score 19 or better they "pass"; if they score 14 through 18, they must retake the exam or take the dreaded Math 001; and if they score 13 or below they *must* take the dreaded Math 001. Let's write a program that takes in a score and gives back the good or bad news. Since the logic is fairly obvious here, we'll go straight to a QuickBASIC program. It seems clear that we could use either decision structure here, but in the spirit of the current section, let's use SELECT...END SELECT.

```
'----------------------------------------------------------------
'       Program title: C03EX06.BAS
'       Author:        Quantitative Placement Service
'       Date:          Sept. 1, 1990

'       Provides quantitative placement information
'       to freshmen at State U.
'----------------------------------------------------------------

'Introduce and get score.

       CLS
       PRINT "Welcome to State U. This program will"
       PRINT "interpret your Quantitative Exam score."
       PRINT
       INPUT "Please enter your score (0-25) --> ", score
       PRINT

'Print out placement data.

       SELECT CASE score
             CASE 25
                    PRINT "A perfect score! Have you considered"
                    PRINT "a math/computer science major?"
             CASE 19 TO 24
                    PRINT "This is a passing score. You have"
                    PRINT "passed SU's quantitative requirement."
             CASE 14, 15, 16, 17, 18
                    PRINT "You have not passed. You must either"
                    PRINT "retake the exam, or you must enroll in"
                    PRINT "Math 001."
             CASE 0 TO 13
                    PRINT "You have not passed. You must enroll in"
                    PRINT "Math 001."
             CASE IS < 0
                    PRINT "A negative score is not possible. Please"
                    PRINT "restart the program."
             CASE ELSE
                    PRINT "A score over 25 is not possible. Please"
                    PRINT "restart the program."
       END SELECT

'Say goodbye.

       PRINT
       PRINT "Thanks and good luck at SU."

END
```

Sample output follows.

```
Welcome to State U. This program will
interpret your Quantitative Exam score.

Please enter your score (0-25) --> 12

You have not passed. You must enroll in
Math 001.

Thanks and good luck at SU.
```

PRACTICE 3.4

1. What is the output of the program segment below?

```
FOR counter = 1 TO 4
    READ num
    SELECT CASE num
        CASE 2, 4
            LET x$ = "is "
        CASE 5 TO 9
            LET x$ = "This "
        CASE IS > 9
            LET x$ = "fun!"
        CASE ELSE
            LET x$ = "sure "
    END SELECT
    PRINT x$;
NEXT counter
DATA 7, 3, 2, 10
```

2. A *prime number* is a whole number 2 or greater that can only be divided evenly by 1 and by itself (e.g., 2, 3, 5, etc., but not 1, 4, 6, etc.). Write a QuickBASIC program that takes in a number from 2 to 20 and then uses the SELECT...END SELECT structure to classify the inputted number as "even and prime," "odd and prime," "even but not prime," or "odd but not prime." (Your cases should simply list the numbers of each type from 2 to 20.)

3.5 Generating Random Numbers

Now that we have both looping and decision structures at our disposal, we can start to do some very interesting things with QuickBASIC, such as *computer simulation* (discussed in the next section). When doing simulation you often need, in addition to various control structures, a *way to generate random numbers*. Structured BASIC provides a way, the **RND** function, which we first encountered in Table 1.2 of Section 1.4.

The RND function is used in any program where we want to have numbers that are chosen *randomly* (RND is short for "random"). Examples include just about any program that plays a *game* and also any program that does *simulation* (e.g., a program that simulates random traffic in a department store). The numbers that the RND function produces are not truly random—they are actually *pseudorandom* in the sense that they are the result of a complicated formula designed to produce numbers that *seem* to have no pattern.

The particular range of random numbers wanted depends on the particular application: to "toss a die," we would want a random integer from 1 to 6; to pick a random location in a diagram of a room, we might want a pair of random numbers representing coordinates. The function RND always produces a random number between 0 and 1, that is, a *proper fraction*; we may then use that number in a formula to get a random number in our desired range. The function RND needs no argument. For example,

```
PRINT RND, RND, RND, RND
```

produces

```
.7055475    .533424    .5795186    .2895625
```

These numbers look pretty random, don't they? On the other hand, *every time* we run that one-line program, it will produce the *same* four numbers, which in some sense isn't very random at all. If you think of QuickBASIC's random number formula (sometimes called a *random number generator*) as generating a *list* of random numbers, then the first time you use the function RND you get the first number on the list (.7055475), the next time you get the second (.533424), and so on. This can be useful: for example, to simulate random traffic in a department store, we might try rearranging exit locations and then see how the *same* random group of customers changes its traffic pattern; to write a program to play *duplicate bridge*, we might have several couples play the *same* randomly chosen hand of cards.

In most of our random number applications, we'll want to produce *different* random numbers each time the program is run. QuickBASIC has a special statement to help us do this:

```
RANDOMIZE TIMER
```

This statement, placed *before* the first use of the RND function, uses the computer's clock to choose the starting point for the RND formula; since the clock's value changes, this amounts to randomizing the starting point. Note: You only need the RANDOMIZE TIMER statement *once* in your program. As an example, here is a program segment, followed by the outputs of three different runs:

```
RANDOMIZE TIMER
PRINT RND, RND, RND, RND
PRINT RND, RND, RND, RND
```

OUTPUT 1

```
.2265894   .2671734   .4876454      .237057
.4438395   .3959407   9.790957E-03              .1952786
```

OUTPUT 2

```
.4641382   .8045269   .1255849      .5732386
.6852946   .9215754   .6828867      .4259915
```

OUTPUT 3

```
3.377932E-02          .4081036      .3773549   .6304286
7.622474E-02          .0612849      .3262582   .3083768
```

Notice several things about these outputs. First, of course, their results are *different*; this is because we used the RANDOMIZE TIMER statement. Second, some of them are printed in *scientific notation* (Outputs 1 and 3): the notation *E-03* means "times 10 raised to the −3 power," that is, move the decimal point 3 places to the left; similarly, *E12* would mean move the decimal point 12 places to the right (the letter *E* is short for "exponent"). Scientific notation is useful for representing either very small or very large numbers (you may use it while inputting, too). Finally, printing the scientific notation took enough space so that the next numbers had to be moved over one whole column; that's why the spacing looks odd.

Changing the Range of Random Numbers

As mentioned above, we'll frequently want random numbers in some range other than 0 to 1. To do this, we'll need to develop a few formulas. The basic idea is to first *multiply* to change the *size* of the range and then *add* to shift the *starting point*. For example, beginning with the range of RND,

$$0 \leq \text{RND} < 1$$

we can *multiply* RND by 10 to stretch the range from length 1 to length 10.

$$0 \leq 10 * \text{RND} < 10$$

If we add 5 to that, our random numbers will *start* at 5 and end at 10 beyond that, that is, at 15.

$$5 \leq 10 * \text{RND} + 5 < 15$$

Suppose we wanted to generate random numbers from −25 to 25, a range of *size 50* and *starting point −25*. The formula would be:

```
50 * RND - 25
```

In general, the formula for random numbers (random *real* numbers: both integers *and* fractions) in a range of given *size* and with a given *starting point* is:

size * RND + startingPoint

EXAMPLE 7

The Lucky Leprechaun Shoppe sells souvenirs of Ireland and is having a special St. Patrick's Day sale. Each customer is to be given a random discount between 10% and 50%. The algorithm is straightforward.

1. Introduce program and get purchase price
2. Compute random discount between 10% and 50%
3. Compute discounted price
4. Print results

The variables we'll need are *purchase* (the purchase price) and *discount* (the discount percentage). In Step 2, we'll be sure to first use RANDOMIZE TIMER to guarantee a different discount each time the program is run. In Step 3, we'll remember to *divide the percentage by 100* before multiplying it by the purchase price to get the amount to deduct; the appropriate expression for the discounted purchase price is:

```
purchase - (purchase * discount / 100)
```

Here's a program that does the job:

```
'-----------------------------------------------------------------
'       PROGRAM NAME:   C03EX07.BAS
'       AUTHOR:         S. T. Patrick
'       DATE:           March 17, 1992

'This program inputs a purchase amount, computes a random
'discount between 10% and 50%, and prints the discount and
'final price.
'-----------------------------------------------------------------

'Introduce program and get purchase amount

   CLS
   PRINT ">>>>> Welcome to the Lucky Leprechaun Shoppe <<<<<"
   PRINT
   PRINT ">>>>> It's our great St. Paddy's Day sale!!! <<<<<"

   PRINT
   PRINT
   INPUT "What is the amount of your purchase? $", purchase

'Compute discount and discounted price

   RANDOMIZE TIMER
   LET discount = 40 * RND + 10  'a random number from 10 to 50

   LET purchase = purchase - (purchase * discount / 100)
   LET purchase = CINT(purchase * 100) / 100 'round to nearest
                                             'penny
```

```
'Print results

    PRINT
    PRINT
    PRINT "YOUR LUCKY LEPRECHAUN DISCOUNT IS"; discount; "%."

    PRINT
    PRINT
    PRINT "Your final cost: $"; purchase

    PRINT
    PRINT
    PRINT ">>>>>>> HAPPY ST. PATRICK'S DAY!! <<<<<<<"

END
```

Here's sample output for the program:

```
>>>>> Welcome to the Lucky Leprechaun Shoppe <<<<<"

>>>>> It's our great St. Paddy's Day sale!!! <<<<<


What is the amount of your purchase? $49.95


YOUR LUCKY LEPRECHAUN DISCOUNT IS 34.36871 %.


Your final cost: $ 32.78


>>>>>>> HAPPY ST. PATRICK'S DAY!! <<<<<<<
```

Run this program several times (C03EX07.BAS on the SAMPLES disk) to see that you get a different discount in the range 10% to 50% each time.

Random Integers

Sometimes we want to restrict our random numbers to be *integers* (i.e., whole numbers); for instance, our output in the last example would look nicer if we only allowed whole number percentages. In card-playing applications, we would have to have whole numbers—there is no 4.16792 of hearts!

The natural thing to do when we have fractions but want integers is to *round off*. We might, for instance, want to round the percentage in the above output, 34.36871, to the nearest whole number, which is 34. In other words, maybe we should replace the line that computes the discount by the following:

```
LET discount = CINT(40 * RND + 10)
```

This is *close* to the right idea, but there is one problem: not all numbers are *equally likely*. For instance, the only way to get a discount of 10% is for the value of *40 * RND + 10* to be between 10 and 10.5 (it can't be less than 10); and we get 20% if the value falls between 19.5 and 20.5. That means that a 20% discount is about twice as likely as 10% because its range of numbers is twice as big!

Maybe using INT instead of CINT would work better, because each integer would get an interval of length 1 which rounded to it (e.g., we'd get 10 if *40 * RND + 10* was between 10 and 11, 20 if it was between 20 and 21). That works great for every number except *50*, because we aren't generating random numbers from 50 to 51. To get it exactly right, we can generate numbers in the range 10 to *51* and then use INT to round them down.

```
INT(41 * RND + 10)
```

Try replacing the original discount formula in C03EX07.BAS with the above formula to get whole number discounts from 10% to 50%.

Developing these formulas was fairly tricky, but now we can simply apply the appropriate one where it's needed. Just remember that the formulas for generating random numbers in a given range are *different* depending on whether you want *random real numbers* (numbers with fractional parts) or *random integers*. The two formulas are as follows:

FORMULAS FOR RANDOM NUMBERS IN A GIVEN RANGE

1. To generate *random real numbers* in the range *lowNum* to *highNum*, the formula is:

   (highNum − lowNum) * RND + lowNum

2. To generate *random integers* in the range *lowInt* to *highInt*, the formula is:

   INT((highInt − lowInt + 1) * RND + lowInt)

For example, to generate *real numbers* in the range 1.4 to 5, the formula would be: 3.6 * RND + 1.4. To generate *integers* in the range 50 to 100, the formula would be: INT(51 * RND + 50).

EXAMPLE 8

The following program segment prints a random time of day by generating a random hour from 1 to 12 and random minutes from 0 to 59 (both numbers are *integers*). The RANDOMIZE TIMER statement guarantees different random results each time the segment is run.

```
RANDOMIZE TIMER
LET hour = INT(12 * RND + 1)
LET minutes = INT(60 * RND)
PRINT "The doctor will see you at";
PRINT minutes; "minutes past"; hour; "."
```

Sample output follows.

```
The doctor will see you at 14 minutes past 3 .
```

PRACTICE 3.5

1. Give the range of random numbers generated by each of the following formulas and indicate whether the numbers generated are *any numbers* or *only integers*:

   (a) `5 * RND + 17`
   (b) `INT(101 * RND)`
   (c) `20 * RND - 8`
   (d) `INT(21 * RND - 10)`
   (e) `RND`
   (f) `INT(RND)`

2. Write down formulas for random numbers in each of the following ranges:

   (a) any number from 0 to 100
   (b) any integer from 18 to 65
   (c) any number from $-\frac{1}{2}$ to $\frac{1}{2}$
   (d) any integer from -15 to 30

3.6 An Introduction to Simulation

We end this chapter with a brief look at an important—and fun—application of computer programming. **Computer simulation** is the use of a computer to mimic as closely as possible some real-life event. Have you ever played Flight Simulator on a computer? If so, you've seen a very nice example of computer simulation. In fact, simulation is one of the computer's most important uses in science and industry and is especially exciting when combined with graphics. Although we're not yet in a position to do any very fancy simulations, in this section we'll look at a few fairly simple examples to get acquainted with the idea.

EXAMPLE 9

Let's write a program that simulates flipping a coin. We'll ask users how many times they want to flip the coin, and then we'll keep track of how many times heads comes up.

How do we simulate a coin flip, anyway? Well, if we think of heads and tails as being instead, say, the numbers 0 and 1, we can use the QuickBASIC random number generator! Although we'll generate a random sequence of 0s and 1s, think of it as a random sequence of heads and tails. Then we can use a *counter* to keep track of the number of heads. Here's an algorithm:

1. Introduce the program and find out how many flips are desired
2. Initialize the random number generator and initialize a counter of the number of heads
3. For each flip:
   a. Generate a random 0 or 1

b. If it's a head (i.e., a 0)
   Increase the head counter by 1 and print out "head"
   Otherwise
   Print out "tail"

4. Say how many heads came up

The program can look like this:

```
'------------------------------------------------------------
'    Program Title: C03EX09.BAS
'    Author:        Bobby Riggs
'    Date:          June 15, 1990

'    A simulation program for coin flipping that tosses
'    a coin as many times as the user wants and counts the
'    number of heads that come up.
'------------------------------------------------------------

'Introduce and get number of flips desired.

    CLS
    PRINT "This program simulates the tossing of a coin."
    PRINT
    INPUT "How many flips would you like? ", numFlips
    PRINT

'Initialize the random number generator and the head counter.

    RANDOMIZE TIMER
    LET headCounter = 0

'Flip 'em

    FOR flip = 1 TO numFlips
           LET outcome = INT(RND * 2)
           IF outcome = 0 THEN
                  LET headCounter = headCounter + 1
                  PRINT "Head    ";
           ELSE
                  PRINT "Tail    ";
           END IF
    NEXT flip

'Say how many heads came up.

    PRINT
    PRINT
    PRINT "There were"; headCounter; "heads out of ";
    PRINT "the"; numFlips; "flips."

END
```

Here's sample output:

```
This program simulates the tossing of a coin.

How many flips would you like? 30

Head    Tail    Tail    Tail    Head    Tail    Head    Head    Head    Tail
Head    Tail    Tail    Head    Tail    Tail    Head    Tail    Head    Head
Head    Tail    Head    Tail    Head    Head    Tail    Tail    Head    Head

There were 16 heads out of the 30 flips.
```

If you understand this program, then you've opened the door for doing lots of simulations. For example, can you see now how you could simulate the roll of a die, or, of more use, the roll of two dice? It would simply involve generating two random whole numbers each from 1 to 6, right? You can work this out now or in Practice 3.6, Exercise 2 at the end of this section.

Already, you're seeing that the use of a random number generator will be central to many simulation programs. The idea, of course, is to translate whatever random event you are trying to mimic into numbers (e.g., "head" = 0, "tail" = 1) and then use the random number generator. Time for another example.

EXAMPLE 10

Now, let's look at a simulation that's both more interesting and more challenging. Suppose that we have a circular dart board 2 feet in diameter centered on a 2-foot-square "backing." The board has a bull's-eye in the middle whose diameter is 6 inches. Let's write a program that simulates throwing a dart at the board. For simplicity, we'll assume that the dart *always* hits the backing, so it can either hit the bull's-eye, miss the bull's-eye but hit the board, or miss the board (but hit the backing).

This is a little harder than flipping coins or rolling dice, but again, the key is the translation of this event (throwing a dart) into numbers and then going from there. We'll need a bit of elementary geometry. A natural way to refer to locations on a drawing of a dart board is by using a *coordinate system*. Figure 3.1 shows the center of the board at point (0,0) and uses two variables: x measures left-right position with respect to the center, y measures up-down position with respect to the center. We've labelled several other points on the board (the unit of measure we've used is *feet*).

We can now describe the various possible outcomes of tossing a dart by using the coordinate system. For instance, hitting the backing amounts to generating a pair of random numbers (*not* necessarily

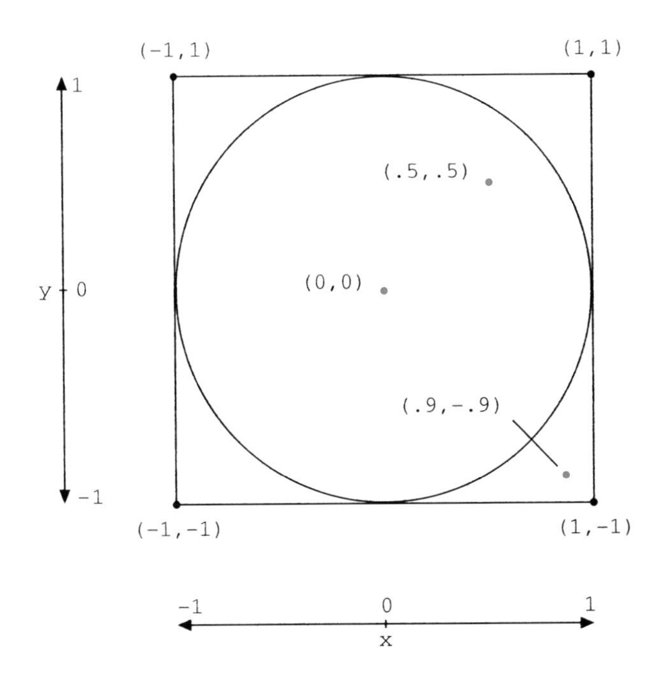

FIGURE 3.1

A Coordinate System for a Dart Board

whole numbers, though) each between -1 and $+1$. For example, (0,.6) would mean that you were perfect left and right, but too high for the bull's-eye. Get the idea?

How, then, do we distinguish "misses," "hits," and "bull's-eyes"? Notice that a bull's-eye is a pair (x,y) whose distance to (0,0) is less than or equal to 3 inches or .25 feet ("liners" count), which is the radius of the bull's-eye section. Likewise, we're on the board if the distance from (x,y) to (0,0) is less than or equal to 1 foot. So the outline of our algorithm is:

1. Introduce the program and initialize the random number generator
2. Throw the dart, that is, generate a pair (x,y) of random numbers each between -1 and $+1$
3. a. If the distance from (x,y) to (0,0) is less than or equal to .25, then "bull's-eye!"
   b. Otherwise, if this distance is less than or equal to 1, then "hit the board, but no bull's-eye"
   c. Otherwise, "sorry, missed"

As we review this outline, the first difficulty we see is in Step 2; we need to compute random numbers between -1 and $+1$ that are not necessarily whole numbers. But remember—we just studied this problem in the previous section. The formula is:

```
2 * RND - 1
```

We'll simply use this formula *twice* to generate the two numbers x and y.

The only problem left is to remember how to compute distances in a coordinate system for Step 3. Once again, we need some basic geometry, this time the *Pythagorean Theorem*. That ancient theorem tells us here that the distance from a point (x,y) to (0,0) is equal to the value of the following expression:

$$\sqrt{x^2 + y^2}$$

With this valuable piece of information, we can compute the distances in Step 3 and write the program.

```
'------------------------------------------------------------------
'     Program Title: C03EX10.BAS
'     Author:        Eric Bristow
'     Date:          November 23, 1991

'     This program simulates a random toss of a dart at a
'     dart board and determines whether the dart hits the
'     bull's-eye, the board, or the backing.
'------------------------------------------------------------------

'Introduce the program and initialize the random number
'generator.

     CLS
     PRINT "Get ready to throw a dart."
     PRINT

     RANDOMIZE TIMER

'Compute the coordinates of the random toss.

     INPUT "When you're ready, hit return.", a$
     PRINT
     LET x = 2 * RND - 1
     LET y = 2 * RND - 1

'Classify the throw.

     LET distance = SQR(x ^ 2 + y ^ 2)
     IF distance <= .25 THEN
            PRINT "Bull's-eye!! Nice shot!"
     ELSEIF distance <= 1 THEN
            PRINT "Hit the board, but no bull's-eye."
     ELSE
            PRINT "Hey, you missed the board!"
     END IF

END
```

Here's what the output might be:

```
Get ready to throw a dart.

When you're ready, hit return.

Bull's-eye!! Nice shot!
```

Two final remarks about this example. First, when we add graphics to our abilities, this and lots of other programs will take on much more life. We will be able to draw a picture of the dart board on the monitor and then watch each dart hit (see Chapter 10, Programming Problem 5). Second, it turns out that you can use the idea in this program to get an estimate for the famous number pi! If you're curious, see Programming Problem 13 at the end of this chapter.

EXAMPLE 11

Let's finish this section with a simple stock market simulation. The real Dow-Jones Average (a number representing the average value of a certain collection of stocks) fluctuates daily under a myriad of different forces, but in our simplified simulation let's assume there are two forces at work: first, that there's a tendency for the average to change randomly up or down from day to day; second, that the change on one day affects the following day, causing a momentum that makes the next day's change tend to be in the same direction.

We'll assume that the first force is a random change in the Dow-Jones Average varying between plus or minus 25 points and that the momentum force is half the size of the previous day's change. We'll simulate the changes in the Dow-Jones Average during the month of February 1993, assuming that the average is 1548.2 on January 31 and that it went up 7.8 points that day. The results will be printed in table form. Here's an algorithm:

1. Store initial value of Dow-Jones Average and initial change; initialize random number generator
2. Print table heading (table will have one line for each business day, showing new average and change from previous day)
3. For each business day in February (say there are 19):
   a. Compute the momentum force
   b. Generate the random force
   c. Add the forces to get the change
   d. Compute the new average
   e. Print the day, average, and change

A QuickBASIC program for this task follows.

```
'---------------------------------------------------------------
'    Program Title:        C03EX11.BAS
'    Author:               Donald Trump
'    Date:                 January 24, 1993

'    This program simulates the Dow-Jones Average for February
'    1993, assuming the change for a given day depends on the
'    change for the previous day and on random forces. A table
'    is printed showing the average and change for each of 19
'    business days.
'---------------------------------------------------------------

'Initialize values and random number generator.

     LET average = 1548.2
     LET change = 7.8
     RANDOMIZE TIMER

'Print table heading

     CLS
     PRINT "  DOW-JONES AVERAGE  FEBRUARY 1993"
     PRINT
     PRINT "BUSINESS DAY", "AVERAGE", "CHANGE"
     PRINT "------------", "-------", "------"

'Compute the changes and new averages for each business day;
'print results on one table line for each day.

     FOR day = 1 TO 19
            LET momentumForce = .5 * change
            LET randomForce = INT(51 * RND) - 25
            LET change = momentumForce + randomForce
            LET change = CINT(10 * change)/10   'round to nearest
                                                'tenth
            LET average = average + change
            PRINT day, average, change
     NEXT day

END
```

Here is what sample output might look like:

```
DOW-JONES AVERAGE  FEBRUARY 1993

BUSINESS DAY  CHANGE        AVERAGE
------------  ------        -------
1             -15.1         1533.1
2             -29.5         1503.6
3             -6.8          1496.8
4             -24.4         1472.4
5               3.8         1476.2
6               3.9         1480.1
7              20           1500.1
8              24           1524.1
9             -5            1519.1
10            -4.5          1514.6
11            -4.2          1510.4
12            -18.1         1492.3
13            -12.1         1480.2
14            -13.1         1467.1
15              9.4         1476.5
16            -12.3         1464.2
17              2.8         1467
18            -2.6          1464.4
19            -2.3          1462.1
```

It should be clear that a stock market simulation program that a brokerage house, or the government, or a doctoral student in economics would actually use would be a great deal more complicated than this, but the general principle behind it would be the same. Designing, writing, and testing a larger program would take more time—but the ideas you've learned up to this point would all apply. We shall look at some techniques for putting together bigger programs in the next chapter.

PRACTICE 3.6

1. What is the following program segment simulating?

```
LET quarter = INT(2 * RND)
LET dime = INT(2 * RND)
LET nickel = INT(2 * RND)
LET penny = INT(2 * RND)
```

2. Write a QuickBASIC program that simulates rolling two dice. It should simply inform the user, "You rolled ______ and ______."

Chapter Summary

In this chapter, we've learned about *decision making* in computer programming. Whenever there are two or more possible courses of action, depending on the situation at hand, we need to use a decision control structure.

The *IF...END IF* decision structure has a simple, direct syntax. It lets us choose a course of action (from as many alternatives as we need), depending on whether one or more *conditions* are true or false. Though the structure has various forms, they are all easy to understand and write.

More complex conditions can be described by combining one or more *simple conditions* together using *logical operators*; the resulting condition is called a *compound condition*. We learned about three logical operators: *AND*, *OR*, and *NOT*.

The *SELECT...END SELECT* structure, QuickBASIC's second decision structure, may be easier to use than IF...END IF when there are a large number of alternatives or when the alternatives fall naturally into cases.

Finally, we learned about generating random numbers using the *RND* numeric function; we were then introduced to the important idea of computer *simulation*, which makes frequent use of decision structures and random numbers.

Review Questions

1. Explain each term briefly and give an example:

(a) decision structure
(b) condition
(c) relational operator
(d) truth value
(e) logical operator
(f) compound condition
(g) RND
(h) simulation

2. Make up two examples, different from the ones you have seen in this chapter, that need decision structures. In one, the IF...END IF structure should be more appropriate; in the other, the SELECT...END SELECT structure should be more appropriate.

Programming Problems

Write down an algorithm for each problem and then a QuickBASIC program using "good style" (i.e., the program should reflect the design of your algorithm through appropriate use of comments, spacing, indentation, and meaningful variable names).

1. Write a program that takes in from the keyboard an annual salary and classifies it as "low income," "middle income," or "high income" depending on whether it is below $10000; at least $10000 but below $40000; or at least $40000. Use only simple conditions.

2. Write a program that takes in an indoor temperature and classifies it as "comfortable" if it's between 62 and 76 and "uncomfortable" otherwise. Use a compound condition.

3. Use the SELECT...END SELECT structure to write a simple language translation program. It should ask the user for a number from 1 to 10 and then return the Spanish word for that number. A sample output would be as follows:

```
Please type in a number from 1 to 10 --> 4
The Spanish word for 4 is cuatro.
```

4. The DATA lines of a program contain first the number of students in Psychology 100, followed by each student's name and his or her scores on the midterm and final exams. Write a program that prints out a table showing, on each line, name, midterm score, final-exam score, average, and the designation "honors" (an average of 80 or better), "passing" (an average between 79 and 60), or "failing" (an average of 59 or below). Use the following data to test your program:

```
DATA 5
DATA A. Freud, 87, 96, S. Freud 45, 57, K. Jung, 78, 75
DATA I. Pavlov, 87, 93, B. Skinner 65, 72
```

Check your output against the following:

```
          FINAL GRADES - PSYCHOLOGY 100

NAME        MIDTERM  FINAL  AVERAGE  MARK
----        -------  -----  -------  ----
A. Freud      87       96     91.5   HONORS
S. Freud      45       57     51     FAILING
K. Jung       78       75     76.5   PASSING
I. Pavlov     87       93     90     HONORS
B. Skinner    65       72     68.5   PASSING
```

5. Modify Programming Problem 9 in Chapter 1 as follows: the new program should ask users their name, their age, *and* whether they have had their birthday yet this year. The program responds with their year of birth and how old they'll turn in the year 2000.

6. Write a simple *text analyzer* as follows: the DATA lines contain first the number of words and then the words themselves (separated by commas) of some text. The user inputs a starting letter, and the program responds with how many words in the text start with that letter (upper or lowercase). For example, if the DATA lines are

```
DATA 8
DATA Four, score, and, seven, years, ago, our, fathers
```

and if the user enters "s" (or "S"), the program responds with 2. Note: You will need some string functions here. See Section 1.5.

7. "Unit pricing," which is now required shelf information in grocery stores in many states, shows the price of an item in a unit size so that different sizes and brands can be compared. Write a unit pricing program that takes in the price and size (in ounces, say) of some item A, the price and size of item B, and returns the message: "Item ________, at a unit price of ________, is a better deal than Item ________, at a unit price of ________."

8. Write a program that inputs three words, alphabetizes them by switching their values around, and then prints them out in alphabetical order (see Example 4 in Section 3.2).

9. The tax bracket program in Practice 3.2, Exercise 2 was oversimplified. The way it really works is that one pays 0% tax on the first $10000 of income, 15% on the *excess* of that up to $25000, and then 24% on the excess of *that*. So, for example, a person with a $43000 adjusted gross income would pay 15% of $15000 (=$25000 − $10000) and 24% of $18000 (=$43000 − $25000). Write a program that takes in the adjusted gross income and returns the correct income tax owed.

10. (a) Write a program that simulates drawing a single card from a standard deck. Since a playing card has two attributes ("suit" and "face value"), you will need to generate two random whole numbers. The output should simply be "You drew a jack of spades," or whatever.
    (b) Modify part (a) so that the user draws five cards (for poker, say)—but notice that your program is not an entirely accurate simulation, since it allows the user to draw the same card more than once. We will see how to fix this problem in Chapter 7, Programming Problem 7.

11. Modify Problem 4 above as follows: the table should first contain "honors" students, then below them "passing" students, then at the bottom "failing" students. You will need the RESTORE statement (introduced at the end of Section 2.6).

12. Write a "random walk on a line" simulation program. A little mouse starts walking at 0 and then goes either one step right (+1) or one step left (−1). He takes 100 such steps randomly. Write a program that shows his position throughout the 100 steps.

13. In Example 10 of this chapter, we simulated throwing a dart at a dart board. If we ignore the bull's-eye and simply concentrate on whether the dart does or does not hit the board, we have a way of estimating the number pi. The idea is: since the area of a circle is pi * radius squared and since our dart board has a radius of 1 foot, the area of our dart board is pi square feet. On the other hand, the area of the backing is 4 square feet. Since our dart shooting is random, if we shoot a bunch of darts, the *proportion* that hit the board should be approximately the *ratio* of these two areas, that is,

    proportion of "hits" = pi / 4 , approximately

    Therefore,

    pi = 4 * proportion of "hits," approximately

    Write a program, then, that starts with the user inputting the number of darts to be tossed and then returns an estimate for pi (which is 3.14159 to five decimal places) based on that many tosses. Be sure to experiment with the number of tosses: 100 tosses probably won't give you a great estimate, but 10000 tosses should work fairly well.

CHAPTER

4

MORE ON ALGORITHM DESIGN AND PROGRAM TESTING

CHAPTER PREVIEW In this chapter, we'll learn more about the three-stage process of computer programming: algorithm design and refinement, translation of the algorithm into a program, and testing and debugging of the program. We'll focus especially on the refinement process (*top-down algorithm design*) and on techniques for finding and correcting errors in our programs, including how to use the QuickBASIC debugger.

4.1 The Three-Stage Process of Program Writing

In Section 1.6, we observed that there are *three main stages* in the process of writing a computer program to solve a particular problem. In this chapter, we'll study the process in more detail. First, let's reiterate the three stages:

Stage 1: Design an algorithm and refine it as needed

Stage 2: Translate the algorithm into a computer program

Stage 3: Test and debug the program

Beginning programming students often believe that Stage 2 is the most important, in fact, that it is the *only* stage. It is very common to see beginners sit down at the keyboard, start "composing," and assume they are done as soon as *any* output (right or wrong!) is obtained. But the truth of the matter is this:

> ***Stages 1 and 3 are the heart of programming. If you are using a good language like Structured BASIC, then Stage 2 is by far the easiest. The key to successful programming is good algorithm design at the beginning and thorough program testing at the end.***

From the very beginning, we have emphasized the importance of algorithm design. In Section 1.6, we discussed the concept of an algorithm (a step-by-step recipe to solve a problem) and the idea of *refining* an algorithm until its steps are readily translatable into QuickBASIC code. If the problem we are faced with is relatively easy and short (as most of ours have been up to now), the algorithm design isn't hard; sometimes, we even feel that we can "do it in our heads," though this is generally *not* a good practice. However, as the problems we face become longer and more challenging, careful algorithm design and refinement become more crucial. When it comes time to translate an algorithm into QuickBASIC, we must make use of the concept of **modularity**: the separation of individual steps of the algorithm into sections of program code, producing a *structured program*. Finally, we must thoroughly test our programs. The larger the program, the more likely it is to have errors that we can detect only through running the program repeatedly, using carefully thought-out *test data*.

You will be on your way to successful programming if you always remember that *three stages are involved* (not just one!) and always concentrate on doing each stage with care.

In the remainder of this chapter, we shall look more closely at the three-stage process of writing good programs.

4.2 Stage 1: Top-Down Algorithm Design

When we need to write a program to solve a problem, we always start by making sure we understand the problem; then we write an algorithm for solving the problem. As we've said before, at this stage, we shouldn't worry about every little detail; instead, we should begin with a *broad outline* of the steps we think are necessary to reach a solution. This broad outline is called a **level-1 algorithm**.

For many computer programs, a perfectly reasonable level-1 algorithm is:

1. Input the data
2. Process the data
3. Output the results

Of course, not every program fits into this mold, but many do—so it's worth keeping the above in mind as a frequent starting place for algorithm design.

Notice now that, in all likelihood, each of the above steps is itself several—perhaps many—individual steps, depending on how complicated the problem at hand is. Obviously, this level-1 algorithm cannot possibly be translated into computer code; it lacks any detail. It must be *refined*. The process of starting with a level-1 algorithm like the one above and going through a *step-by-step refinement* of it is called **top-down algorithm design**. The idea is, quite simply, that we take a problem and break it into subproblems, then break those subproblems into subproblems, and so on until the algorithm has enough detail to be readily translated into computer code. Example 1 shows this process in action.

EXAMPLE 1

Let's write a program that simulates a cash register at the checkout counter of a grocery store. The program asks how many items are being bought, then asks the cost of each item and whether or not it is taxable (at 7%), and finally gives the bill, accepts payment, and gives back change due if any.

Right away, we see that the three-step level-1 algorithm proposed above doesn't quite fit here, because the item prices must be brought in and *processed* one at a time. Therefore, we begin with a more detailed level-1 algorithm, as follows.

LEVEL-1 ALGORITHM

1. Find out the number of items
2. Find out the price and "taxability" of each item, computing the sums of taxable items and of nontaxable items
3. Compute the tax on the sum of the taxable items, compute the total owed, and output both
4. Find out the amount paid and compute and output the amount of change due

Take a good look at this algorithm—it's all in plain English; there is no discernible QuickBASIC code. Certainly, we cannot yet translate this algorithm into a computer program—but it *is* an *outline* of what needs to be done. When we finally do write our program (in the next section), it will probably have four main sections; and this level-1 algorithm will be our guide for bringing *modularity* to our program. In this way, the program will be easy to read and understand; its outline will be clear.

Notice also that although Step 1 is clear each of the others needs *refinement*. Steps 3 and 4 look fairly easy, involving only assignments of values, one input of data (the amount paid), and some output of results. Step 2 is more complicated: we must do something for each item, including making a decision.

Now is the time, when refining our level-1 algorithm, to think about *what variables are needed*. In this case, the quantities that can change from one run of the program to the next are the number of items, the price of each item, the totals of the taxable and nontaxable items, the tax due, the grand total, the payment, and the change due—all of which are numbers. Also, we need to keep track of whether each item is taxable ("Y" or "N," which is a string). So, using *meaningful* names, let's have numeric variables *numItems, price, taxableSum, nontaxableSum, tax, total, payment,* and *change*, and a string variable *taxable$*. We're now ready to move to the next level of refinement. We'll call the refinement of a level-1 algorithm a **level-2 algorithm**, the refinement of a level-2 algorithm a **level-3 algorithm**, and so on.

LEVEL-2 ALGORITHM

Variables: *numItems, price, taxable$, taxableSum, nontaxableSum, tax, total, payment, change*

1. Input *numItems*
2. For each item:
   a. Input *price*
   b. Ask whether it's taxable
   c. If it is taxable
         Add that *price* into *taxableSum*
      Otherwise
         Add that *price* into *nontaxableSum*
3. Compute *tax* = 7% of *taxableSum*,
   compute *total* = *tax* + *taxableSum* + *nontaxableSum*,
   and print out *tax* and *total*
4. Input *payment* and compute and print out
   change = *payment* − *total*

Although our level-2 algorithm is still in English, notice that it is starting to look something like a QuickBASIC program! Recall that this mixture of English words and BASIC code is called *pseudocode*. The pseudocode provides a *transition* from the ordinary English of our level-1 algorithm to the QuickBASIC program that we will write. In our level-2 algorithm, Step 1 is *already* QuickBASIC, and the other steps haven't far to go. Seeing that Step 2 will require a FOR...NEXT loop, we will need a loop-counter variable, *item*.

We are very close to writing the program. At this point, we should identify any extra tasks that need to be performed. For instance, we will want to introduce the program to the user; we will want to round *tax* to the nearest cent before computing the total; and we will want to say thank you at the end. So let's refine once more, writing a final version of our algorithm that will translate quite directly into QuickBASIC.

LEVEL-3 ALGORITHM

Variables: *numItems, item, price, taxable$, taxableSum, nontaxableSum, tax, total, payment, change*

1. a. Introduce the program
   b. Input *numItems*
2. For each *item*:
   a. Input *price*
   b. Input *taxable$*
   c. If *taxable$* = "Y", then
      Let *taxableSum* = *taxableSum* + *price*
      Otherwise
      Let *nontaxableSum* = *nontaxableSum* + *price*
3. a. Let *tax* = .07 * *taxableSum*
   b. Round off *tax*
   c. Let *total* = *taxableSum* + *nontaxableSum* + *tax*
   d. Print *tax* and *total*
4. a. Input *payment*
   b. Let *change* = *payment* − *total*
   c. Print *change*
   d. Say "thanks"

Although this is still pseudocode, it's very close to QuickBASIC. Writing the program in the next section will be very easy, given the work already done.

This process may seem lengthy to you—but it is absolutely worth it! The truth is that *careful algorithm design and refinement saves time and energy in the long run*. The reason is simple: if you don't take care at this point, you will likely write a program that is not well-designed and that will not work properly. Then you'll spend twice as much time fixing things you should have had right in the first place.

How much refining should you do? That depends on the situation. The following is a good rule to program by:

> ***You should* always *write a* level-1 algorithm*; then you should* always list your variables *and refine your algorithm to a* level-2 algorithm. *The amount of additional refinement needed depends on the difficulty of the problem at hand.***

We have said enough for the moment about this first stage in writing a program. Let's turn now to the stage that should be the easiest if we've done the first stage properly.

4.3 Stage 2: From Algorithm to Program

One of the great strengths of Structured BASIC, as we have often said before, is that the language allows us to translate our procedure for solving a problem into computer code in a very natural way. Having written a list of the variables needed and a careful algorithm (level-2 or higher), we can usually write the QuickBASIC program without much difficulty. At this point, we should have *two basic goals* in mind:

> First, we want to write a program *that does, in a sensible way, what it is supposed to do.*
>
> Second, we want to write a program *that is readable and clearly organized* so that we and others can easily see what it is doing. This is important when we are testing the program for errors or when, later on, we or others return to the program to modify it.

But here's the point: *our algorithm makes it easy for us to achieve both these goals.* We produce a *correct* program by translating the *details* of the algorithm into QuickBASIC code, and we produce a *clearly organized* program by using the *outline* of the algorithm (i.e., the level-1 algorithm) to break the program into logical sections. This latter technique is called *modularity* and is an absolutely essential component of successful programming. Finally, we must always use *good programming style* (as introduced in Section 2.7: use of comments, blank lines, indentation, and meaningful variable names).

When we put all this together, we have written a **structured program**, that is, one that solves a problem in a clear, logical manner and that we or someone else can easily understand when reading it from top to bottom. Combining sensible algorithm design with a structured language such as QuickBASIC makes writing easy-to-read, logical programs a much easier task than in the days of old-style BASIC, with its line numbers and GOTO statements!

Let's complete this process by translating our cash register simulation algorithm into a QuickBASIC program. Our algorithm indicates that there will be four main sections. The details of the solution, including the variables we need (each with a meaningful name), are clearly listed. The following is a preliminary version of the program (testing will probably result in some revisions):

```
'-------------------------------------------------------------
'    Program title: C04EX01A.BAS
'    Author:        C. Chavez
'    Date:          Sept. 23, 1992

'    Simulates a cash register in a grocery store. It must
'distinguish between taxable and nontaxable items, putting a
'7% tax on the former.
'-------------------------------------------------------------
```

```
'Introduce the program and get the number of items.

     CLS
     PRINT "Welcome to Grand Onion!"
     INPUT "How many items do you have? ", numItems

'Get price and taxability of each item, accumulate a taxable
'sum and a nontaxable sum.

     FOR item = 1 TO numItems
            INPUT "Price --> $", price
            INPUT "Taxable? (Y/N) ", taxable$
            IF (taxable$ = "Y") THEN
                   LET taxableSum = taxableSum + price
            ELSE
                   LET nontaxableSum = nontaxableSum + price
            ENDIF
     NEXT item

'Compute and print out the tax and total.

     LET tax = .07 * taxableSum
     LET tax = CINT(100 * tax) / 100  'Round off to nearest cent
     LET total = taxableSum + nontaxableSum + tax

     PRINT "The tax on these items is $"; tax
     PRINT "The total you owe is $"; total

'Get payment and give back change.

     INPUT "How much is your payment? $", payment
     LET change = payment - total
     PRINT "Your change due is $"; change
     PRINT "Thanks for shopping with us!"

END
```

Compare this program with the level-3 algorithm—it is almost a direct translation, using correct QuickBASIC syntax and good programming style. It is certainly easy to read and understand. The question now is: *does it work*? If it does, the next question is: *how does the output look*—is *it* readable and nice looking? To answer these questions, we must now *test and debug* our program. It is almost certain that what we have written thus far will *not* be the finished product. Even if the program basically works properly, we are bound to find small problems to fix and small improvements to make. Let's take on that task now.

4.4 Stage 3: Testing and Debugging

Once you've typed the word *END* and saved the program you have just written, the real fun (and sometimes the frustration) begins. At this point, it's time to run the program to find out whether it does what you've designed it to do. Let us say at the outset that the more *careful* you have been about *algorithm design*, the more likely you are to have fun rather than frustration at the time of running. On the other hand, it's safe to say that almost no program works *perfectly* the first time it's run. Let's talk about some of the things that can go wrong.

First, the program can have errors ("bugs"). Second, the output of the program may not be in a suitable form. We'll discuss both in turn.

There are two kinds of errors that can occur in a computer program: *syntax errors* and *logical errors*. A **syntax error** is an error in the use of the QuickBASIC language itself; it is a grammatical or spelling mistake that prevents the compiler from understanding what was typed (see Step 7 of Section WS2.3 for a brief discussion of the compiler). For example, each of the following contains a QuickBASIC syntax error:

1. `PRIMT "Hi there!"`
2. `PRINT "Hi there!`
3. ```
   IF num = 7
       LET num = num + 1
   END IF
   ```
4. `LET b + c = a`

Do you see what's wrong with each of these? QuickBASIC *does* report syntax errors to you when it detects them, which can occur at different stages of the programming process. Recall that QuickBASIC has a "Smart Editor" (see Step 9 of Section WS2.3), which tries to find syntax errors as soon as you've entered a line; the editor either reports errors to you immediately or *corrects* them if it can (a very nice feature indeed!). So, for example, QuickBASIC will report the errors in lines 3 and 4 immediately after they are entered, and it will simply correct line 2 for you. Some syntax errors, however, cannot be detected by the Smart Editor; these will not surface until compilation time, that is, when you try to run the program. The error in line 1 is of this type. You would do well to type each of these yourself to see what happens.

Because syntax errors prevent a program from running, they *must* be corrected before any output is obtainable. That's the bad news; the good news is that a good compiler (such as QuickBASIC's) points out these errors to you so that they are *usually* (but not always) easy to fix. We'll have more to say about this below.

A **logical error** is exactly what you think: an error in the logic of your algorithm. Logical errors cannot, of course, be detected by the compiler, since it cannot know what problem you are attempting to solve. As long as your grammar is correct, the compiler is happy. Hence, *logical errors are, in general, more difficult to find and correct than are syntax errors.* Here is an example of a fairly obvious logical
   ```

error, given that *sum* is supposed to be the sum of five inputted numbers:

```
FOR counter = 1 TO 5
    INPUT number
    LET sum = number
NEXT counter
PRINT "The sum is"; sum
```

This segment compiles without difficulty (i.e., it contains no *syntax* errors), but of course it doesn't "work," because the logic of the LET statement is wrong. No matter which five numbers are typed in, what will be the output of this segment? We shall discuss below how you can try to find and fix logical errors.

Besides errors, the other problem that usually arises upon first running a program is that the output does not look the way you would like it to—and, usually, this part of testing and debugging is easy and fun. Often, it's a matter of adding blank lines to the output (PRINT by itself), making messages easier to read, lining up columns in a table, and so forth—but sometimes it entails using more sophisticated techniques (which we shall discuss in Chapter 9). Let's just say here that you *will* do at least a little of this kind of debugging with every program you write.

Let's go through a *testing and debugging procedure*, which you can use with any new program.

1. Find and correct all syntax errors.

Read the error message the compiler has given you; usually, this tells you right away what needs fixing. However, since the compiler is trying to understand incorrect language, it may not always be able to pinpoint exactly what you've done wrong. If you get an error message during *editing*, the error is almost certainly on the line you've just entered. If, on the other hand, you get this message during compilation, the error is either on the highlighted line or *on some previous line* (but, for whatever reason, the compiler was unable to detect the error when it occurred). In this case, you must look carefully at the highlighted line and then work backwards line by line until you find the error. For an example showing lots of syntax errors, see Practice 4.4, Exercise 1 at the end of this section.

If you simply can't find an indicated error, try deleting (temporarily) the highlighted line, recompile, and see if the error goes away. If it does, then it was almost certainly on that (now deleted) line. Retype the line, compile again, and hope for the best. If all else fails, ask someone else to look at the program for you (it's easy to be blind to our own mistakes!) or simply put it aside and come back to it later.

Repeat all this until you have no more syntax errors. Now you have a grammatically correct program, but *does it work*? That is, is it *logically* correct?

2. Design a set of *test data* representing all the possible kinds of data that your program might encounter.

Now, you have to put your new program "through its paces." Start with data simple enough for you to calculate relatively easily "by hand" what the computer is supposed to be doing. If this data works well, put in more complicated data to see how it is handled. At this point, you should be playing the role of the program's "worst enemy," trying all the different possibilities for incoming data that you can imagine. If all this works, you *probably* have no logical errors, though there may be problems that you simply haven't foreseen. Spend time on this process!

3. Find and correct all logical errors, using the techniques of careful reading, hand-tracing, inserting extra PRINT statements, "commenting out" lines, and/or using the QuickBASIC debugger.

Finding logical errors can sometimes be quick and easy and sometimes very difficult. The first step is simply to *read through your program carefully*. It helps to get a printout of the program and look at it on paper rather than on the monitor. Very often, you'll see that you didn't write what you meant to write.

Let us mention here a very common logical error that can occur when using QuickBASIC but can often be caught through careful reading: *the misspelling of an occurrence of a variable*. In some computer languages, such as Pascal, programmers must "declare" their variables, that is, at the beginning of the program, they must write down the names of all their variables. In such languages, the subsequent misspelling of a variable in the program becomes a syntax error. In QuickBASIC, however, variables are not declared, so the compiler can only assume that the misspelling is a *new* variable. Here's an example:

```
LET sum = 0
FOR counter = 1 TO 5
    INPUT number
    LET sum = sum + namber
NEXT counter
PRINT sum
```

It's easy for your eye to skip over such misspellings—but, of course, they "kill" the program. What is the value of *namber*, and hence *sum*, throughout this segment? Always keep the possibility of this error in mind.

If a careful reading gives you no clues, try **hand-tracing** your program. Also called "playing computer," the idea is that you work through your program exactly as the computer does (only *much* more slowly), going line by line and using the data that revealed the error to you in the first place. Definitely use paper and pencil for this. Divide your paper into two sides, one showing the current value of each variable and one showing any output. Concentrate on doing what each line actually says to do, *not* what you think it is *supposed* to do (that's exactly the problem, right?). Hand-tracing, if done carefully, almost always reveals the source of logical errors.

Another quite helpful technique is *to temporarily insert extra PRINT statements*. For example, in our segment above, which is supposed to compute the sum but doesn't, you might try inserting a "PRINT sum" statement *inside* the loop. You would then have:

```
FOR counter = 1 TO 5
    INPUT number
    LET sum = number
    PRINT sum
NEXT counter
PRINT sum
```

Running the segment in this form clearly reveals the problem: the sum is not accumulating! Now, you can fix the problem, delete the extra line, and run it again.

This technique can be used in various ways. For instance, if you suspected that some option of a decision structure (IF...END IF or SELECT...END SELECT) is not working properly, you can put in an extra PRINT statement (e.g., PRINT "In ELSE clause") to signal that you have entered that option. Try this technique; the basic idea is that the more you *see* of what your program is doing, the better you will understand it.

A last debugging technique to be mentioned here is that of *commenting out* one or more lines. If you want to (temporarily) remove part of your program—usually in order to see if the trouble disappears when that part is gone—you can simply place the comment mark (') at the beginning of each line you wish to remove. Since those lines are now comments, the compiler skips over them. If that seems to isolate the error, you can then remove the comment marks one at a time, hence "zeroing in" on the problem.

All the above techniques apply no matter what computer language you use. As a QuickBASIC user, however, you have an additional and very helpful tool: the built-in *QuickBASIC Debugger*. We will devote the next section of this chapter to learning to use this facility—but for now, be aware that it is another option for debugging a program.

Finally—as with syntax errors—if all else fails, either have a friend look at your program or put it away for a while and take a break!

4. Once all errors are corrected, look at the output and make whatever changes are necessary to get it looking the way you want.

As we said previously, this will consist of things like adding blank lines to the output via PRINT, lining up columns, and so on. We will say much more about this in Chapter 9.

5. Now, retest the program a final time, that is, repeat Steps 1 through 3.

It may well be that in making changes in Step 4 you have introduced *new* errors (aaarghh!). You *must* retest the program in its final form. Also, look at the program itself to be sure that its organization and style are still as you want them to be. When you've confirmed all this, *save* the program and "rest on your laurels."

Let's test and debug our cash register simulation program now. It's saved as C04EX01A.BAS (see the previous section; and it's on the SAMPLES disk, of course). Upon running, we discover (happily) that there are no syntax errors. Now it's time to input test data. Let's start with data that we can easily hand-check.

```
Welcome to Grand Onion!
How many items do you have? 4
Price --> $5.00
Taxable? (Y/N) Y
Price --> $2.00
Taxable? (Y/N) N
Price --> $5.00
Taxable? (Y/N) Y
Price --> $4.00
Taxable? (Y/N) N
The tax on these items is $ .70
The total you owe is $ 16.70
How much is your payment? $20.00
Your change due is $ 3.30
Thanks for shopping with us!
```

Comparing our hand-computed results with the output indicates that the program seems to perform correctly so far. Let's try again, with different data.

```
Welcome to Grand Onion!
How many items do you have? 2
Price --> $3.50
Taxable? (Y/N) y
Price --> $1.80
Taxable? (Y/N) n
The tax on these items is $ 0
The total you owe is $ 5.30
How much is your payment? $6.00
Your change due is $ .70
Thanks for shopping with us!
```

That's not right! What went wrong? Well, this error is fairly easy to find: the user typed in "y" as the response to "Taxable?" but the test in the IF...END IF only allows for uppercase Y. We can change this by making the condition compound:

```
IF (taxable$ = "Y") OR (taxable$ = "y") THEN
```

Now, here's some other data that might cause trouble:

```
Welcome to Grand Onion!
How many items do you have? 1
Price --> $3.49
```

```
Taxable? (Y/N) N
The tax on these items is $ 0
The total you owe is $ 3.49
How much is your payment? $3.00
Your change due is $ -.49
Thanks for shopping with us!
```

Minus 49 cents in change? The arithmetic is correct, of course, but our program really should be able to handle the situation where the customer "shorts" the clerk. One solution is another decision structure at the end.

```
INPUT "How much is your payment? $", payment
LET change = payment - total
IF payment > total THEN
    PRINT "Your change due is $"; change
ELSEIF payment < total THEN
    PRINT "I'll need $"; - change; "more please"
END IF
```

Of course, this new section has to be tested (try all *three* possibilities: change due, shorted, and exact payment).

Here's one more little problem we might stumble upon, with "ordinary" data:

```
Welcome to Grand Onion!
How many items do you have? 4
Price --> $12.89
Taxable? (Y/N) Y
Price --> $10.00
Taxable? (Y/N) N
Price --> $5.89
Taxable? (Y/N) Y
Price --> $3.45
Taxable? (Y/N) N
The tax on these items is $ 1.31
The total you owe is $ 33.54
How much is your payment? $35.00
Your change due is $ 1.459999
Thanks for shopping with us!
```

Change due is $1.459999? This is not our fault: it has to do with the way in which the computer stores numbers. We can fix it, though, by rounding off the change to the nearest cent:

```
LET change = CINT(change * 100) / 100
```

At this point, we believe we have a program that works properly (although testing alone can't guarantee this—there can always be a bug that doesn't show up for our choice of test data). One point: Notice that we forgot to initialize the two sum variables before the loop begins. Although this didn't create bugs for us here, since QuickBASIC automatically initializes numeric variables to 0, in another situation we might not be so lucky. Therefore, we should initialize *taxableSum* and *nontaxableSum*.

It's now time to improve the appearance of the output. Certainly, we could use some blank lines in it. Also, we might like to have it say something like the following:

```
Item # 1
     Price --> $
     Taxable? (Y/N)
Item # 2
```

(and so on)

Other than that, the program seems to be in fairly good shape—so let's make the above changes and see what we've got.

```
'----------------------------------------------------------------
'    Program title: C04EX01B.BAS
'    Author:        C. Chavez
'    Date:          Sept. 23, 1992

'    Simulates a cash register in a grocery store. It must
'distinguish between taxable and nontaxable items, putting a
'7% tax on the former. This is a refinement of C04EX01A.BAS.
'----------------------------------------------------------------

'Introduce the program and get the number of items.

     CLS
     PRINT "Welcome to Grand Onion!"
     PRINT
     INPUT "How many items do you have? ", numItems
     PRINT

'Get price and taxability of each item, accumulate a taxable
'sum and a nontaxable sum.

     LET taxableSUM = 0
     LET nontaxableSUM = 0
     FOR item = 1 TO numItems
          PRINT "Item #"; item
          INPUT " Price --> $", price
          INPUT " Taxable? (Y/N) ", taxable$
          PRINT
          IF (taxable$ = "Y") OR (taxable$ = "y") THEN
               LET taxableSum = taxableSum + price
          ELSE
               LET nontaxableSum = nontaxableSum + price
          ENDIF
     NEXT item

'Compute and print out the tax and total.

     LET tax = .07 * taxableSum
     LET tax = CINT(100 * tax) / 100 'Round off to nearest cent
     LET total = taxableSum + nontaxableSum + tax
```

```
    PRINT "The tax on these items is $"; tax
    PRINT
    PRINT "The total you owe is $"; total
    PRINT

'Get payment and give back change (or get more money if needed).

    INPUT "How much is your payment? $", payment
    PRINT
    IF payment > total THEN
            LET change = payment - total
            LET change = CINT(change * 100) / 100
            PRINT "Your change due is $"; change
            PRINT
    ELSEIF payment < total THEN
            PRINT "I'll need $"; - change; "more please"
            PRINT
    END IF
    PRINT "Thanks for shopping with us!"

END
```

Remember that at this point we *must* again thoroughly test the program, since we may have introduced new problems while fixing the old ones. We won't write that all down here—but when you're testing your own programs you must *not* be satisfied with one quick run. Here's a sample of what the program now does:

```
Welcome to Grand Onion!

How many items do you have? 2

Item # 1
    Price --> $2.00
    Taxable? (Y/N) y

Item # 2
    Price --> $1.50
    Taxable? (Y/N) n

The tax on these items is $ .14

The total you owe is $ 3.64

How much is your payment? $3.00

I'll need $ .64 more please

Thanks for shopping with us!
```

In summary, the testing and debugging stage of programming can be difficult and time-consuming, but, once again, if you were careful during Stage 1 (algorithm design), your job in Stage 3 will usually be much easier. If you do the job right, you end up with a correctly functioning program with attractive output—and that, as you know already, is an enjoyable and satisfying experience!

PRACTICE 4.4

1. The following segment contains 13 QuickBASIC syntax errors! Find and correct them.

```
CLR
IMPUT "Type in a number: num
IF num => 0 AND =< 10
    LET num + 3 = num
OTHERWISE
    PRINT 'Out of range!'
PRINT num
```

2. The following segment, which is supposed to compute the product of a specified number of inputted numbers, is free of syntax errors but contains four *logical* errors. Fix the errors so that the program segment works properly.

```
INPUT howMany
For k = 0 TO howMany
    LET product = num * num
    INPUT num
NEXT k
PRINT product
```

4.5 Using the QuickBASIC Debugger

In Section 4.4, we discussed various techniques for finding and correcting logical errors in programs—techniques such as careful reading, hand-tracing, adding extra PRINT statements, and commenting out lines. We emphasize again: you can apply these techniques no matter what computer language you use and no matter what the "programming environment" is. However, since you are currently using QuickBASIC, you may also find it helpful to learn to use the debugging system that is built into the QuickBASIC environment. This system has both simple and advanced techniques; we will go over some of the simpler ones and let you pursue the more advanced topics on your own.

We will demonstrate how to have a program execute one line and then wait, execute the next line and again wait, and so on, so that we can "step" through the program at our own pace. We shall also cover how to "watch" the values of any variables we want while the program runs and how to set points where we want the program to halt. That is,

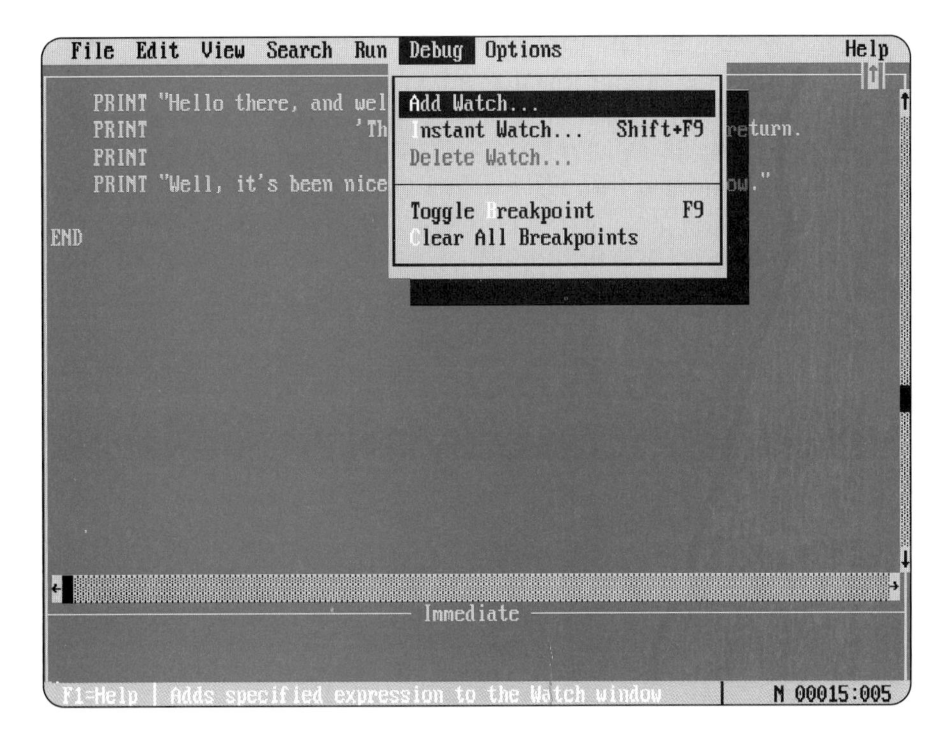

FIGURE 4.1

The *Debug* Menu

we can "automatically" perform some of the techniques from the last section using the QuickBASIC debugger.

This should be a *hands-on* experience. *Go to a computer and start up QuickBASIC.* We assume that you are using Version 4.5 with the Short Menu option selected or version 4.0 (if you see more options or slightly different options than we discuss, don't worry). Before loading a program, look at the blank QuickBASIC screen. Notice the *Reference Bar* at the bottom: it shows (among other things) that you can "step" through a program by pressing the **F8** function key repeatedly. Always remember to look at the Reference Bar; it contains useful information at all stages of the programming process.

Now, pull down the **Debug Menu** by pressing **ALT-D**. You should see the options *Add Watch, Instant Watch,*[1] *Delete Watch, Toggle Breakpoint*, and *Clear All Breakpoints*, as shown in Figure 4.1.

Before trying these options on a sample program, we want to explain the two main ideas which appear here. First, you can **watch** the value of a variable (as many as you want) either by having Quick-BASIC show that variable in the **Watch Window** (this is the *Add Watch* option) or by having it display a dialog box containing the variable's name and value (this is *Instant Watch*). Second, you can set a **Break-point** at any line of your program; each time that line is encountered, the program will halt (so that you can "watch" a variable, for example). When you are ready to continue running the program, you press **F5**. It's really quite easy!

[1] This option is available only in Version 4.5.

Let's try some of these techniques. Get your SAMPLES disk and open the program named C03EX05.BAS. Look it over and run it once or twice to refresh your memory. Now—so it doesn't get tedious—*change* the first line of DATA from 16 to, say, 6 (making *classSize* smaller). As you work through the following steps, you'll be using the Debug Menu and several function keys. Below is a list of these keys, together with brief descriptions, on which we'll elaborate in the steps that follow.

Key	Function
F4	Move between output and QuickBASIC screens
F5	Continue running program from current statement
F8	Step through the program
F9	Set or clear a breakpoint at cursor location
Shift-F9	Instant watch of variable at cursor location (Version 4.5 only)

Now, with the program C03EX05.BAS, carry out the following steps. You can refer to the above function key descriptions as needed.

Stepping

Step through the program entirely by pressing **F8** repeatedly; enter **80** and **100** when you're asked for the lower and upper limits. Notice that whenever a statement involves input or output, QuickBASIC goes to the output screen and then returns immediately to the QuickBASIC screen. This can be irritating, but it's unavoidable. If you want to see the output screen at any time, just press **F4**. You can always *move back and forth* between the QuickBASIC and output screens by *pressing F4*.

Stepping allows you to watch the "flow" of the program, which can be fun. For example, in C03EX05.BAS, when the condition in the IF...END IF statement is false, you see the program move directly to the END IF line. Simply watching the flow can sometimes help you debug a program.

Watching

Now, let's step through again, but this time we'll first add a watch variable and also do an "Instant Watch" on two other variables during the stepping process. Pull down the Debug Menu (**ALT-D**) and select the *Add Watch* option. In the dialog box that appears, type in **student** and press **<Enter>**. Look near the top of the screen; a new window, the *Watch Window*, has opened up, in which the name of the program and the variable name *student* are displayed. As the program runs, the current value of *student* will continue to be displayed in this window. Now, step through the program again (**F8**). Notice that when you enter the loop, *student* gets the value 1, and each time through the loop it increments.

Version 4.5 users only: After two (or so) times through the loop, place the cursor under the variable *name$* and then select the option *Instant Watch* from the Debug Menu (or press **Shift-F9**). The dialog box now displayed contains the current value of *name$*. Notice also that the cursor is now on the option *Add Watch*. Press **<Enter>**; now *name$* is also in the Watch Window. Place the cursor under *score* and again ask for Instant Watch (**Shift-F9** or the Debug Menu). Pressing **<Enter>** after the dialog box appears adds *score* to the Watch Window also; pressing **<Esc>** clears the dialog box without adding it to the Watch Window. Go ahead and step through the rest of the program (**F8**), noticing the changing values of the variables in the Watch Window. It's fun, right?

Watching the flow of the program and the values of certain variables is exactly what you do when you hand-trace a program as described in the previous section. Moreover, having "watch variables" is an alternative to using extra PRINT statements to display the values of variables. QuickBASIC makes doing things like this easy.

Although stepping through a program is informative, if the program is of any size at all, stepping takes a long time. To deal with this, QuickBASIC also allows you to run the program as usual (i.e., at "full speed") but to set *breakpoints* where the program will pause. Let's check this out.

Breakpoints

Put the cursor, say, on the line "NEXT student." Now select the *Toggle Breakpoint* option from the Debug Menu (or press **F9**). The line you are on becomes a breakpoint: the program will halt each time it encounters that line. Start the program up as you normally do; it will execute until it hits your breakpoint. Look at the "watch variables" that you set previously. To start the program again, press **F5** or select the *Continue* option from the Run Menu. The program runs until it hits the breakpoint again, and so on.

Remember that if you are at a breakpoint and you would like to get a look at the output screen, you can do so by pressing **F4**. To *remove* a breakpoint, put the cursor on that line and press **F9** (or use the Debug Menu). Experiment with this a little; it's quite handy for debugging.

Also, remember the *Reference Bar* at the bottom of the screen! It usually displays relevant function keys.

Here, we've looked at the simplest, but probably the most useful, features of the QuickBASIC debugger. There are other features, as well. You can have the computer "trace" your program by executing it at the rate of about one line per second (you might call this "automatic stepping"); you can have it "remember" the last twenty lines and then step backwards through them; you can watch *conditions* as well as variables (to see whether they are true or false); you can set "watchpoints," which cause the program to halt when a condition becomes true; and so on. Feel free to experiment with any of these features: a good way to proceed is to select the *Full Menus* option from the Options Menu and then pull down the *Debug Menu* and use the Help System (**F1**) to find out about these other features.

We'll finish this section with a very brief look at another QuickBASIC feature that can occasionally be useful when creating or debugging a program. The *Immediate Window* near the bottom of the

QuickBASIC screen allows you to test a single line of code. The Immediate Window is different from the View Window in that *whenever you press* ***<Enter>****, the current line is executed.* So if you type

```
PRINT 45 * 34
```

in the Immediate Window and then press **<Enter>**, the output screen will show "1530." This means, for example, that you can use the Immediate Window as a hand calculator if you left yours at home! The function key **F6** *toggles* you between the View Window and the Immediate Window; try this now by pressing **F6** and then entering the PRINT statement shown above (you press **F6** again to return to the View Window).

In short, QuickBASIC makes the often difficult job of finding and correcting logical errors a little easier by offering a built-in debugging system. We've shown how to step through a program, how to watch the values of variables, and how to set up breakpoints. We can also use the Immediate Window to test single statements. If you learn to use some or all of these features, your debugging sessions will be shorter and more fun.

PRACTICE 4.5

1. The file C04PC01.BAS on the SAMPLES disk is a modification of the coin-flipping program of Example 9 in Section 3.6, which has a logical error in it. Using the QuickBASIC Debugger to watch the variables *outcome* and *headCounter*, trace the program (with the **F8** key) and find the error.
2. Use the Immediate Window to find the square root of 10.

Chapter Summary

In this chapter, we've focused on the idea that computer programming is a *three-stage process*: algorithm design and refinement, translation of the algorithm into a computer program, and testing and debugging of that program. The first and third stages are the most challenging.

Stage 1 involves first *understanding* the problem; then writing an outline of a solution to the given problem (a *level-1 algorithm*); and then the subsequent refinement of that outline (including a *listing of the variables* needed), until the algorithm has enough detail to be readily translated into a computer language. The refinement process is called *top-down algorithm design*. These refined algorithms (*level-2*, *level-3*, etc.) are written in *pseudocode*, and their separate sections give the solution *modularity*.

In *Stage 2*, we translate the detailed algorithm into a "first-draft" program. The pseudocode becomes "real code" and the modularity of the algorithm produces a *structured program*. If the algorithm was designed with care, this stage is easy. We must, of course, remember to use good programming style.

Stage 3, testing and debugging, can be a lengthy process—but, again, careful algorithm design greatly eases the work. The testing process involves finding and correcting all *syntax errors;* designing a set of *test data;* running the program with the test data in order to find and correct all *logical errors* (by careful reading, hand-tracing, using extra PRINT statements, commenting out lines, and/or using the Quick-BASIC Debugger); adjusting the output to look as desired; and last, fully retesting the final version of the program once more.

QuickBASIC provides a *built-in debugging facility* for finding and correcting logical errors. Among its features are the capabilities to *step* through a program, to *watch* the values of any specified variables, and to set *breakpoints,* which cause the program to pause. In addition, the QuickBASIC *Immediate Window* can be used to test short segments in isolation.

Review Questions

1. Explain each term briefly:

   (a) top-down algorithm design
   (b) level-1 algorithm
   (c) level-2 algorithm
   (d) pseudocode
   (e) modularity
   (f) structured program
   (g) syntax error
   (h) logical error

2. Write a short QuickBASIC program segment containing both syntax and logical errors. Remember that in order for there to be logical errors at all, you must state what the segment is supposed to do.

3. Discuss various techniques for finding and correcting logical errors. Include a brief description of some of the features of the QuickBASIC Debugger.

Programming Problems

1. The program C04PB01.BAS on your SAMPLES disk is designed to compute correct postage charges using the following rules:

   Weight less than or equal to 1 ounce . . . . .25 cents

   For each additional ounce or fraction thereof. . . . . .20 cents

   Special delivery, add a $2 surcharge.

   The program requires rounding *up.* Since INT(num) rounds *num* down, -INT(-num) will round it up. Test this with several values to see whether it works.

   The problem here is that the author was not careful with either the algorithm design or the actual coding into QuickBASIC, so the program contains several syntax and logical errors. Your job is to test and debug the program. You should use enough test data to be convinced that the program is working properly.

Note: For Problems 2 through 6, write a level-1 algorithm, refine it as much as needed (including listing the necessary variables), translate the final algorithm into a structured QuickBASIC program, and thoroughly test and debug the program.

2. The Acme Widget Company needs a weekly payroll program. Each DATA line of the program (except the first, which shows the number of employees) contains the following information on an employee: name, five-digit identification number, hourly wage, and hours worked that week.

The program should produce a table, with one line per employee, showing name, identification number, gross pay, and net pay. Net pay is computed as follows: for gross pay under $100, withhold no tax (so net = gross); for gross of at least $100 but less than $400, withhold 12% of gross for taxes; for gross $400 and over, withhold 18%.

The program should include "error traps" to catch bad data for the hourly wage and hours worked. Specifically, if the hourly wage is less than $3 or more than $20, the program should display the message "Bad data for Employee #________." It should do the same if the hours worked are less than 0 or more than 80.

Test the program with the following data, *plus* two or three more employees that you add yourself:

Albert Brooks, 18654, 4.55, 37.5
Carol Kane, 17863, 7.30, 40
David Bowie, 16845, 8.20, 30
Elvis Presley, 14587, 8.80, 22
Frank Sinatra, 14276, 3.50, 14

3. Write a computerized card catalog system for a library. DATA statements contain the number of books on the first line; each line thereafter contains three items about a book: call number, author, and title. Users are first asked whether they will enter a call number, an author, or a title (C or A or T). Having chosen, they then enter the information, and the program searches the data for that book. If, for example, a user enters an author and that author has more than one book in the library, then all of that author's books should be listed. If no entry is found, the program says, "I'm sorry, we don't seem to have that book," or some other appropriate message.

Try your program with the following data:

```
DATA 6
DATA BF173F645, FREUD SIGMUND, THE EGO AND THE ID
DATA PS3515E37S9, HEMINGWAY ERNEST, THE SUN ALSO RISES
DATA N5300J3, JANSON HORST, HISTORY OF ART
DATA PS3568075P6, ROTH PHILIP, PORTNOY'S COMPLAINT
DATA PS3570Y45A23, TYLER ANNE, THE ACCIDENTAL TOURIST
DATA PS3570Y45B74, TYLER ANNE, BREATHING LESSONS
```

4. In Programming Problem 6 of Chapter 3, we encountered a simple "text analyzer" that counted occurrences of a specified letter at the beginning of words. Now, let's write one that counts *all* appearances of a specified letter in a text.

The First DATA line contains the number of remaining DATA lines. Each line thereafter contains some text (note that the data should be enclosed in quotes, since commas may well appear as punctuation in the given text). The user types in a letter, and the program responds with the number of occurrences of that letter (upper or lowercase), the total number of *letters* (A–Z and a–z) in the text, and the reduced ratio of these two quantities (e.g., "1 in every 15.7 letters is a 't' ").

Try your program with the data below. (Hint: You'll need nested loops, and the inner loop will involve the LEN function—see Table 1.4 in Section 1.5).

```
DATA 4
DATA "This land is your land, this land is my land,"
DATA "From California to the New York Island."
DATA "From the Redwood Forest to the Gulf Stream water,"
DATA "This land was made for you and me!"
```

5. Write a day-by-day bank account balance program for some period of time. Users first enter the number of days to be considered and the starting balance in the account. Then, for each day, users indicate whether they made a withdrawal, a deposit, or no transaction, and—if it's either of the first two—what the amount of the transaction was. The program returns the new balance and goes on to the next day. At the end of the specified period, the program returns the *average daily balance* in the account over that period, then stops.

Here might be a typical output (without introductory output, etc.):

```
How many days in this period? 4
What is the starting balance? $346.57
For each day enter W for withdrawal, D for deposit,
or N for no transaction:

Day # 1 Transaction: (W/D/N) W
        Amount? $42.85
        New balance is $ 303.72

Day # 2 Transaction? (W/D/N) N

Day # 3 Transaction? (W/D/N) D
        Amount? $150.00
        New Balance is $ 453.72

Day # 4 Transaction? (W/D/N) W
        Amount? $89.76
        New Balance is $ 363.96

Average daily balance for the period is $ 356.28
```

6. Write a program that classifies triangles. The user enters the lengths of the three sides of a triangle (in any order), and the program responds with one of three messages:

1. `These lengths do not form a triangle.`
2. `This is a right triangle.`
3. `This is not a right triangle. Its largest angle is ________ degrees.`

Obviously, we need to know some math to do this one. First, notice that if the longest of the three "sides" is as long or longer than the sum of the other two, there is no triangle. But if a triangle exists, how do we check whether it is a *right* triangle? We turn to the Pythagorean Theorem for the answer: if the longest side is labelled c (and the other two a and *b*), a triangle has a right angle exactly when

$$a^2 + b^2 = c^2$$

Finally, if it isn't a right triangle, we can use the so-called Law of Cosines to get the largest angle. Specifically, that law says that

cosineOfC = (a² + *b*² − c²) / (2 * a * *b*)

We can then use QuickBASIC's built-in arctangent function to get c:

sineOfC = SQR(1 − (cosineOfC)²)

c = ATN(sineOfC / cosineOfC)

Last of all, to convert the answer from radians to degrees, multiply by 180 and divide by pi (=3.14159 approximately). Be sure to test an "obtuse" triangle (i.e., a triangle having an angle over 90 degrees). Here, you must add 180 to get the right answer. Have fun!

CHAPTER

5

Conditional Looping Structures

CHAPTER PREVIEW

In this chapter, we'll learn the difference between *conditional* and *unconditional* looping. The FOR...NEXT loop introduced in Chapter 2 is unconditional; now, we shall learn to use a conditional looping structure, the *DO...LOOP*, which has various natural forms depending on how it's being used. It plays an important role in many situations, including the processing of data and the creation of "error-resistant" software.

5.1 Conditional versus Unconditional Looping

The FOR...NEXT loop, which we studied in Chapter 2, is called an *unconditional loop* because you decide *before the loop starts* how many times it will be executed. But what if we *don't know* before a loop begins how many times it is to execute? What if "it depends"? Well, QuickBASIC provides a very flexible *conditional looping structure* called the **DO...LOOP**, which lets us decide after each iteration whether we want to continue or terminate, depending on whether some condition is true or false. Let's begin by looking at a simple example.

EXAMPLE 1

As a start at simulating the card game Blackjack, let's write a program that takes in positive whole numbers from the keyboard until their sum exceeds 21, then stops and prints out the final sum.

This program obviously needs a loop to take in one number after another, but the FOR...NEXT structure won't do, since we want to loop *until the sum exceeds 21*—that is, we want to loop until the condition *sum* > *21* changes from false to true. This loop is conditional! An algorithm follows.

1. Introduce the program and initialize a variable *sum*
2. Repeat:
    a. Input a number
    b. Add it into *sum*

    Until *sum* exceeds 21
3. Print out *sum*

That's all there is to that problem. When we find ourselves saying "repeat" in an algorithm, it's a sure sign that we need a loop. Whether we need an unconditional loop (FOR...NEXT) or a conditional loop depends on the situation. Here, since we want to "repeat *until*" something happens, we know that we need a conditional loop: the DO...LOOP structure. We'll need two variables: *sum* and *number*. Here's a corresponding QuickBASIC program:

```
'-----------------------------------------------------------------
'      Program title: C05EX01.BAS
'      Author:        B. Maverick
'      Date:          Jan. 14, 1992

'      Takes in numbers from the keyboard and adds them up until
'a sum of 21 is exceeded. This is a start at simulating
'Blackjack.
'-----------------------------------------------------------------
```

```
'Introduce program and initialize sum.

      CLS
      PRINT "This program takes in positive whole numbers"
      PRINT "until their sum exceeds 21."
      PRINT

      LET sum = 0

'Get the numbers and compute the sum until it's over 21.

      DO
          INPUT "Type a number --> ", number
          LET sum = sum + number
      LOOP UNTIL sum > 21

'Print out the sum.

      PRINT
      PRINT "The sum is"; sum; "."

END
```

Here's sample output:

```
This program takes in positive whole numbers
until their sum exceeds 21.

Type a number --> 7
Type a number --> 10
Type a number --> 6

The sum is 23 .
```

Take a close look at the middle section of this program. The form of the control structure here is:

```
DO
      .
      .
      .
LOOP UNTIL sum > 21
```

The idea is very simple; once again, we see that one of the nice things about Structured BASIC is that the way it says things is close to the way we think about them.

We need to discuss three issues that arise in this example. The first is the matter of *initialization of variables*. Let us repeat here a cardinal rule, which was first stated in Section 2.4:

Always *initialize variables before they are used; in particular, any variable that will be updated* inside *a loop must be initialized properly* before *the loop.*

The variable *sum* in this Example is an accumulator whose value is updated inside the loop; so it must be initialized, here to 0, before the loop begins. In this case, it so happens that we would get away with it if we failed to initialize *sum* (since QuickBASIC automatically initializes numeric variables to 0)—but under many circumstances, as we've already seen (e.g., Example 4 in Section 2.4) and will see, failure to initialize can lead to bugs of all sorts.

Second, the variable (or variables) in the condition that is controlling the loop *must be updated in the loop*, for the loop will terminate only when the truth value of the condition *changes*. So in our example, *sum* gets a new value each time through the loop, and the loop will terminate when that value finally exceeds 21. To see the necessity of updating, look at this segment:

```
LET num = 5
DO
    PRINT "Going...";
LOOP UNTIL num = 6
PRINT "Gone!"
```

What will happen? Well, the condition *num* = 6 is always false since *num* starts at 5 but then is *never updated* inside the loop, so the output is:

```
Going...Going...Going...Going...Going...Going...
Going...Going...Going...Going...Going...Going...
```

(and so on)

For obvious reasons, this is called an **infinite loop**. It's time to tell you what to do when you accidentally write and run one of these (and you will!).

To stop a running program (such as one with an infinite loop), you press* Ctrl-Break*, that is, you hold down the* Ctrl *key and then press the* Break *key.

Finally, the actual form of the DO...LOOP could have been different in this example if we had phrased the problem differently. For instance, we could easily have said: "Let's add up numbers as long as (i.e., while) the sum is less than or equal to 21." That would have been fine; the resulting QuickBASIC code might have looked like:

```
DO
     :
LOOP WHILE sum <= 21
```

The point is that in whatever way we think about a conditional loop, QuickBASIC can translate our thoughts directly into code. It turns out, in fact, that there are *five* versions of the DO...LOOP; we use whichever one makes the most sense at the time. We shall discuss these five versions in the next section.

So, when do you use FOR...NEXT (i.e., an unconditional loop) and when do you use DO...LOOP (i.e., a conditional loop)? The choice usually follows easily and naturally from the circumstances of the problem at hand, but a rule of thumb is:

> ***If you know*** before ***starting a loop how many times it is to execute (i.e., for a fixed range of values of a certain variable), then use a FOR...NEXT loop. If you do*** not ***know before starting a loop how many times it is to execute (i.e., it depends on some condition), then use a DO...LOOP.***

Again, this distinction is not difficult to make. With a little practice, you will pick the correct looping structure simply by looking at your algorithm and choosing the code that fits it most naturally. It's just common sense!

PRACTICE 5.1

1. What is the output of each of these segments?

(a)
```
FOR k = 3 TO 7
   PRINT k
NEXT k
```

(b)
```
LET k = 3
DO
   PRINT k
   LET k = k + 1
LOOP UNTIL k = 7
```

2. What is the output of each of these segments?

(a)
```
LET a$ = "STOP"
DO
   PRINT "Testing"
LOOP UNTIL a$ = "STOP"
```

(b)
```
LET a$ = "STOP"
DO
   PRINT "Testing"
LOOP WHILE a$ = "STOP"
```

(c)
```
LET a$ = "STOP"
DO UNTIL a$ = "STOP"
   PRINT "Testing"
LOOP
```

3. Write a QuickBASIC program that takes in words from the keyboard until a word is typed that starts with *n*, at which point the program stops.

5.2 The DO...LOOP Structure

In this section, we'll make clear the syntax and operation of the DO...LOOP control structure and look at some examples of using it.

The DO...LOOP is a conditional looping structure, that is, it causes a block of statements to execute over and over until some condition changes its truth value. There are *five basic forms* the DO...LOOP can take. The first four involve the words *UNTIL* or *WHILE* and look as follows:

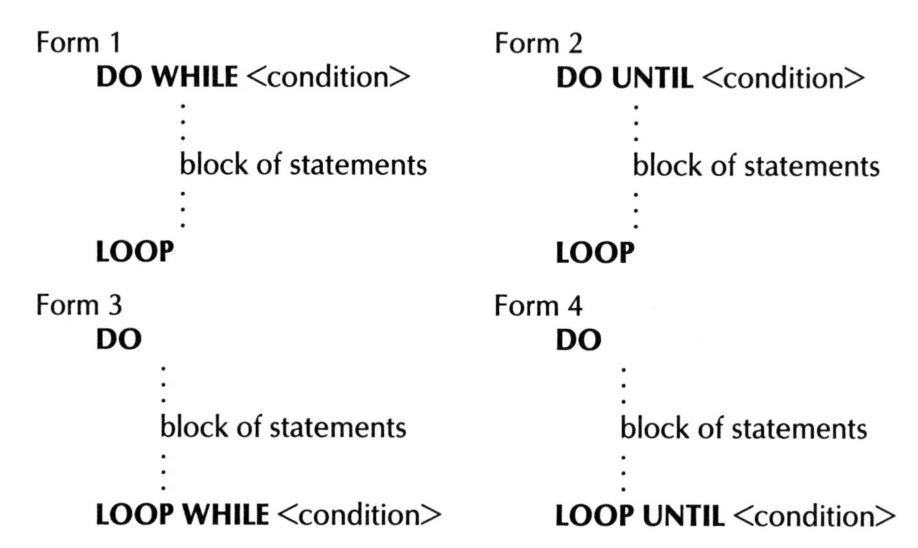
Form 1
DO WHILE <condition>
block of statements
LOOP
Form 2
DO UNTIL <condition>
block of statements
LOOP
Form 3
DO
block of statements
LOOP WHILE <condition>
Form 4
DO
block of statements
LOOP UNTIL <condition>

The operation of these forms is, as always, exactly what you would expect. Form 1, for example, checks the condition immediately (since the condition is at the top). If the condition is false, the next statement that QuickBASIC will execute is the first line after the LOOP line. If it's true, the block of statements is executed and then the condition is rechecked and the process begins again.

Let's examine Form 4. The block of statements executes once for sure (since here the condition is at the bottom). Then the condition is checked. If it's true, the loop ends (because of the word *UNTIL*). If it's false, the block of statements executes again and the process continues.

Carefully work through Forms 2 and 3 on your own. Identify the operation exactly—take time to do that!

Forms 1 and 2 are called **pre-checked** loops since the condition is at the top. Notice that, depending on the truth value of the condition, a pre-checked loop *may not execute even once*. This is why, again, *initialization* of the variable or variables in the condition is so crucial (for example, look again at Practice 5.1, Exercise 2c).

Forms 3 and 4 are called **post-checked** loops since the condition is at the bottom. Notice that a post-checked loop always executes at least once (see, for example, Practice 5.1, Exercise 2a).

The fifth form of the DO...LOOP structure allows you to put the controlling condition *inside* the loop using the **EXIT DO** statement. The syntax is, again, very simple:

Form 5

```
DO
    :
    block of statements
    :
    IF <condition> THEN
        EXIT DO
    END IF
    :
    block of statements
    :
LOOP
```

The operation of this form is exactly what you'd expect. If the condition is satisfied, the EXIT DO statement is executed, causing the loop to terminate. As with Forms 1 to 4, the next statement that QuickBASIC will execute is the first line after the LOOP line.

Form 5 fits naturally with many algorithms. For instance, the loop in Example 1 of the previous section could just as well have been written as follows:

```
DO
    INPUT "Type in a number --> ", number
    LET sum = sum + number
    IF sum > 21 THEN
        EXIT DO
    END IF
LOOP
```

If at this point you're worried about deciding how to choose from *five* different kinds of DO...LOOP structures, we say again: relax! All you have to do is write your algorithm, and the form (or forms) best fitted to that algorithm will emerge naturally when it comes time to write the QuickBASIC code. The examples that follow will help make this clearer.

EXAMPLE 2

A very common use of the DO...LOOP is to give the user of a computer game or other interactive program the chance to use the program over and over without having to restart it. The basic algorithm is:

1. Do introduction and necessary initializations
2. Play game (or whatever)
3. Ask if user wants to go again
4. If yes, *repeat*, starting from Step 2
   Otherwise, end program

Steps 2 through 4 can be expressed in BASIC code very naturally using a DO...LOOP:

```
DO
    :
    :
    code to play game
    :
    :
    INPUT "Want to play again (Y/N)?", answer$
LOOP WHILE answer$ = "Y"
```

Get the idea? Let's add this feature to the dart-throwing program (Example 10) in Section 3.6. In that program, users were allowed to throw only one measly dart. If they wanted to throw another, they had to restart the program. Let's improve that program now as suggested above.

```
'------------------------------------------------------------------
'      Program Title: C05EX02.BAS
'      Author:        Eric Bristow
'      Date:          November 23, 1991

'      This program simulates random tosses of darts at a
'dart board and determines whether each dart hits the
'bull's-eye, the board, or the backing.
'------------------------------------------------------------------

'Introduce the program and initialize the random number
'generator.

      CLS
      PRINT "Get ready to throw some darts!"

      RANDOMIZE TIMER

      PRINT
      INPUT "When you're ready, hit return.", a$

'Loop to allow user unlimited number of tosses

      DO

             'Compute the coordinates of the random toss.
             LET x = 2 * RND - 1
             LET y = 2 * RND - 1

             'Classify the throw.
             LET distance = SQR(x ^ 2 + y ^ 2)
             PRINT
```

```
            IF distance <= .25 THEN
                  PRINT "Bull's-eye!! Nice shot!"
            ELSEIF distance <= 1 THEN
                  PRINT "Hit the board, but no bull's-eye."
            ELSE
                  PRINT "Hey, you missed the board!"
            END IF

            'Ask about another toss.
            PRINT
            INPUT "Want to throw another (Y/N)? ", answer$

      LOOP WHILE answer$ = "Y"

'Say goodbye.

      PRINT
      PRINT "Okay, bye. Have a nice day."

END
```

Sample output might be:

```
Get ready to throw some darts!

When you're ready, hit return.

Hit the board, but no bull's-eye.

Want to throw another? Y

Hey, you missed the board!

Want to throw another? Y

Bull's-eye!! Nice shot!

Want to throw another? N

Okay, bye. Have a nice day.
```

Try this program (C05EX02.BAS on your SAMPLES disk). It's certainly more fun than the original, one-dart version. As we mentioned in Chapter 3, this program will be even more fun when we add graphics to it (see Programming Problem 5 of Chapter 10).

In the above example, notice that most but not all of the program is contained inside the DO...LOOP. This is standard: there are usually introductions and initializations at the beginning of a program that need to be done once only, and there is often a final printout at the end. The point is simple but important:

> *If something is to be done only once, it should* not *lie within a loop. If it is to be repeated some number of times, it* should *lie within a loop.*

Surprisingly, beginning programmers can lose sight of this idea. Make sure it "sinks in" for you.

You will find yourself using this "Do you want to go again?" DO...LOOP often when you write **interactive software**, that is, programs with which users interact via the INPUT statement. It's simply a convenient option for the user to have. However, to make the loop as error-resistant as possible, you will have to do some extra work. For example, notice that in our dart program, if the user types "y" instead of "Y," the program terminates! We'll discuss ways to make software reasonably error-resistant in Section 5.4 below.

Let's end this section with an example concerning personal finances.

EXAMPLE 3

Compound interest plays a role in many financial matters. Savings accounts, credit cards, mutual funds, and mortgages, to name just a few, all involve compound interest. The basic idea is that starting with some initial amount of money (the *starting principal*) and a rate of interest, additional money is earned (or, if we're talking about a loan, charged), and then that new money is added to the principal producing a *new* principal. Then the process begins again. The point is that the principal keeps changing!

Let's do a straightforward application of compound interest. Suppose that you have $1,000 (a graduation gift from Aunt Wilma), which you would like to put away and let grow in a savings account. Given the initial principal ($1,000), the annual interest rate that you can earn (say, 8.9%), and the amount of money you would like to have at the end (say, $2,500), write a program that will print out a table of years gone by and current balance in the account, stopping when you reach your goal. For simplicity, assume that the interest you earn is "compounded annually," that is, once a year your old principal gets replaced by the new one. The algorithm could be:

1. Introduce and get the initial data (starting principal, interest rate, and goal)
2. Print headings for table (years passed and current principal)
3. Repeat the following while principal is less than goal:
    a. Increase the year counter
    b. Compute the interest earned
    c. Add interest to principal to get new value of principal
    d. Print row of table

It looks as if we'll need variables *principal, rate, goal, interest,* and *year.* All the steps are straightforward except perhaps Step 3b, where we must remember that since *rate* is entered as a percentage (say, for example, 8.9), we must divide it by 100 to convert it to its actual value (in the example, .089). So we have:

```
LET interest = rate / 100 * principal
```

If you read the algorithm carefully, there's one other problem—as it's written, the first line of the table is *not printed*! Having a DO...LOOP incorrectly handle the *first case* or *last case* is a common mistake, called an **off-by-one error**. The way to correct this is to see whether we could have designed it better; if not, we can handle the first or last case separately *outside the loop.* In this example, we can simply add one step to our algorithm between Step 2 (printing the table headings) and Step 3 (the loop):

2½. Print first line of table

Here's a QuickBASIC program for this algorithm:

```
'---------------------------------------------------------------
'   Program title: C05EX03.BAS
'   Author:        Donald Trump
'   Date:          June 14, 1992

'Computes a table of balances in a savings account until a
'financial goal is met. Illustrates compound interest at work.
'---------------------------------------------------------------

'Introduce program and get initial values.

    CLS
    PRINT "This program prints out a table of how much money"
    PRINT "you will have in a savings account as it grows"
    PRINT "earning compound interest. It will stop when the"
    PRINT "goal you have indicated has been reached."
    PRINT
    INPUT "What is your initial investment? ", principal
    INPUT "What interest rate applies (%)? ", rate
    INPUT "And how much is your goal? ", goal
    LET year = 0

'Print table headings.

    CLS
    PRINT "      COMPOUND INTEREST AT"; rate; "%"
    PRINT "      -------------------------"
    PRINT "YEAR", "BALANCE IN THE ACCOUNT"
    PRINT "----", "----------------------"
```

```
'Print first line of table.

    PRINT year, "         $"; principal

'Print line of table showing year and new principal, for each
'year that principal < goal (round interest to nearest dollar).

    DO WHILE principal < goal
        LET year = year + 1
        LET interest = rate / 100 * principal
        LET interest = CINT(interest)
        LET principal = principal + interest
        PRINT year, "         $"; principal
    LOOP

END
```

Sample output might look like this:

```
This program prints out a table of how much money
you will have in a savings account as it grows
earning compound interest. It will stop when the
goal you have indicated is reached.

What is your initial investment? 1000
What interest rate applies (%)? 8.9
And how much is your goal? 2500
```

(new screen)

```
    COMPOUND INTEREST AT 8.9%
    -------------------------
YEAR        BALANCE IN THE ACCOUNT
    ----    ----------------------
 0                  $ 1000
 1                  $ 1089
 2                  $ 1186
 3                  $ 1292
 4                  $ 1407
 5                  $ 1532
 6                  $ 1668
 7                  $ 1816
 8                  $ 1978
 9                  $ 2154
 10                 $ 2346
 11                 $ 2555
```

For a look at the other side of compound interest (i.e., borrowing money), see Programming Problem 7 at the end of this chapter.

This program requires a DO...LOOP because, when we start, we have no idea how many lines our table will have. The table ends *conditionally*, so the conditional looping structure is appropriate. What would the right structure be for a specified *number of years* rather than a goal?

Lots of situations involving data occur in which we do not know beforehand how much data is to be processed. Here again, conditional looping is the correct tool. We shall look more closely at this idea in the next section.

PRACTICE 5.2

1. What is the output of this segment?

```
LET x = 5.2
DO
    PRINT x
    LET x = x - .4
    IF x < 4.1 THEN
        EXIT DO
    END IF
LOOP
PRINT "End."
```

2. You could say that the DO...LOOP structure actually has *six* forms, the sixth being as follows:

```
PRINT "Again ";
DO
   PRINT "and again ";
LOOP
```

Why don't we want to use this sixth form?

3. Write five DO...LOOP segments (preceded by initializations), each using a different one of the five forms and each producing the output:

```
1 2 3 4 5 6 7 8 9 10
```

While you're at it, write a FOR...NEXT segment for this output as well.

5.3 Processing Data Using Flags and Trailers

Processing data is one of the most common uses of computers in today's world. No matter what is being done with the data (*sorting* it into some order, *searching* it for certain entries, performing *calculations* on it such as averaging, etc.), loops must certainly play a role. Whether a conditional or an unconditional looping structure is appropriate depends on how we know when to *stop processing*. Let's look at a simple example.

EXAMPLE 4

If you look back at Example 3 at the beginning of Section 2.4 (C02EX03.BAS on the SAMPLES disk), you'll find a program that averages gasoline prices (per gallon) among various local service stations. Notice that the first question asked of the user is:

```
INPUT "How many prices do you have? ", howMany
```

With this information, a FOR...NEXT loop can be set up. But suppose instead that we do not wish to ask users "how many?" at the beginning (for example, the list of prices might be quite long and it would be inconvenient to count them). Instead, we could ask users to send a *signal* when all the data has been entered, perhaps some number that could not possibly be a gasoline price. Such a signal is called a **flag** (or **sentinel**). Let's rewrite that program, using, say, −99 as a flag to stop processing. An algorithm would be:

1. Introduce the program and initialize the sum and the "how many" counter
2. Repeat:
   a. Get a price
   b. If it's −99, then
      Stop processing
      Otherwise
      Add the price to the sum, and increase the "how many" counter by 1
3. Compute and print out the average

We'll need variables *sum, howMany, price,* and *average*. Here's a program:

```
'-----------------------------------------------------------
'     Program title: C05EX04.BAS
'     Author:        J. P. Getty
'     Date:          March 23, 1992

'     Computes the average of various inputted gasoline prices.
'Uses the flag -99 to end processing.
'-----------------------------------------------------------
```

```
'Introduce and initialize variables.
      CLS
      PRINT "This program finds the average price of a gallon"
      PRINT "of regular gas in town."
      PRINT

      LET sum = 0
      LET howMany = 0

'Get the data and compute the sum.

      PRINT "Type in the prices, in cents, one by one."
      PRINT "To end, type -99."
      PRINT

      DO
            INPUT "(-99 to end)--> ", price
            IF price = -99 THEN
                  EXIT DO
            ELSE
                  LET sum = sum + price
                  LET howMany = howMany + 1
            END IF
      LOOP

'Calculate and print the average (rounding to the nearest
'tenth).

      LET average = sum / howMany
      LET average = CINT(10 * average) / 10
      PRINT
      PRINT "The average price is"; average; "cents."

END
```

An output might be:

```
This program finds the average price of a gallon
of regular gas in town.

Type in the prices, in cents, one by one.
To end, type -99.

(-99 to end)--> 104.8
(-99 to end)--> 107.9
(-99 to end)--> 102.7
(-99 to end)--> -99

The average price is 105.1 cents.
```

Be sure to notice that you *must* tell users what the flag is! In fact, as we did above, it's a good idea to keep reminding them what it is (suppose there was so much data that eventually the introduction went off the screen, for example)—it can be frustrating if you've forgotten how to halt a program you're using and there's no way to find out.

Let us make two more remarks about this example. First, in the DO...LOOP section, we chose to put the EXIT DO statement in the ELSE option of the IF...END IF structure. Notice, however, that each of the pieces of code that follow does exactly the same thing; it's up to you which you prefer.

```
DO
    INPUT price
    IF price = -99 THEN
        EXIT DO
    END IF
    LET sum = sum + price
    LET howMany = howMany + 1
LOOP
```

```
DO
    INPUT price
    IF price = -99 THEN
        EXIT DO
    ELSE
        LET sum = sum + price
        LET howMany = howMany + 1
    END IF
LOOP
```

Second, notice that it is very important to test for the flag *before* using the input. For example, the following loop *looks* reasonable, but in fact it adds the flag −99 into the sum! (The counter *howMany* is wrong, too.)

```
'Example of an incorrect use of a flag
    DO
        INPUT price
        LET sum = sum + price
        LET howMany = howMany + 1
    LOOP UNTIL price = -99
```

This is another example of an *off-by-one error*, because we perform an operation one too many or one too few times (in our example, both LET statements are executed one too many times). The following is a good rule to program by:

When writing a loop, you should always check to see that it starts and stops at precisely the right points.

Flags can appear in various forms. A string can serve as a flag just as well as a number, provided that it is matched with a string variable. Take this little segment, for example:

```
PRINT "Want to come in? Then say the secret words!"
DO
    INPUT "--> ", guess$
    IF guess$ = "swizzle stick" THEN
        EXIT DO
    ELSE
        PRINT "Nope!"
    END IF
LOOP
PRINT "That's right! Come on in!"
```

Either users eventually guess "swizzle stick," or they get frustrated trying. This segment might remind you of an experience you could well have had with computers: have you ever forgotten your *password* when trying to sign onto a network of computers or get money out of an automatic teller machine? Well, a password program is much like the segment above, which keeps giving you another chance to remember. See Programming Problem 8 at the end of this chapter.

Let's summarize the basic idea about using flags:

To process a list of data, you must use a loop. If at the start you know the number of data items, then you can use an unconditional (i.e., FOR...NEXT) loop. Otherwise, you need a flag to signal that the end of the data has been reached, and you use a conditional DO...LOOP, which continues processing until the flag is encountered.

The use of flags can produce easy-to-use interactive programs. It's nice not to have to say right up front how many data items you want to process. It turns out that this technique is also very handy when we are using the READ and DATA statements first introduced in Section 2.6. For example, suppose that in our gasoline price example above (Example 4), we decided to use READ and DATA rather than have the program be interactive. To do this, we simply put the −99 flag as the *last item* of data. The loop section would then look like:

```
DO
     READ price
     IF price = -99 THEN
        EXIT DO
     ELSE
        (and so on)
```

The data section would be:

```
DATA 104.8, 102.9, 107.9, 102.4, -99
```

Used in this manner, at the end of a list of data items, a flag is often called a **trailer**. Earlier, when we were processing READ/DATA statements with the FOR...NEXT loop (see Section 2.6), we encountered the idea of a *header*, which is the *first* data item and which tells us *how many times to loop*. Now that we have the conditional DO...LOOP, we have the option of using a *trailer*, which is the *last* data item and tells us to *stop looping*. Note how convenient the use of a trailer is: if the data changes, and even if the *number* of data items changes, the trailer need not change at all!

Let's look at another use of trailers, which your favorite telephone company might implement.

EXAMPLE 5

When you call information to get a phone number, what happens? You tell the operator the name, he or she types it in to the computer, and then the program *searches* through the data for that name. If the program finds the name, it gives back the phone number; if it doesn't find the name, it returns you to the operator. Although there are different ways of searching through data (see Section 7.3 for a full discussion of this matter), we'll look at the way that starts from the beginning and goes straight through the data, called a **linear search**. If the name is found, great—but if not, the program will come upon the trailer that has been placed at the end of the data, which signals that the search has ended unsuccessfully. Let's write a program that a phone company could use for this purpose. An algorithm would be:

1. Introduce the program and accept the desired last and first names as input
2. Repeat:
   a. Read the last name from the list
   b. If trailer is found then exit the loop; otherwise, read the first name and phone number
   c. If the desired name is found, give back the number and then exit the loop

We will need variables *lastWanted$* and *firstWanted$* (which the user inputs), and *last$*, *first$*, and *number$* (for the data). Notice that we use a string variable for the phone number, since the number contains a dash. Notice, also, that our algorithm handles the first data item separately, since it might be the trailer. If we tried to read in groups of three (last name, first name, phone number), we would get the OUT OF DATA error—do you see why? Let's use EOD (standing for "end of data") as the trailer. The program follows.

```
'-------------------------------------------------------------
'    Program title: C05EX05.BAS
'    Author:        Lily Tomlin
'    Date:          August 23, 1991

'    Simulates a telephone information service by searching a
'list of names and phone numbers to find a desired number or
'to report that that number is not listed.
'-------------------------------------------------------------

'Introduce and get desired name.

        CLS
        PRINT "Information!"
        PRINT
```

```
    PRINT "What name please? (Last name first, separated by"
    INPUT "a comma please.)--> ", lastWanted$, firstWanted$
    PRINT

'Look through the list for this person's name or report that
'it is not present if the end of the list is reached.

    DO
        READ last$
        IF last$ = "EOD" THEN
            PRINT "I'm sorry. I have no such listing."
            EXIT DO
        END IF
        READ first$, number$
        IF (last$ = lastWanted$) AND (first$ = firstWanted$) THEN
            PRINT "The number is "; number$
            EXIT DO
        END IF
    LOOP
    PRINT
    PRINT "Thank you for using our company!"

'-----------------------------------------------------------------
'Data Section: Names and phone numbers; "EOD" indicates end of data.

    DATA Adams, John, 555-3486, Buchanan, James, 555-9865
    DATA Carter, James, 555-1274, Eisenhower, Dwight, 555-0987
    DATA Ford, Gerald, 555-2376, Garfield, James, 555-3752
    DATA Kennedy, John, 555-3756, Lincoln, Abraham, 555-9632
    DATA Polk, James, 555-7837, Reagan, Ronald, 555-3487
    DATA Wilson, Woodrow, 555-2867
    DATA EOD
'-----------------------------------------------------------------

END
```

Sample output could be:

```
Information!

What name please? (Last name first, separated by
a comma please.) --> Polk, James

That number is 555-7837

Thank you for using our company!
```

Or possibly:

```
Information!

What name please? (Last name first, separated by
a comma please.) --> Dukakis, Michael

I'm sorry. I have no such listing.

Thank you for using our company!
```

Try this program (C05EX05.BAS on the SAMPLES disk). The trailer EOD works perfectly even if the data needs changing. We shall see more of this idea in Chapter 8, when we study the use of *files* to store our data.

One thing that might strike you upon running this program is that it is rather "sensitive to errors" on input. For example, if the user types in

`Carter, Jimmy` or `CARTER, JAMES`

the program responds with "I'm sorry"—but, of course, the program *should* give us James Carter's phone number. This problem isn't unique to this program; the fact is that, in general, *string data is especially sensitive to errors*. In the final section of this chapter, we will look at some techniques for making your programs error-resistant.

PRACTICE 5.3

1. What is the output of each segment?

(a)
```
LET p = 1
DO
    READ x
    IF x = 0 THEN
        EXIT DO
    ELSE
        LET p = p * x
    END IF
LOOP
PRINT p
DATA 3, 5, 2, 1, 4, 0
```

(b)
```
LET a$ = ""
DO
    READ b$
    IF b$ = "EOD" THEN
        EXIT DO
    ELSE
        LET b$ = LEFT$(b$,1)
        LET a$ = a$ + b$
    END IF
LOOP
PRINT a$
DATA National, Basketball
DATA Association, EOD
```

2. Write a QuickBASIC program that reads a list of numbers from data lines until the flag −111 is reached; the program then prints out the largest number in the list.

5.4 Writing Error-Resistant Software

We have seen that interactive programs can easily "do the wrong thing" if the responses of the user don't fit with how the program has been written. A simple example is the following dialogue after a program has done its job once:

```
Do you want to go again? yes
Okay, goodbye and have a nice day!
```

This kind of thing can be irritating. How does it happen? Well, it's probably not a programming error as such, but rather what we might call "error-prone code." If the code for this dialogue is, say,

```
DO
    .
    .
    .
    INPUT "Do you want to go again? ", answer$
LOOP WHILE answer$ = "YES"
```

then the simple fact that the user typed "yes" instead of "YES" is enough to wreck things. Fortunately, there are several techniques for making software **error-resistant** (also called **robust**). Since this can become a lengthy and complex topic, we'll confine ourselves here to two techniques:

1. Using *string functions* to "simplify" string input
2. Using *DO...LOOP* structures to "trap" input errors

First, let's focus on the "Do you want to go again?" dialogue. The problem that occurs most often is that the response to this question is close to but not *exactly* what is wanted (e.g., "yes" instead of "YES"). But here's the point: if a user types in something that starts with a Y, upper or lowercase, then she or he almost certainly *wants* to go again.

Hence, we can make use of the two string functions LEFT$ and UCASE$ (see Section 1.5) to "pick off" the *Y*.

```
DO
    .
    .
    .
    INPUT answer$
    LET answer$ = UCASE$(LEFT$(answer$, 1))
LOOP WHILE answer$ = "Y"
```

The function LEFT$(answer$, 1) picks off the leftmost character of *answer$*; then the function UCASE$ converts that character to uppercase. Even if the user types in "yes indeedy pie," the program works properly!

Of course, you can *never* make your software error-*proof*! In this example, what happens if the user types "sure!" or "You must be kidding!"? Of course, these are unlikely responses—you should try to write your programs to handle correctly the kind of input that a (marginally) reasonable person might enter.

Finishing with this example, you might decide to concentrate on *N* rather than *Y*. This code could be:

```
DO
    .
    .
    .
    INPUT answer$
LOOP UNTIL UCASE$(LEFT$(answer$, 1) = "N"
```

Now "sure!" works, but, alas, "You must be kidding!" still doesn't. Once again, you'll never be able to get it perfect.

EXAMPLE 6

As a second example of using string functions, let's think about how we might make the telephone information service program (Example 5 in the previous section) a little more error-resistant. First, we can certainly avoid trouble by entering all the data in uppercase letters and then using the UCASE$ function to process input, as we did above. The first line of data would now read:

```
DATA ADAMS, JOHN, 555-3486, BUCHANAN, JAMES, 555-9865
```

In addition, we could add flexibility by focusing on the last name and first *initial* only, perhaps printing out the names and numbers of anyone with that last name and first initial—this avoids complications arising from nicknames, for example. (A "real" program for giving phone information would have to be more sophisticated than this, especially in a large city, where, for example, asking for the number of SMITH, JOHN would give you the number of every James, Janet, Jeff, etc. Smith in town.) A more error-resistant program follows.

```
'-------------------------------------------------------------
'   Program title: C05EX06.BAS
'   Author:        Lily Tomlin
'   Date:          August 23, 1991

'   Simulates a telephone information service by searching a
'list of names and phone numbers to find a desired number or
'to report that that number is not listed. This is a
'somewhat more error-resistant version than C05EX05.BAS.
'-------------------------------------------------------------

'Introduce and get desired name.

    CLS
    PRINT "Information!"
    PRINT
    PRINT "What name please? (Last name first, separated by"
    INPUT "a comma please.) --> ", lastWanted$, firstWanted$
    PRINT

'Capitalize last name and pick off first initial.

    LET lastWanted$ = UCASE$(lastWanted$)
    LET initWanted$ = UCASE$(LEFT$(firstWanted$, 1))

'Look through list for the last name and first initial or report
'that they are not present if the end of the list is reached.

    DO
        READ last$
        IF last$ = "EOD" THEN
            PRINT "I'm sorry. I have no such listing."
            EXIT DO
        END IF
        READ first$, number$
        LET init$ = LEFT$(first$, 1)
        IF (last$ = lastWanted$) AND (init$ = initWanted$) THEN
            PRINT last$; ", "; first$; " --> "; number$
            EXIT DO
        END IF
    LOOP
    PRINT
    PRINT "Thank you for using our company!"

'-------------------------------------------------------------
'Data Section: Names and phone numbers; "EOD" indicates end of data.

    DATA ADAMS, JOHN, 555-3486, BUCHANAN, JAMES, 555-9865
    DATA CARTER, JIMMY, 555-1274, EISENHOWER, DWIGHT, 555-0987
    DATA FORD, GERALD, 555-2376, GARFIELD, JAMES, 555-3752
```

```
    DATA KENNEDY, JOHN, 555-3756, LINCOLN, ABRAHAM, 555-9632
    DATA POLK, JAMES, 555-7837, REAGAN, RONALD, 555-3487
    DATA WILSON, WOODROW, 555-2867
    DATA EOD
'-----------------------------------------------------------------

END
```

Sample output for this program could be:

```
Information!

What name please? (Last name first, separated by
a comma please.) --> Carter, Jimmy

CARTER, JAMES --> 555-1274

Thank you for using our company!
```

As usual, you should try this program to verify that it *is* more robust (i.e., more error-resistant) than C05EX05.BAS. Of course, you could go further. For example, you might want the program to check the last name and first initial (as this one does) and, if nothing is found, have it return to the beginning of the list and search for all parties with that last name (so that, say, if you typed in "Rosalynn Carter," it would supply you with Jimmy's number, perhaps among others). See Programming Problem 9 at the end of this chapter.

Let's turn now to our second technique for resisting input errors: the use of DO...LOOP structures to "trap" input errors. The idea is simple: use a DO...LOOP to make the user reenter bad data until the data is correct. A simple example should make this clear.

EXAMPLE 7

Let's write a program that takes in test scores (in the range 0–100) until a flag of −99 is entered; the program then returns the average score. The program should reject any inputted data that is out of the range 0–100 (except, of course, our flag −99, which gets "special treatment"). All this should be familiar to you, except for the "data error trap" part. It should look something like this:

```
INPUT "score --> ", score
:
:
DO WHILE (score < 0) OR (score > 100)
    INPUT "Reenter please --> ", score
LOOP
```

Notice that this will be a loop within a larger loop: the outer loop for picking up and processing the scores; the inner loop for rejecting obviously faulty scores. Let's go ahead and write a QuickBASIC program.

```
'----------------------------------------------------------------
'      Program title:      C05EX07.BAS
'      Author:             I. Newton
'      Date:               October 12, 1992

'      Computes average of test scores, rejecting input which
'is obviously faulty.
'----------------------------------------------------------------

'Introduce program and initialize variables.

      CLS
      PRINT "Type in test scores to get the average."
      PRINT "Type -99 to stop input"
      PRINT

      LET sum = 0
      LET howMany = 0

'Pick up the scores and accumulate the sum. Reject scores
'that lie outside the range 0 to 100 (except -99).

      DO
            INPUT "(-99 to end) score --> ", score
            IF score = -99 THEN
                  EXIT DO
            ELSE
                  DO WHILE (score < 0) OR (score > 100)
                         INPUT "Reenter please --> ", score
                  LOOP
                  LET sum = sum + score
                  LET howMany = howMany + 1
            END IF
      LOOP

'Compute the average, round it off to the nearest tenth,
'and print it out.

      LET average = sum / howMany
      LET average = CINT(10 * average) / 10
      PRINT
      PRINT "The average is"; average; "."

END
```

Here's sample output:

```
Type in test scores to get the average.
Type in -99 to stop input.

(-99 to end) score --> 78
(-99 to end) score --> 84
(-99 to end) score --> 576
Reenter please --> 57
(-99 to end) score --> 93
(-99 to end) score --> -67
Reenter please --> 677
Reenter please --> 67
(-99 to end) score --> -99

The average is 75.8 .
```

We can use DO...LOOP structures to trap input errors in almost any setting. As a second (and last) example of this, let's consider a different approach to the "Do you want to go again?" situation. One way to handle this is to insist on certain input and reject anything else. Here's a segment that allows either upper or lowercase *Y* or *N*, but nothing else:

```
INPUT "Do you want to go again? (Y or N) ", answer$
LET answer$ = UCASE$(answer$)
DO UNTIL (answer$ = "Y") OR (answer$ = "N")
    INPUT "Again? (Y or N please!) ", answer$
    Let answer$ = UCASE$(answer$)
LOOP
```

Sample dialogue from the output of this segment might be:

```
Do you want to go again? (Y or N) yes
Again? (Y or N please!) y
```

How does this approach compare with the "picking off the first letter" approach that we discussed at the beginning of this section? Well, this latest approach has the advantage that it can't go wrong (unless, of course, the user manages to confuse the meanings of *Y* and *N*—not likely!); but it has the disadvantage of being somewhat harsh, inflexible, "computerlike." If you say yes to "Do you want to go again?," it should simply go again, right? Perhaps you should experiment with both ways of doing things in your programs and see which you are more comfortable with.

In general, then, we have seen that the conditional looping structure, the DO...LOOP, is ideal for trapping input errors. The idea is simple: loop until you get acceptable data. That, together with the thoughtful use of string functions, can make your programs much more resistant to input errors.

PRACTICE 5.4

1. For each of the following cases, write down four different strings, all of which will cause the loop to *end*:

   (a)
```
DO
    .
    .
    .
    INPUT "Again? ", a$
LOOP UNTIL UCASE$(LEFT$(a$, 1)) = "N"
```

   (b)
```
DO
    .
    .
    .
    INPUT "Again? ", b$
LOOP UNTIL LEFT$(b$, 2) = "no"
```

2. What input error is being trapped by this segment (i.e., what is "bad data" here)?

```
INPUT "Type a number: ", num
DO UNTIL num = INT(num)
   INPUT "Reenter please: ", num
LOOP
```

3. Write a QuickBASIC program that asks users to type in, one by one, ten words that start with *t* (or *T*). If they type in a word starting with anything else, it should be rejected. The output would be something like:

```
Type in 10 words starting with "t":
Word #1 --> top
Word #2 --> Tom
Word #3 --> horse
Try again: word #3 --> tizzy
```

   (and so on)

Chapter Summary 

In this chapter, we've learned about the difference between conditional and unconditional looping. The central idea is that if you know *before* the loop begins how many times it will repeat, you use an unconditional looping structure (e.g., *FOR...NEXT*), whereas if the looping process will end when some condition changes truth value, you use a conditional looping structure.

In QuickBASIC, the only conditional looping structure that we need is the *DO...LOOP*, which has five different basic forms: two pre-checked forms (DO WHILE and DO UNTIL), two post-checked forms (LOOP WHILE and LOOP UNTIL), and a form in which the check is in the body of the loop (the *EXIT DO* statement). You should use whichever form fits most naturally with your algorithm.

One very common use of the DO...LOOP is to enclose an interactive program in a "Do you want to go again?" loop. Another very important use is to process data in which the number of items to be processed is not known at the start. Here, a *flag* is used to signal that the processing is to end. When the READ and DATA statements are used, the flag at the end of the data is called a *trailer* (as contrasted with a *header*, which is used when processing data with the FOR...NEXT loop). Finally, DO...LOOP structures, sometimes in conjunction with string functions, can be used to make programs much more resistant to input errors.

Review Questions

1. Explain each term briefly and give an example:

(a) unconditional loop
(b) conditional loop
(c) infinite loop
(d) pre-checked loop
(e) `EXIT DO`
(f) flag
(g) trailer
(h) error trap

2. What kind of loop (FOR...NEXT or DO...LOOP) would you use in writing a program to solve each of the following problems? Explain briefly.

(a) Find the highest price among 154 prices of this year's domestic and imported car models.
(b) Find out how long it takes to accumulate $5,000, starting with $1,000 earning compound interest at a 9.5% annual rate.
(c) Search the words in a text until 10 occurrences of the word *and* are found.
(d) Count how many of the first 1,000 words in a text start with a vowel.

3. Discuss briefly why string data is more prone to input error than numeric data and what techniques can help cut down on such errors. Give an example or two to illustrate your points.

Programming Problems

Write an algorithm for each problem, list the variables you need, refine the algorithm as much as necessary, and then write a modularized, well-formatted, well-documented QuickBASIC program to solve the problem. Test and debug each program carefully.

1. You are saving your pocket change each day, hoping to get to $20. Write a program that takes in the amount you save each day and prints out "You made it! You've got $____.____" when you've saved $20 or more.

2. Write a program that instructs users to type in words at the keyboard one at a time (i.e., hitting <Enter> after each word), typing "STOP" when they are done; the program then returns the message "The longest word you typed in had ________ characters." You will need the LEN string function (see Table 1.4 in Section 1.5).

3. The DATA lines below contain the names of some 1992 car models and their sticker prices. Write a program that allows the user to type in a price range and that then returns a table of names and prices that fall in that range.

```
DATA Ford Festiva, 8150, Ford Tempo, 10600, Geo Prism, 9789
DATA Chevy Malibu, 12564, Dodge Colt, 8794, Yugo, 4800
DATA Buick Regal 15799, Buick Skylark, 9501, Suburu GL, 11788
DATA Honda Civic, 10566, Honda Accord, 15987
DATA Nissan Stanza, 12458, Hyundai Excel, 6800
DATA EOD
```

For your convenience, you'll find this data in the file C05PB03.BAS on your SAMPLES disk. Copy it to your own disk and start from there.

4. Take *any* interactive program that you have written previously in this course (for example, Programming Problems 2 through 5 and 7 through 9 in Chapter 2; Programming Problems 1 through 3 and 7 through 10 in Chapter 3) and add "Do you want to go again?" Think carefully about what things at the beginning and at the end should *not* be contained in the loop. Make your loop reasonably resistant to input errors. Notice that having added a large loop to your program, much of your indenting needs to be revised.

5. The following problem was first encountered in Chapter 2, Programming Problem 11. We now have a more natural approach to it.

   In 1988, the city of Yonkers, New York, was found in contempt of court in a case concerning housing discrimination. The judge in the case fined the city $100 for the first day that it refused to comply with his ruling; the fine was then to double every day thereafter. The entire 1988 annual budget of Yonkers was $337 million. In how many days would the city have gone broke if it ignored the order? (Remember, the fines were not only doubling each day, they were also accumulating. The second day the city owed $100 + $200 = $300, the third day $300 + $400 = $700, and so on.)

6. Write a program for meteorologists that takes in daily high temperatures in Los Angeles over some period of time until −999 is typed in; the program then returns the highest high and the average high over that period. Include an error trap for entries below 0 and above 120.

7. Compound interest can help you if you are saving money, but it helps the bank even more if you take out a loan (since, of course, banks will *always* charge a higher rate on loans than they will pay on savings). Write a program that takes in the amount of a loan, the *monthly* interest rate (for example, 1.75%), and the proposed monthly payment. The output is a table showing the months passed and (we hope) the decreasing principal. The table should end when the loan is paid off. The main formula for this problem is:

   new principal = old principal + interest charged − payment

   Notice that if the payment is too small, you will never pay off the loan. Try this out and see what happens. Here's the beginning of a sample output:

```
How big is the loan? $ 1000
What is the monthly interest rate (%)? 1.75
How big a monthly payment? $ 50

MONTH            PRINCIPAL

  0               1000.00
  1               967.50
  .
  .
  .
```

8. (a) Write a program that simulates a (simplified) automatic teller machine. Your machine should:

- Ask for the card number (seven digits)
- Ask for the password until the correct one is given
- Ask whether deposit or withdrawal is desired
- Ask how much is to be deposited or withdrawn
- Ask "Do you want another transaction?"

The DATA lines for this program contain card numbers followed by passwords (a "real" teller would also probably "know" the account balance and would adjust that balance after the transaction, but that is impossible for us to do at this time, since we can't get the program to change what's in a DATA line. See Example 2 in Section 8.2 for a way to handle this.)

Test your program with the following data (contained in the file C05PB08.BAS on the SAMPLES disk) which uses −1 as a trailer:

```
DATA 1125673, IGGY, 1546793, LOVER, 2356321, GROUCH
DATA 1548735, DIVER, 3254712, SPIKE, 5367832, FUNFUN
DATA 3874562, DAISY, 4986742, RUNNER
DATA -1
```

(b) Most "real" teller machines only allow the customer to enter the wrong password three times or so before simply withholding the card (since it might well be stolen). Modify your program so that it allows entry of only three incorrect passwords.

9. Modify the telephone information program (C05EX06.BAS in Section 5.4) so that it first searches the data for the desired last name and first initial, but if unsuccessful then searches for the last name only. Only after both searches are unsuccessful does it say "sorry!"

10. Example 1 in Section 5.1 was described as a start at simulating the card game Blackjack. Write a program now that comes much closer to simulating "one-hand" Blackjack as follows:

(a) The player is dealt two cards, that is, the program generates two random numbers between 1 and 13, 1 standing for Ace, 2 for 2, and so on, and 11 for Jack, 12 for Queen, and 13 for King.

(b) Add appropriate values to an accumulating sum. The values are 2 for 2, 3 for 3, and so on, and 10 for Jack, Queen, or King, and either 11 or 1 for Ace (11, unless that puts the sum over 21).

(c) Ask the user if they want to get another card ("hit") or stop there ("stand pat"). The user can continue to be dealt additional cards, but if the sum goes over 21, the user has "busted" and the game ends.

11. Continuing with Problem 10, one-hand Blackjack is not too exciting. Now add a dealer (i.e., second player) to your program who plays after the user is done. The only difference is that the dealer always takes another card as long as the sum is below 17 and always "stands pat" if the sum is 17 or over. High total (not over 21) wins, and the dealer wins if the totals tie. In addition, put a "Want to play another hand?" loop around the program.

CHAPTER

6

SUBPROGRAMS AND USER-DEFINED FUNCTIONS

CHAPTER PREVIEW **In this chapter, we'll learn how a complex program can be built out of a collection of smaller, simpler program segments by using two QuickBASIC structures, *subprograms* and *user-defined functions*; we'll also see how data is passed among the different pieces that make up a program by employing *parameters* and *arguments*.**

6.1 Modularity

Most of the programs you have written and read so far have been fairly short, not much more than a page or two of BASIC code. However, the vast majority of programs used today in business, industry, education, government, and elsewhere are much longer—they may be 10 pages or even 100 pages long. And the longer a program is, the more difficult it is to design, to test, and to read. An important technique for designing and testing long programs uses a *formalized notion of modularity.* So far, we have used the word *modularity* to mean the process of building a program from smaller, simpler program segments; we formalize this idea by introducing ways to build a program from program segments that are actually *separate* from our main program. We can test these segments separately and use them more than once—even in more than one program! In this chapter, we'll learn about two QuickBASIC structures that help us do this: *subprograms* and *user-defined functions.*

In Chapters 1 and 4, we learned techniques for designing algorithms to solve problems using the computer. We always begin with a *level-1 algorithm,* which simply outlines the major steps needed to solve the given problem. In more complicated problems, there may be quite a few such steps; and in QuickBASIC it is possible then to have a main program whose lines are those steps exactly. Let's look at an example of this idea.

EXAMPLE 1

Suppose you want to write a program called CSTutor that allows a user to choose from a list of computer science terms (*operating system, software, programming language, sequential execution, control structure,* etc.) and that returns an explanation of the chosen term. Your *level-1 algorithm* might look like this:

1. Introduce the program to the user
2. Print out the list of terms available:
   a. Operating system
   b. Software
   c. Programming language
   ⋮
3. Allow the user to choose from the terms until she or he wants to quit

Using the formalized idea of modularity, the corresponding QuickBASIC program might look like this:

```
CALL IntroduceProgram
DO
    INPUT "Press return to see a list of terms:", r$
    CALL ListTerms
    INPUT "Desired term (enter number): ", termNum
    PRINT
    SELECT CASE termNum
       CASE 1
           CALL ExplainOperatingSystem
       CASE 2
           CALL ExplainSoftware
       CASE 3
           CALL ExplainProgrammingLanguage
       .
       .
       .
   END SELECT
   INPUT "Do you want another term? (y/n) ", again$
   LET again$ = UCASE$(LEFT$(again$, 1))
LOOP UNTIL again$ = "N"
```

The underlined words in the program are the names of **subprograms**, which, together with the **main program** shown above, make up the whole program. That is, IntroduceProgram, ListTerms, ExplainOperatingSystem, ExplainSoftware, and ExplainProgrammingLanguage are subprograms, which are stored separately and which the main program "calls" when needed.

What do these subprograms look like? Well, IntroduceProgram might look like this:

```
SUB IntroduceProgram

    CLS
    INPUT "Hi! What's your name? ", name$
    PRINT "Welcome to the Computer Tutor, "; name$; "!"
    PRINT "Now you can type in terms about the computer"
    PRINT "and I'll explain them to you."
    PRINT "Sound like fun?"
    PRINT

END SUB
```

The subprogram ExplainSoftware might look like:

```
SUB ExplainSoftware

    PRINT "The term software refers to any program"
    PRINT "written for the computer. A piece of"
    PRINT "software usually serves a specific purpose,"
    PRINT "such as word processing, data manipulation"
    PRINT "('spreadsheet'), communications, and so on."

END SUB
```

6.2 Syntax and Operation of Subprograms

The subprograms illustrated in Example 1 are particularly simple. Their syntax is as follows:

SUB <subprogram name>
:
list of statements
:
END SUB

In addition to the above format, which is used to *define* a particular subprogram, we see that the main program must be able to **call** a subprogram, i.e., there must be a statement that says to *execute* the body of a particular subprogram. The syntax of the **CALL** statement is:

CALL <subprogram name>

EXAMPLE 2

Continuing with the CSTutor program, suppose instead that we have a simpler main program, consisting of the following lines, which calls the subprogram IntroduceProgram twice:

```
PRINT "LINE BEFORE FIRST CALL"
CALL IntroduceProgram
PRINT "LINE BEFORE SECOND CALL"
CALL IntroduceProgram
PRINT "LINE AFTER SECOND CALL"
```

Output from this program is shown below.

```
LINE BEFORE FIRST CALL
Hi! What's your name? Simon
Welcome to the Computer Tutor, Simon!
Now you can type in terms about the computer
and I'll explain them to you.
Sound like fun?

LINE BEFORE SECOND CALL
Hi! What's your name? Garfunkel
Welcome to the Computer Tutor, Garfunkel!
Now you can type in terms about the computer
and I'll explain them to you.
Sound like fun?

LINE AFTER SECOND CALL
```

This program can be found in the file C06EX02.BAS on the SAMPLES disk. If you start QuickBASIC and open this program, you'll see the main program, but you won't see the subprogram IntroduceProgram. That's because subprograms are stored in *separate windows* from the main program and from each other; we'll learn more about that in the next section. For now, try *running* the program: you'll know then that the subprogram is *somewhere*, because you'll see its output!

It might also be helpful to *step* through this program by using the function key **F8**; remember that you can move back and forth between the program and its output by pressing **F4** (for a review of how to use these keys, see Section 4.5). Now, you *will* be able to see the subprogram IntroduceProgram, because its window will be displayed whenever you step through its statements.

Another function key for stepping through programs, **F10**, steps through each individual line of the main program but executes each *complete subprogram* immediately. This is useful in debugging for viewing the flow of control in the main program without being distracted by the subprograms; also, it reflects the point of view that, once you've written a subprogram, the corresponding CALL to that subprogram can be thought of as being a *new BASIC statement*, which you can use whenever you like. Indeed, a BASIC statement can be thought of as a *built-in subprogram*: the BASIC statements we've been using all along, like INPUT or PRINT, can be regarded as calls to segments of code that are internal to the QuickBASIC system and that carry out the task described by that statement. Thus, defining subprograms allows us, in effect, to add new statements to the BASIC language.

If you look at the file C06EX02.BAS, you'll see one more statement associated with subprograms (and with *user-defined functions*, which we'll look at in Section 6.7). For each subprogram that is *called* somewhere in the program, the main program contains a **DECLARE** statement, which declares the existence of the subprogram and initializes some internal checking procedures. Its syntax is:

DECLARE <subprogram name> **( )**

The nice thing about DECLARE statements is that the QuickBASIC system types them in *automatically* whenever you save your program—so you never have to remember to include them! (By the way, if the parentheses at the end of the DECLARE statement look weird, don't worry: we'll explain their use in Section 6.4.)

Now that you have some idea of what a subprogram looks like; of how the main program calls a subprogram; and why you might want to use subprograms to make a long program easier to design, debug, and read; let's discuss how to create and use subprograms in QuickBASIC.

PRACTICE 6.2

If you did not do so while reading Section 6.2, now is the time to try out C06EX02.BAS on the SAMPLES disk (even if you did, be sure to do Exercise 4 below).

1. *Run* the program several times, noting which output lines come directly from the main program and which come from the subprogram invoked by the CALL statement.
2. Use the **F8** key to *step through* the program. Notice that the main program is displayed when its lines are being executed and the subprogram is displayed when *its* lines are being executed.

3. Use the **F10** key to step through the program. Notice that all the lines of the subprogram are executed immediately, which is the difference between using **F10** and **F8.**
4. *Modify the main program* to add a third CALL statement (exactly like the other two CALL statements). Run and step through the modified version to see how it works.

6.3 Windows and Subprograms in QuickBASIC

We must now address how we "get at" subprograms in the QuickBASIC system: how we type them in and how we access their "windows" when we want to modify them. Continuing with the CSTutor program described in Example 1, assume we've typed in the main program as well as the subprograms IntroduceProgram and Explain Software. How do we enter the subprograms ListTerms and Explain OperatingSystem?

As we've already observed, subprograms in QuickBASIC are not entered in the same editing area, or **window**, as the main program. There is one window for the main program and separate windows for each subprogram. Although there are several ways to enter a new subprogram, here we'll describe how to do this using the QuickBASIC menus. Read through our description first, then try this method in Practice 6.3.

> *Note: To take advantage of QuickBASIC's methods for handling subprograms, you must use* **Full Menus** *rather than* **Easy Menus**, *which we assumed you've been using so far. Selecting the option* **Full Menus** *from the Options Menu toggles back and forth between Easy Menus and Full Menus.*[1]

To enter a new subprogram, you need the **New Sub...** option from the **Edit Menu**. Choose this by pressing **Alt-E-S** (if QuickBASIC "beeps" at you when you try this, you haven't activated Full Menus). Alternatively, press **ALT-E** to get the Edit Menu, then use the **arrow** keys to select the *New Sub...* option. Either way, you'll then get a menu asking you for a name. If, for example, you enter **ListTerms**, QuickBASIC puts you in a new editing area, or window, and it fills in the opening and closing lines of the subprogram ListTerms. You may now fill in the *body* of the subprogram.

When you're done entering your new subprogram, you'll probably want to switch back to the window that contains the main program. To move between the various windows containing your main program and your subprograms, you need the *View Menu* (there are also "shortcuts" using function keys, which we'll describe below).

---

[1] You should only need to do this once: the next time you start QuickBASIC it will select the option (Full or Easy) that you used in your previous session. This option appears only in Version 4.5.

The View Menu contains three choices having to do with subprograms: *SUBs*, *Next SUB*, and *Split*. The first choice, *SUBs*, will give you a dialog box listing all the windows you have: your main program and whatever subprograms you've created. You can use the **arrow** keys to select the window you want and then press <Enter>. Pressing the function key **F2** is a shortcut for bringing up the SUBs dialog box.

The *Next SUB* option in the View Menu provides an alternative way to change windows: each time you choose this option you are switched to the *next* window (if you have only two windows, you switch to the other one). Pressing **Shift-F2** is a shortcut; thus, pressing **Shift-F2** repeatedly *cycles* you through all the windows.

The *Split* option in the View Menu lets you divide the viewing screen into two regions, so that you can look at two windows simultaneously (it's actually a *toggle*: to go back to a single window you select the View-Split option again); there is no shortcut function key for this. Once you've split the screen into two windows, you can use the function key **F6** (which was introduced in Section WS2.4) to move between these two windows (and the Immediate Window, which is always there). The View-Split option allows you to look, for instance, at your main program and a subprogram simultaneously.

Sound complicated? It's not really, in fact it's like many things involving computers: confusing today, second nature tomorrow—after you've tried it out a few times! Remember, too, that QuickBASIC tries to help you: it provides reminders in the Reference Bar at the bottom of the screen—and you can always "browse" through the menus until you find what you want.

PRACTICE 6.3

Be sure to do this practice exercise! It's a "hands-on" session showing you how to create and work with subprograms in the QuickBASIC system; for that reason, it's somewhat longer than the usual practice exercises.

The file C06PC03.BAS on the SAMPLES disk contains a main program like that in Example 1 (but with only two of the three CASE clauses shown there) and the subprograms IntroduceProgram and ExplainSoftware, as shown in Section 6.1. In this Practice, you'll try the new QuickBASIC commands described in this section by adding the two subprograms ListTerms and ExplainOperatingSystem, which are needed to complete the program.

(a) Start QuickBASIC and open the program C06PC03.BAS; read over the main program to get a feel for what it's doing. Notice that we have commented out the CALL statement for the subprogram ExplainOperatingSystem, because it doesn't exist yet; you'll remedy this in part (d). We did not comment out the call to ListTerms because the first thing you'll do in part (b) is add that subprogram. If you haven't yet done so, be sure to activate *Full Menus* from the Option Menu.

(b) Prepare to create a new subprogram by pressing **Alt-E-S**; enter the name *ListTerms*; then fill in the body of that subprogram as shown below. Be sure to *indent* the body of the subprogram as shown, as you would for a control structure.

```
SUB ListTerms
'Displays a list of terms for which the program
'provides descriptions.

    CLS
    PRINT
    PRINT "You may choose from the following terms:"
    PRINT
    PRINT "  1. Operating system"
    PRINT "  2. Software"
    PRINT
    PRINT

END SUB
```

(c) *Run* the modified program several times to confirm that it's working properly (try requesting both terms 1 and 2); if you need to move between the various windows to make corrections, press **Shift-F2**.

(d) Repeat the steps in parts (b) and (c) above to add the subprogram ExplainOperatingSystem. Design the body of the subprogram yourself: it should consist of several PRINT statements that explain what an operating system is (remember to use good programming style!). When you retest this latest modification as described in part (c), be sure to *first remove the comment symbol* (i.e., the single quote) from the line in the main program that calls this subprogram (use **Shift-F2** to cycle to the main program window).

(e) Try the other method of moving between your windows: press **F2** (unshifted) and use the **arrow** keys to highlight the different windows. As you do this, notice that a description of the highlighted window appears at the bottom of the dialog box.

(f) With the main program window showing (use **F2** or **Shift-F2** if necessary), select the *Split* option from the View Menu to split the screen into two windows: notice that both windows show your main program but that the cursor is in the top window. Move the cursor to the "Author" line in the program heading and add the words **and me** at the end of that line; notice that the change doesn't show in the other window until you move the cursor off that line. Now move the cursor to the other window by pressing **F6**. Next, press **Shift-F2** to bring one of the subprograms into that window; notice that you can now view (and edit!) both the main program (in window 1) and the subprogram (in window 2)!

(g) With the screen still split into two view windows, try using **F8** to step through the program; notice that QuickBASIC uses the two windows to show whichever program part (main program or subprogram) contains the line that is currently being executed. If you wish, step through the program again, this time using **F10**. When you're done stepping through the program, use the View-Split option to return to a single window.

(h) *Save* your program (under any name you like) on your data disk; after saving, look at the main program—it should now contain two new DECLARE statements.

6.4 Parameters and Arguments

The CSTutor program in Example 1 is somewhat unusual in that it requires no variables. We have seen, however, that just about every computer program *does* require variables—in fact, that's one thing that makes computer programs able to tackle so many tasks successfully. Now, if you want to break your program into subprograms, and if your program involves variables, then the data in those variables may have to be *passed back and forth* among the main program and the subprograms. In this section, we shall learn how to do this in QuickBASIC. Let's look at an example.

EXAMPLE 3

Suppose you are writing a main program that at various times during its execution must draw a horizontal bar whose length and thickness and the character it is built from may vary as the program moves along (an example of such a program would be one that prints a *bar graph* for some list of data).

One way to handle this situation is to write a *subprogram* that will draw the bar each time it is needed. So, as discussed in the last section, we select the *New Sub...* option from the Edit Menu, name the subprogram something like *DrawBar,* and then type in the subprogram (see Table 1.4 in Section 1.5 for the definition of the STRING$ function).

```
SUB DrawBar (char$, howLong, howThick)
'This subprogram draws a horizontal bar of length howLong
'and thickness howThick, using the character char$.
'The cursor is left at the beginning of the next line.

    FOR i = 1 TO howThick
        PRINT STRING$(howLong,char$)
    NEXT i

END SUB
```

The underlined words in parentheses in the heading of our subprogram are called the *parameters* of the subprogram. We see that the subprogram DrawBar has three parameters: *char$*, *howLong*, and *howThick*. Notice that we do *not* call them variables, and there is an important reason for this: a variable is a memory location but a parameter of a subprogram is not. Instead, a **parameter** is a *place-holder* that is *replaced* by either a variable or a constant value *when the subprogram is called* using the CALL statement. Until a call occurs, a parameter is really nothing *but* a place-holder; you can think of it simply as a name that will be replaced by a value or by a variable name when the subprogram is called.

In the DrawBar subprogram above, the general form of subprograms using parameters is evident. The syntax of the subprogram definition is as follows:

SUB <subprogram name> (list of parameters)
:
list of statements
:
END SUB

The DECLARE statement is shown below. Note that QuickBASIC automatically appends the symbol "!" to each numeric variable; just as "$" indicates a string variable, "!" indicates a *numeric* variable.[2] Note also that the empty parentheses in the DECLARE statement we saw in Section 6.2 just meant that that subprogram had no parameters.

DECLARE <subprogram name> (list of parameters)

The CALL statement is as follows:

CALL <subprogram name> (list of arguments)

The **arguments** describe the values or variables that will be substituted for the parameters. The list of parameters and list of arguments must *match* in length and data types. For instance, any call to DrawBar must have three arguments, the first a string and the second and third numeric.

Let's see what happens when our subprogram DrawBar gets called by the main program. First, suppose that there's a call like this:

```
CALL DrawBar("*", 20, 3)
```

The "*", 20, and 3 are the *arguments* of this CALL statement. In this case, since these three arguments are constant values rather than variable names, the parameters *char$*, *howLong*, and *howThick* are

[2] Actually, the symbol "!" indicates a special kind of numeric variable, called a *single-precision* variable—which is what we've been using all along. If you want to learn about the different kinds of numeric variables, look up the hyperlink Data Types in either the Contents or Index of the QuickBASIC Help system. There is also a discussion of data types in Section 8.5.

replaced by the *values "*"*, *20*, and *3*. What will the output be? Just what you would expect:

```
********************
********************
********************
```

Now, let's look at a different type of call to DrawBar. Suppose this time that our main program contains the following lines:

```
LET border$ = "*"
LET longNum = 20
LET wideNum = 3
CALL DrawBar(border$, longNum, wideNum)
```

It's clear that this call will produce *exactly the same output* as the previous one—but what happens to the parameters *char$*, *howLong*, and *howThick* is different! This time they get replaced by the *variables border$*, *longNum*, and *wideNum* from the main program, that is, they aren't simply given values. Instead, they actually *become* the memory locations *border$*, *longNum*, and *wideNum*. In the next section, we'll focus on these two different ways to pass data between the subprogram and the main program. In the meantime, the file C06EX03.BAS on the SAMPLES disk contains a program that lets you try the subprogram DrawBar with various types of arguments (see Practice 6.4, Exercise 3).

PRACTICE 6.4

1. Consider the following main program (on the left) and subprogram (on the right):

```
LET x = 5                        SUB MysterySub (num1, num2)
LET y = 3                            LET temp = num1
PRINT x, y                           LET num1 = num2
CALL MysterySub (x, y)               LET num2 = temp
PRINT x, y                       END SUB
```

   (a) What is the output of the main program?
   (b) Name each of the parameters and each of the arguments.
   (c) What task does the subprogram perform?

2. Answer the same questions for the following main program and subprogram:

```
LET name$ = "George Bush"          SUB SecretSub (word$, num)
LET x = 4                              FOR i = 1 TO LEN(word$) STEP num
CALL SecretSub(name$, 3)                   PRINT MID$(word$, i, 1);
CALL SecretSub("abcde", x)             NEXT i
CALL SecretSub(name$, x-2)             PRINT
                                   END SUB
```

3. Start QuickBASIC and open the program C06EX03.BAS on the SAMPLES disk. Run it several times and study it carefully; in the

main program, look especially at each of the CALL statements in which DrawBar is called and notice whether the arguments are constants, variables, or expressions.

6.5 Passing by Value and by Reference

As we saw in the preceding section, there are two methods for moving data back and forth between a subprogram and the main program: *pass by value* and *pass by reference* (the terms *call by value* and *call by reference* are sometimes used).

Pass by value If an argument in the CALL statement is a *constant value*, that is, a number, a string in quotes, or an expression (e.g., 2, "Hello", 3*x−5), then the corresponding parameter in the subprogram is assigned that value.

Pass by reference If an argument in the CALL statement is a *variable*, then the corresponding parameter in the subprogram is *replaced* by that variable; the parameter becomes that memory location. In other words, *both* names—the name of the variable that is the argument *and* the name of the parameter—refer to the very same memory location (hence the phrase *pass by reference*).

Are the people who wrote QuickBASIC just trying to confuse you by providing these two different possibilities? No—the fact is that both types of data passing are necessary for different situations. The first situation is fairly clearcut. With a CALL statement like

```
CALL DrawBar("*", 20, 3)
```

all we can do is give the values "*", 20, and 3 to the parameters *char$*, *howLong*, and *howThick*. That is, if an argument is a constant or an expression (i.e., *not* a variable) then pass by value is the only way that makes sense.

However, although pass by value works fine for moving data from the main program to the subprogram, it can't move data the other way! If our subprogram is producing data that the main program wants to use, then pass by reference is our only hope. Let's look at another example.

EXAMPLE 4

Using the subprogram DrawBar, suppose we want a main program that inputs a character, a length, and a thickness, and then calls DrawBar to draw a bar to those specifications. The following would work:

```
PRINT "This program draws a bar to your specifications."
PRINT "Please enter a character, a length, and a thickness:"
INPUT char$, howLong, howThick
CALL DrawBar(char$, howLong, howThick)
```

A nice enhancement of this program would be to *check for valid input;* in other words, check that *char$* is a single character and that *howLong* and *howThick* are positive numbers. Although we could insert some lines after the INPUT statement to do this, the readability of the program would suffer. Instead, let's write our own special input statement (i.e., subprogram) that will accept only valid input.

```
    SUB ValidInput(ch$, num1, num2)
    'This subprogram inputs ch$, num1, and num2, but
    'accepts only valid input, i.e., ch$ must be a single
    'character, and num1 and num2 must be positive

        DO
            INPUT ch$, num1, num2
            IF LEN(ch$) = 1 AND num1 > 0 AND num2 > 0 THEN
                EXIT DO
            ELSE
                PRINT "*** BAD INPUT - START AGAIN ***"
            END IF
        LOOP

    END SUB
```

All we need to do now is replace the INPUT statement in the main program by a CALL to ValidInput, and our subprogram will do the job.

```
PRINT "This program draws a bar to your specifications."
PRINT "Please enter a character, a length, and a thickness:"
CALL ValidInput(char$, howLong, howThick)
CALL DrawBar(char$, howLong, howThick)
```

This works precisely because we pass by reference this time, that is, parameter *ch$* becomes the location *char$*, parameter *num1* becomes the location *howLong*, and parameter *num2* becomes the location *howThick*. These memory locations get filled in by the INPUT statement in the subprogram, and, because each parameter refers to the same memory location as its corresponding argument, the effect is to fill in the arguments themselves, thus passing data back to the main program. If you'd like to run this program, it's in the file C06EX04.BAS on the SAMPLES disk.

If you find these ideas difficult, here's some good news. If you do the natural thing when calling a subprogram, in most cases QuickBASIC will automatically pick the appropriate data passing method. If you write

```
    CALL DrawBar("#", 12, 5)
```

QuickBASIC will give those values to the parameters because it has no other choice. But if you say

```
CALL ValidInput(char$, howLong, howThick)
```

QuickBASIC will replace *ch$* by *char$*, *num1* by *howLong*, and *num2* by *howThick*—which is exactly what you want to happen!

Let's summarize some of what we've learned about parameters of a subprogram, arguments of a CALL statement, and the passing of data between the main program and a subprogram.

1. If a subprogram gets data from the main program or sends data back to it, then the subprogram must have *parameters* (one or more) declared in the subprogram heading.
2. When a subprogram that has parameters is called by the main program, the CALL statement must include *arguments*, one for each parameter, in the same order as the parameters are, and each of the corresponding type (numeric or string).
3. Any given argument in a CALL statement can be a variable, a constant, or an expression. If it is a variable, QuickBASIC will *pass by reference*, that is, the corresponding parameter in the subprogram will become that variable. If an argument is *not* a variable, QuickBASIC will *pass by value*, that is, the corresponding parameter in the subprogram will be given the value of that argument.

Admittedly, these are not the easiest ideas that we've encountered; but, as usual, if you work with them for a while, they will become quite natural.

PRACTICE 6.5

For each of the arguments in each of the CALL statements in the first two exercises of Practice 6.4, determine whether the argument is being passed by reference or passed by value.

6.6 Local Variables

If you look back at Examples 1 and 3, you will see that the subprograms IntroduceProgram and DrawBar each contain a variable that is not a parameter but rather is just used "locally" in that subprogram. We are referring to the variable *name$* in IntroduceProgram and *i* in DrawBar. Such variables are called **local variables**. They exist nowhere but in the subprogram itself. If the main program that calls DrawBar contains a variable named *i*, it is a completely *different variable*, even though it has the same name. For example, this main program might include the following program segment for drawing a triangle:

```
FOR i = 1 TO 10
    CALL DrawBar("#", i, 1)
NEXT i
```

Since the two variables named *i* are totally independent, no problems arise.

In fact, except for the connection between parameters and arguments, *all* variables in QuickBASIC are "local," whether they are in the main program or any subprogram. This means, then, that to pass data between subprograms and the main program we *must* use parameters and arguments. (Actually, QuickBASIC provides several other ways to pass data; in Section 8.8 we'll look at one of these ways, the DIM SHARED statement.)

PRACTICE 6.6

List all the local variables in the subprograms in Exercises 1 and 2 in Practice 6.4.

6.7 User-Defined Functions

In Section 6.2, we noted that one way to view subprograms is as a way to insert additional statements that are not "built-in" to the BASIC language. For example, the built-in statement PRINT does a variety of things, but it does not allow us to print a bar of specified length and thickness, using a specified character. By writing the subprogram DrawBar in Example 3, we created an additional statement we could use, namely, "CALL DrawBar," which did that task.

In fact, all the BASIC statements (PRINT, INPUT, etc.) are essentially "built-in" subprograms—when the statement "PRINT x" is executed, the variable x plays the role of an argument; and the computer actually executes a whole sequence of instructions, which compute the value of x and then cause that value to be printed as output. If BASIC does not provide a statement to carry out a particular task, we can create a *user-defined* statement by writing a subprogram to do the task.

In addition to *statements*, we know that QuickBASIC also provides a variety of built-in *functions*, for example, CINT, SQR, LEFT$, LEN, and so on, that compute numeric or string *values*. As with statements, we may sometimes find that we need a certain function that QuickBASIC simply doesn't provide. Examples that we've already encountered include: a function to compute a random integer in a given range, a function to round *up* a real number to the next whole number, and a function that returns the uppercase first character in a string.

Just as subprograms allow us to create new BASIC statements, QuickBASIC provides a structure that allows us to create new BASIC *functions*, called the **user-defined function**. It is quite similar to the subprogram structure in its syntax and the way it is handled in the editor—but there are a couple of important differences. Let's begin by looking at an example.

EXAMPLE 5

We have already written several programs that required a random integer in a specified range, say from *low* to *high*, where "low" and "high" are integers. Here's a QuickBASIC function with two parameters, *low* and *high*, that computes a random integer in the range *low* to *high*, using the formula we developed in Section 3.5 (the file C06EX05.BAS on the SAMPLES disk contains a program that lets you see this function in action):

```
FUNCTION RandInt (low, high)
'This function computes a random integer in the range
'low to high.

    LET RandInt = INT(RND * (high - low + 1)) + low

END FUNCTION
```

Note the similarity to the *subprogram* structure in the opening and closing lines—the only difference is that the words *SUB...END SUB* have been replaced by the words *FUNCTION...END FUNCTION*. Functions follow *exactly* the same rules as subprograms regarding parameters and local variables.

There is one important *difference* between subprograms and functions. Namely, since a function computes a *value*, every function definition *must* contain a line where the name of the function is assigned a value. In this example, that is the *only* line of the function definition. In other words, if our function name is "Zibbledorf," somewhere in the body of the function definition, there must be a line such as

```
LET ZibbleDorf = ....,
```

or

```
INPUT ZibbleDorf,
```

or

```
READ ZibbleDorf,
```

(and so on)

We use a user-defined function the same way we use a built-in function. For example, if we want to make *x* a random number from 1 to 10, then, using the function RandInt given above, we write:

```
LET x = RandInt(1, 10)
```

It's important to notice that a function, whether it's built-in or user-defined, is never a whole statement by itself—it's simply a *value*, numeric or string, that can be *used* in a BASIC statement. This is in contrast to subprograms, in which case "CALL SubprogramName" *is* an entire statement.

EXAMPLE 6

In many of the programs in this text that request a yes/no reply from the user, we've replaced the user's response by its first letter, uppercase (for instance, the main program in Example 1 of Section 6.1). This allowed us to simplify conditions that use the response (e.g., LOOP UNTIL ans$ = "N"). Now, we'll define a function that computes the first character in a string, uppercase. Note: A function that computes a value that is a *string* must have a name ending in "$" (as is the case for built-in functions). Here's a function that does the job:

```
FUNCTION FirstCap$ (word$)
'This function returns the first character,
'capitalized, from word$

    LET FirstCap$ = UCASE$(LEFT$(word$, 1))

END FUNCTION
```

Of course, function definitions can be longer.

EXAMPLE 7

The following function computes "n factorial" (also denoted "n!"), that is, the product 1 * 2 * 3 * . . . * n (also see Example 4 in Section 2.4):

```
FUNCTION Factorial (n)
'For n a positive integer, this function computes
'the product 1 * 2 * 3 * ... * n

    LET product = 1
    FOR i = 2 to n
        LET product = product * i
    NEXT i
    LET Factorial = product

END FUNCTION
```

Thus, the output of the statement "PRINT Factorial(6)" would be 720 (=1 * 2 * 3 * 4 * 5 * 6). In the definition of this function, notice that we use local variables, *product* and *i*. As mentioned above, these follow the same rules that were described for subprograms.

Let's summarize what we've learned about user-defined functions.

1. A user-defined function computes a *value*. The general format for defining a function is:

   FUNCTION <function name> (list of parameters)
   :
   list of statements
   :
   END FUNCTION

2. The name of the function must indicate whether its value is numeric or string, that is, the name of a function that returns a string value must end in "$."

3. The list of statements in the definition of a function must contain *at least one* statement that assigns a value to the function's name.
4. We use user-defined functions in the same way that we use built-in functions or any other numeric or string expression. For instance,

```
PRINT RandInt(1, 10)
```

or

```
IF FirstCap$(ans$) = "N" THEN
```

(and so on)

In general,

FunctionName(list of arguments)

is an *expression*, not a whole *statement*; we do *not* use CALL with user-defined functions.

PRACTICE 6.7

Consider the following main program (on the left) and user-defined function (on the right):

```
PRINT Round(3.2)        FUNCTION Round (num)
LET x = 4.9                 LET Round = -INT(-num)
LET x = Round(x)        END FUNCTION
PRINT x
```

(a) What is the output of this program?
(b) What task does this function perform?
(c) List all the parameters, arguments, and local variables that appear.
(d) For each use of the function in the main program, determine whether the argument is being passed by reference or by value.

6.8 Functions in QuickBASIC

The way we enter functions in QuickBASIC is similar to the way we enter subprograms. Choose *New Function...* from the Edit Menu (for subprograms, we choose *New Sub...*). As with subprograms, you are directed to enter the name of your function, then given a new "window" in which to enter it. Once you've entered the function definition, you can move between windows by using options from the *View Menu* (or the function key **F2**), exactly as we did for subprograms in Section 6.3.

6.9 Programming Style

The style conventions we use with subprograms and user-defined functions are analogous to what we have been doing all along (see the examples in this chapter for models):

1. Give subprograms, user-defined functions, and their parameters *meaningful names*.
2. Immediately following the first line of a subprogram or function, provide a *comment* describing what it does.
3. Separate the body of the subprogram or user-defined function from the heading and descriptive comment with a *blank line*; do the same to separate the body from the closing line.
4. *Indent* the body of the subprogram or user-defined function.
5. Within the body of the subprogram or user-defined function, follow the same rules of style that we have used all along.

6.10 Techniques for Testing

As you begin writing more complex programs using subprograms and user-defined functions, you'll find that it's important to test the individual pieces as you write them. There are several useful techniques for doing this.

EXAMPLE 8

Suppose we wish to write a program that prints a *banner*, that is, the user enters a string (e.g., "Happy Birthday") and the program prints it out in large block letters that are written sideways. A good approach would be to design a main program that inputs a string and then, for each letter, calls a subprogram to print the corresponding block letter.

To test an individual subprogram, we might enclose it in a very simple program that does nothing more than call the subprogram so we can see how it works. Sometimes called a **driver program**, it is sometimes discarded after being used to "drive" our subprogram until we are confident that it is correct. For instance, a "driver" to test a subprogram named BlockA might be as simple as this:

```
CALL BlockA
END
```

However, we may wish to test the main program *before* its subprograms are written. The problem here is that our main program may contain the line "CALL BlockF," but BlockF may not yet be written. In this case, we may want to use **stubs**. For example, we could quickly create the following subprogram:

```
SUB BlockF
   PRINT "F"
END SUB
```

This is called a "stub" for the subprogram BlockF, because it contains that subprogram's opening and closing lines and very little else! The use of such stubs allows us to partially test the main program before all the subprograms are written. Of course, testing is never complete until you've written all the pieces and thoroughly tested the whole package!

Suppose the banner program is assigned to a *team* of students, with one person working on the main program and other team members working individually on the subprograms for each letter. Suppose, for instance, that Albert has written and tested a main program stored in a file called BANNER.BAS, while Betty has written and tested the subprogram BlockF using a driver program called TESTF.BAS. How does Betty get her subprogram BlockF into Albert's file BANNER.BAS containing the main program? More generally, if subprograms are designed and tested using driver programs as described above, how does the programmer assemble all the pieces into one file?

As you might expect, QuickBASIC provides a way to *move* a subprogram from one file to another; once again, the method requires that you activate the *Full Menus* option from the Options Menu. In the following example, we'll take you through the steps necessary to copy a subprogram from one file to another (if you want to pursue the banner idea, see Programming Problems 1 and 7 at the end of this chapter).

EXAMPLE 9

(This is a "hands-on" example: do it at a computer.) In Example 1 of Section 6.1, we began discussing a program called CSTutor that permitted the user to choose from a list of computer terms; the program then printed an explanation of the chosen term. In Practice 6.3, you modified the file C06PC03.BAS, which contained the main program for that example plus several subprograms. Suppose that someone else has independently written a subprogram called ExplainProgrammingLanguage, has tested it using a driver program, and has saved it in a file named C06EX09.BAS on the SAMPLES disk. Here are the steps you should follow to copy the subprogram ExplainProgrammingLanguage *from* the file C06EX09.BAS *to* your file C06PC03.BAS, which contains the main program:

1. First, select *Open Program...* from the File Menu to open the file C06PC03.BAS, which contains the main program (in general, you should *open* the file that you want to copy the subprogram *to*).
2. Next, choose *Load File...* from the File Menu. You'll be prompted for a file name: enter the name of the file containing the subprogram to be moved,[3] C06EX09.BAS in this case. (Don't worry—your main file is still there: the file you first *open* is considered the "main module"; the file you then *load* is treated as an "auxiliary" module.)
3. Press function key **F2** to get the SUBs dialog box—you'll see that both files and all their subprograms are listed. Use the

[3] You may also notice that this menu offers you three options for "Load as"—the default option, Module, is the correct one here.

arrow keys to highlight the subprogram to be moved (Explain-ProgrammingLanguage in this case)—*don't* press <Enter> yet!

4. After highlighting the subprogram, use the **Tab** key several times until the word *Move* at the bottom of the dialog box is highlighted—*now* press **<Enter>**.
5. You'll now see yet another dialog box asking you to "Choose destination module"—use the **arrow** keys to select the file containing the main program (e.g., C06PC03.BAS) and press **<Enter>**. The SUBs dialog box will reappear; it should show that the subprogram has been moved.
6. At this point, you may wish to delete the file that originally contained the subprogram (from QuickBASIC that is, *not* from your disk). This can be done by using the **arrow** keys to highlight the file name (C06EX09.BAS in this example) and then the **Tab** key to select the *Delete* box; when you press **<Enter>** this time, you'll be asked if you want to save the file; *select No* unless you want the subprogram *permanently* removed from the file.
7. When you're finished moving the subprogram, press **Esc** to clear the SUBs dialog box.

One final comment about moving subprograms (and user-defined functions, of course) from one file to another: If, in this example, the "destination file" C06PC03.BAS already contained a subprogram named ExplainProgrammingLanguage (for example, it might have a stub that was used in testing), then QuickBASIC will not permit you to load another file that also contains a subprogram with that name. In this situation, you would begin at Step 6 above to *delete* the stub with that name; only then could you proceed with Step 1, to move the real subprogram ExplainProgrammingLanguage from C06EX09.BAS to C06PC03.BAS.

PRACTICE 6.10

This practice requires a computer.

1. In this section, you copied the subprogram ExplainProgrammingLanguage into the file C06PC03.BAS. Now, you should further modify C06PC03.BAS to *use* this subprogram, that is, so that the program provides an explanation of the term *programming language*. You will need to add *programming language* to the list of terms in the subprogram ListTerms and to add a third CASE clause in the main program to CALL the new subprogram ExplainProgrammingLanguage. Be sure to *test* your modified program!
2. (a) In QuickBASIC, write a little program containing a single subprogram named PrintBye that simply prints the word *Bye*. The main program should clear the screen and then

call the subprogram. Test this program and then save it under the name TESTBYE.BAS.

(b) Choose the *New Program* option from the File Menu. Write another little program containing a single subprogram named PrintHi that simply prints the word *Hi*. The main program should clear the screen and then call the subprogram. Test this program and then save it under the name GREETINGS.BAS.

(c) Follow the steps described in this section to *move* the subprogram PrintBye to the program GREETINGS.BAS. When you're done, delete the loaded file TESTBYE.BAS.

(d) After you've successfully completed Step (c), add a line to the main program so that it also calls PrintBye. Test the program; the output should now consist of two lines, "Hi" and "Bye." Save the program in this form.

Chapter Summary

In this chapter, we've introduced the important idea of *formal modularity*—building a complex program out of smaller, simpler program segments that are actually *separate* from each other. QuickBASIC provides two structures that help us do this: *subprograms* and *user-defined functions*.

A *subprogram* is a self-contained program segment that is given a name and can be "called" one or more times by the main program (or by other subprograms) using the CALL statement.

A *user-defined function* is also a self-contained program segment that is given a name; but, unlike a subprogram, a user-defined function computes a numeric or string *value*. For that reason, the body of a user-defined function must always contain at least one statement that assigns a value to the name of the function. A user-defined function is used the same way that a built-in function is used—as an *expression* that is *part* of a complete statement.

The sharing of data among the different pieces of a program is accomplished through the use of *parameters* and *arguments*. In the definition of a subprogram (or user-defined function), we may specify a list of *parameters*, which are "place-holders" that will be replaced by values or variables when the subprogram is called. These values or variables are the *arguments*—they and their corresponding parameters must have matching types.

The way in which a parameter is replaced by its argument *differs* depending on whether that argument is a *constant value* or a *variable name*. These two different ways of passing data from an argument to a parameter are called *pass by value* and *pass by reference*.

If the argument is a constant value (or an expression that can be evaluated to give a constant value), we simply assign that value to the parameter, that is, we *pass by value*.

If the argument is a variable name, the parameter is replaced by that variable, that is, the parameter name *refers* to the actual memory location corresponding to the argument; hence, we say that we *pass by reference*. This way of passing data is the *only* way to send data from the subprogram back to the main program (or to whatever other program part that did the "calling").

You must be aware that if your argument is a variable, it is possible to have it changed by the subprogram. Otherwise, you can usually simply fill in your arguments in whatever seems to be the natural way, without worrying about whether you are passing by reference or by value.

Since the notion of modularity allows us to build a large program out of many small parts, it is important to learn to design and test the parts individually, using techniques such as *driver programs* and *stubs*, finally assembling all the pre-tested pieces and testing the whole package one last time.

Review Questions

1. Explain each of these ideas briefly, giving examples where appropriate:
   (a) formal modularity
   (b) subprogram
   (c) user-defined function
   (d) parameter
   (e) argument
   (f) pass by value
   (g) pass by reference
   (h) local variable
   (i) driver program
   (j) stub

2. Each statement in the list below illustrates a call to one of the examples of subprograms or user-defined functions that were discussed in this chapter. Assume that the variables *a$*, *b$*, *x*, and *y* were previously assigned the values "*", "#", 4, and 10, respectively. For each statement, determine whether each argument is being passed by value or by reference and describe the result of the calling statement.
   (a) `CALL DrawBar(a$, x, y)`
   (b) `CALL DrawBar("+", y, x-2)`
   (c) `CALL ValidInput(b$, x, y)`
   (d) `LET a$ = FirstCap$("hi")`
   (e) `PRINT RandInt(0, y)`
   (f) `PRINT RandInt(x, Factorial(x))`

Programming Problems

Note: Problems 1 and 2 do not require the use of parameters.

1. Write a program containing three subprograms that print the following in block letters: E, S, and T. After testing each subprogram, write a final program that calls these routines to print the word *TESTS*. (You may wish to have the subprograms print the block letters *sideways* to look like a banner.)

2. (a) Write and test a function, Face$, that randomly chooses the face value of a playing card from a standard deck; thus, its value is one of the following *strings*: Ace, 2, 3, 4, 5, 6, 7, 8, 9, 10, Jack, Queen, King.
   (b) Write and test a function, Suit$, that randomly chooses the suit of a playing card from a standard deck; thus, its value is one of the following strings: Clubs, Diamonds, Hearts, Spades.
   (c) Write a program that uses the above functions, Face$ and Suit$, to randomly select and print *two* cards (e.g., 2 of Diamonds and Jack of Clubs); have the program then print whether the two cards are identical, different in suit only, different in face value only, or different in both suit and face value.

3. The DATA statement shown below lists revenues (in thousands of dollars) for the Acme Floppy Disk Company for the first six months of its existence.

```
DATA 11, 15, 12, 12, 8, 3
```

   Using the subprogram DrawBar from Example 3, design a program that will print a bar graph with one bar for each data item. The bars should be two lines thick and the length of each should match its corresponding data item (hence, the bar graph will be printed *sideways*). For characters, use the digits 1 through 6, so that each bar will show the month whose revenues it represents; separate each bar with one blank line.

4. (a) Write and test a function named Max, having two numeric parameters, that returns the larger value of the two parameters (if they are equal, it returns their common value).
   (b) Write a program that reads a list of numbers from a DATA statement and then prints the largest value; use the function Max each time you wish to compute the larger of two values.
   (c) Add to the program above a function named Min that returns the *smaller* of two numeric values; then modify the main program to print both the largest *and* smallest values that it reads.

5. *Automatic teller machines* (also known as ATMs) perform many of the duties of bank tellers, such as making deposits and paying bills—but perhaps their most convenient feature is that they dispense *cash*. Most ATMs, however, limit such withdrawals to some amount like $100 and dispense only $20 and $5 bills.
   (a) Write and test a subprogram, ValidInput, that inputs an amount of money to be withdrawn but, like the subprogram in Example 4, will accept only valid inputs. In this case, an amount of money is valid only if it is a whole number divisible by 5 and it lies in the range 5 to 100.
   (b) Write and test a subprogram, Dispense, that takes a valid withdrawal amount and determines the correct number of $20 and $5 bills to dispense; thus, a withdrawal amount of $55 would correspond to two $20 bills and three $5 bills (this subprogram will require three parameters: one for the withdrawal amount, one for the number of $20 bills, and one for the number of $5 bills).
   (c) Use these two subprograms to write a program that simulates an ATM that does withdrawals only; if you wish, you may add other features to make it more like a real ATM.

6. (a) Write and test a function, Reverse$, that takes a string and returns that string spelled *backwards*; thus, *Reverse$("Quick")* is "kciuQ."

(b) Use Reverse$ in a program that inputs a string and determines whether it is a *palindrome*, that is, whether it is the same spelled backwards or forwards (e.g., *noon* is a palindrome).

Note: Problems 7 and 8 involve larger programs, which may be suitable for team projects.

7. This problem involves designing a more sophisticated banner printer than the one described in Problem 1. The person running the program should be asked to input a *string* to be printed and the following information concerning the attributes of the block letters: a *character* to print them with, their *height*, and their *width*. (Note: *Width* is a reserved word in QuickBASIC, so don't use it as a variable name.) At the very least, you will need a subprogram for each block letter (remember to print the letters *sideways*), with one parameter for each of the three attributes. The block letters should be at least two characters thick, and you should test each block letter routine separately, being sure to try different sets of attributes. You may wish to limit the letters that you print to those that can be printed with no *diagonal bars*, which are: A, C, E, F, G, H, I, J, L, O, P, S, T, U.

After you've tested each letter routine and the main program (printing to the screen), you'll probably want the final version to display input prompts and other messages on the screen, while the actual banner prints on the printer. You can use the QuickBASIC statement LPRINT to do this. LPRINT behaves like the PRINT statement *except* it prints to the printer rather than to the screen.

8. Write a *data analyzer* that allows the user to choose among several operations to be performed on a list of numbers stored in DATA statements. The available operations should include: printing the list; printing those values that fall within a specified subrange; computing the mean; computing the standard deviation (see Chapter 2, Programming Problem 13); computing the highest value; computing the lowest value; and any other operations you would like to include. In addition to routines to perform each operation, include a routine that prints a menu listing the available operations; allow the user to make choices from the menu as many times as he or she wishes.

CHAPTER

7

ARRAYS

CHAPTER PREVIEW In this chapter, we'll learn how to store a whole list (or whole table, etc.) of data items in memory using an *array*. Because the list is stored together in a sequence of memory locations, arrays can easily be created, manipulated, and printed using loops. Arrays can be one-dimensional (lists), two-dimensional (tables), or three-dimensional and higher. We'll study two of the most important tasks performed on arrays: *searching* the array for some item and *sorting* the array into some order. Finally, we'll learn how to pass arrays as parameters to subprograms and user-defined functions.

7.1 Introduction

Up to this point, when we've been concerned with processing data of some kind, our level-1 algorithms have usually looked something like this:

1. For each item of data:
   a. Take in the item
   b. Process the item
2. Return the results

For example, to find the sum of a bunch of numbers, we take in each number, add it into an accumulating sum, and then essentially "throw that number away" by placing the next data item in the same memory location—since once our number is added into the sum, we have no more need for it. The same story goes for other tasks we've performed, such as finding averages, finding the biggest or smallest item in a list, finding the alphabetically first or last string in a list, and so on.

Can every data processing task be done in this manner, that is, take in, process, and then throw away each item? Well, let's look at a simple example where this approach simply doesn't work.

EXAMPLE 1

Let's write a program that takes in a list of numbers (the list can be any length) and prints it out in reverse order. For example, if you enter the data in the order

4 7 2 6 8 3 6

the program returns

```
6  3  8  6  2  7  4
```

Sounds easy enough, right? But wait! This time, we can't simply take in number 4, process it, and then throw it away. We've got to *hang on to it* until *all* the items are in, then print them all out, including the 4, in reverse order. How can we do this?

Notice that we *can* handle this problem if the list always has some *fixed number of items*. For example, here's a program for lists of seven numbers:

```
INPUT num1, num2, num3, num4, num5, num6, num7
PRINT num7, num6, num5, num4, num3, num2, num1
```

Although this works, it has so little flexibility that it's practically useless. Though it may surprise you, the fact is that we do not as yet *have the ability to solve the problem* inherent here, which is, how to handle lists of varying lengths. What we need is a way to store a whole list of items in memory. Happily, Structured BASIC provides us with a way to do just this: the **array data structure**.

An **array** is a *sequence of memory locations* all with the *same name* and all holding the same type of data, but each with a *different number* (called its **index**) labelling it. In general, a **data structure** is a way to organize a set of data for storage in memory. Arrays are the first such structures we've encountered (aside from simple variables, which we've used since Day One; we shall see another data structure—*record variables*—in Chapter 8).

In the next section, we'll take a close look at the idea of an array, but for now, let's look at how an array solves our problem in Example 1.

```
DIM num(1 TO 30)

PRINT "How many numbers in your list"
INPUT "(no more than 30 please)? ", howMany

PRINT "Type them in please:"
FOR index = 1 TO howMany
       INPUT "---> ", num(index)
NEXT index

PRINT "Here they are in reverse order:
FOR index = howMany TO 1 STEP -1
       PRINT num(index); "    ";
NEXT index
```

That does the trick. Don't worry about the DIM statement—we'll go over that in the next section. (It just tells the compiler that *num( )* is an array that can hold up to 30 numbers labelled *num(1)*, *num(2)*, and so on, up to *num(30)*.) Sample output for the above follows.

```
How many numbers in your list
(no more than 30 please)? 5
Type them in please:
---> 3
---> 7
---> 1
---> 8
---> 2
Here they are in reverse order:
2  8  1  7  3
```

How does it work? The five numbers in this run were stored in five locations (see Figure 7.1). All five locations have a name of the form *num( )*, but each has a different *index* (*1* through *5*) inside the parentheses. We store all the data in memory so that we can manipulate it however we need to (in this case, print it out backwards).

3	7	1	8	2
num(1)	num(2)	num(3)	num(4)	num(5)

FIGURE 7.1

The First Five Locations of the Array *num*

Arrays are a very powerful tool. In the following section, we'll look closely at their syntax and operation; and, in subsequent sections, we'll see how to use them for various important tasks such as sorting or searching a list. We'll also introduce arrays whose *dimensions* are two (these are called "tables" or "matrices") or higher.

7.2 One-Dimensional Arrays

As we've said, arrays allow us to store an entire list of data in the computer's memory. We repeat:

> ***An* array *is a sequence of memory locations all with the same name, all holding the same type of data, but each having its own number (called its "index" or "subscript").***

For example, an array named *score( )*, which is supposed to hold six numbers, might look like that in Figure 7.2. The numbers in the boxes are, of course, the current values of *score(1)*, *score(2)*, and so on. A second example might be an array *word$( )*, which is to hold five words (see Figure 7.3).

As you can see, the idea of an array is not complicated at all—but it turns out to be a *very* useful tool in programming!

To use an array in QuickBASIC, you must first *declare* that array, that is, you must notify the compiler that you want to set up an array; then you must tell it the array's name and its indices. You do all this with the **DIM statement** (DIM is short for "dimension"). To store a *list* of items, you use a **one-dimensional array**: an array in which each box has *one* index (in Section 7.4, we'll look at arrays in which each box has two or more indices). For one-dimensional arrays, the dimension statement normally has the form:

DIM <variable name> **(**<lowest index> **TO** <highest index>**)**

For example, the statement

```
DIM price (1 TO 20)
```

tells the compiler that an array named *price* with lowest index 1 and highest index 20 should be created and that it is to hold numeric data (since *price* is a numeric variable name). The compiler then sets aside 20 locations labelled *price(1)*, *price(2)*, and so on through *price(20)* and *initializes* all 20 locations to the value 0. For another example, the statement

```
DIM name$(0 TO 45)
```

causes the compiler to set aside 46 locations, labelled *name$(0)*

FIGURE 7.2

A Numeric Array

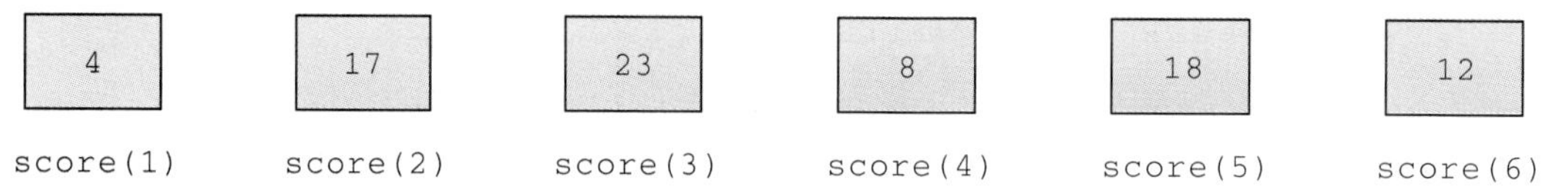

4	17	23	8	18	12
score(1)	score(2)	score(3)	score(4)	score(5)	score(6)

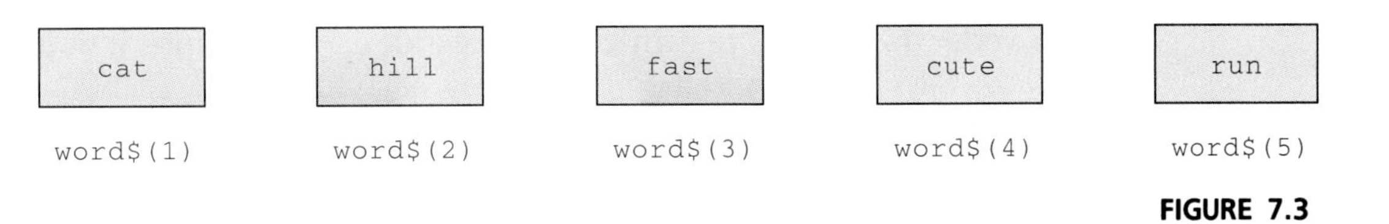

FIGURE 7.3

A String Array

through *name$(45)*, and to initialize them all to the "empty string," that is, the string with no characters in it.

We should remark here that a commonly used variation of the DIM statement explicitly states only the *highest* index, and the compiler *assumes a lowest index of 0*. Hence, the statement

```
DIM itemNum(25)
```

will cause a numeric array with 26 locations, labelled *itemNum(0)*, *itemNum(1)*, and so on through *itemNum(25)*, to be created. Though you will see this variation elsewhere, in this text we shall follow the practice of always explicitly stating both the lowest and highest indices.

The DIM statement permits you to use *variables* or *arithmetic expressions* inside the parentheses. For example, the following segment is perfectly "legal":

```
INPUT "How many names do you have? ", howMany
DIM name$(1 TO howMany)
```

When you declare an array this way, that is, with a variable or expression for the highest and/or lowest index, it is called a **dynamic array**. Dynamic means "changing," that is, the size of the array can change from one run of the program to the next. If, on the other hand, the lowest and highest indices are both constants, then the array is said to be a **static array**; its size does *not* change from run to run. Dynamic array dimensioning has the advantage of setting up the right number of locations each time but the disadvantage (for our purposes usually slight) of the program taking more time to run, since the array gets set up while the program is running. You should use whichever method seems best in a given situation.

Once you have declared an array using the DIM statement, you can then use the individual locations of the array in exactly the way you use simple variables. For example, if you have declared an array by the statement

```
DIM price(1 TO 20)
```

thus setting up 20 numeric variables labelled *price(1)* through *price(20)*, you can have statements like

```
INPUT price(1), price(2)
LET price(3) = price(2) + price(1)
PRINT "The total is: $", price(3)
```

However, you will usually use arrays in conjunction with *loops*. This is because the power of arrays lies in their ability to store lots of data under a single name with a changing index. For example, if you want to store 20 prices in memory, all you have to say is:

```
FOR item = 1 TO 20
    INPUT price(item)
NEXT item
```

Very handy! And if there are 20,000 prices instead of 20 (say you're working for the nationwide OK-Mart), the code is just as simple:

```
DIM price(1 TO 20000)

FOR item = 1 TO 20000
    INPUT price(item)
NEXT item
```

(Of course, with *this* much data you wouldn't want to use the standard INPUT statement. You would either use the READ and DATA statements or an input file—see Chapter 8.)

Now, it's time to look at our new tool in action. The three examples that follow each use arrays in a different but essential way.

EXAMPLE 2

In Programming Problem 3 of Chapter 5, you were to write a program that read the names and sticker prices of different models of automobiles and then allowed the user to pick a price range and see which models were in that range. Suppose you wanted to allow the user to pick *more than one range*. Without the ability to store and hold the data in memory, you would have to keep *rereading* the data, that is, you would need the RESTORE statement. Now, you have a better way—the use of arrays! You can store the data in arrays, once and for all; then it's available for as many searches as are desired. Let's write an algorithm for this, assuming that, at most, 20 models are listed.

LEVEL-1 ALGORITHM

1. Store all the model names and prices in memory
2. Introduce the program to the user
3. Repeat the following:
    a. Find out the desired price range
    b. Search the list of prices for cars in that range, printing out the ones that are
    c. Ask the user if another range is desired

   Until the user wants to quit

The algorithm isn't too complicated: we need two arrays—one a string, the other numeric—to hold the data. These arrays—which we can call *name$* and *price*—are examples of *parallel arrays,* because looked at index by index they represent different attributes of some common item. For example, *name$(1)* and *price(1)* have as values the name and price of the first car in our list, *name$(2)* and *price(2)* the name and price of the second car, and so on. Parallel arrays pop up quite often, so take a moment to make sure you understand this idea.

We also need *counter, howMany, highPrice, lowPrice*, and *again$* for the "Do you want to go again?" question. We'll use a trailer to signal the end of the data and read it in with a DO...LOOP. Let's refine our algorithm.

LEVEL-2 ALGORITHM

Parallel arrays: *name$*(1 to 20), *price*(1 to 20)
Variables: *counter, howMany, highPrice, lowPrice, again$*

1. Repeat:
    a. Increment *counter*
    b. Read each *name$(counter)* and *price(counter)*

   Until the trailer is reached
2. Introduce the program
3. Repeat:
    a. Get *highPrice* and *lowPrice* from user
    b. For each *name$(counter)* and *price(counter)*:
        If *lowPrice* <= *price(counter)* <= *highPrice*
            Print *name$(counter)* and *price(counter)*
    c. Ask user if he or she wants to go again

   Until *answer$* is no

As always, it should be easy for us to write the program now, as below.

```
'-------------------------------------------------------------
'    Program title: C07EX02.BAS
'    Author:        Lee Iacocca
'    Date:          November 8, 1992

'    This program lets users find out which car models are
'    in their price range. DATA may contain at most 20 models and
'    should be followed with an EOD trailer.
'-------------------------------------------------------------

'Declare the arrays and read the data into them.

     DIM name$(1 TO 20), price(1 TO 20)

     LET counter = 0
     DO
            READ word$
            IF word$ = "EOD" THEN
                   EXIT DO
```

```
              ELSE
                     LET counter = counter + 1
                     LET name$(counter) = word$
                     READ price(counter)
              END IF
       LOOP

       LET howMany = counter

  'Data section: limit of 20 models (name, price);
  'last data item must be "EOD".

       DATA Ford Festiva, 8150, Ford Tempo, 10600, Geo Prism, 9789
       DATA Chevy Malibu, 12564, Dodge Colt, 8794, Yugo, 4800
       DATA Buick Regal, 15799, Buick Skylark, 9501, Subaru GL, 11788
       DATA Nissan Stanza, 12458, Hyundai Excel, 6800
       DATA EOD

  'Introduce the program.

       CLS
       PRINT "           Welcome to AUTOLIST"
       PRINT
       PRINT "If you type in your desired price range, we will"
       PRINT "be glad to list the current models that are"
       PRINT "in that range."
       PRINT

  'Get the desired range and search the list for the autos that
  'are in that range.

       DO
              INPUT "Type in your upper limit --> $", highPrice
              INPUT "Type in your lower limit --> $", lowPrice
              PRINT
              PRINT "Here are the models in this price range:"
              PRINT
              PRINT "MODEL",, "LIST PRICE"
              PRINT
              FOR counter = 1 TO howMany
                     LET thisPrice = price(counter)
                     IF (thisPrice >= lowPrice) AND (thisPrice <= highPrice) THEN
                            PRINT name$(counter),, thisPrice
                     END IF
              NEXT counter
              PRINT
              INPUT "Want to put in a new range? ", again$
       LOOP UNTIL UCASE$(LEFT$(again$, 1)) = "N"

       PRINT
       PRINT "Have a nice day!"

  END
```

Sample output might be:

```
        Welcome to AUTOLIST

If you type in your desired price range, we will
be glad to list the current models that are
in that range.

Type in your upper limit --> $10000
Type in your lower limit --> $7000

Here are the models in this price range:

MODEL                    LIST PRICE

Ford Festiva              8150
Geo Prism                 9789
Dodge Colt                8794
Buick Skylark             9501

Want to put in a new range? yes

Type in your upper limit --> $6000
Type in your lower limit --> $4000

Here are the models in this price range:

MODEL                    LIST PRICE

Yugo                      4800

Want to put in a new range? no thanks

Have a nice day!
```

Arrays are the perfect tool for this program, since we want to hold onto the data to allow the user to ask repeated questions about it. We enter the data into the computer's main memory once and for all at the beginning of the program—then it's there for us to use throughout the rest of the program. What we actually do to the data in this program is *search* it for certain items; we will have more to say about this extremely common task in the next section.

We have one other minor comment about this program. In the FOR...NEXT loop near the end of the program, notice that we have the following line:

```
LET thisPrice = price(counter)
```

This line essentially "renames" the variable *price(counter)*. Why would we bother to do this? The reason can be found in the next line of the program (the IF line); the condition in this line is so long that we need a shorter variable name to make the line fit on the screen. The first thing needed for a readable program is a *visible* program!

Once students learn about arrays, they often come to believe that they need to use them in every program they write. This is *not* true! You've read and written many programs that don't require their use. So, here is a rule of thumb for using arrays:

> ***You should store a list of data in an array if your task requires you to hold on to that list. Examples of such tasks are repeated searches through the list and rearrangements of the list. You do* not *need to use an array if the task allows each data item to be processed and then "thrown away." Examples of such tasks are finding a sum, finding an average, and doing a single search.***

Now, let's look at an example where we use an array to keep track of several different counts. The example also illustrates the usefulness of being able to start the indexing wherever we want.

EXAMPLE 3

This time, our data consists of the daily low temperature recorded in Nome, Alaska, for each day in the first quarter of 1989. We know that these lows were always in the range −20 degrees to 20 degrees. Our task is to print out a frequency table, that is, for each temperature in the range, we must list how many times it occurred as the low.

Notice that we only need to do *one* search through the data, so *it* need not be stored in an array. However, we need to keep track of 41 counts! (Why, you ask? Because there are 41 temperatures between −20 and 20 inclusive.) An excellent way to do this is to create *an array of counters*, one for each temperature. Let's write an algorithm for doing that.

LEVEL-1 ALGORITHM

1. Declare and initialize to 0 an array of 41 counters, one for each possible temperature
2. Read through the list of temperatures, each time increasing by one the counter that has that particular temperature as its index
3. Print out a table with the results, showing only those temperatures that occurred at least once

We'll need variables *temperature* and *day* and an array *count( )*, of which *temperature* will be the index. One more important point comes up here. If a temperature typed into the DATA statement falls out of the range −20 to 20, the attempt to increase the corresponding counter will cause the run-time error "Subscript Out of Range" (for example, we can't increment *count(21)* since there *is* no *count(21)*!). For this reason, we should definitely include an error trap (see Section

5.4), which will sift out such data; in fact, let's include a counter *outCount*, which keeps track of how many stray data items there are. We're now ready to refine.

LEVEL-2 ALGORITHM

Arrays: *count*(−20 to 20)
Variables: *day, temperature, outCount*

1. Declare *count* and for each *temperature* from −20 to 20 set *count(temperature)* to 0 (one DIM statement will do all this)
2. For each *day* (1 to 90):
   a. Read the *temperature*
   b. If temperature is in the proper range then
      Increase that *count(temperature)* by one
   Otherwise
      Increase *outCount* by one
3. Print a table heading and then for each *temperature*:
   If *count(temperature)* > 0 then
      Print *temperature* and *count(temperature)*
4. Finally, print the number of data items that were out of range.

We're now ready to write the program.

```
'--------------------------------------------------------------
'    Program title: C07EX03.BAS
'    Author:        Willard Scott
'    Date:          May 23, 1989

'    Prints a frequency table of the daily low temperatures in
'    Nome, Alaska, during Jan-March 1989 (program assumes that
'    all temperatures lie between -20 and 20 and keeps track of
'    the number of DATA items that are out of range).
'--------------------------------------------------------------

'Declare and initialize the count array and the out-of-range counter.

    DIM count(-20 TO 20)
    LET outCount = 0

'Read the temperatures and keep count of the frequencies.

    FOR day = 1 TO 90
            READ temperature
            IF (temperature >= -20) AND (temperature <= 20) THEN
                    LET count(temperature) = count(temperature) + 1
            ELSE
                    LET outCount = outCount + 1
            END IF
    NEXT day
```

```
'Print out the table of results. Split output into two sections
'and stop screen scrolling in the middle for readability.

     CLS
     PRINT "1st QUARTER 1989 DAILY LOWS - NOME, ALASKA"
     PRINT
     PRINT "TEMPERATURE", , "FREQUENCY"
     PRINT

     FOR temperature = -20 TO 0
            IF count(temperature) > 0 THEN
                   PRINT temperature, , count(temperature)
            END IF
     NEXT temperature

     INPUT "Press Enter to continue", go$
     FOR temperature = 1 TO 20
            IF count(temperature) > 0 THEN
                   Print temperature, , count(temperature)
            END IF
     NEXT temperature

     IF outCount > 0 THEN
            PRINT
            PRINT outCount; "temperatures out of the range -20 to 20."
     END IF

'Data Section

     DATA -12,-15,-20,-12,-5,-5,0,4,6,3,8,-1,-4,-12,0,8,12,11
     DATA 4,1,-4,-12,-18,-20,-21,-19,-15,-12,-10,-6,-6,-10,0,4
     DATA 8,7,8,12,15,15,10,12,7,0,-5,-4,-2,-9,-15,-20,-17,-13
     DATA -6,-3,0,0,7,12,13,9,12,18,20,14,12,6,0,4,-3,-2,-12
     DATA -6,-1,5,12,13,20,23,20,18,12,7,15,14,20,18,19,20,15,12

END
```

With this data, the output would be:

```
1st QUARTER 1989 DAILY LOWS - NOME, ALASKA

TEMPERATURE                 FREQUENCY

-20                         3
-19                         1
-18                         1
-17                         1
```

```
 .
 .
 .
 18                3
 19                1
 20                5

 2 temperatures out of the range -20 to 20.
```

There is one section in the program that wasn't in our algorithm but instead was a result of our debugging session: if we didn't manually stop it, the top part of our table scrolled off the screen before we had a chance to read it. Seeing this, we decided to add "Press Enter to continue" somewhere near the middle of the table. Remember, just about every program you ever write will give you a few surprises when you run it, and you'll have to go back and make the necessary adjustments.

We'll end this section with a simulation.

EXAMPLE 4

Let's write a program that simulates drawing one playing card from a standard deck. If you wrote this program earlier (in Programming Problem 10 of Chapter 3), you certainly found that you needed long SELECT...CASE or IF...END IF statements to print out the correct words (e.g., "2 of Clubs," "King of Diamonds," etc.). A better way to proceed is to store the 13 "face values" in one array and the 4 "suits" in another. If we do this, we won't need any decision structures at all! Let's write an algorithm.

1. Declare two string arrays *value$( )* and *suit$( )* and read the names into them
2. Introduce the program and generate two random numbers, one between 1 and 13 and the other between 1 and 4
3. Write the value and suit associated with those two random numbers

We'll need two arrays *value$*(1 to 13) and *suit$*(1 to 4), a *counter* for the reading-in loop, and two numeric variables for the two random numbers. Let's go ahead with it!

```
'-------------------------------------------------------------
'     Program Title:  C07EX04.BAS
'     Author:         Edmond Hoyle
'     Date:           January 15, 1991

'     Simulates the drawing of one card from a standard deck.
'-------------------------------------------------------------
```

```
'Declare the arrays and read the names into them.

     DIM value$(1 TO 13), suit$(1 TO 4)

     FOR counter = 1 TO 13
         READ value$(counter)
     NEXT counter
     FOR counter = 1 TO 4
         READ suit$(counter)
     NEXT counter

'Data Section.

     DATA Ace,2,3,4,5,6,7,8,9,10,Jack,Queen,King
     DATA Spades,Hearts,Diamonds,Clubs

'Introduce program and generate two random numbers.

     RANDOMIZE TIMER
     CLS
     PRINT "Get ready to draw a card!"
     PRINT
     INPUT "Press Enter when you're ready. ", go$
     LET vIndex = INT(13 * RND) + 1
     LET sIndex = INT(4 * RND) + 1

'Print out the answer.

     PRINT
     PRINT "You drew the "; value$(vIndex); " of "; suit$(sIndex); "."

END
```

An output might be:

```
Get ready to draw a card!

Press Enter when you're ready.

You drew the King of Hearts.
```

Of course, this program can be jazzed up considerably. Drawing one card is not of much interest; drawing 5 or 13 can be. See Programming Problem 7 at the end of this chapter.

Two of the most important uses of arrays are the searching and sorting of data. We take a close look at these two tasks in the next section.

PRACTICE 7.2

1. Describe exactly what the compiler does when it encounters each of the following statements:
   (a) `DIM price(1 TO 25)`
   (b) `DIM lastName$(1 TO 1000)`
   (c) `DIM num(-100 TO 100)`
2. What is the output of the following program segment?

```
DIM num(1 TO 5)
DIM word$(1 TO 5)

FOR item = 1 TO 5
    READ num(item), word$(item)
NEXT item

PRINT word$(4); num(2); word$(1)

DATA 7, sale, 4, zoo, 12, dog, 5, auto, 3, tree
```

3. Write a program that takes in 20 numbers from the keyboard and then prints out every other one in reverse order (i.e., it prints out the last, then the third from the last, etc.).

7.3 Searching and Sorting

In the last section, we saw that one-dimensional arrays are a natural way to store lists of numbers or strings. Once a list has been stored in an array, it can be **searched** and **sorted**, that is, *search* for an item in the list or *sort* the list into order (increasing, decreasing, alphabetical, etc.). Computer scientists have estimated that these two tasks may account for at least 25% of *all* computer time used in the world today! It shouldn't come as a surprise, then, that the development of efficient algorithms to search and sort lists has been important to programming and has generated a great number of exciting new ideas in computer science. Let's learn a little about some of these ideas now.

Searching and sorting algorithms generally fall into two categories: *elementary algorithms,* which correspond to simple, intuitive methods, and *advanced algorithms,* which arise out of more inventive approaches. The advantage of the elementary algorithms is that, being relatively simple, they are fairly easy to program and debug. The advanced algorithms are usually trickier to program and debug, but they are much more efficient, that is, they will do the same job in considerably less time. Elementary algorithms are called for if the lists they apply to are reasonably short, so that running time is not an issue. If one wants to search or sort a long list, efficiency becomes crucial, and it's worth the trouble to program one of the more advanced algorithms.

Searching

In this section, we'll discuss a few elementary algorithms in detail, and we'll also say a little about more advanced algorithms. Let's start with *searching*.

Suppose you were handed a pile of student exams and were asked to find the one by Mary Smith. You probably would simply look through the exams, from first to last, until you found Mary Smith's exam or reached the bottom of the pile. This is the essence of the simplest search algorithm, called **Linear Search**.

The general problem we want to solve is: given a list (of numbers, strings, or whatever) and given an item to search for in that list, determine whether the item appears in the list and, if so, where it appears. The Linear Search algorithm consists of comparing the item to each entry on the list, starting with the first entry and continuing until either the item is found or the end of the list is reached. This algorithm can be implemented using a DO...LOOP, assuming that we have a list of numbers already stored in an array called *numList( ),* which is indexed from 1 to *howMany*. After this program segment is executed, the variable *position* will have the value 0 if the item has not been found; but if the item *is* found, *position* will contain the first position of the item in the list. Look at the following segment carefully:

```
LET position = 0
LET count = 0
DO
    LET count = count + 1
    IF item = numList(count) THEN
        LET position = count
        EXIT DO
    ELSEIF count = howMany THEN
        EXIT DO
    END IF
LOOP
```

Linear Search is quite simple to program. Notice that as the list grows in length, the search will take longer. For a list with *n* entries, we may have to do as little as one comparison (if *item* matches the first entry) or as many as *n* comparisons (if *item* either matches the last entry or isn't found). Thus, on average, a successful search will require about $n/2$ comparisons, whereas an unsuccessful search will require *n* comparisons.

In fact, we've done linear searches previously in this text. As long ago as Example 2 in Chapter 3, when we searched for the top scores on a math test, the algorithm was Linear Search. Remember the telephone information service (Examples 5 and 6 in Chapter 5)? Again, the method was Linear Search. This algorithm is very natural to use under many circumstances.

While Linear Search is the only search algorithm we'll look at in detail, notice that it is *not* the algorithm that most of us would use to search through really *long* lists, like the list of names and numbers in a phone book. In that case, and knowing that the names are *in order*, we're more likely to begin our search in the middle (i.e., open the phone book somewhere in the middle) and move about halfway forwards or backwards, depending upon how close we are to the item of our search, and continue this process until we find what we're looking for. Again, notice that this technique depends on the list being *in order*—a condition that is frequently true of lists such as phone books, dictionaries, and the like.

The technique of starting in the middle and repeatedly moving halfway forwards or backwards until the item is found (or determined not to be in the list) is called the **Binary Search** algorithm—"binary" because we keep chopping the list in half. Binary Search is a "divide-and-conquer" technique, which means that we accomplish our search by dividing the data in half, then dividing that half in half, and so on. It is somewhat more difficult to program and so is not worth the bother for short lists, but its increased efficiency makes it an important tool for searching long, ordered lists. On average, the Binary Search algorithm requires about log(n) comparisons for a list of n elements, whether or not the item is in the list. (In fact, the particular logarithm here is $\log_2(n)$, the "base-2" logarithm; 2 is the proper base, since we are cutting the list in half each time.) If you're not familiar with logarithms, the table below shows some sample values to help you compare the efficiency of Linear Search and Binary Search.

n	$n/2$	$\log(n)$
25	12.5	4.64
2,500	1,250	11.29
25,000	12,500	14.61

Thus, a typical (successful) search for a name in the Saratoga Springs, New York, telephone book, which has about 25,000 entries, would require more than 12,000 comparisons using Linear Search; the same search using Binary Search would require about 15! How's *that* for a difference?

Coding Binary Search into a programming language can be a bit tricky, and we won't go into the details here. However, we can certainly write a level-1 algorithm for it and let you take it from there.

BINARY SEARCH

Given: A sorted list of data and a particular data item, called the "search item."

Task: Find the position of an occurrence in the list of the search item, or report that it is not in the list.

Procedure:

Repeat:

1. Look at a list item that lies at or near the center of the (remaining) list.
2. Compare this list item with the search item. If the search item is the list item, you are done. If the search item precedes the list item in the order of the list, restrict your search to the part of the (remaining) list preceding the list item. If the search item lies after the list item, restrict your search to the part of the (remaining) list following the list item.

Until the search item is located or the entire list has been checked unsuccessfully.

One final word before moving on to sorting algorithms. Computer scientists use the word **complexity** to describe the approximate number of steps a program takes to complete its task in terms of the number n of data items it is processing. For example, we saw above that if we are searching through n items, Linear Search takes, on average, about $n/2$ steps, whereas Binary Search takes, on average, about $\log(n)$ steps. People say, then, that "Linear Search is an $n/2$ algorithm" whereas "Binary Search is a $\log(n)$ algorithm." Since the value of $\log(n)$ is less than the value of $n/2$, Binary Search will, in general, run more quickly than Linear Search.

The issue of algorithm complexity does not loom large when you are a beginning programmer. However, as you progress and the problems you deal with become harder, the complexities of your algorithms become more and more crucial.

Sorting

Now, let's turn our attention to *sorting*. Clearly, putting a pile of exams into order (by grade or name) is a more complicated task than finding the exam of a particular student. It shouldn't be surprising then that algorithms for sorting are generally more complex than algorithms for searching. We will describe two *elementary* sorting algorithms in detail; we'll also compare their efficiency (i.e., complexity) with the efficiency of *advanced* sorting algorithms.

Almost all sorting algorithms, elementary or advanced, require that we swap entries in the list to put it into order. For example, if we have a string array whose five entries are B, A, C, D, E, then swapping the first and second entries would bring the list into alphabetical order. We have seen before (e.g., in Example 4 of Chapter 3) that to do this we need a *third*, temporary location. For example, if we want to swap the values in array locations *list(1)* and *list(2)*, we use a location *temp*:

```
LET temp = list(1)
LET list(1) = list(2)
LET list(2) = temp
```

Now, for the general problem. Given a list, *sort it into some order* that makes sense in terms of the entries—usually increasing or decreasing for numbers and alphabetical for strings. As you'll see, both of the sorting algorithms we'll describe are based on a sequence of steps that brings at least one entry into its proper position in the list. This sequence is then repeated until *all* entries have been put into their proper position, that is, until the list is completely sorted.

The first algorithm, **Selection Sort**, is one that many people might use intuitively to sort a pile of exams into order (for illustration, assume we are sorting the exams into increasing order by grade—lowest grade at the beginning, highest grade at the end). We start by looking through the pile for the exam with the lowest grade. When we find it, we put it at the beginning. If we were doing this in QuickBASIC, with the exam grades in an array, we would swap the lowest grade with the grade in the first position. Then, the first position would have the correct entry, but the rest of the list would still be unsorted. If we repeat this process on the remaining, unsorted portion of the list, we'll bring the second entry into its correct position. If we continue, each time repeating the process on the portion of the list that remains unsorted, eventually we will have the whole list in order. See Figure 7.4 for an example using a list of five grades; on each line, we show the next pair of entries to be swapped (in this example, though, there is no swap needed in either the third or fifth line).

FIGURE 7.4

Example of Selection Sort

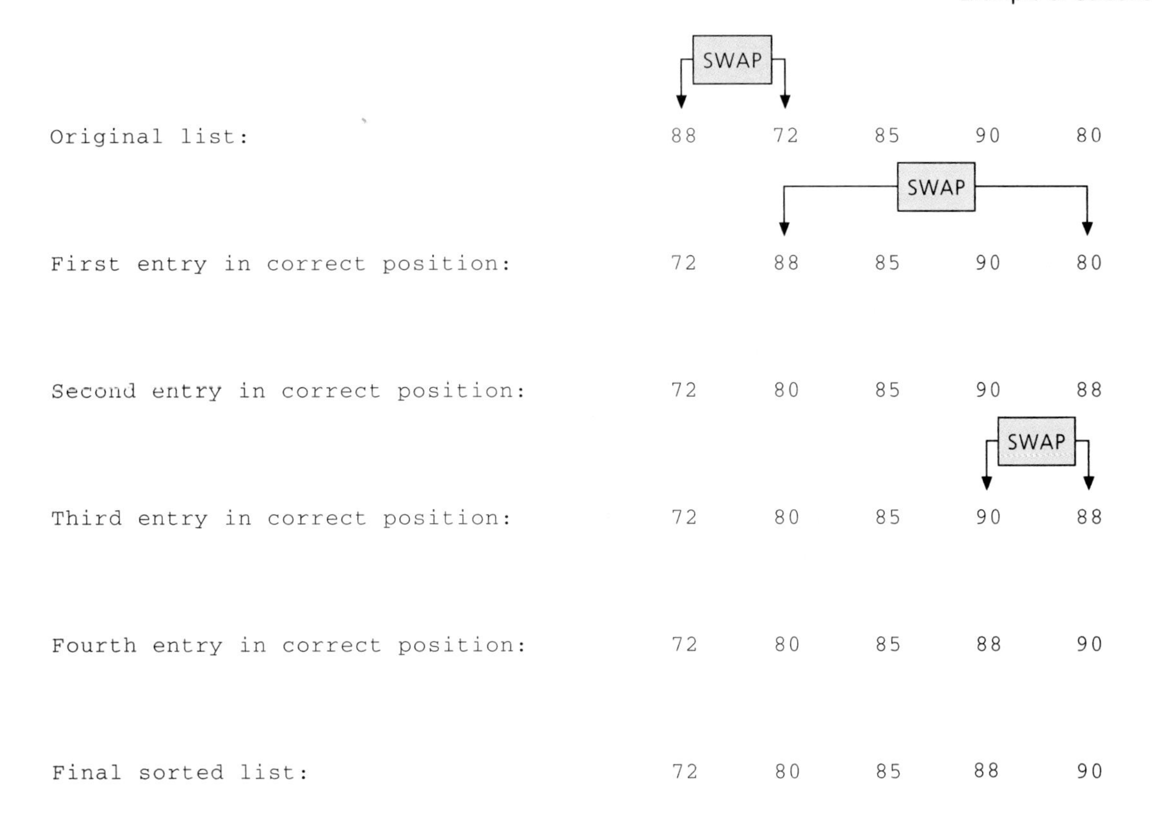

Thus, each stage requires scanning all the entries that remain, finding the smallest one, and swapping it with the first entry (in that portion of the list) to put it in its correct place. This is done using a loop. We repeat this process until we have used up the entire list—hence, we need *nested loops*. Notice, by the way, that once we have the next-to-last entry in its correct position (the fourth entry in the example above), the last entry will be in the correct place, too—there's no other place left! Let's write a Selection Sort algorithm.

SELECTION SORT

For each starting position (from left to second from right):

a. For each remaining position to the right,
   check if that position holds the smallest data item so far; if so, "remember" that position
b. Swap the values in the starting position and the position holding the smallest data item

Here is a QuickBASIC implementation of the Selection Sort algorithm:

```
FOR startPos = 1 TO howMany - 1
    LET smallPos = startPos
    FOR currentPos = startPos + 1 TO howMany
        IF numList(currentPos) < numList(smallPos) THEN
            LET smallPos = currentPos
        END IF
    NEXT currentPos
    LET temp = numList(startPos)
    LET numList(startPos) = numList(smallPos)
    LET numList(smallPos) = temp
NEXT startPos
```

Read through this carefully to make sure you understand what's going on. Even though this algorithm is "elementary," it requires some attention in order to understand it.

Although searching requires comparisons only, sorting requires both comparisons and swaps. To assess the efficiency of sorting algorithms, we can estimate their complexity, which now includes both comparison steps and swapping steps. For Selection Sort, it's easy to see that there is at most one swap for each position except the last—so for a list of n elements, there will be, at most, $n - 1$ swaps. It is harder to count the number of comparisons, since at each stage we do roughly as many comparisons as there are entries on the remaining portion of the list. One can show that the total number of comparisons is approximately $n^2/2$. Thus, for example, to sort a list with 10 entries using this algorithm will require about 9 swaps and 50 comparisons.

The other elementary sorting algorithm we'll describe is called **Bubble Sort**, because entries tend to "bubble" to their correct place —unlike Selection Sort, where they are put there directly. The basic idea of Bubble Sort involves repetition of the following process: move through the list from beginning to end comparing *adjacent pairs* of entries and swap them if they are not in the correct order. Let's carry out this process on the list from the last example (see Figure 7.5).

As you can see, the list is not yet sorted—80 and 88 are out of order. Are any entries *guaranteed* to be in the correct position? Yes! Notice that entries (like 88) keep getting moved to the right until they are compared with a bigger entry. Thus, the biggest entry is guaranteed to be moved all the way to the end of the list—its correct position. Therefore, one stage of Bubble Sort, like one stage of Selection Sort, is sure to bring at least one entry to its correct position, namely, the last position. To be sure that all the entries arrive at their correct positions, we repeat the process on the remaining list until finally all entries are in their correct positions. Here is a QuickBASIC implementation of Bubble Sort:

```
FOR lastPos = howMany TO 2 STEP -1
    FOR currentPos = 1 TO lastPos - 1
        IF numList(currentPos + 1) < numList(currentPos) THEN
            LET temp = numList(currentPos)
            LET numList(currentPos) = numList(currentPos + 1)
            LET numList(currentPos + 1) = temp
        END IF
    NEXT currentPos
NEXT lastPos
```

Even though Bubble Sort *looks* simpler than Selection Sort, let's examine it for complexity—how many comparisons and swaps does *it* require? As in Selection Sort, we repeatedly look at lists that have one less entry each time. And, again as in Selection Sort, we do roughly as many comparisons as there are entries in the remaining portion of the list, for a total of about $n^2/2$ comparisons. There are, however, *many*

FIGURE 7.5

Example of Bubble Sort

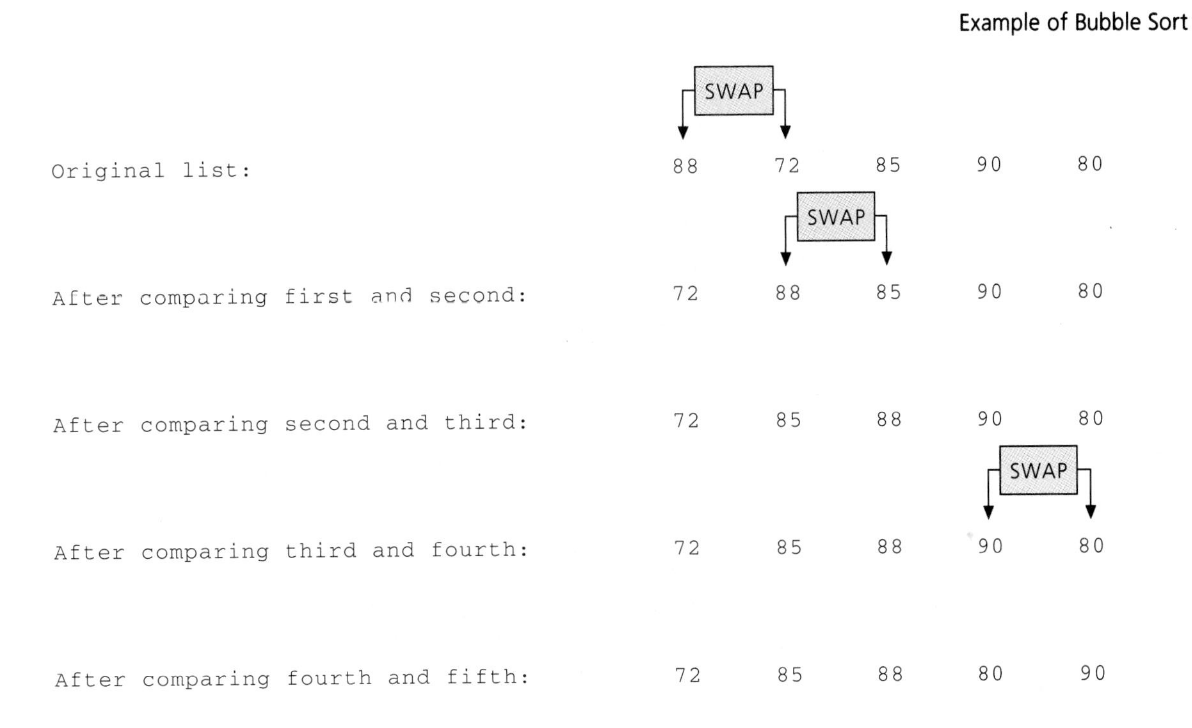

more swaps, since an entry is never moved more than one position to the left or right in any one swap. In fact, if you look at the IF...END IF segment above, you'll see that each comparison may result in a swap if the entries are out of order. Thus, there may be as many as $n^2/2$ swaps in Bubble Sort, compared with $n - 1$, at most, for Selection Sort. Hence, in general, Bubble Sort takes more steps than Selection Sort to complete its work.

EXAMPLE 5

The QuickBASIC program C07EX05.BAS on the SAMPLES disk lets you watch these two sorting techniques in action and compare their performance. Try it out!

Most advanced sorting algorithms use divide-and-conquer techniques, similar to the idea underlying the Binary Search algorithm—repeatedly cut the size of the list in half, sorting as you go. These advanced algorithms (e.g., Quick Sort, Merge Sort, Heap Sort, and others) all cut the number of comparisons required for a typical list to approximately $n \log(n)$, compared with $n^2/2$ for the elementary sorting algorithms. Depending on the particular algorithm and the particular list, the number of swaps required ranges from about n (as in Selection Sort) to about $n \log(n)$. Since as n gets larger $n^2/2$ grows much more rapidly than either n or $n \log(n)$, the reduced number of comparisons makes the advanced algorithms substantially faster for long lists. Below is a table comparing n, $n \log(n)$, and n^2; the values of $n \log(n)$ are rounded to the nearest integer.

n	n^2	$n \log(n)$
25	625	116
2,500	6,250,000	28,219
25,000	625,000,000	365,241

To get a sense of the relative size of these numbers, let's consider units of a millionth of a second. Then, 625,000,000 corresponds to 625 seconds or a little over 10 minutes. In contrast, 365,241 corresponds to less than half a second. If each comparison takes a millionth of a second, the elementary sorts will spend about 5 minutes doing comparisons on a list with 25,000 entries, whereas the advanced sorts will use less than a second (the complete programs do more than just compare, so the total times will be longer). Remember that these differences in efficiency only become noticeable for long lists. Thus, it would not make sense to program one of the (fairly tricky) advanced sorting algorithms for a list of 25 numbers—but it *would* make sense for a list of 2,500 numbers, not to mention lists like the New York City phone book with its 5 million or so entries!

EXAMPLE 6

A nifty program on your SAMPLES disk, C07EX06.BAS, uses graphics and sound to allow you to watch various different sorting techniques do their job (this program is written by the Microsoft Corporation).

Definitely run it and watch! Two remarks: First, Selection Sort is referred to as "Exchange Sort"; second, try to get a color monitor to watch this program (it's more fun!).

We've probably said enough about searching and sorting for now. Although this section has perhaps been a bit more technical than most of the others, concepts such as program efficiency, complexity, and binary (divide-and-conquer) algorithms are important for you to start thinking about, now that you're no longer a beginner. Next, we shall look at another important object: the multidimensional array.

PRACTICE 7.3

1. Play a secret number guessing game. Have a friend of yours pick a number between 1 and 30 and you try to guess it in no more than five guesses. Using a binary (i.e., divide-and-conquer) searching technique, you *should* always be able to get it in five guesses. Try this game a few times (verbally or with paper and pencil—*don't* write a program).

   Now, try the game with the new numbers listed below.

Friend picks number between 1 and	You guess it in at most
100	7 guesses
500	9 guesses
1,000	10 guesses
10,000	14 guesses

   Have fun! Think about how this last search would go if you used Linear Search ("Is it 1? . . . Is it 2? . . ."). This game will probably impress you with the amazing efficiency of binary algorithms.

2. Sort ("by hand") the set of numbers below from lowest to highest using two algorithms: Selection Sort and Bubble Sort. Show the new order after each swap.

   34 23 56 7 24 13 21 37

   For example, using Selection Sort, your first two lines should be:

   ```
   34  23  56   7  24  13  21  37
    7  23  56  34  24  13  21  37
   ```

3. Try to imagine, in rough outline only, how you might design a binary sorting algorithm. It might help to watch Quick Sort, Heap Sort, or Merge Sort while running the program C07EX06.BAS on your SAMPLES disk.

7.4 Multidimensional Arrays

All the arrays we've looked at so far have been *one-dimensional*, that is, each has been a *list* of data items that we keep track of by using a *single index*. But not all data can be easily organized into a list, so we

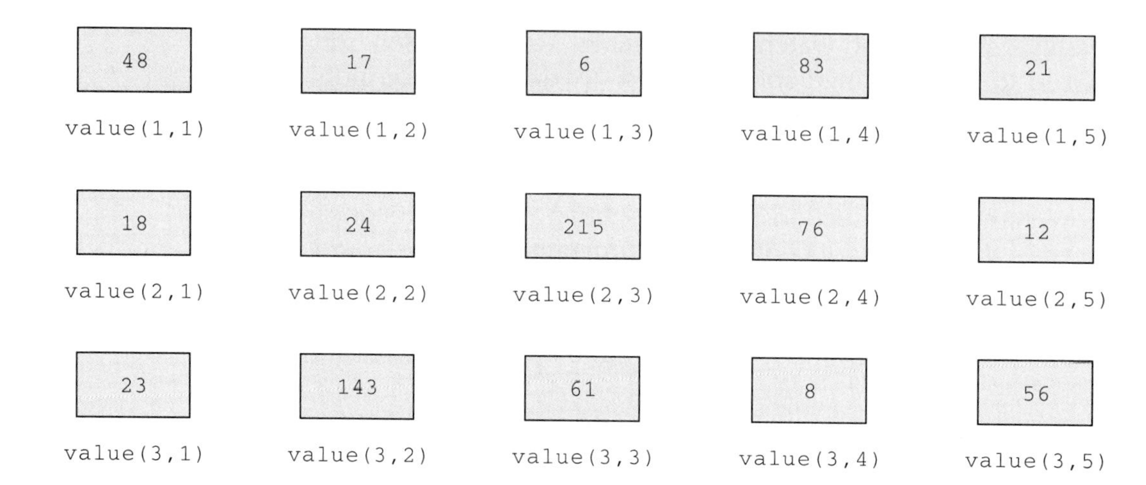

FIGURE 7.6

A Two-Dimensional Numeric Array

may want to use an array in which each data item has two, or three, or maybe even more indices. Figure 7.6 displays a two-dimensional numeric array called *value( )*, with three rows and five columns of numbers, which was set up using the following statement:

```
DIM value(1 TO 3, 1 TO 5)
```

Of course, a two-dimensional array can hold string data just as well. Figure 7.7 displays a string array *word$( )* with two rows and four columns, which was set up using the following statement:

```
DIM word$(1 TO 2, 1 TO 4)
```

FIGURE 7.7

A Two-Dimensional String Array

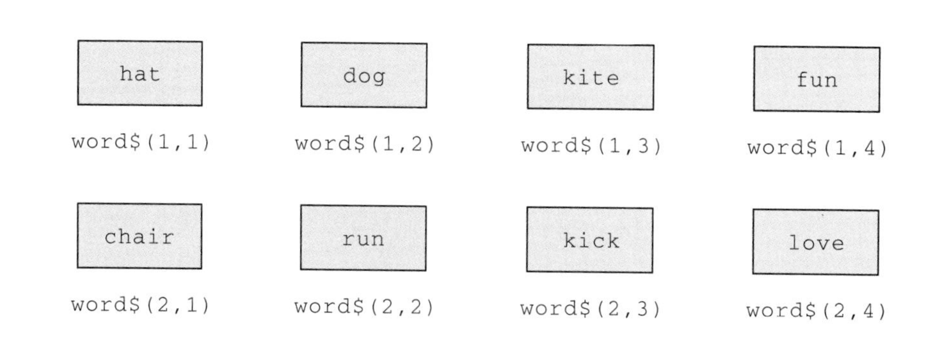

EXAMPLE 7

As a simple first example, let's compute, store in memory, and then print out a *multiplication table* for the numbers 0 through 9. Since this data is in the form of a table, the natural data structure for storing it is a *two-dimensional array,* indexed by the two numbers being multiplied. Thus, we will want to make a declaration something like:

```
DIM mult(0 TO 9, 0 TO 9)
```

Since the idea here is pretty straightforward, let's go ahead with the QuickBASIC code, as below.

```
'-----------------------------------------------------------------
'     Program title: C07EX07.BAS
'     Author:        Isaac Newton
'     Date:          March 23, 1991

'     Computes, stores in a two-dimensional array, and then prints
'     out a multiplication table for the numbers from 0 to 9.
'-----------------------------------------------------------------

'Declare two-dimensional array and then compute and store its entries.

     DIM mult(0 TO 9, 0 TO 9)

     FOR firstNum = 0 TO 9
            FOR secondNum = 0 TO 9
                   LET mult(firstNum, secondNum) = firstNum * secondNum
            NEXT secondNum
     NEXT firstNum

'Print out the table with headings.

     CLS
     PRINT "    MULTIPLICATION TABLE"
     PRINT "    ===================="
     PRINT
     PRINT "X   0   1   2   3   4   5   6   7   8   9"
     PRINT
     FOR firstNum = 0 TO 9
            PRINT firstnum; "   ";
            FOR secondNum = 0 TO 9
                   PRINT mult(firstNum, secondNum);
                   IF mult(firstNum, secondNum) < 10 THEN
                          PRINT " ";
                   END IF
            NEXT secondNum
            PRINT
     NEXT firstnum

END
```

Notice that one little complication in this program is lining up the columns of the table properly; that's why the IF...END IF block is needed in the last loop. QuickBASIC has a statement called PRINT USING, which makes lining up columns much easier—see Section 9.2.

Now, let's look at a somewhat more involved example that uses a two-dimensional array.

EXAMPLE 8

Suppose you are the treasurer for a fundraising drive that will last two weeks. One of your jobs is to keep track, each day for the next 14 days, of the money that comes in from each of eight different sources. This data organizes itself naturally into a table with, say, 8 columns (one for each source) and 14 rows (one for each day); so, again, we can use QuickBASIC to store and analyze this data in a two-dimensional array, that is, an array with two indices, one for the day and one for the source. The declaration of the array will look like:

```
DIM income(1 TO 14, 1 TO 8)
```

Notice that Day 1 has eight sources associated with it, Day 2 has another eight sources, and so on. For example, then, reading the data in from DATA statements will involve *nested loops*:

```
FOR day = 1 TO 14
    FOR source = 1 TO 8
        READ income(day, source)
    NEXT source
NEXT day
```

Building on this idea, let's write a program that stores this data in a two-dimensional array and then allows users to compute a total for whichever row or column they desire. That is, if they want to know the total that came in from Source 5, they can find out; if they want to know how much money came in on Day 10, the program will tell them. Let's design an algorithm.

LEVEL-1 ALGORITHM

1. Read the data into an array that has two indices, one for *day* and one for *source*
2. Introduce the program
3. Ask the user whether she or he wants a sum for a particular day or a sum for a particular source
4. If a "day-sum" is wanted, then
    a. Find out which day
    b. Add up for that day over all sources
    c. Print out the answer

    But if a "source-sum" is wanted, then
    d. Find out which source
    e. Add up for that source over all days
    f. Print out the answer
5. Ask if another sum is wanted

Not too bad. We'll need the array *income( )* with the two indices *day* and *source*, the two variables *dayWanted* and *sourceWanted*, a *total*, and a string variable for the day or source choice and for the "Do you want to go again?" choice. So, let's refine.

LEVEL-2 ALGORITHM

Arrays: *income(1 TO 14, 1 TO 8)*
Variables: *day, source, dayWanted, sourceWanted, total, choice$*

1. For each *day* and *source*, read in *income(day, source)*
2. Introduce the program
3. Repeat:
   a. Print out a table showing the data
   b. Ask whether day or source is wanted
4. If day is wanted, then
   a. Find out *dayWanted*
   b. For each *source*
      get *total* of *income(dayWanted, source)*
   c. Print out *total*

   Otherwise
   d. Find out *sourceWanted*
   e. For each *day*
      get *total* of *income(sourceWanted, day)*
   f. Print out *total*
5. Ask "Do you want another sum?"

Before we write the program, we need to make one more observation. As is often a problem when using arrays, our program will produce the "Subscript Out of Range" run-time error if the user enters a number other than 1 through 14 for *dayWanted* or other than 1 through 8 for *sourceWanted.* Hence, an error trap is called for here. We have chosen to place it in the subprogram GetInput, which is then called twice by the main program.

```
'--------------------------------------------------------------
'     Program title: C07EX08.BAS
'     Author:        Jerry Lewis
'     Date:          Sept. 30, 1991
'
'     Prints out a table of money collected in the fund drive and
'     allows the user to compute totals over rows or columns.
'--------------------------------------------------------------

'Read the data into a two-dimensional array.

     DIM income(1 TO 14, 1 TO 8)
     FOR day = 1 TO 14
         FOR source = 1 TO 8
             READ income(day, source)
         NEXT source
     NEXT day
```

```
'Data Section (each line contains 2 days of income)

     DATA 23,12,34,17,10,25,40,16,21,26,55,12,34,45,16,42
     DATA 21,56,16,38,76,36,53,10,34,41,40,20,16,83,14,15
     DATA 45,56,83,34,12,36,45,41,18,27,63,41,49,51,12,16
     DATA 23,65,13,45,48,51,32,35,16,48,72,56,41,38,12,47
     DATA 48,23,28,12,18,82,34,67,81,47,31,26,17,25,56,42
     DATA 65,14,54,24,56,88,31,14,47,45,52,61,52,47,12,37
     DATA 24,55,84,44,19,87,35,36,17,42,54,21,48,39,55,38

'Introduce the program.

     CLS
     PRINT "This program displays the income collected over "
     PRINT "14 days from 8 sources for the fundraising drive. "
     PRINT "It allows you to compute the total for any day"
     PRINT "or any source."
     PRINT
     INPUT "Press enter to continue.", choice$

'Print out the table and let the user choose a total.

     DO
         CLS
         PRINT "            Income from Fundraiser"
         PRINT
         PRINT " Source #   1   2   3   4   5   6   7   8"
         PRINT "Day #"
         FOR day = 1 TO 14
             IF day < 10 THEN
                 PRINT " ";
             END IF
             PRINT "  "; day; "     ";
             FOR source = 1 TO 8
                 PRINT income(day, source); " ";
             NEXT source
             PRINT
         NEXT day
         PRINT

         PRINT "Do you want the total for a particular day"
         INPUT "or a particular source? (D/S) ", choice$
         LET choice$ = UCASE$(LEFT$(choice$, 1))
         PRINT

        'If the choice was day:

        IF choice$ = "D" THEN
            PRINT "Which day (1-14)? ";
            CALL GetInput(dayWanted, 1, 14)
            LET total = 0
```

```
            FOR source = 1 TO 8
                LET total = total + income(dayWanted, source)
            NEXT source
            PRINT
            PRINT "The total for Day #"; dayWanted;
            PRINT "is $"; total; "."

        'but if it was source:

        ELSE
            PRINT "Which source (1-8)? ";
            CALL GetInput(sourceWanted, 1, 8)
            LET total = 0
            FOR day = 1 TO 14
                LET total = total + income(day, sourceWanted)
            NEXT day
            PRINT
            PRINT "The total for Source #"; sourceWanted;
            PRINT "is $"; total; "."
        END IF

        'Ask about another total.

        PRINT
        INPUT "Want another total (Y/N)? ", choice$
        LET choice$ = UCASE$(LEFT$(choice$, 1))
    LOOP UNTIL choice$ = "N"

    PRINT
    PRINT "Thank you."

END

SUB GetInput(value, low, high)
'An input routine that traps bad input values.

        DO
            INPUT "", value
            IF (value >= low) AND (value <= high) THEN
                EXIT DO
            ELSE
                PRINT "Value must be in the range"; low; "to"; high; ": ";
            END IF
        LOOP

END SUB
```

Sample output could be:

```
This program displays the income collected over
14 days from 8 sources for the fundraising drive.
It allows you to compute the total for any day
or for any source.

Press return to continue.
```

(new screen)

```
          Income from Fundraiser

   Source #   1   2   3   4   5   6   7   8
Day #
    1        23  12  34  17  10  25  40  16
    2        21  26  55  12  34  45  16  42
    3        21  56  16  38  76  36  53  10
    4        34  41  40  20  16  83  14  15
    5        45  56  83  34  12  36  45  41
    6        18  27  63  41  49  51  32  35
    7        23  65  13  45  48  51  32  35
    8        16  48  72  56  41  38  12  47
    9        48  23  28  12  18  82  34  67
   10        81  47  31  26  17  25  56  42
   11        65  14  54  24  56  88  31  14
   12        47  45  52  61  52  47  12  37
   13        24  55  84  44  19  87  35  36
   14        17  42  54  21  48  39  55  38

Do you want the total for a particular day
or for a particular source? (D/S) D

Which day (1-14)? 5

The total for Day # 5 is $ 352 .

Want another total (Y/N)? N

Thank you.
```

Arrays with three or more dimensions are not as common as those with one or two—but they can be helpful at times. For example, suppose in Example 7 that you actually had *five different* fund drives going on at once. In this case, you would need a *third dimension* for your array *income( )* to take care of the five separate drives. Thus, your array declaration would look like:

```
DIM income(1 TO 5, 1 TO 14, 1 TO 8)
```

A simple way to think of this is that it consists of 5 *pages*, each containing 14 rows and 8 columns.

To help with this multidimensional concept, suppose you wanted to write a program to simulate three-dimensional tic-tac-toe. You would want to have a string array *pos$( )* (for "position") declared as follows:

```
DIM pos$(1 TO 3, 1 TO 3, 1 TO 3)
```

The first dimension is the "level," the second the row, and the last the column. The *values* of the array can be "X", "O", or "" (i.e., the empty string). See Figure 7.8 for this three-dimensional array.

Writing a program in which a user goes up against the computer in playing three-dimensional tic-tac-toe would be a challenge but certainly not impossible. After all, people have written programs that make the computer a world-class chess player, and chess is, of course, a great deal more complicated than tic-tac-toe. The point here is, though, that if you *were* to write the tic-tac-toe program, you would certainly want to employ a three-dimensional array. See Programming Problem 10 at the end of this chapter.

FIGURE 7.8

A Three-Dimensional Array

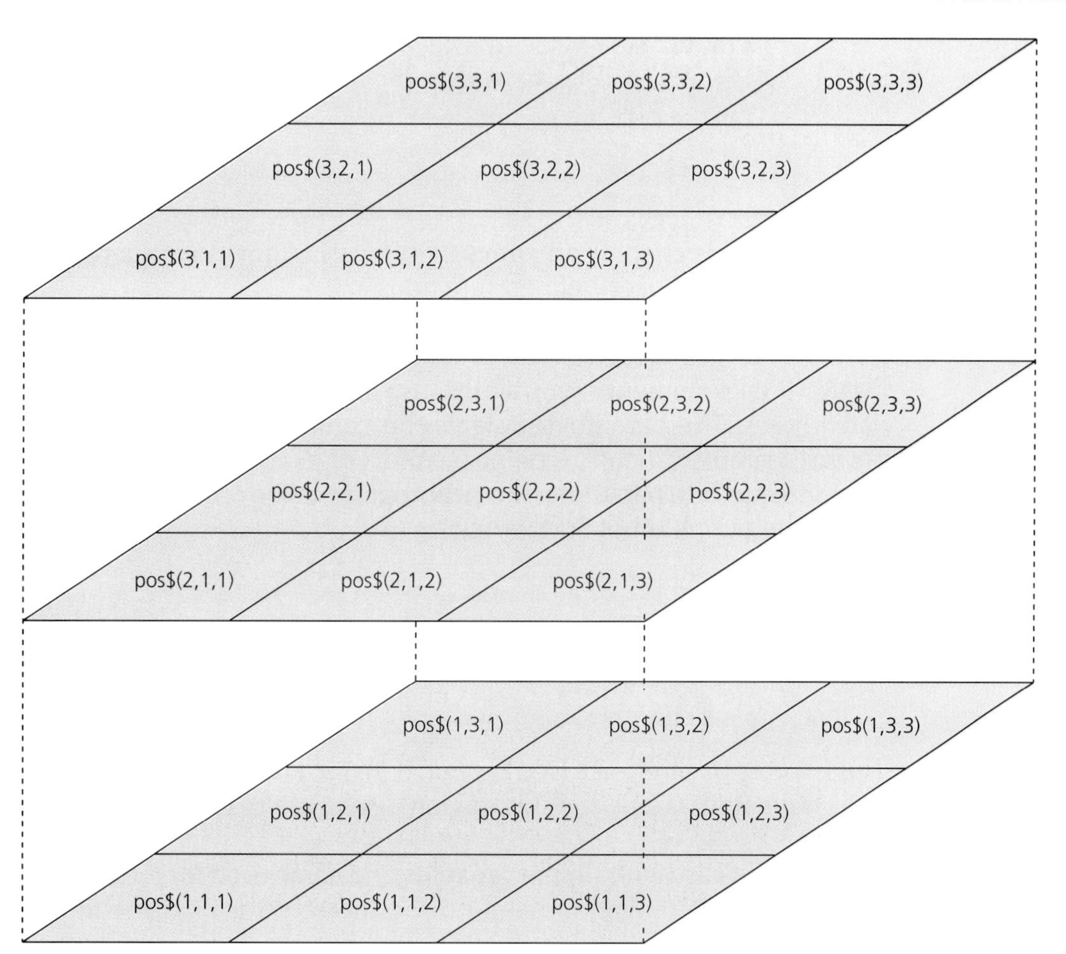

PRACTICE 7.4

1. Describe exactly what the compiler does when it encounters each of the following:

   (a) `DIM num(1 TO 10, 1 TO 15)`
   (b) `DIM item$(1 TO 4, 1 TO 7, 1 TO 5)`

2. (a) Draw a picture (as in Figure 7.6) of the array in the program segment below.
   (b) Trace the segment and fill in the values as they are read.
   (c) Finally, show the output of the segment.

```
DIM table(1 TO 4, 1 TO 5)

FOR row = 1 TO 4
    FOR col = 1 TO 5
        READ table(row, col)
    NEXT col
NEXT row

LET sum = 0
FOR pos = 1 TO 4
    LET sum = sum + table(pos, pos)
NEXT pos
   PRINT sum

DATA 6, 3, 7, 1, 12, 4, 8, 4, 2, 7, 9, 10, 1, 4, 7
DATA 11, 5, 8, 2, 9
```

7.5 Using Arrays in Subprograms and User-Defined Functions

We'll finish this chapter on arrays by discussing how to use arrays in subprograms and user-defined functions.

To pass an array as a parameter to a subprogram—both as an argument in the CALL statement and as a parameter in the SUB or FUNCTION statement—you simply *use the array name* including the *parentheses*. The parentheses signal the compiler that an array, and not just a simple variable, is being passed. For example, if we want the array *list( )* to be a parameter in a subprogram called Sort, then the first line of the definition of Sort would be:

```
SUB Sort(list( ))
```

And if we wanted to use *list( )* as an argument in a call to Sort, when calling the subprogram from the main program, we would write:

```
CALL Sort(list( ))
```

This is a pass by reference (see Section 6.5). That is, no new copy of the array is created; rather, the subprogram uses the already existing array locations.

As is the case with simple variables, the *name* used for the array in the subprogram definition need not be the same as its name in the main program. Suppose, for example, that we have *two* arrays, *mathScore( )* and *verbScore( ),* in our main program and we want to sort *both* of them. The subprogram heading can *still* be

```
SUB Sort(list( ))
```

but now the two calls in the main program will look like

```
CALL Sort(mathScore( ))
```

and

```
CALL Sort(verbScore( ))
```

At the time of the first call, *list( )* becomes a *temporary new name* for the array *mathScore( )*; then, at the second call, it becomes a temporary new name for *verbScore( )*.

One more remark before looking at a programming example: You can always pass *individual locations* of an array as parameters *exactly* as you pass simple variables. For example, if you want to pass the fifth box in an array *name$( )* to a function whose definition begins with

```
FUNCTION FirstCap$(word$)
```

then the call in the main program would look something like

```
LET initial$ = FirstCap$(name$(5))
```

The simple string variable *word$* in the function corresponds to the simple string variable *name$(5)* in the main program.

If you wanted to use the function on every name in the list, then *initial$* might be an array itself, and the main program might have a segment like the following:

```
FOR count = 1 TO howMany
    LET initial$(count) = FirstCap$(name$(count))
NEXT count
```

It's time to look at a program that passes arrays to subprograms and user-defined functions.

EXAMPLE 9

Let's write a *data analyzer* program. It should take in a list of numbers from the keyboard and then offer the user a variety of different options for analyzing the data. Among these could be: find the mean (i.e., average), find the standard deviation (see Chapter 2, Programming Problem 13), find the range (i.e., highest value − lowest value), sort the list, search the list for specific values, find the median (i.e., middle value when sorted in order), and so on.

Sounds like quite a chore, right? But remember, if we take a modular approach to the problem—that is, if we break the problem into small, manageable pieces—then we can build it up piece by piece until the whole thing is there. *Subprograms and user-defined functions are the perfect organizational tool here.* And, of course, we will use a one-dimensional array to store the data. Let's write an algorithm.

LEVEL-1 ALGORITHM

1. Introduce the program to the user
2. Store the data
3. Repeat:
    a. Present the user with a menu of options:
        Find mean
        Find standard deviation
        Find range
        Sort data
        Search data for an item
        Find median
    b. Perform the chosen task

   Until the user wants to quit

We can easily organize this program by writing a main program that looks essentially like the above algorithm and by assigning the various optional tasks to subprograms or user-defined functions.

```
'-----------------------------------------------------------------
'    Program Title: C07EX09.BAS
'    Author:        J. Bernoulli
'    Date:          October 17, 1992

'    Gives the user a menu of options for analyzing a list of
'    numbers.
'-----------------------------------------------------------------

'Main program begins. Introduce program to user.

     CLS
     PRINT "Welcome to DATA ANALYZER !!"
     PRINT
     PRINT "This program will give you various options for"
     PRINT "analyzing any list of numbers that you have."
     PRINT "We hope you find it useful!"
     PRINT

'Store the data.

     PRINT "First, we must get your data from you."
     INPUT "How many numbers do you have? ", howMany

     DIM numList(1 TO howMany)

     PRINT
     PRINT "Now type in your data items one at a time:"
     FOR count = 1 TO howMany
         PRINT "Item #"; count; "-->";
         INPUT " ", numList(count)
     NEXT count
```

```
      PRINT
      PRINT "Thank you!"
      PRINT
      INPUT "Press enter to continue.", answer$

'Display the menu, let the user choose, and perform that task.

    DO
        CLS
        PRINT "Here are your options for analyzing your data:"
        PRINT
        PRINT "      A. Find the mean."
        PRINT "      B. Find the standard deviation."
        PRINT "      C. Find the range."
        PRINT "      D. Sort the data (low to high)."
        PRINT "      E. Search the data for an item."
        PRINT "      F. Find the median."
        PRINT
        INPUT "Your choice? (A-F) ", answer$
        LET answer$ = UCASE$(LEFT$(answer$, 1))
        PRINT

        SELECT CASE answer$
            CASE "A"
                PRINT "The mean is"; Mean(howMany, numList())
            CASE "B"
                PRINT "The standard deviation is";
                PRINT SD(howMany, numList())
            CASE "C"
                PRINT "The range is"; Range(howMany, numList())
            CASE "D"
                CALL Sort(howMany, numList())
                PRINT "Here is the sorted data:"
                FOR count = 1 TO howMany
                    PRINT numList(count); " ";
                NEXT count
                PRINT
            CASE "E"
                CALL Search(howMany, numList())
            CASE "F"
                PRINT "The median is"; Median(howMany, numList())
            CASE ELSE
                PRINT "Sorry, "; answer$; " is not an option"
        END SELECT

        PRINT
        INPUT "Do you want to choose another option? ", answer$
        LET answer$ = UCASE$(LEFT$(answer$, 1))
    LOOP UNTIL answer$ = "N"

    PRINT
    PRINT "Thank you for using DATA ANALYZER !!"

END    'of the main program.
```

Here's sample output:

```
Welcome to DATA ANALYZER !!

This program will give you various options for
analyzing any list of numbers that you have.
We hope you find it useful!
First, we must get your data from you.
How many numbers do you have? 6

Now type in your data items one at a time:
Item # 1 --> 13
Item # 2 --> 8
Item # 3 --> 23
Item # 4 --> 17
Item # 5 --> 4
Item # 6 --> 21

Thank you!

Press enter to continue.
```

(new screen)

```
Here are your options for analyzing your data:

A. Find the mean.
B. Find the standard deviation.
C. Find the range.
D. Sort the data (low to high).
E. Search the data for an item.
F. Find the median.

Your choice? (A-F) A

The mean is 14.33333

Do you want to choose another option? No thanks

Thank you for using DATA ANALYZER !!
```

Look closely at the SELECT...END SELECT section of this program. In every CASE but the last one, a call is made either to a user-defined function (Mean, SD, Range, and Median) or to a subprogram (Sort and Search). Each time, the function or subprogram "must be told" both the number of data items (*howMany*) and the items themselves (*numList( )*), so that those are passed as parameters to the functions or subprograms.

What about these functions and subprograms? Let's look at two of them. First, the function Mean:

```
FUNCTION Mean (howMany, numList())
    LET sum = 0
    FOR count = 1 TO howMany
        LET sum = sum + numList(count)
    NEXT count
    LET Mean = sum / howMany
END FUNCTION
```

We've certainly seen this task performed many times before. Notice that we've chosen to use the names from the main program (*howMany* and *numList( )*) for the two arguments of the function, but, as always, that was not necessary. We could have called them *fred* and *ethel( )* if we wanted. But that wouldn't have been good programming practice, right? Variable names should be meaningful!

Here's a way to do the Sort subprogram. We've chosen to use the Selection Sort algorithm as discussed in Section 7.3.

```
SUB Sort (howMany, numList())
    FOR startPos = 1 TO howMany - 1
        LET smallPos = startPos
        FOR currentPos = startPos + 1 TO howMany
            IF numList(currentPos) < numList(smallPos) THEN
                LET smallPos = currentPos
            END IF
        NEXT currentPos
        LET temp = numList(startPos)
        LET numList(startPos) = numList(smallPos)
        LET numList(smallPos) = temp
    NEXT startPos
END SUB
```

Take a few minutes to run this program (C07EX09.BAS on your SAMPLES disk). You'll discover that the only options that have been written are the two above. It will be *your* job to write the other four—see Programming Problem 9 at the end of this chapter!

PRACTICE 7.5

What is the output of the following program:

```
'Main program
    READ n
    DIM list(1 TO n)
    FOR k = 1 TO n
        READ list(k)
    NEXT k
    CALL Rev(n, list( ))
    PRINT list(4)
    DATA 6
    DATA 34,23,12,62,41,51
END
```

```
SUB Rev(num, array( ))
   DIM temp(1 TO num)
   FOR i = 1 TO num
     LET temp(i) = array(num-i+1)
   NEXT i
   FOR i = 1 TO num
     LET array(i) = temp(i)
   NEXT i
END SUB
```

Chapter Summary

In this chapter we've learned about storing data in an *array*, which is a sequence of adjacent memory locations all with the same name, all holding the same type of data (numeric or string), but each with its own *index*. Whenever it is necessary to *hold* a list of data in memory (as opposed to processing and then throwing out one data item at a time), you should use an array.

When you use an array, you must *declare* that you are using it by putting a DIM statement near the beginning of your program. This statement tells the compiler the name of the array (and the name itself tells the compiler the data type); how many memory locations it contains (including how they will be labelled: "1 TO 10," "−100 TO 100," etc.); and *initializes* all those locations (to 0 for numbers, to the empty string for strings).

Arrays can be *one-dimensional* (lists), *two-dimensional* (tables, matrices), *three-dimensional* (pages of tables, etc.), or higher if needed. The choice of the number of dimensions is usually easy, fitting naturally with the organization of the data.

Two of the most important tasks performed on an array of data are *searching* and *sorting*. There are many *algorithms* for each of these, some *elementary*, which are relatively easy to program but may work slowly on larger lists, and some *advanced*, which are harder to program but may work much more quickly. We looked specifically at *Linear Search*, *Selection Sort*, and *Bubble Sort*, all of which are elementary. The advanced algorithms, such as *Binary Search* and *Quicksort* usually employ some *divide-and-conquer* strategy. We can discuss the efficiency of any given algorithm in terms of its *complexity*, which means the approximate number of steps it takes to complete the given task in terms of the number of data items put in.

Finally, we learned how to pass arrays to and from subprograms and user-defined functions. Arrays are always passed by reference, and the signal to the compiler that the named parameter or argument is an array is that it is followed by "( )."

Review Questions

1. Explain each term briefly and give an example:

(a) array
(b) index
(c) DIM statement
(d) Linear Search
(e) sorting algorithm
(f) complexity of an algorithm
(g) two-dimensional array

2. In each case, explain briefly whether or not (and *why*) a list of numbers *must* be stored in an array in order to perform the given task:

(a) find the average
(b) find the range (highest to lowest)
(c) arrange in descending numerical order
(d) find the median (the numerically "middle" value)

3. Give an example (different from the ones in the text), together with an appropriate DIM statement, of data that would naturally be stored in a:
   (a) one-dimensional array
   (b) two-dimensional array
   (c) three-dimensional array

Programming Problems 

1. The DATA statements below contain the high temperatures recorded each day of June 1991 in Gotham City. Write a program that stores these temperatures in an array and then allows the user to pick any time period during the month and find out what the average high temperature was during that period. The data is:

```
DATA 67,75,78,72,68,79,81,83,79,73,76,81,87,85,82
DATA 73,65,64,59,67,74,78,78,81,86,89,87,82,78,75
```

   Here's possible output:

```
Welcome (and so on)
What is the date of the first day of your time period? 7
What is the last day? 15
The average high temperature over that period was 80.8 .
Want another time period? no thanks
Okay. Goodbye!
```

2. Write a program that reads a list of up to 40 words from DATA statements, stores them in an array, and then allows users to see all words starting with the letter of their choice. Make up your own data, which should end with a trailer. Possible output (without the introduction) might be:

```
What starting letter? c
The words starting with c in our list are:
cat        cow        cart
Want another starting letter? no chance
Have a nice day!
```

3. Write a simple number sorting program. The user types in a list of numbers at the keyboard and the program returns them in ascending numerical order. You may use any sorting algorithm you wish.

4. Tiny-Mart is doing an inventory of the 12 items it sells. The first line of DATA below contains the *quantities* on hand of each item; the second and third lines contain the selling price of each item. Write a program that calculates and prints out the present (gross) worth of each item and the total (gross) worth of the store's present whole stock.

```
DATA 21,12,6,13,4,15,23,5,10,34,28,21
DATA 5.98,12.50,4.75,15.35,25.90,7.98,5.60,8.98
DATA 25.50,12.40,7.90,5.95
```

5. The program C05EX06.BAS in Chapter 5 simulates a telephone information service. One drawback to that program is that the user can ask for only one piece of information. By storing the data in three arrays (*last$*, *first$*, and *number$*), allow the user to ask for more than one number. (Start by simply copying C05EX06.BAS from the SAMPLES disk to your own program disk.)

6. Write a "word opposites" game for children. Two lists of words are stored in string arrays; the second list contains the opposites of the words in the first list, but in a different order. You also need a numeric array, *position*, which tells where in the second list the opposite of each first-list word is (for example, if the opposite of the first word is fifth in the second list, then *position(1)* is 5).

   The game goes as follows: The first word in List 1 is displayed somewhere on the screen, and somewhere else the first word in List 2 is shown. The child says yes or no to whether they are opposites; if he or she says no and no is the correct answer, then the second word in List 2 is displayed, and so on. Once the opposite to this first word has been found (or pointed out by the computer), the game moves on to the second word in the first list. Got it? This is a little tricky, but fun! Try to make your output as "friendly" as possible.

7. Write a program that simulates drawing 5 cards from a standard deck. In Example 4 of this chapter (C07EX04.BAS), we simulated drawing *one* card. The problem now is that we must avoid the possibility of drawing the same card twice; we must keep track of what's been drawn already. Here's a suggestion: in addition to the two string arrays already in C07EX04.BAS, add a two-dimensional numeric array, *drawn*, which has, say, 4 rows and 13 columns. This array should hold all 0s to start with, but each time a card is drawn, the corresponding location in *drawn* gets changed to, say, 1. Each time you draw a new card, check to see whether there's a 1 or a 0 in the corresponding location in *drawn*. A 0 indicates a new card, and the program must therefore change that location to 1. A 1 indicates that the card has already been drawn, so the program must generate two new random numbers.

   Note that once this program is written, it can easily be changed to dealing out 7 cards, or 13 cards, or even the whole deck!

8. Each page of a teacher's gradebook contains rows and columns: each row usually containing the grades on the various tests, reports, and so on for one student. The DATA contained in C07PB08.BAS on your SAMPLES disk shows such a page. Copy that data to your disk and write a program that allows the teacher to choose either a certain row (i.e., student) or a certain column (i.e., test, etc.) and find out the average of that row or column. Your program should include a "Want more information?" option.

9. Complete the data analyzer program in Example 9 of this chapter (C07EX09.BAS). Copy the program from your SAMPLES disk and write the remaining four subprograms or functions. Standard deviation was introduced in Programming Problem 13 of Chapter 2. The median is the "middle value" in a list, which means that *after* the list is sorted into order, the median is the middle item in the list if there are an odd number of items, or is the average of the *two* middle items if the list contains an even number of items.

10. (a) Write a program that simulates a tic-tac-toe game. Have the user play against the computer, and have the computer choose its moves randomly (though it cannot, of course, move where the user has already moved). The computer should "know" when someone has won (this part of the program takes some real thought!).

(b) Modify the program in part (a) so that it plays *three-dimensional* tic-tac-toe (see the end of Section 7.4).

(c) Modify the program in part (a) so that, rather than choosing moves randomly, the computer chooses the best move based on the current state of the board. If that doesn't do you in, do the same thing to the program in part (b)!

CHAPTER

8

DATA FILES

CHAPTER PREVIEW **In this chapter, we'll learn how to get data into a program from a file (rather than from the keyboard or from DATA statements) and how to output data to a file (rather than to the monitor screen). This will enable us to work with much larger data sets than we have previously. We'll see that there are two different kinds of "data files": *sequential* and *random-access*. Sequential files are a bit easier to understand, while random-access files are more flexible for use in complex programs.**

8.1 Introduction

With the ideas we've learned in the previous chapters, we now have the tools to write a wide variety of programs, ranging from short and sweet to large and complex. Indeed, many professional programmers use QuickBASIC to write the complex software required by business today.

One feature common to most business software is that it deals with *large sets of data*. Whether it uses employee records, merchandise inventory, or statistical data, most commercial software is designed to process large quantities of information; its output is also usually quite extensive.

The control structures we've learned, together with the techniques of modularity made possible by using subprograms, simplify the task of writing complex programs. Arrays, which we learned about in the last chapter, help us deal with long lists and tables of data, but only *within* the program; we don't yet have an effective way to store extensive *output* from a program or to deal with lengthy *input* to a program. In this chapter, we'll learn how to store large data sets in *files*.

As we've already seen, a *file* is a set of information that is electronically stored on a disk (hard or floppy). Files can hold many different kinds of information, such as computer programs or text documents. Files have some similarities with *arrays*: they both consist of a *sequence* of storage locations. There is, however, one very important *difference* between files and arrays: Arrays store data in sequences of memory locations in the computer's *internal memory*; this data is *lost* when the computer is turned off (or when the program in which they're used finishes). Files, on the other hand, are stored on a disk, so data stored in a file can be saved even when the computer is turned off. Think how crucial this is for all the data maintained by schools, government, and industry!

QuickBASIC programs can work with two kinds of data files: *sequential* and *random-access*. **Sequential files** are simply *ASCII* files, that is, they contain simple text characters like the files we discussed in Workshop 1. We'll see that input/output operations with sequential files are similar to input from the keyboard and output to the monitor screen. Random-access files are more complex in their structure but offer more flexibility in terms of programming; we'll see that random-access files behave, in some sense, like arrays.

8.2 Sequential File Output

The simplest introduction to files is to learn how to print output to a file rather than on the monitor screen. Let's begin with an example.

EXAMPLE 1

The program below prints a table showing the amount of tip one might leave in a restaurant for a variety of subtotals and percentages. For example, the table shows that for a subtotal of \$20 a 15% tip would be \$3.

```
'-----------------------------------------------------------------
'        TITLE:   C08EX01A.BAS
'        AUTHOR: Julia Child
'        DATE:    9/15/92

'This program prints a table showing tip amounts for a variety of
'subtotals and tip percentages.
'-----------------------------------------------------------------

'Print table heading

    CLS
    PRINT SPACE$(10); STRING$(50, "$")
    PRINT SPACE$(10); "TIP VALUES FOR GIVEN SUBTOTALS AND TIP PERCENTAGES"
    PRINT SPACE$(10); STRING$(50, "$")
    PRINT
    PRINT
    PRINT "SUBTOTAL", "10%", "15%", "20%", "25%"
    PRINT "--------", "---", "---", "---", "---"

'Print one row for each subtotal from $10 to $100 in $10 increments.

    FOR subtotal = 10 TO 100 STEP 10
        PRINT "$"; subtotal,
        PRINT "$"; .1 * subtotal,
        PRINT "$"; .15 * subtotal,
        PRINT "$"; .2 * subtotal,
        PRINT "$"; .25 * subtotal
    NEXT subtotal

END
```

Here's how the output from this program looks:

```
          $$$$$$$$$$$$$$$$$$$$$$$$$$$$$$$$$$$$$$$$$$$$$$$$$$
          TIP VALUES FOR GIVEN SUBTOTALS AND TIP PERCENTAGES
          $$$$$$$$$$$$$$$$$$$$$$$$$$$$$$$$$$$$$$$$$$$$$$$$$$

SUBTOTAL      10%           15%           20%           25%
--------      ---           ---           ---           ---
$ 10          $ 1           $ 1.5         $ 2           $ 2.5
$ 20          $ 2           $ 3           $ 4           $ 5
$ 30          $ 3           $ 4.5         $ 6           $ 7.5
$ 40          $ 4           $ 6           $ 8           $ 10
$ 50          $ 5           $ 7.5         $ 10          $ 12.5
```

```
$ 60      $ 6       $ 9        $ 12      $ 15
$ 70      $ 7       $ 10.5     $ 14      $ 17.5
$ 80      $ 8       $ 12       $ 16      $ 20
$ 90      $ 9       $ 13.5     $ 18      $ 22.5
$ 100     $ 10      $ 15       $ 20      $ 25
```

Any program that prints to the screen can be altered to print to a file by making the following three changes:

STEPS FOR PRINTING TO A SEQUENTIAL OUTPUT FILE

1. First, we must identify the file name that will be used and permit the program to perform the necessary initializations by using an OPEN statement. We will see four variations of the OPEN statement in this chapter, but the version we need for performing *output to a sequential file* is shown below.

   OPEN "<file name>" **FOR OUTPUT AS** #<file number>

   Any legal file name may be used (with or without drive prefix) and the number may be any integer from 1 to 255. This number is used in subsequent statements whenever you want to refer to the file. For instance, the OPEN statement below sets up a file named A:ANSWERS.DAT for sequential output with reference number 1. Notice that you must put quotes around the file name.

   ```
   OPEN "A:ANSWERS.DAT" FOR OUTPUT AS #1
   ```

2. Next, each PRINT statement must be modified so that output goes to the appropriate file instead of to the screen. This is done by adding the phrase "#*<file number>*," right after the word *PRINT*. For example, instead of writing

   ```
   PRINT "HELLO THERE"
   ```

   we would write

   ```
   PRINT #23, "HELLO THERE"
   ```

   to print the string "Hello there" in file number 23 rather than on the screen.

3. When you're through with the file, you signal that fact with the **CLOSE** statement; this also releases the file's reference number so that it can be used in a subsequent OPEN statement. To close file number 17, we would write

   ```
   CLOSE #17
   ```

Here's how we would modify the program in Example 1 to print its output to a file on the A-drive named C08EX01B.DAT.[1] Modified BASIC statements have been highlighted.

```
'---------------------------------------------------------------
'       TITLE:  C08EX01B.BAS
'       AUTHOR: Julia Child
'       DATE:   9/15/92

'This program prints a table showing tip amounts for a variety of
'subtotals and tip percentages.
'The table is printed to a file named A:C08EX01B.DAT.
'---------------------------------------------------------------

'This statement initializes the file A:C08EX01B.DAT as file #1.

    OPEN "A:C08EX01B.DAT" FOR OUTPUT AS #1

'Print table heading

    PRINT #1, SPACE$(10); STRING$(50, "$")
    PRINT #1, SPACE$(10); "TIP VALUES FOR GIVEN SUBTOTALS AND TIP PERCENTAGES"
    PRINT #1, SPACE$(10); STRING$(50, "$")
    PRINT #1,
    PRINT #1,
    PRINT #1, "SUBTOTAL", "10%", "15%", "20%", "25%"
    PRINT #1, "--------", "---", "---", "---", "---"

'Print one row for each subtotal from $10 to $100 in $10 increments.

    FOR subtotal = 10 TO 100 STEP 10
        PRINT #1, "$"; subtotal,
        PRINT #1, "$"; .1 * subtotal,
        PRINT #1, "$"; .15 * subtotal,
        PRINT #1, "$"; .2 * subtotal,
        PRINT #1, "$"; .25 * subtotal
    NEXT subtotal

'We're done now so we close the file.

    CLOSE #1

END
```

[1] DAT is short for "data" and is a commonly used suffix for identifying data files. Other reasonable suffixes for sequential files include *SEQ*, *TXT* (since they are text, i.e., ASCII, files), or *INP* and *OUT* (to indicate whether they are for input or output of data).

There are several things to note about the modified program. The first and most important is that when the line "OPEN A:C08EX01B.DAT FOR OUTPUT AS #1" is executed, the program will create a new, *empty* file named C08EX01B.DAT on the A-drive; if a file by that name already exists, that file will be used. What's *important* about this is that when we begin to print new data in the file, *the file's previous contents will be erased!* Below, we'll see a variant of the OPEN statement that allows us to *add* data to an existing file without erasing its original contents.

The second thing to notice about the modified program is that we deleted the CLS statement—that statement clears the output screen, but since our output is being sent to a file, we have no need for the statement. There are times, of course, when some of your program's output will be to the screen and some will be to a file, but it's important to distinguish between the two. In this case, the output will be displayed in the file C08EX01B.DAT just as it appeared on the screen with the original version of the program.

A final thing to note is that when you run this program, you don't see any output! That's because the output was printed to the file rather than to the screen. The question now is, How do you get a look at the file while you're testing your program? In Section 8.4, we'll learn how to use the File Menu to "load" a data file for editing—but if we only want a peek, it may be easier to use the DOS command TYPE. QuickBASIC will let you do this without exiting the QuickBASIC system by using the **Dos Shell** option from the File Menu (this option is available only when using Full Menus). If you select this option, you'll be placed in the operating system, where you can execute any DOS command (e.g., DIR or TYPE C08EX01B.DAT) *without* ending your QuickBASIC session; to *return* to QuickBASIC you simply type the word **EXIT**.

EXAMPLE 2

Let's write a bank account program that we will modify and expand in subsequent examples in this chapter. For the first phase, we'll write subprograms that allow users to record deposits and withdrawals in a file; the main program will present users with a list of the available transactions. Each time users have new entries to add, they simply run the program and are allowed to enter their transactions. For this reason, it is important that we write the program in such a way that the old data file is *not* destroyed. To do this, we use the word **APPEND** instead of *OUTPUT* in the OPEN statement, for example:

```
OPEN "A:BANK.DAT" FOR APPEND AS #1
```

Here are the two subprograms from C08EX02.BAS that allow users to make deposits or withdrawals (the main program repeatedly lets them choose one of the two transactions):

```
SUB MakeDeposit
'Input and record deposit in C08EX02.DAT

    'Input date and transaction amount

        INPUT "Enter month (1 to 12): ", month
        INPUT "Enter date:            ", date
        INPUT "Enter year (2 digits): ", year
        PRINT
        INPUT "Enter amount of deposit: $", amount

    'Record transaction in C08EX02.DAT

        OPEN "C08EX02.DAT" FOR APPEND AS #1
        PRINT #1, year, month, date, "D", amount
        CLOSE #1

END SUB
```

```
SUB MakeWithdrawal
'Input and record withdrawal in C08EX02.DAT

    'Input date and transaction amount

        INPUT "Enter month (1 to 12): ", month
        INPUT "Enter date:            ", date
        INPUT "Enter year (2 digits): ", year

        PRINT
        INPUT "Enter amount of withdrawal: $", amount

    'Record transaction in C08EX02.DAT

        OPEN "C08EX02.DAT" FOR APPEND AS #1
        PRINT #1, year, month, date, "W", amount
        CLOSE #1

END SUB
```

Suppose that the first time we run this program we have two deposits, one on 10/1/92 for $100, and another on 10/15/92 for $45.50. After running the program with this data, the file C08EX02.DAT would look as follows:

```
92      10      1       D      100
92      10      15      D      45.5
```

If we then ran the same program a second time, entering a withdrawal of $39.95 on 10/5/92, the file C08EX02.DAT would be changed as follows:

```
92      10      1       D      100
92      10      15      D      45.5
92      10      5       W      39.95
```

As predicted, the new data has been *appended* to the old; if we had used the word *OUTPUT* instead of *APPEND*, the old data would have been lost.

An important thing to notice in these first two examples is that we open the file *just before* we're about to use it and we close it *as soon as* we're done with it. We do this because many programs do both input *and* output with the same sequential file, but a file can only be opened for *one* of these operations at a time (input *or* output, not both). By opening and closing the file right before and after we use it, we don't have to worry later in the program whether the file was opened in some earlier program segment.

There is a useful alternative to the PRINT # statement if you intend to use the output file later as an *input* file, either in the same program or in another. If, instead of saying PRINT #, you say **WRITE #**, the output data is printed to the file, with *commas* separating the data items on each line and with string output in *quotes*.

EXAMPLE 3

The following program segment illustrates the difference between using PRINT # and WRITE #:

```
LET a = 1
LET b$ = "two"
LET c = 3

OPEN "C08EX03.DAT" FOR OUTPUT AS #1
PRINT #1, a, b$, c
WRITE #1, a, b$, c
CLOSE #1
```

Here's what the contents of C08EX03.DAT look like after we run this segment:

```
 1             two            3
1,"two",3
```

The second line of output may not be as attractive as the first, but, for the purposes of *inputting*, it's better. In the next section, we'll see that inputting from a sequential file is analogous to reading from a DATA statement, in that the data items on each line must be separated by commas (you may also recall that the use of quotes around string data was permitted in DATA statements); the WRITE statement formats data in exactly this way.

PRACTICE 8.2

Assuming that each of the following four program segments are run *consecutively*, indicate what the contents of the file C08PC02.DAT would be at the end of each segment:

(a)
```
OPEN "C08PC02.DAT" FOR OUTPUT AS #1
PRINT #1, "HELLO", 33.5, "GOODBYE"
CLOSE #1
```
(b)
```
OPEN "C08PC02.DAT" FOR APPEND AS #1
PRINT #1, "TODAY", -1243, "TOMORROW"
CLOSE #1
```
(c)
```
OPEN "C08PC02.DAT" FOR APPEND AS #1
WRITE #1, "HELLO", 33.5, "GOODBYE"
CLOSE #1
```
(d)
```
OPEN "C08PC02.DAT" FOR OUTPUT AS #1
WRITE #1, "TODAY", -1243, "TOMORROW"
CLOSE #1
```

8.3 Sequential File Input

Just as a program can output its data to a sequential (i.e., text) file rather than to the monitor screen, so can a program *input* its data from a *file* rather than from the keyboard. The steps involved in writing this kind of program are as follows:

STEPS FOR USING A SEQUENTIAL INPUT FILE

1. First, we must *create* the file that will contain our input data. In the previous section, we saw that this can be done by creating the file as a sequential *output* file using the WRITE statement. Alternatively, the file can be created separately using a text editor or word processor; in Section 8.4, we'll learn how to do this using the QuickBASIC editor.
2. Once the data file has been created, we use an OPEN statement to set it up as a sequential input file. The syntax is as follows:

   OPEN "<file name>" **FOR INPUT AS** #<number>

   If the file was created in the same program as an output file, it must be *closed* as an output file before we open it as an input file: a file may *not* be used *simultaneously* for both sequential input and sequential output.
3. Each time we wish to input from the file that we've opened, we use a statement of the following form:

   INPUT #<number>, <list of variables>

For example, the following statement would input a string and a number from a sequential file that had been opened as number 12:

```
INPUT #12, word$, num
```

4. As with output files, we use a CLOSE statement to signal that we are done using the file for input. If we wish, that same file can then be opened for input or appending later in the program.

EXAMPLE 4

As a simple example, the program segment below writes several lines to a sequential output file and then inputs the lines from the file and prints them on the screen.

```
'Open file C08EX04.DAT, write three data lines to it, then close it.

    OPEN "C08EX04.DAT" FOR OUTPUT AS #1
    WRITE #1, "Euphrates", 1739
    WRITE #1, "Columbia", 1232
    WRITE #1, "Mississippi", 2348
    CLOSE #1

'Print heading on screen

    CLS
    PRINT " RIVER", "LENGTH IN MILES"
    PRINT " =====", "==============="
    PRINT

'Now open C08EX04.DAT for input, input the three lines and print to screen,
'then close the data file.

    OPEN "C08EX04.DAT" FOR INPUT AS #1
    FOR river = 1 TO 3
        INPUT #1, riverName$, numMiles
        PRINT riverName$, numMiles
    NEXT river
    CLOSE #1
```

After we run this program segment, the data file C08EX04.DAT looks like this:

```
"Euphrates",1739
"Columbia",1232
"Mississippi",2348
```

Output to the screen looks like this:

```
  RIVER           LENGTH IN MILES
  =====           ===============

Euphrates         1739
Columbia          1232
Mississippi       2348
```

An important question about inputting from files is the following: how can we tell when we've input *all* the data from the file? For instance, if you try to input from a file but there's no data left, you'll get a run-time error, as you might expect. The last example was designed to handle three data lines, no more, no less.

One way to deal with this is to remember the similarity between sequential input files and DATA statements (mentioned at the end of Section 8.2). In Chapter 2 we introduced the idea of a *header* and in Chapter 5 the idea of a *trailer*. Below are two modifications of the previous segment, one using a header and the other a trailer to indicate how much data there is. In each case, the new lines are highlighted.

```
'Modification using header

    OPEN "C08EX04.DAT" FOR OUTPUT AS #1
    WRITE #1, 3
    WRITE #1, "Euphrates", 1739
    WRITE #1, "Columbia", 1232
    WRITE #1, "Mississippi", 2348
    CLOSE #1
              .
              .
              .
    OPEN "C08EX04.DAT" FOR INPUT AS #1
    INPUT #1, numRivers
    FOR river = 1 TO numRivers
        INPUT #1, riverName$, numMiles
        PRINT riverName$, numMiles
    NEXT river
    CLOSE #1
```

```
'Modification using trailer

    OPEN C08EX04.DAT" FOR OUTPUT AS #1
    WRITE #1, "Euphrates", 1739
    WRITE #1, "Columbia", 1232
    WRITE #1, "Mississippi", 2348
    WRITE #1, "EOD"
    CLOSE #1
            :
            :

    OPEN "C08EX04.DAT" FOR INPUT AS #1
    DO
        INPUT #1, riverName$
        IF riverName$ = "EOD" THEN
            EXIT DO
        END IF
        INPUT #1, numMiles
        PRINT riverName$, numMiles
    LOOP
    CLOSE #1
```

The simplicity of this example makes the use of headers and trailers a bit artificial, but you should still be able to see how they make it easier to input all the data from the file. You can find all three versions of these programs in the files C08EX04A.BAS, C08EX04B.BAS, and C08EX04C.BAS on the SAMPLES disk.

QuickBASIC actually provides a built-in function that acts like a trailer for sequential data files. The function is called

EOF (file number)

where *file number* is the number assigned to the file when it was opened. This function returns one of the values *true* or *false* depending on whether or not the end of the data has been reached (EOF is short for "end of file"). We generally use this function as a condition of the DO...LOOP in which we input all the data in the file. The basic format of such a loop would be:

DO UNTIL EOF (file number)
:
Input data from file #file number
Process data from file #file number
:
LOOP

A final modification of Example 4 (which can be found in the file C08EX04D.BAS) would be:

```
'Modification using EOF function

    OPEN "C08EX04.DAT" FOR OUTPUT AS #1
    WRITE #1, "Euphrates", 1739
    WRITE #1, "Columbia", 1232
    WRITE #1, "Mississippi", 2348
    CLOSE #1
              .
              .
              .
    OPEN "C08EX04.DAT" FOR INPUT AS #1
    DO UNTIL EOF(1)
        INPUT #1, riverName$, numMiles
        PRINT riverName$, numMiles
    LOOP
    CLOSE #1
```

This last segment is simpler to write and understand than either of the two previous modifications. Nonetheless, each technique is appropriate to particular problems, so you should remember all three ways to keep track of the end of data in a sequential input file: *headers, trailers*, and the *EOF function*.

EXAMPLE 5

Let's modify the bank account program of Example 2 so that it permits users to get printouts of their deposits, withdrawals, or their account balance. To do this, we must do two things. First, we must modify the subprograms MakeDeposit and MakeWithdrawal so that they WRITE to the data file (now called C08EX05.DAT) rather than PRINT to it. Second, we must add the new options to the menu in the main program and then write a subprogram for each new transaction.

The algorithm for the subprogram ListDeposits is fairly straightforward (ListWithdrawals is very similar).

1. Open the file C08EX05.DAT for input
2. Repeat the following for each line in C08EX05.DAT:
    a. Input all the data on the line
    b. If it's a deposit, print the information on the screen
3. Close the file C08EX05.DAT when done

Notice that we don't know in advance how many lines there are in the file C08EX05.DAT because users can make as many deposits and withdrawals as they wish; nevertheless, the EOF function will make it easy for us to write Step 2. Below is a refinement of our algorithm into pseudocode, which is then fairly easy to translate completely into BASIC.

```
OPEN "C08EX05.DAT" FOR INPUT AS #1
DO UNTIL EOF(1)
    Input a line of data from #1
    If deposit, then print info on screen
LOOP
CLOSE #1
```

The new subprograms—ListDeposits, ListWithdrawals, and ShowBalance—are listed in the program segment below (the complete program is in the file C08EX05.BAS). The parameter *month$( )* is an array created in the main program containing the names of each of the months (e.g., *month$(1)* = "January").

```
SUB ListDeposits (month$())
'List all deposits recorded in C08EX05.DAT

    'Print heading for display
    CLS
    PRINT SPACE$(14); STRING$(10, ">");
    PRINT " LIST OF DEPOSITS ";
    PRINT STRING$(10, "<");
    PRINT
    PRINT
    PRINT , "     DATE", "     DEPOSIT AMOUNT"
    PRINT

    'Input each line in C08EX05.DAT; print if deposit
    OPEN "C08EX05.DAT" FOR INPUT AS #1
    DO UNTIL EOF(1)
        INPUT #1, year, monthNum, date, type$, amount
        IF type$ = "D" THEN
            PRINT , month$(monthNum); date; ","; year + 1900, "$"; amount
        END IF
    LOOP
    CLOSE #1

END SUB
```

```
SUB ListWithdrawals (month$())
'List all withdrawals recorded in C08EX05.DAT

    'Print heading for display
    CLS
    PRINT SPACE$(14); STRING$(10, ">");
    PRINT " LIST OF WITHDRAWALS ";
    PRINT STRING$(10, "<");
    PRINT
    PRINT
    PRINT , "     DATE", "     WITHDRAWAL AMOUNT"
    PRINT
```

```
    'Input each line in C08EX05.DAT; print if withdrawal
    OPEN "C08EX05.DAT" FOR INPUT AS #1
    DO UNTIL EOF(1)
        INPUT #1, year, monthNum, date, type$, amount
        IF type$ = "W" THEN
            PRINT , month$(monthNum); date; ","; year + 1900, "$"; amount
        END IF
    LOOP
    CLOSE #1

END SUB
```

```
SUB ShowBalance
'Calculate and print current balance

    'Set up matrix to record date transaction currently being processed;
    'start balance at 0
    DIM ymd(1 TO 3)
    LET balance = 0

    'input data from C08EX05.DAT, keeping track of balance
    OPEN "C08EX05.DAT" FOR INPUT AS #1
    DO UNTIL EOF(1)
        INPUT #1, ymd(1), ymd(2), ymd(3), type$, amount
        IF type$ = "D" THEN
            LET balance = balance + amount
        ELSE '(withdrawal)
            LET balance = balance - amount
        END IF
    LOOP
    CLOSE #1

    'Clear screen and print current balance
    CLS
    PRINT "CURRENT BALANCE: $"; balance

END SUB
```

After entering several deposits and withdrawals, the file C08EX05.DAT might look like this:

```
92,10,1,"D",100
92,10,15,"D",45.5
92,10,23,"W",39.95
92,11,3,"W",15
92,11,5,"D",100
92,12,15,"W",50
```

If we now ask for a list of deposits, the output would be:

```
>>>>>>>>>>  LIST OF DEPOSITS  <<<<<<<<<<

     DATE                    DEPOSIT AMOUNT

October 1, 1992                  $ 100
October 15, 1992                 $ 45.5
November 5, 1992                 $ 100
```

If we asked for the current balance, the output would be:

```
CURRENT BALANCE: $ 140.55
```

In reading the subprograms, notice again that we always open and close the file *promptly*, just before and immediately after we use it.

In the next section, we'll learn another way to prepare a sequential input file.

PRACTICE 8.3

1. Assume that you've created a data file named WORDS1.DAT containing the following data:

```
Hello Goodbye
Today,Tomorrow
```

Show the output of the following program segment (be careful!):

```
OPEN "WORDS1.DAT" FOR INPUT AS #1
FOR count = 1 TO 3
       INPUT #1, word$
       PRINT word$, LEN(word$)
NEXT count
CLOSE #1
```

What would happen if you had the FOR...NEXT loop execute four times rather than three?

2. Suppose, now, that you "fix" the above data file by separating the two words on the first line with a comma:

```
Hello,Goodbye
Today,Tomorrow
```

(a) Add an appropriate *header* to the data file and then write a loop that will read all the data in the file and print it on the monitor screen.
(b) Repeat part (a) using a *trailer* instead of a header.
(c) Repeat part (a) using the EOF function to detect the end of the data.

8.4 Using the QuickBASIC Editor to Create Sequential Input Files

The methods we've seen so far for creating a sequential output file, closing it, and then reopening it for use as a sequential input file can be unnecessarily cumbersome in some applications. If we know in advance precisely what our data is, and especially if it's lengthy, we'd probably prefer to type the data directly into a file, much the way you type an English composition directly into a word processor.

If you already use a word processor for writing papers, you can now use it to create data files for use as sequential input files—but there are three important things to remember:

1. The data file must be stored as an *ASCII* file (many word processors store files in a special way that saves formatting information as well as the text itself).
2. The data items on each line must be separated by commas, as they are in a DATA statement.
3. Use *headers* or *trailers* (as discussed in Example 4 of Section 8.3) rather than the EOF function.

The reason for the last recommendation is technical. Some word processors and text editors differ in the characters they use to mark the end of a file, which can cause the EOF function to give incorrect results. In any case, using your own headers or trailers helps to guarantee that you won't get an "Out of Data" error when you try to use the file for sequential input to a program. If you keep these three things in mind, your programming task should be a little easier.

You can use the QuickBASIC system as a simple word processor or "text editor"[2] to create data files, but keep in mind the three points mentioned above. For instance, BASIC programs are *not* stored as ASCII files, so you'll need to learn how to use the QuickBASIC menus to create a *text file*. By the way, the problem with the EOF function that we mentioned above *does* occur when you use the QuickBASIC editor to create a file, so be *sure* to use headers or trailers.

HOW TO USE QuickBASIC TO PREPARE TEXT FILES

1. First, activate the *Full Menus* option from the Options Menu. The *Files Menu* should now contain the following three options:

   Create File—to create and edit a new file

   Load File—to load an existing file from disk into memory

   Unload File—to remove a file that is currently in memory

[2] The difference between a *text editor* and a *word processor* is that, while both provide an environment for entering and editing text, only the latter provides options for sophisticated document formatting, such as underlining, subscripts, italics, and so on.

These three options, together with the *Save As* or *Save* options are all you need to create text files for use as data files (you can also write letters to Mom, etc.).

2. To create a new text file, select the *Create File* option from the Files Menu. A dialog box will appear, prompting you for the name of the file and whether you want it to be created as "Module," "Include," or "Document." Enter your file name and use the **Tab** key to highlight *Document*. Important: Don't forget to choose the "Document" option; this choice turns off the Smart Editor and makes the file a *text* file.
3. You can now use the QuickBASIC editor to enter your data. Be sure that you use *commas* to separate multiple data items on the same line; and remember to use headers or trailers.
4. When you're done editing your file, *save* it as usual. To remove it from memory (i.e., from the QuickBASIC system), use the *Unload File* option from the Files Menu.
5. With the *Load File* option from the Files Menu, you can do additional editing on a file you've already created, if you wish.

You can actually have several files in memory at the same time; they are not removed unless you explicitly "unload" them. As with subprograms, you can use the function key **F2** to see a list of all the files you currently have in memory.

EXAMPLE 6

The data below is from a file called C08EX06.DAT that was created using the techniques described above; each line lists a brand of cereal, its cost per ounce, a rating of 1 to 5 for its fiber content (1 = worst, 5 = best), and its number of calories per ounce (information is from *Consumer Reports*, October 1989, pp. 642–645).

```
Fiber One, 15, 5, 57
Cheerios, 22, 4, 106
Wheaties, 15, 4, 105
Rice Krispies, 21, 1, 110
Cap'n Crunch's Crunch Berries, 17, 3, 113
Nabisco Cream of Rice, 10, 2, 103
EOD
```

This file can now be used for sequential input to a BASIC program (the file C08EX06.BAS contains a little program that simply reads all the data and prints it on the screen).

How do you choose between these two ways to create data files, that is, when should you create the file as a sequential output file and when should you simply use a text editor and type in the data yourself? The main issue is whether all the data will be known *in advance* of running the program. In Example 5 (the bank book), the data was *not* known in advance; the user could continue to add new data while running the program; thus, the file had to be created, while the program was running, as a sequential output file. On the other hand, if the data for Example 6 is complete, it's simpler to create the data file separately using a text editor rather than to write a BASIC program to input the data and write it to the file.

PRACTICE 8.4

This practice requires a computer.

1. Use the *Load File* option from the File Menu to load the file C08EX06.DAT. Add the following data line to the file (anywhere before the EOD trailer) and then save the file (information is from *Consumer Reports*, October 1989, pp. 642–645):

```
Grape-Nuts, 14, 4, 96
```

2. Open the program C08EX06.BAS and run it to see that the new data is handled correctly.

8.5 Random-Access Files and Records

Sequential files are fairly simple to understand and use, and they meet the requirements of most "casual" users who write programs that perform input and output to files. They do have some limitations, however, for any program that makes heavy use of files, like an accounting program for a large business or a database program that maintains an electronic card catalog for a library. These limitations include the inability to open a file for input *and* output simultaneously, and the fact that the data in the file must always be read in order, from first to last, with no possibility of skipping directly to, say, the 20th data item. Indeed, this second point is why they are called *sequential* files: the data can only be read *in sequence* from beginning to end.

By contrast, a **random-access file** is one in which the data can be accessed in any order (i.e., in "random" order). While sequential files are in some ways analogous to DATA statements, random-access files share some similarities with *arrays*. For instance, we can input the value of the fifth data item directly, without having to look at the first four (for this reason random-access files are sometimes also called **direct-access files**). In fact, random-access files are even slightly more flexible than arrays because each entry can actually consist of several data items of differing types. Nonetheless, as you read on about random-access files, it will be helpful to think of them as arrays of data that happen to be stored in a file.

Random-access files store data quite differently than sequential files; in particular, numeric data in a random-access file is not stored as text characters. The data items in random-access files are stored using a data structure called a *record*: roughly speaking, a **record** is a "composite variable" used to represent a typical data item in the file (very shortly, we'll learn the QuickBASIC statements used for setting up records). To use a random-access file to store data, we must first define the type of record we will be using for that file. It's easiest to see how to do this in the context of an example.

EXAMPLE 7

Suppose we want to write a program that will create and perform several operations on a file containing data about various countries, namely, their populations and capital cities. A typical data item in this file has three parts: the country's name, its population (in millions), and its capital. The following BASIC statement defines a record data structure that could be used to represent such a data item (note the use of the word *title* rather than *name* for the country's name; this is because *name* is a BASIC reserved word). Each record of this type will contain *three* pieces of information.

```
TYPE CountryType
    title AS STRING * 25
    population AS SINGLE        'population in millions
    capital AS STRING * 20
END TYPE
```

Having used the TYPE...END TYPE statement to *define* the record type called CountryType, we now wish to declare a *record variable* to hold data having this record type. Recall that, in Chapter 7, we used the DIM statement to declare array variables. Well, the DIM statement can actually be used to make several different kinds of variable declarations (use the QuickBASIC Help system if you want to see all the details). In particular, the following variation of the DIM statement can be used to declare record variables:

```
DIM country AS CountryType
```

The variable *country* is sometimes called a **user-defined variable.** Up until now, we have discussed only two types of variables, string and numeric, which were designated by the presence or lack of the character "$" at the end of the variable name. The variable *country* is more complex; it is actually a *composite* or *compound* variable made up of three *elements* (*title*, *population*, and *capital*), each of which is in turn described a little more carefully than simply as "string" or "numeric." Table 8.1 lists all the fundamental variable types, usually called *elementary data types*.

There are a variety of things to observe in Table 8.1. First, the groupings of the data types indicate that they fall into three categories: *whole number* (INTEGER and LONG), *real number* (SINGLE and DOUBLE),[3] and *string* (STRING and STRING * <*length*>). The "numeric" and "string" variables that we've been using all along have actually had the implicit data types SINGLE and STRING, respectively.

[3] Real-number variables are also called *floating-point* variables.

TABLE 8.1 Elementary Data Types in BASIC

Name	Description
INTEGER	Integers in the range −32,768 to 32,767
LONG	Integers in the range −2,147,483,648 to 2,147,483,647
SINGLE	Real numbers accurate to 7 digits, in the range 1.4E − 45 to 3.4E + 38 (approximately), not counting sign
DOUBLE	Real numbers accurate to 15 digits, in the range 4.9E − 324 to 1.8E + 308 (approximately), not counting sign
STRING	Variable-length string (up to 32,767 characters)
STRING * <*length*>	Fixed-length string, having a specified number of characters

In addition to declaring arrays or records, the DIM statement can actually be used to create a variable having any one of the types described in Table 8.1. For example, the following statement declares a double-precision variable called *bigNum*:

```
DIM bigNum AS DOUBLE
```

However, our main use of the DIM statement (in addition to setting up arrays) will be to create *record variables* for use with random-access files.

You may wonder why QuickBASIC bothers with the last data type in Table 8.1, the *fixed-length string*; after all, if a variable of type STRING can be any length, why would you want to declare a string variable of fixed length? It turns out that with random-access files, it's useful to be able to set the length of strings. In fact, except for the data type STRING, each of the other data types listed in Table 8.1 requires a *fixed number of bytes* for each variable of that type (for example, variables of type INTEGER each require 2 bytes, variables of type SINGLE use 4 bytes, and fixed-length strings require 1 byte per character). Random-access files make use of this fact to calculate the position of each record, which is why we can access data items directly. (We won't need to know all the technical details, such as the number of bytes used for each type, so don't worry.)

PRACTICE 8.5

For each of the following data descriptions, name the *elementary data type* you think would be most appropriate for representing it (for example, for "birth year of a person," INTEGER would probably be the most appropriate choice):

(a) body temperature for a human being
(b) state capitals (to be stored in a random-access file)
(c) the squares of the integers from 1 to 1,000

(d) the square roots of the integers from 1 to 1,000, accurate to 2 decimal places
(e) the square roots of the integers from 1 to 1,000, accurate to 10 decimal places

8.6 Syntax and Operation of the Record Data Structure

Before we continue with files, let's look at the syntax and operation of the TYPE...END TYPE statement and the DIM statement. The general format of the TYPE...END TYPE statement is shown below; the record type name and element names may be any legal variable names, and the data type names are any of the names that appear in Table 8.1.

TYPE <record type name>
<element name 1> **AS** <data type name>
<element name 2> **AS** <data type name>
<element name 3> **AS** <data type name>
⋮
END TYPE

While the record type name may be any legal variable name, we strongly recommend that you always use a word ending with *Type* to distinguish the *type* of record from a record *variable* of that type. For instance, in Example 7, our record type name was *CountryType*, and a record variable of that type was called *country*.

Important: A TYPE...END TYPE statement defining a record that will be used with a random-access file may* not *have any elements that have data type STRING; only* fixed-length *strings may be used with random-access files.

We can use the DIM statement to declare a variable having either one of the elementary data types or having a record data type that was previously defined using a TYPE...END TYPE statement.

DIM <variable name> **AS** <elementary data type>
or
DIM <variable name> **AS** <record data type>

Variables having elementary data types that are declared with DIM statements can be used, like any variable, in statements such as INPUT, PRINT, LET, and so on. But how do we use a record variable, which is really a composite of its elements? After all, a variable like *country* in Example 7 has three different elements, each of which represents a different kind of data. To refer to a particular element of a record variable, we use a composite name consisting of the variable name, followed by a period, and then the element name. For instance, the following names would be used to refer to each of the elements of the composite variable *country*:

country.title
country.population
country.capital

Each of the three names above is used exactly like a regular variable name in INPUT statements, LET statements, as an argument in calls to functions and subprograms, and so on. Notice, also, that when we use the DIM statement to declare a string variable, we don't need the "$" suffix on the variable name.

EXAMPLE 8

The program segment below shows how we might input values for the record variable *country*. To make it easy to read, we've included the TYPE...END TYPE and DIM statements, and we've highlighted the lines that use the record variable *country*.

```
'Define CountryType record and declare variable of that type

     TYPE CountryType
            title AS STRING * 25
            population AS SINGLE              'population in millions
            capital AS STRING * 20
     END TYPE

     DIM country AS CountryType

'Let user input data for countries; keep track of number of
'countries and total population (for computing average later)

     CLS
     LET numCountries = 0
     LET populationSum = 0

     DO
            PRINT "Enter name of country (<Enter> to quit)";
            INPUT ": ", country.title
            IF country.title = SPACE$(25) THEN
                   EXIT DO
            END IF
            LET numCountries = numCountries + 1
            PRINT "Enter population of "; country.title;
            INPUT ": ", country.population
            LET populationSum = populationSum + country.population
            PRINT "Enter capital of "; country.title;
            INPUT ": ", country.capital
            PRINT
     LOOP
```

```
'Print total number of countries and average population

     PRINT
     PRINT
     IF numCountries > 0 THEN
            PRINT "NUMBER OF COUNTRIES:", numCountries
            PRINT
            LET average = populationSum / numCountries
            LET average = CINT(average * 10) / 10
            PRINT "AVERAGE POPULATION: ", average; "million"
     ELSE
            PRINT "... No countries entered ..."
     END IF
```

Notice that the loop is terminated by the user pressing **<Enter>** when he or she is prompted for a country title. With our usual string variable, the value assigned in that case would be the empty string. However, since the variable *country.title* has type "STRING * 25," it will be filled out to length 25 with spaces, which explains the line "IF country.title = SPACE$(25) THEN." Below is some sample output for this program segment; see if you can figure out why the input lines look the way they do.

```
Enter name of country (Return to quit): Indonesia
Enter population of Indonesia                :177.4
Enter capital of Indonesia                  :Jakarta

Enter name of country (Return to quit): Luxembourg
Enter population of Luxembourg               :0.4
Enter capital of Luxembourg                 :Luxembourg

Enter name of country (Return to quit): Ghana
Enter population of Ghana                    :14.4
Enter capital of Ghana                      :Accra

Enter name of country (Return to quit):

NUMBER OF COUNTRIES:          3

AVERAGE POPULATION:           64.1 million
```

The reason the colon (which was the prompt in the INPUT statements) appears so many spaces after the requests for population and capital is that the variable *country.title* is a *fixed-length string* of length 25; the extra spaces fill it out to that length. Admittedly, this looks a little clumsy—but, luckily, QuickBASIC provides the RTRIM$ string function (which was not mentioned in Chapter 1) to help us out.

RTRIM$(*string expression*) Returns the value of its string argument, with all spaces on the *right* end of the string removed.

LTRIM$(*string expression*) Returns the value of its string argument, with all spaces on the *left* end of the string removed.

Below is a modification of the DO...LOOP in Example 8 that uses the function RTRIM$ to improve the appearance of the output. Modified lines have been highlighted.

```
DO
    PRINT "Enter name of country (Return to quit)";
    INPUT ": ", country.title
    IF RTRIM$(country.title) = "" THEN
       EXIT DO
    END IF
    LET numCountries = numCountries + 1

    PRINT "Enter population of ";RTRIM$(country.title);
    INPUT ": ", country.population
    LET populationSum = populationSum + country.population
    PRINT "Enter capital of "; RTRIM$(country.title);
    INPUT ": ", country.capital
    PRINT
LOOP
```

This is how the output looks after we make the above changes:

```
Enter name of country (Return to quit): Mozambique
Enter population of Mozambique: 15.1
Enter capital of Mozambique: Maputo
```

Another advantage of this modification is that if we decide to change the length of the strings in our TYPE...END TYPE statement, we don't have to change the IF...THEN condition used for exiting the loop. Complete programs for both versions of Example 8 can be found in the files C08EX08A.BAS and C08EX08B.BAS on your SAMPLES disk.

There's one final comment to make about the TYPE...END TYPE and DIM statements, regarding their use in programs that have subprograms or user-defined functions. TYPE...END TYPE statements are permitted *only in the main program*; you may *not* define record data structures with the TYPE...END TYPE statement in subprograms or user-defined functions. However, once you've defined a record data structure in the main program with a TYPE...END TYPE statement, you can use the DIM statement *anywhere in your program* to declare record variables having that record type; if you use DIM to declare a record variable in a subprogram, the variable will be treated as a *local* variable.

In the next section, we'll learn how to use records in conjunction with random-access files. Although this is the only use of records that will be discussed in this text, you can actually use record variables in any program, even a program that doesn't use files at all. In large, complex programs, record variables are very useful for storing data in an organized, structured way, which aids ease of program design and readability.

PRACTICE 8.6

In Example 6 of Section 8.4, we looked at data on cereals. For each cereal, we gave its brand name (e.g., "Fiber One"), its cost (in cents) per ounce, a rating of 1 to 5 for its fiber content, and its number of calories per ounce.

1. Use the TYPE...END TYPE statement to define a record type (with four elements) for this data; be sure to use fixed-length strings.
2. Use the DIM statement to declare a record variable having the type you defined in Exercise 1.
3. Write a sequence of four INPUT statements that permit the user to give values to the variable you declared in Exercise 2.
4. Write a segment that describes the fiber content of the cereal entered in Exercise 3 as "excellent," "good," "fair," "poor," or "bad." For example, for the cereal Fiber One, output would be as follows:

```
Fiber One has excellent fiber content.
```

Use the RTRIM$ function so that your output won't have any extra spaces after the cereal name.

8.7 Using Random-Access Files

A random-access file stores on disk a collection of records all having the same record type; as we mentioned in Section 8.6, in this case, only fixed-length data types are allowed in the TYPE...END TYPE statement, that is, any type from Table 8.1 *except* STRING. For instance, the record type *CountryType* of Examples 7 and 8 satisfies this requirement. Remember also that the data in random-access files is stored differently than in text files; nonetheless, you can imagine the records being stored one after another in the file. If we set up a random-access file to hold records of type *CountryType*, you might imagine it looking as below after we had put some record data into it. (We've placed the actual file contents in boldface and used italics to show the record number of each record and the names of each element; the record numbers and element names are *not* contained in the file.)

Record Number	*Title*	*Population*	*Capital*
1	**Indonesia**	**177.4**	**Jakarta**
2	**Luxembourg**	**.4**	**Luxembourg**
3	**Ghana**	**14.4**	**Accra**
4	**Mozambique**	**15.1**	**Maputo**

Because we used only fixed-length data types, each record occupies exactly the same number of bytes. This is the key idea behind random-access files: by requiring that the length of all the records in the file be the same, QuickBASIC is able to say precisely where each record in the file begins. Thus, it can, for example, locate the third record without having to look at the first two. For now, though, let's see how to set up a random-access file and then how to output records to the file.

STEPS FOR SETTING UP A RANDOM-ACCESS FILE

1. Before setting up the file, we must first define the record type for the kind of records we want to store in the file; we do this using the TYPE...END TYPE statement as described in the previous two sections (again, no elements of type STRING are permitted—only fixed-length strings may be used).
2. Next, we use DIM statements to declare variables of the record type defined in Step 1.
3. Now that we've defined our record type and have declared one or more record variables of that type, we're ready to set up our random-access file. This is done by using yet another variant of the OPEN statement. The syntax is as follows:

OPEN "<file name>**" FOR RANDOM AS #** <file number> **LEN = LEN(**record variable**)**

This statement sets up a random-access file, gives it a reference number, and, finally, declares the size of the records that this file will hold. Notice that you do not need to calculate the size of the records yourself; it is equal to the value of the expression "LEN(*record variable*)".

Continuing with the program in Example 8, here is how we could open a random-access file called C08EX08.DAT to hold records of type *CountryType*, once we had declared a variable *country* of that type:

```
OPEN "C08EX08.DAT" FOR RANDOM AS #1 LEN = LEN(country)
```

Once we open our random-access file, how do we output and input data to and from the file? With sequential files, we used PRINT #, WRITE #, and INPUT #, but these statements are *not* used with random-access files. Instead, we use the GET statement for input and the PUT statement for output.

To use GET and PUT, we must specify the file reference number and the variable name, as we did with input and output statements for sequential files. However, with random-access files, we must also specify *where in the file* we want the input/output to occur. For instance, we can input the fourth record in random-access file opened as number 2 into a record variable named *numRecord* as follows:

```
GET #2, 4, numRecord
```

Let's see the syntax of the GET and PUT statements; then we'll learn more about them by looking at examples.

GET #<*file number*>,<*record number*>,<*record variable*> **Inputs the** indicated record (i.e., indicated by *record number*) from the file (indicated by *file number*) into the specified *variable*.

PUT #<*file number*>, <*record number*>, <*record variable*> **Outputs** the value of the specified record *variable* into the file indicated by *file number*, at the position indicated by *record number*.

GET and PUT input or output all the elements of a record in one fell swoop. The following statement would PUT (i.e., output to the file) the complete contents of a record variable called *testRecord* at position 23 in file number 7:

```
PUT #7, 23, testRecord
```

In both the GET and PUT statements, you can omit the *record number* argument; in that case, the input/output occurs at the position immediately following the current record number (i.e., the position following the most recent GET or PUT statement; for the *first* such statement, this would be position 1). For example, the following pair of statements would GET (i.e., input) a record value from position 19 and then PUT (i.e., output) a record value in position 20:

```
GET #1, 19, record1
PUT #1, , record2
```

EXAMPLE 9

Let's modify the program of Example 8 so that it records the data on each country in a file called COUNTRY.DAT. In this version, we'll omit the section that prints the total number of countries and average population. (Modifications are highlighted.)

```
'Define CountryType record and declare variable of that type

     TYPE CountryType
          title AS STRING * 25
          population AS SINGLE               'population in millions
          capital AS STRING * 20
     END TYPE

     DIM country AS CountryType

'Set up random-access file to store data

     OPEN "COUNTRY.DAT" FOR RANDOM AS #1 LEN = LEN(country)

'Let user input data for countries; record data in file

     CLS
     DO
          'input data for next country
          PRINT "Enter name of country (Return to quit)";
          INPUT ": ", country.title
          IF RTRIM$(country.title) = "" THEN
             EXIT DO
          END IF
          PRINT "Enter population of "; RTRIM$(country.title);
          INPUT ": ", country.population
          PRINT "Enter capital of "; RTRIM$(country.title);
          INPUT ": ", country.capital
          PRINT

          'record data in file
          PUT #1, , country
     LOOP
```

If we run this program and enter data for several countries, it will be recorded in the file COUNTRY.DAT in the order in which it's entered. For example, suppose that the first time we run this program, we enter the following data:

```
Indonesia, 177.4, Jakarta
Luxembourg, 0.4, Luxembourg
Ghana, 14.4, Accra
```

This data will be recorded in the new file COUNTRY.DAT in the order that we entered it. Suppose that we now run the program *again*, entering data for two additional countries as shown below:

```
Mozambique, 15.1, Maputo
Greece, 10.1, Athens
```

This data will also be recorded in COUNTRY.DAT in the order in which we entered it—but it will be recorded at the *beginning* of the file, *wiping out* any data that was there already! Thus, the file would now contain information on the following countries (in order): Mozambique, Greece, Ghana; the information on Indonesia and Luxembourg would be wiped out. This would happen because, when you first OPEN a file, the record position is set at 0, that is, preceding the first piece of data in the file.

Clearly, this won't do—and, as you might expect, there's a way out. Obviously, we'd like to have the new data appended to the *end* of the file, preserving the records already there. We can do this by calculating the position of the last record in the file and then, in our PUT statements, specifying record numbers starting at the next position. To do this, we need another function:

> **LOF**(*file number*) Returns the length, in bytes, of the indicated file (LOF stands for "length of file").

For instance, if random-access file number 1 had 5 records, each 30 bytes long, then the value of LOF(1) would be 150. That relationship, namely,

length of file = (length of a single record) * (total number of records)

is the key to finding the position of the last record, since that is the same as the number of records. Rearranging the above equation gives us the following:

position of last record = total number of records
= (length of file)/(length of a single record)

This last expression can be computed using functions we've introduced in this chapter, giving us the following useful formula:

position of last record = LOF(**file number*****)/LEN(*****record variable*****)***

Using this formula, we can fix our program as below, so that it will *append* new records to the end of the existing file each time it's run (new lines are highlighted).

```
LET lastPos = LOF(1)/LEN(country)
DO
    'input data for next country
    PRINT "Enter name of country (Return to quit)";
    INPUT ": ", country.title
    IF RTRIM$(country.title) = "" THEN
       EXIT DO
    END IF
    PRINT "Enter population of "; RTRIM$(country.title);
```

```
        INPUT ": ", country.population
        PRINT "Enter capital of "; RTRIM(country.title);
        INPUT ": ", country.capital
        PRINT

        'record data in file
        LET lastPos = lastPos + 1
        PUT #1, lastPos, country
    LOOP
```

EXAMPLE 10

Let's modify the above program segment so that, after users have finished entering data on new countries, they can see a list of all countries in the file having populations in a given range. The complete program is in the file C08EX10.BAS, but the new part is shown below. Remember that we already have the current value of the variable *lastPos* from the previous segment; we can use the GET statement in a FOR...NEXT loop to input each record and print it if its value is in the appropriate range.

```
INPUT "Enter minimum population: ", min
INPUT "Enter maximum population: ", max

CLS
PRINT , "COUNTRY", "CAPITAL", "POPULATION"
PRINT , "-------", "-------", "----------"
FOR position = 1 TO lastPos
    GET #1, position, country
    IF country.population >= min AND country.population <= max THEN
        PRINT , RTRIM$(country.title), RTRIM$(country.capital),
        PRINT country.population
    END IF
NEXT position
```

If we enter data for the countries Indonesia, Luxembourg, Ghana, Mozambique, and Greece, and then ask for the countries with populations between 10 and 20 million, this is the output:

```
              COUNTRY       CAPITAL    POPULATION
              -------       -------    ----------
              Ghana         Accra       14.4
              Mozambique    Maputo      15.1
              Greece        Athens      10.1
```

The last thing we'll mention here concerns using the same random-access data file in more than one program. This is something you may well want to do—but be sure to use the *same record definition* in each program that uses the same random-access data file. This is necessary because once the file is created, the length of each record is fixed; if you later use a different record definition in another program, its elements may have different lengths, and the original file will be destroyed.

PRACTICE 8.7

This practice is a continuation of Practice 8.6, in which you set up a record variable to store information about cereals.

1. Using the data type and record variable you set up in Practice 8.6, use the OPEN statement to set up a random-access file to store records of that type.
2. In Practice 8.6, Exercise 3, you wrote a sequence of INPUT statements that let the user enter values for your record variable. Add a PUT statement at the end of that segment that will record the data in the file.
3. Suppose, now, that a program has been written that permits the user to record information for an arbitrary number of cereals in the data file. Use the formula we developed in this section to write an expression representing the position of the last record in the file.
4. Modify the segment you wrote in Practice 8.6, Exercise 4, so that it asks the user for a number from 1 to the value computed in Exercise 3 above, GETs the data recorded at that position in the file, and then prints the sentence describing the fiber content of the cereal.

8.8 Using Record Variables in Subprograms

We have now seen how to set up a random-access data file and how to use the GET and PUT statements to input and output data to and from the file. In this final section, we'll discuss how to use random-access files in larger programs, particularly in conjunction with subprograms. We'll see that the main thing to understand is how to use record variables in subprograms.

File access statements (e.g., OPEN, GET, PUT) can be used anywhere in a program, including in subprograms and user-defined functions. The first (and most important) issue we must address is how to share data from a *file* with subprograms and the main program. Recall from Chapter 6 that we use *parameters* to share data, and that each data item can be a value or a variable. Now the data from random-access files can be stored in *record variables*, so we need to learn how to use record variables as parameters.

In several examples in the previous section, we used a record type called *CountryType*. Now, suppose we wanted to create a subprogram GetData to input data for particular countries, which would then be used by the main program. We could give that subprogram a parameter *newCountry* of type *CountryType* as follows:

```
SUB GetData(newCountry AS CountryType)
```

In the parameter specification, we must indicate that *newCountry* is a record variable; if we omit "AS CountryType," the compiler will assume that *newCountry* is simply a plain numeric variable. In general, the syntax for specifying a parameter with a record type is as follows (the ellipses—"..."—indicate that the subprogram may have more than one parameter):

SUB <subprogram name>**(. . . ,** <variable name> **AS** <data type>**, . . .)**

or

FUNCTION <function name>**(. . . ,** <variable name> **AS** <data type>**, . . .)**

The DECLARE statement that is automatically inserted when you save or compile the program will substitute the word *ANY* for the actual data type; as with other DECLARE statements, you can just ignore it! Here's what the DECLARE statement would be for the above SUB definition:

```
DECLARE SUB GetData(newCountry AS ANY)
```

In addition to sharing data, subprograms often make use of *local variables*. If we wish to use a record variable as a local variable in a subprogram, we must put a DIM statement in the subprogram to declare that variable (remember, though, that the TYPE...END TYPE statement that defines the record type must be in the *main* program). If we wanted a local record variable named *country* in the above subprogram, we would simply put a DIM statement at an appropriate spot in the subprogram, for example:

```
SUB GetData(newCountry AS CountryType)

    'Set up local record variable for use in subprogram
    DIM country AS CountryType
        .
        .
        (rest of subprogram)
        .
        .

END SUB
```

In subprograms that access a random-access file, you'll almost always need a "generic" record variable, just so that you can easily GET and PUT data in the file. One way to do this is to declare the variable *locally* in each case (as shown above), that is, use a similar DIM statement in each subprogram. Rather than have many identical DIM statements, you can use yet another variant of DIM that permits you to declare a variable once in the main program that can then be used in any subprogram or user-defined function. To do this, simply say DIM SHARED instead of DIM. Here is how you might declare a "shared" variable of type *CountryType*:

```
'Set up a shared variable; must be done in main program
DIM SHARED country AS CountryType
```

The variable *country* may now be used in any of the subprograms of that program. *Be careful* about using shared variables, because they are like hidden parameters; in other words, if they are changed in one subprogram, then the next time you use them—either in another subprogram or in the main program—they *remain* changed! We tend to use them only as a "generic" variable for use in GET and PUT statements.

To illustrate these ideas, we'll create a program that will manage an electronic telephone directory that is stored in a random-access file. But first, let's summarize the three ways we discussed for using record variables in subprograms:

USING RECORD VARIABLES IN SUBPROGRAMS

1. As *parameters*: To define a parameter with record type in a subprogram or user-defined function, we add the qualifier "AS <*record type*>" after the parameter name; the corresponding DECLARE statement will say "AS ANY."
2. As *local variables*: To have a local variable with record type in a subprogram or user-defined function, we simply declare it with a DIM statement, just as we would in the main program.
3. As *shared variables*: We can declare a record variable in the main program that will be recognized (i.e., "shared") by all subprograms and user-defined functions by using the DIM SHARED statement to declare it (this statement may be used *only* in the main program).

EXAMPLE 11

Let's design a program that will allow students to set up a personal telephone directory containing the names and extensions of their friends and permit them to look up and add entries. Typical operations that we might want are:

1. Look up a name and print the corresponding extension
2. Look up an extension and print the corresponding name
3. Print all listings for a given letter of the alphabet (e.g., all listings for names starting with *B*)
4. Add a new listing

Notice that every subprogram will need to access the file, so it probably makes sense to set up a generic shared variable for input and output. The main program will set up the record type (remember that we may use the TYPE...END TYPE statement only in the main program), declare the shared record variable, open a random-access file for that type, and then permit the user to choose an operation. We can then call subprograms to carry out each operation. Below are the statements from the main program that set up the record type, declare the shared variable, and open the file.

```
TYPE EntryType
    lastName AS STRING * 20
    firstName AS STRING * 20
    extension AS STRING * 4
END TYPE

DIM SHARED entry AS EntryType

OPEN "PHONE.DAT" FOR RANDOM AS #1 LEN = LEN(entry)
```

Notice that we open our file at the beginning of the program. When we discussed sequential files, we recommended that you open and close them at exactly those times in the program when you needed to use them; this was because sequential files could not be used simultaneously for both input and output. Random-access files *can* be used simultaneously for both input and output; and, in a program like this, which is designed specifically for using a file, it makes sense simply to open the file once at the beginning and close it once at the end of the program. The rest of the main program will present the user with a menu of operations to choose from.

Let's look, now, at one or two of the subprograms. The program that looks up a given name should input a name, search the file for entries with that name, and print out either the listing it finds or a message that no listing was found. We decided to ask only for the *last* name and then have the program print out all entries with that name; not only is this a little simpler to write than if we asked for the full name, but it avoids the problem of nicknames (e.g., if the user enters the first name "Sue" but the listing has "Susan"). The algorithm outline is:

1. Get last name to look up
2. For each listing in the file
    a. Compare listing's last name with last name that was entered
    b. If last names match, then print the listing
3. If no matches are found, say so

To do Step 3, we decided to keep a count of the number of entries found and to print that out at the end. Below is our subprogram; note that, since it doesn't share information with the main program, it needs no parameters (it uses the shared variable *entry* to get data from the file).

```
SUB LookUpName
'Print listing for given name

    CLS
    INPUT "Enter last name of entry to look up: ", lastName$
    LET lastName$ = UCASE$(lastName$)

    'Print all entries with that name
    LET lastPos = LOF(1) / LEN(entry)
    LET numFound = 0
    PRINT
    FOR position = 1 TO lastPos
        GET #1, position, entry
        IF RTRIM$(entry.lastName) = lastName$ THEN
            LET numFound = numFound + 1
            PRINT RTRIM$(entry.lastName); ", ";
            PRINT RTRIM$(entry.firstName); ": ";
            PRINT entry.extension
        END IF
    NEXT position
    PRINT
    PRINT "Number of entries found: "; numFound

END SUB
```

Although we use DO...LOOPs to search sequential files, we can often use FOR...NEXT loops to search random-access files. This is possible because we can calculate the exact number of records in a random-access file by using the formula developed in Section 8.7.

Let's now think about how to add a listing to our file. The simplest algorithm would be:

1. Get data for new listing
2. Move to end of file and PUT new listing in file

But let's make this algorithm a little more sophisticated. First, it makes sense to check whether the listing is already present to avoid duplicate listings. Second, it seems preferable to keep the listings in alphabetical order rather than simply putting new listings at the end of the file (this decision will also affect the subprogram that prints all listings starting with a specified letter). Our revised algorithm is:

1. Get data for new listing
2. Check current file to see if listing is there
    a. If listing is there, say so
    b. If name is there, but extension is different, give user the option of changing the extension

   c. If name is not there, then find correct location for new listing (i.e., look for first listing that is alphabetically *after* new listing)
3. If listing isn't there, then, starting at end of file, shift all entries down one position to make room for new entry; insert new entry at proper position (found in Step 2c)

This algorithm is complicated enough to warrant separate subprograms for each of the three main steps; the subprogram for the entire algorithm will call these three auxiliary subprograms. Here's the subprogram, AddNewListing, which calls subprograms GetData, CheckFile, and Insert to carry out Steps 1 to 3:

```
SUB AddNewListing
'Inputs and adds a new entry to the file, keeping alphabetical order

    'Set up record variable for new entry

        DIM newEntry AS EntryType

    'Get data for new entry

        CLS
        CALL GetData(newEntry)
        PRINT

    'Check listing to see if entry is already there

        CALL CheckFile(newEntry, newPos)

    'If newPos is not zero, then it equals position for new entry,
    'so insert new entry there

        If newPos > 0 THEN
            CALL Insert(newEntry, newPos)
        END IF

    'for testing, print out whole list

        PRINT
        LET lastPos = LOF(1) / LEN(entry)
        FOR position = 1 TO lastPos
            GET #1, position, entry
            PRINT RTRIM$(entry.lastName); ", ";
            PRINT RTRIM$(entry.firstName); ": ";
            PRINT entry.Extension
        NEXT position

END SUB
```

Like the subprogram LookUpName, AddNewListing does not need to share its data with the main program; notice that the variable *newEntry* was declared locally. On the other hand, AddNewListing *will* need to share the information about the new entry with the three auxiliary subprograms; therefore, they each have a record parameter of type *EntryType*, so that we can pass the variable *newEntry* as an argument. Below is the subprogram Insert; notice also that it and AddNewListing both make use of the generic shared variable *entry*.

```
SUB Insert (newEntry AS EntryType, newPos)
'Insert newEntry at indicated position, moving latter entries down first
'to make room

    LET lastPos = LOF(1) / LEN(entry)
    FOR position = lastPos TO newPos STEP -1
        GET #1, position, entry
        PUT #1, position + 1, entry
    NEXT position
    PUT #1, newPos, newEntry
    PRINT
    PRINT "Entry added to directory."

END SUB
```

Be sure to try this program, which is contained in the file C08EX11.BAS.

Many commercial programs are analogous to this last example, in the sense that their job is to perform a variety of operations on a data file. These operations may include inserting or deleting entries, searching for a particular entry, sorting the file entries in one or more ways, and so on. To complete our study of records and random-access files, let's look at two statements that will help us work with record variables and will thus be useful in programs that use random-access files.

LET *<record variable 1>* = *<record variable 2>* Assigns to *record variable 1*, element by element, all the values of *record variable 2*.

SWAP *<variable 1>*, *<variable 2>* Exchanges the values of the two specified variables. Any type of variable may be used (e.g., numeric or string, simple or record), so long as the two variables have *exactly the same type*. If they are record variables, then the values of each of their elements will be exchanged.

What's nice about these statements is that they let us assign (or swap) an entire record variable—which is really a composite having several values—in one fell swoop. We have, of course, been using LET for simple variables since Chapter 1. SWAP is new, but recall that we discussed the process of swapping the values of two variables in Sections 3.2 and 7.3.

It's worthwhile to compare LET and SWAP with statements like INPUT and PRINT. INPUT and PRINT can handle only *individual elements* of a record variable, which makes sense if you think about it. LET and SWAP (and, for that matter, GET and PUT) can handle a complete record variable all at once. Let's look at an example that adds sorting options to the program discussed in Example 9 (which inputted data on countries and stored it in a random-access file).

EXAMPLE 12

In Example 9, we wrote a program that inputted information about countries (their populations and capitals) and stored it in the random-access file COUNTRY.DAT. New entries were appended to the end of the file. In the program C08EX12.BAS, we've added three subprograms: one to sort the file alphabetically by country, one to sort the file by population size, and one to print the file contents on the screen. To keep things as simple as we could, we based our sorting subprograms on the Selection Sort algorithm discussed in Section 7.3. Here is the subprogram that sorts alphabetically by country (the subprogram for sorting by population is very similar):

```
SUB SortByCountry
'Sorts file entries alphabetically by country

    DIM startCountry AS CountryType
    DIM smallCountry AS CountryType
    DIM currentCountry AS CountryType

    LET lastPos = LOF(1) / LEN(Country)

    FOR startPos = 1 TO lastPos - 1
        GET #1, startPos, startCountry
        LET smallPos = startPos
        LET smallCountry = startCountry
        FOR currentPos = startPos + 1 TO lastPos
            GET #1, currentPos, currentCountry
            IF currentCountry.title < smallCountry.title THEN
                LET smallCountry = currentCountry
                LET smallPos = currentPos
            END IF
        NEXT currentPos
```

```
        PUT #1, startPos, smallCountry
        PUT #1, smallPos, startCountry
    NEXT startPos

END SUB
```

If you carefully compare this subprogram to the Selection Sort algorithm of Section 7.3, you'll see that we've changed it a little (in addition to the obvious introduction of files and records). In the original algorithm, the entries were stored in an array, and we designed the algorithm to do as few swaps as possible (instead, it kept track of *positions* of entries, since it was quicker to record a position than to swap). This time, as we did our comparisons, we recorded both the position and the *value* of record variables (using the LET statement); we never actually used the SWAP statement. That's because we really needed to swap *file entries* rather than record variables, and we did that with two PUT statements at the end of the subprogram. Here's how the output would look if we entered several countries and then sorted alphabetically:

```
COUNTRY        CAPITAL        POPULATION
=======        =======        ==========

France         Paris           55.9

Ghana          Accra           14.4

Greece         Athens          10.1

Indonesia      Jakarta         177.4

Luxembourg     Luxembourg      .4

Mozambique     Maputo          15.1

Pakistan       Islamabad       107.5
```

Although this subprogram is a little tricky to understand, it illustrates some important ideas—so read it carefully enough to get a good sense of what it does. Among the ideas illustrated by this subprogram is the following:

> ***"File-access" statements (i.e., OPEN, CLOSE, GET, PUT, READ #, PRINT #, and WRITE #) are by far the slowest statements in any program, so try to minimize the number of times you use them.***

In the sorting subprogram above, we recorded the values of record variables in order to avoid having to GET the same file entry more than once on each pass through the list.

PRACTICE 8.8

1. Continuing from Practices 8.6 and 8.7, modify your DIM statement (using the DIM SHARED statement) so that your record variable will be recognized by any subprograms that the program might contain.
2. Write a subprogram that prints out the names of all the cereals in the file that have ''good'' or ''excellent'' fiber content.

Chapter Summary 

In this chapter, we've seen how to use *data files* for input and output of program information. Using data files permits us to deal with large sets of data that could not be handled well if we had to input from the keyboard and output to the screen. Another equally important feature of files is that their data is stored on a disk, which means it is saved even when the computer is turned off. QuickBASIC provides two different kinds of data files: *sequential* and *random-access.*

Sequential files are text files and are easier to learn to use. They are called ''sequential'' because the data in them must be accessed in order; you can't read the 100th item without reading the first 99.

To use a sequential file, you must choose a name for it and then OPEN it in one of three ways.

OPEN "<file name> " *FOR OUTPUT AS* #<number>
Prepares the file to receive output; any previous data in the file will be lost.

OPEN "<file name> " *FOR APPEND AS* #<number>
Prepares the file to receive output; any previous data in the file will remain, while new data will be put at the end of the file (i.e., ''appended'').

OPEN "<file name> " *FOR INPUT AS* #<number>
Prepares the file to be used for INPUT statements.

A sequential file may *not* be used simultaneously for input and output. To avoid confusion about which purpose your file is currently opened for, you should open the file at the point in the program when you need to use it and close it (using the CLOSE statement) as soon as you're finished with that use.

Input and output operations on sequential files are performed by using analogues of the INPUT and PRINT statements that specify the file's reference number and by using the WRITE statement.

INPUT #<number>, <variable>
Inputs the variable from the specified file.

PRINT #<number>, <list of expressions>
Prints the expressions in the indicated file in the same format as they would appear if printed on the screen.

WRITE #<number>, <list of expressions>
Prints the expressions in the indicated file, with strings in quotes and with items on each line separated by commas.

A sequential input file may be created in several ways. If a program creates a sequential output file and then closes it, that file may then be reopened, by that program or by some other program, for use as a sequential input file. Alternatively, we may wish to create a sequential file directly, by simply typing in the data and then saving the file. This can be done using any word processor or text editor that allows us to enter the data and then save the file as *text*. QuickBASIC can be used as a text editor to do this, but we must remember to use the *Create File* option and then highlight "Document" in the dialog box that appears. This sets up the file as a text file and turns off QuickBASIC's Smart Editor.

A useful function when inputting data from a sequential data file, EOF(*file number*) gets the value *true* when we reach the end of the data in the file. This function can be used as a condition on a DO...LOOP to read all the data from the file. Alternatively, we can include *headers* or *trailers* in our data file, as we did with DATA statements (you *should* use headers or trailers if your data file was created using a text editor).

For larger, more complex programs that maintain a data file (using it and updating it in various ways), *random-access files* may be a better choice. While they are, at first, somewhat more difficult to understand than sequential files, they are also more flexible, permitting simultaneous input and output. In addition, the name "random-access" indicates that you can access any item in such a file by specifying its position in the file; in that sense, these files are similar to arrays.

Random access is possible because data in the files is organized into *records* (collections of one or more individual pieces of data), with the total record size fixed. Thus, to use random-access files, you need to understand how to use *record variables*, which are composite variables designed to hold these conglomerate pieces of data.

Before you can use a record variable, you must first use a TYPE...END TYPE statement to *define* the kind of record that you want. You can then use a DIM statement to *declare* a record variable of that type. Variables declared using the DIM statement are called *user-defined variables*.

The individual parts of a record variable, called *elements*, may have any legal data type. The elementary data types include INTEGER, LONG, SINGLE, DOUBLE, STRING, and STRING * <*length*>. Only fixed-length strings are permitted for use with random-access files. Once you've defined a record type and set up a variable of that type, you can refer to individual elements by using the variable name followed by the element name, separated by a period:

<variable name> **.** <element name>

As with sequential files, a random-access file must be opened before it can be used. The appropriate OPEN statement is

OPEN "<file name>**" FOR RANDOM AS #**<record number> **LEN = LEN(**record variable**)**

where the indicated record variable is of the type you plan to use with this file. Since we don't need to worry about opening the file for input as opposed to output, we generally OPEN it once when we first need it in the program and then CLOSE it when we're completely done with it.

To perform input and output on a random-access file, we use the statements GET and PUT, respectively,

GET # <file number>**,** <record number>**,** <record variable>
PUT # <file number>**,** <record number>**,** <record variable>

where *<record number>* is the position in the file where we want to input (GET) or output (PUT) the record variable; if *<record number>* is omitted (but don't leave out the comma!), then the input/output occurs at the position immediately following the current record number.

Frequently, we want to *append* data to the end of the file. To do this, we need to know the position of the last record in the file; then we can set the position in the PUT statement to one higher than that. A formula for the position of the last record in the file is:

position of last record = LOF(*file number*)/LEN(*record variable*)

When writing more complex programs that use random-access files, we will often want to use subprograms. To do this, we must know how to use *record variables* in conjunction with subprograms, because these are the kind of variables that we use with random-access files. To use record variables as parameters and arguments in subprograms and user-defined functions, you must declare them in the heading as follows:

SUB <subprogram name>**(. . . ,** <variable number>**AS** <data type>**, . . .)**
FUNCTION <function name>**(. . . ,** <variable number>**AS** <data type>**, . . .)**

Record variables can also be declared as local variables within a subprogram or user-defined function by using a DIM statement. On the other hand, if all you need is a "generic" record variable for file input and output statements, a useful alternative to local record variables are *shared* variables. These are declared in the main program using the DIM SHARED statement; they are recognized by all subprograms and user-defined functions. But be careful about using shared variables, because they are like "hidden parameters": if they are changed by one subprogram, they will remain changed when you use them somewhere else.

When writing longer programs that make extensive use of random-access files and records, it's worth noting that the LET and SWAP statements can be used to assign or exchange all the elements of a record variable at once. Finally, remember that *file-access* (also called *disk-access*) operations are by far the slowest statements in any program; it's worth taking some time to think about ways to minimize the number of times you use statements such as GET and PUT (or INPUT #, PRINT #, and WRITE # for sequential files) in a given program.

Review Questions

Review questions 1 and 2 deal only with sequential files; the rest of the questions deal with sequential and random-access files.

1. Briefly explain each term or idea:
   (a) sequential file
   (b) opening for OUTPUT versus APPEND
   (c) PRINT # versus WRITE #
   (d) opening for INPUT versus OUTPUT
   (e) EOF function

2. All the programs you wrote previous to those in Chapter 8 sent their output to the screen. Explain what changes you would make to such a program so that it sends its output to a sequential file named OUTPUT.DAT.

3. Briefly explain the main differences between sequential and random-access files and give examples in which each type of file would be more appropriate than the other.

4. Briefly explain each term or idea:
   (a) record variable
   (b) INTEGER versus LONG data types
   (c) SINGLE versus DOUBLE data types
   (d) LOF function
   (e) RTRIM$ and LTRIM$ functions
   (f) DIM SHARED statement

Programming Problems

Note: Problems 1 to 5a use sequential files.

1. (a) In Chapter 2, Programming Problem 1, you were asked to write a program that printed a table showing the squares and square roots of the integers from 1 to 20. Modify that program, or write a new one, so that the output is written to a sequential output file called SQUARE.DAT. Remember that you can use the *DOS Shell* option from the File Menu if you want to use the DOS command TYPE to view the data file.
   (b) Modify the program in part (a) so that it first asks the user for a range (i.e., a low number and a high number) and then prints in the file the table for integers in that range. Does it make more sense here to OPEN the file for OUTPUT or APPEND?

2. Write a program that lets users keep a chronological record of their weight. Each time they run the program, they should input their first name, the date, and their weight, and then record the data in a file called WEIGHT.DAT. Does it make more sense here to OPEN the file for OUTPUT or APPEND? Write the program so that when users type out the

file (at the DOS level) to see how they've been doing, it's easy to read (i.e., a neat table with headings on the columns). Note: The heading should be stored in the file along with the actual data; you can do this by entering the heading the first time you run the program.

3. Write a program that helps drivers keep track of their car's gas mileage. The program will maintain a sequential file called GAS.DAT, whose entries record the odometer reading and the number of gallons taken each time the tank is filled. The program should provide drivers with two options: first, they should be allowed to add a new entry (i.e., odometer reading and number of gallons needed to fill tank); second, they should be able to obtain a printout showing the total number of miles traveled, the number of fill-ups for those miles, and the average mileage. For example, suppose that at some point the file contains the following entries:

```
25361.8,9.2
25634.9,8.7
25976.6,10.2
```

Then the total number of miles traveled is 614.8 (= 25976.6 − 25361.8), the number of fill-ups for those miles is 2 (the first fill-up is gas for previous miles), and the average mileage is 32.5 (= 614.8 / 18.9, rounded to one decimal place, where 18.9 is the total amount of gas used). Notice that, since GAS.DAT will be used for both output and input, you should use WRITE # rather than PRINT #.

4. The table below lists information about several brands of PC FAX boards (the information is from *PC Week*, November 13, 1989, p. 156).

Product	Number of bytes	Baud Rate	Price
Smart Fax	640	9600	799
Page Power	640	9600	1295
TR-111	40	9600	1250
EFax Manager	60	4800	545
GammaFax MC	130	9600	795
SuperFax	60	9600	995

(a) Use the QuickBASIC editor to create a data file named FAX.DAT containing the above information; do *not* include headings and do separate data items on the same line by commas, so that this file can be used as a sequential input file in part (b). Also remember to add either a header or a trailer to the file, as recommended in Section 8.4.

(b) Write a BASIC program that allows users to use the data file you created in two ways. They should be able to do the following:

- Get a listing of the entire file on the screen, with headings (see table above)
- Enter a price and get a listing of those products selling for no more than that price

You'll probably want the main program to provide a menu of choices and then use subprograms to carry out each choice.

Note: Problems 5b to 8 use random-access files (Problem 5a uses sequential files).

5. The table below contains the names of some famous baseball batters.

Name	Years Played	At Bats	Hits
Ty Cobb	24	11436	4190
Rogers Hornsby	23	8173	2930
Joe Jackson	13	4981	1774
Pete Browning	13	4795	1664
Ed Delahanty	16	7493	2593
Ted Williams	19	7706	2654
Babe Ruth	22	8399	2873
Lou Gehrig	17	8001	2721
Rod Carew	19	9315	3053
Joe DiMaggio	13	6821	2214

In parts (a) and (b) you are asked to write two programs that perform the *same tasks* but differ in the kinds of files that they use. The programs should do the following:

- Permit the user to add players to the file
- Print out the names, years played, and batting averages of each player (batting average = hits / at bats, rounded to three decimal places)

(a) Write a program to perform the above tasks, using *sequential files*.
(b) Write a program to perform the above tasks, using *random-access files*.

6. In this problem, you will design a program that manipulates a random-access data file containing data on *glass-cleaning products*. For each product, we'll have the following information: its *name*, its *type* (A = aerosol, T = trigger pump, P = plunger pump, and C = can), its *size* in ounces, its *price*, and its *cleaning ability* (from 1 = worst to 5 = best).

(a) Use a TYPE...END TYPE statement to define a record data type to represent this data; be sure to use fixed-length strings, since these records will be stored in a random-access file.
(b) Write a program that lets the user select from the following operations on a random-access file holding data of the type you defined in part (a):
- Add a new product to the file
- Input a product type (A, T, P, or C) and print a table showing all products of that type
- Input a cleaning ability (1 to 5) and print a table showing all products having a cleaning ability as good as or better than the input ability
- Input a unit price (in the range $.05 to $.15) and print a table showing all products having at most that unit price

Test your program with the following data (from *Consumer Reports*, October 1989, p. 614) and any other data you might like to add:

Product	Type	Size	Price	Cleaning Ability
Savogran Dirtex	A	18	$2.29	5
Glass Plus	T	22	$1.75	5
K Mart	P	22	$1.43	4
Glass Wax	C	16	$2.32	4
Windex	T	22	$2.02	3
Kroger	T	22	$1.39	3
Liquid Gold	A	14	$1.96	2
Sparkle	T	25	$1.88	2

7. (a) Design a record data type to hold information about your music collection. Some information you might want to include is: name of artist, name of album, year of album, type of media (record, tape, CD), type of music (rock, jazz, classical, etc.). Now write a program to maintain a file containing this information. Add subprograms to perform the kinds of operations you think are important, for example, add a new entry, print all entries, print all entries in a given category (by a given artist, all CDs, all rock albums, etc.).

(b) Using the subprogram discussed in Example 12 of Section 8.8 as a model, add one or more subprograms that *sort* your file into a given order. For instance, one subprogram might sort the file *chronologically*, another *alphabetically* by artist, another by media type.

8. In an encyclopedia or almanac, find out the following data for each of the fifty states: name, capital, population, land area. Then write a program that will let you record this data in a random-access file and will permit you to sort the data alphabetically by state name, by population, or by land area. Your program should contain subprograms to perform each of these tasks as well as a subprogram to print out a table showing the contents of the file. Since the complete output cannot fit on one screen, design this last subprogram so that it pauses after 20 lines have been printed and the user presses **<Enter>** to see the next 20 lines of the table.

CHAPTER

9

OUTPUT DESIGN AND TEXT GRAPHICS

CHAPTER PREVIEW

In this chapter, we'll learn some techniques for making the output of our programs more readable and better looking. The *PRINT USING* statement helps us print output data in exactly the form we want and is especially handy if we are printing a table. *Text graphics* can be used in practically every program to give the output color and to draw such things as designs, borders, menus, and bar graphs.

9.1 Introduction

When we write a program to perform some task, the single most important goal is that it *work properly*, that is, it must give the user the *correct answers* to the questions asked. After that come other slightly lesser but still important goals. Does the program run quickly and efficiently? Is the program itself easy to read and understand (i.e., is it well structured and well documented)? Is the *output* of the program easy to read, clearly organized, and attractive to the eye?

In this chapter, we'll concentrate on the last of these goals: good output design. If you're writing programs for yourself only, it's nice but not necessary to have attractive and clear output; but if you're writing programs that other people will use, it's essential!

Throughout this text, we've been concerned with producing clear output. We've discussed, for example:

1. Clearing the screen (CLS) at the beginning and perhaps at other times during output
2. Skipping lines (PRINT) to enhance readability
3. Having informative and friendly introductions and user prompts
4. Using commas in PRINT statements to line up columns for a table

In addition, there are other ways to make our output neater and nicer—in fact, downright *fancy* if we want! In this chapter, we'll discuss how to get numeric and string output into the exact form we want with the PRINT USING statement, how to place the cursor wherever we want on the output screen, and how to use QuickBASIC *text graphics* for color. We'll see how to use these techniques for creating menus, drawing bar graphs, and so on. This is fun stuff, so let's get to it!

9.2 The PRINT USING Statement

There are many times when we want the values of the variables we are outputting to have a certain form. For example, we may want numbers rounded to the nearest 100th (e.g., dollars and cents), or we may want a dollar sign in front of each item on a line, or we may want to align the decimal points in columns of numbers. Especially in creating an output table, it can be difficult or at least clumsy using the simple PRINT statement to get things the way we want.

EXAMPLE 1

Look at the following segment, which outputs a table of prices in dollars and cents:

```
FOR row = 1 TO 3
      READ price1, price2, price3, price4
      PRINT price1, price2, price3, price4
NEXT row
DATA 4.55, 10.50, 6.43, 8.00, 12.78, 13.85, 5.00, 15.82
DATA 10.35, 7.00, 4.75, 9.98
```

The output will look like this:

```
4.55      10.5      6.43      8
12.78     13.85     5         15.82
10.35     7         4.75      9.98
```

What we would *like*, of course, would be for it to look like this:

```
$ 4.55    $10.50    $ 6.43    $ 8.00
$12.78    $13.85    $ 5.00    $15.82
$10.35    $ 7.00    $ 4.75    $ 9.98
```

In fact, QuickBASIC includes a statement, **PRINT USING**, that helps you to put output in the form you desire. Shortly, we'll see how to create the table above, but let's start with a simpler example. If you want the variable *cost* (which is less than $1,000) to print out in standard dollars and cents form, you need only say:

```
PRINT USING "$###.##"; cost
```

If *cost* is $45, the output will have the form:

```
$ 45.00
```

Notice that we could not have gotten the ".00" if we had used PRINT rather than PRINT USING. If *cost* is two-thirds of $1,000, then the output will have the form:

```
$666.67
```

Notice that this value has been *rounded off* to the nearest cent without using the CINT function!

Another useful feature of *formatting strings* (such as $###.## in the above example) is that if we use the same formatting string in two or more successive PRINT USING statements, *the decimal points will line up*. For instance, say we had an array *cost( )* and, say, *cost(1)* is $5.74 and *cost(2)* is $87, then the output of

```
PRINT USING "$###.##"; cost(1)
PRINT USING "$###.##"; cost(2)
```

is

```
$ 5.74
$87.00
```

In this example, we used "$###.##" twice. A more convenient option is to store this formatting string in a string variable named, say, *format$*, and then refer to the variable name:

```
LET format$ = "$###.##"
PRINT USING format$; cost(1)
PRINT USING format$; cost(2)
```

Although there are quite a few characters that can be used in the formatting string of a PRINT USING statement, Table 9.1 below lists the ones most commonly used (for others, look up PRINT USING in the QuickBASIC Help System or Reference Manual).

TABLE 9.1 Characters Used in Formatting Strings

Character(s)	Effect When Used in a Formatting String
#	Provides a position for a single digit. Digit positions are filled starting from the right; any unused digit positions on the left are filled with spaces.
.	Prints a decimal point. Digit positions to the right of a decimal point will be filled by rounding off or filling unused positions with zeros.
$	Prints a dollar sign to the left of the leftmost digit position. Thus, dollar signs on successive lines will line up.
$$	Prints a (single) dollar sign in the first *unused* digit position on the left. Thus, dollar signs on successive lines will *not* necessarily line up.
,	When used to the left of the decimal point in the format string (or to the right of the rightmost # if there is no decimal point), causes a comma to be printed after every third digit position to the left of the decimal point.
\ \	Indicates the beginning and ending positions of a field for printing *strings*. If a string to be printed is too long for the field, its rightmost characters will be omitted; if it's too short, the field will be filled out with blanks on the right. (Note that these are *back*slashes.)

Below are some examples of the options listed in Table 9.1.

QuickBASIC Statement	Output
`PRINT USING "###.#"; 134.71`	`134.7`
`PRINT USING "###"; 34.71`	`35`
`PRINT USING "##.##"; 18`	`18.00`
`PRINT USING "$###.##"; 35.6`	`$ 35.60`
`PRINT USING "$$###.##"; 35.6`	`$35.60`
`PRINT USING "#####,.##"; 7462`	`$ 7,462.00`
`PRINT USING "\        \"; "Hi!"`	`Hi!`
`PRINT USING "\        \"; "Hi there!"`	`Hi ther`

The question now becomes: how can we make use of this new tool to print *tables* like the one in Example 1? It turns out that there are *two* separate ways to do it:

Method 1: Use a combination of PRINT TAB and PRINT USING statements

Method 2: Use a single formatting string for a whole line of a table

Let's take a quick look at each of these possibilities. First, the TAB function, which is always used in conjunction with PRINT, simply sets the cursor at the desired column (1–79) on the current line. For example,

```
PRINT TAB(20);
```

sets the cursor at the 20th column of the current line (unless the cursor is already beyond the 20th column, in which case it sets it there in the *next* line). Similarly, the statement

```
PRINT TAB(35); "How are you?"
```

prints the message "How are you?" starting in the 35th column of the current line. The argument in parentheses can be any valid numeric expression. What, for example, is the output of this little segment?

```
FOR num = 1 TO 10
    PRINT TAB(5 * num); "FUN!"
NEXT num
```

Although we can't combine PRINT TAB and PRINT USING into a single statement, we can certainly produce a neat table row using a series of alternating statements, like this:

```
LET format$ = "$##.##"
PRINT USING format$; price1;
PRINT TAB(16);
PRINT USING format$; price2;
PRINT TAB(31);
PRINT USING format$; price3;
PRINT TAB(46);
PRINT USING format$; price 4
```

Though this is a little cumbersome in this setting, the TAB statement can often come in handy. For more about it, use the QuickBASIC Help System or see the Reference Manual.

Method 2 provides a simpler way to handle tables: a single formatting string for the whole row of the table. For example:

```
LET format$ = "$##.##       $##.##       $##.##       $##.##"
PRINT USING format$; price1, price2, price3, price4
```

Let's use Method 2 to give the program segment in Example 1 the output we desire.

```
LET format$ = "$##.##      $##.##      $##.##      $##.##"
FOR row = 1 TO 3
       READ price1, price2, price3, price4
       PRINT USING format$; price1, price2, price3, price4
NEXT row
DATA 4.55, 10.50, 6.43, 8.00, 12.78, 13.85, 5.00, 15.82
DATA 10.35, 7.00, 4.75, 9.98
```

Now the output looks the way we want it to.

```
$ 4.55     $10.50     $ 6.43     $ 8.00
$12.78     $13.85     $ 5.00     $15.82
$10.35     $ 7.00     $ 4.75     $ 9.98
```

Let's look at another fairly simple example for which the output would be impossible to "get right" without PRINT USING.

EXAMPLE 2

Clarence's Computer Supplies is having a sale on various items. If you buy from 1 to 10 units of an item, the unit price is discounted 20%; if you buy 11–25 units, the discount is 35%; and if you buy more than 25, you get a 50% discount on each unit. Let's write a program that prints out the names, list prices, and discount prices of a dozen items for advertising purposes. The data is as follows (item name followed by list price):

printer cable, $18.90, ROM chip, $42.50,
mouse, $121.40, floppy drive, $180.55, box of disks, $11,
RAM expander, $60.35, 1200B modem, $140.50 ,
KingClone PC, $750, word processor, $150,
spreadsheet, $135, FORTRAN, $100, QuickBASIC, $85.30

The algorithm for this is very easy.

1. Print the headings for the table
2. For each sale item:
   a. Read the name and list price
   b. Compute and print those and the three discount prices, which will be .8 (i.e., 100% − 20%), .65, and .5 of the list price, respectively

Not much to it. Let's write the program.

```
'---------------------------------------------------------------
'   Program Title: C09EX02.BAS
'   Author:        J. Galbraith
'   Date:          Sept. 8, 1991

'   Prints out flyer for September computer sale.
'---------------------------------------------------------------

'Print the headings.

    CLS
    PRINT "                    Clarence's Computer Supplies"
    PRINT
    PRINT "               *******BIG FALL CLEARANCE SALE*******"
    PRINT
    PRINT "     ITEM     LIST PRICE         DISCOUNTED UNIT PRICE FOR QUANTITY"
    PRINT
    PRINT "                                 1-10          11-25     MORE THAN 25"
    PRINT

'Set the formatting string and process the data.

    LET  f$ = "\              \  $###.##        $###.##        $###.##      $###.##"
    FOR item = 1 TO 12
         READ name$, price
         PRINT USING f$; name$, price, .8 * price, .65 * price, .5 * price
    NEXT item
    PRINT
    PRINT "               Hope you like CLARENCE'S CLEARANCE !!"
```

```
'Data section.

    DATA Printer cable, 18.9, ROM chip, 42.5, Mouse, 121.4
    DATA Floppy drive, 180.55, Box of disks, 11, RAM expander, 60.35
    DATA 1200B Modem, 140.5, KingClone PC, 750, Word Processor, 150
    DATA Spreadsheet, 135, FORTRAN, 100, QuickBASIC, 85.30

END
```

The output is as follows. Notice how nicely it all works!

```
                 Clarence's Computer Supplies

            *******BIG FALL CLEARANCE SALE*******

    ITEM        LIST PRICE    DISCOUNTED UNIT PRICE FOR QUANTITY

                                1-10       11-25    MORE THAN 25

Printer cable     $ 18.90     $ 15.12    $ 12.28     $   9.45
ROM chip          $ 42.50     $ 34.00    $ 27.62     $  21.25
Mouse             $121.40     $ 97.12    $ 78.91     $  60.70
Floppy drive      $180.55     $144.44    $117.36     $  90.28
Box of disks      $ 11.00     $  8.80    $  7.15     $   5.50
RAM expander      $ 60.35     $ 48.28    $ 39.23     $  30.17
1200B Modem       $140.50     $112.40    $ 91.32     $  70.25
KingClone PC      $750.00     $600.00    $487.50     $375.00
Word Processor    $150.00     $120.00    $ 97.50     $  75.00
Spreadsheet       $135.00     $108.00    $ 87.75     $  67.50
FORTRAN           $100.00     $ 80.00    $ 65.00     $  50.00
QuickBASIC        $ 85.30     $ 68.24    $ 55.44     $  42.65

          Hope you like CLARENCE'S CLEARANCE !!
```

You will find that anytime you want to produce a table as output to one of your programs, the PRINT USING statement will serve you well. With just a little practice, you'll have it down.

PRACTICE 9.2

1. For each PRINT USING statement below, indicate the output it would produce. Note that in part (f) there are four spaces between the backslashes.

(a) `PRINT USING "####"; 587.56`
(b) `PRINT USING "##.#"; 43.32`
(c) `PRINT USING "$####.##"; 78`
(d) `PRINT USING "$$####.##"; 78`
(e) `PRINT USING "#######,.#"; 2654784.88`
(f) `PRINT USING "\    \"; "this is a test"`

2. Write a formatting string f$ and then a PRINT USING statement that would produce the lines of a table, each line being something like this:

```
00456    Flump, Joe    $ 8.75    35.8    $313.25
```

These entries might be employee number, employee name, hourly wage, hours worked this week, total (gross) pay.

9.3 Cursor Movement and Color—QuickBASIC Text Graphics

Have you wished on occasion that your program's output was a little "snappier"? Maybe have nicer colors instead of the usual black and white, or maybe be able to move the cursor around the screen in a different order than the usual row by row, left to right. If so, QuickBASIC has statements that let you include these features in your screen output. In this section, we will learn what these statements are.

The statements we shall discuss are sometimes called *text graphics* statements: we print the same ASCII characters we've been using all along (and perhaps some we haven't used yet), but text graphics statements permit us to print them in a variety of colors and at any location on the screen we wish. In Chapter 10, we shall learn about *medium- and high-resolution graphics,* in which we no longer print the standard characters but rather lines, curves, squares, circles, and so on. Those graphics are a little more involved; the text graphics we do here are not at all complicated.

Before we begin, we need to say a word about graphics adapters. In Section 10.1, we shall discuss in some detail the different graphics adapters available for IBM PC and PS2 computers (and their clones) and the effects they may have on graphics output. However, here, we shall assume that you are using the CGA ("color graphics adapter"). If you are not, you may experience *minor* differences in your output from ours, but no major difficulties should arise. Basically, don't worry!

Color

Let's start with *color.* Suppose you would like your program's output to have yellow characters on a blue background with a black border around the edge of the screen. Well, all you have to do is include the following statement in your program (obviously, *before* the output begins):

```
COLOR 14, 1, 0
```

This does the trick, since 14 is the number associated with yellow, 1 with blue, and 0 with black.

The general format of the COLOR statement for text graphics is as follows:

COLOR <foreground>**,** <background>**,** <border>

The background and border arguments are *optional*; that is, if you want to change only the foreground (or only the foreground and background but not the border), you can omit the argument or arguments that remain unchanged. (*EGA and VGA users note*: The border argument is not used with these adapters. No matter what you say, the border will remain black.)

Below are the available colors and their associated numbers.

Colors in QuickBASIC

Number	Color	Number	Color
0	black	8	gray
1	blue	9	light blue
2	green	10	light green
3	cyan	11	light cyan
4	red	12	light red
5	magenta	13	light magenta
6	brown	14	yellow
7	white	15	high-intensity white

Note: (1) Colors 8–15 are *not* available for the background;
(2) adding 16 to the chosen foreground color will cause the foreground to *blink*!

That's about all there is to it! Sit down at a computer, start up QuickBASIC, and try this out. For example, you might type in the following segment:

```
COLOR 30, 1, 0
CLS
PRINT
PRINT
PRINT "      Hi Mom!!"
PRINT
PRINT
COLOR 12
PRINT "      Love, Junior"
```

Can you see what will happen? Try to figure it out first, then type it in and run it.

There is one subtlety here. Whenever you issue a new COLOR statement that changes the foreground and background, it will affect only *subsequently printed characters* (*not* the whole screen). If you want a new background color for the whole screen (and/or a new border color), you must issue a *CLS statement* after the COLOR statement. Notice this in the segment above. The intention of the *first* COLOR statement is to change foreground, background, and border colors for the whole screen, so the COLOR statement must be followed by the CLS statement. However, the intention of the *second* COLOR statement is to change only the foreground color for the string "   Love, Junior", so the background and border arguments are omitted and no CLS statement follows.

As usual, a little practice makes perfect on this point. Try these two side-by-side segments to see the role that CLS plays in setting colors:

```
COLOR 13, 1
PRINT
PRINT "TESTING"
```

```
COLOR 13, 1
CLS
PRINT
PRINT "TESTING"
```

Let us make one other remark about the COLOR statement. If we want our program to be easier to read, we can always use well-named variables. For example, we could rewrite our previous segment as follows:

```
LET yellow = 14
LET blue = 1
LET black = 0
LET lightRed = 12
LET blink = 16

COLOR yellow + blink, blue, black
CLS
PRINT
PRINT
PRINT "            Hi Mom!!"
PRINT
PRINT
COLOR lightRed
PRINT "          Love, Junior"
```

Cursor Movement

Let's turn to *cursor movement*. Look at the segment above. Notice that to move our "Hi Mom!!" message down the screen and across toward the middle, we need to use lots of PRINT statements and then lots of blanks after the quote. It's true that we could use the TAB function to move horizontally (to the right) on the current row (see Section 9.2)—but wouldn't it be nice if we could simply move the cursor directly to the column *and* row where we want to start the message? We can, with the QuickBASIC statement LOCATE! Its operation is quite simple. Say we want to start our "Hi Mom!!" message in the 10th row (out of 25) at the 35th column (out of 80). We need only say:

```
LOCATE 10, 35
PRINT "Hi Mom!!";
```

The general format of the LOCATE statement is:

LOCATE <row>, <column>

The value for row can range from 1 to 25; the value for column from 1 to 80. If values outside these ranges are used, an error message ("Illegal Function Call") is issued. The row and column arguments can be any valid numeric expressions, provided that they fall in the proper ranges. Can you see what the segment below does? (Hint: Its title would be "Big X." Type it in and try it!)

```
CLS
FOR row = 1 TO 20
    LOCATE row, 4 * row
    PRINT "X";
    LOCATE row, 84 - 4 * row
    PRINT "X"
NEXT row
```

Now, let's rewrite our "Hi Mom!!" segment once again, using our two new QuickBASIC statements COLOR and LOCATE.

```
LET yellow = 14
LET blue = 1
LET black = 0
LET lightRed = 12
LET blink = 16

COLOR yellow + blink, blue, black
CLS
LOCATE 10, 35
PRINT "Hi Mom!!";
COLOR lightRed
LOCATE 17, 28
PRINT "Love, Junior";
```

One remark is worth making: in general it's best, when using the LOCATE statement, to put a *semicolon* (i.e., ";") at the end of the corresponding PRINT statement, since that leaves the cursor immediately to the right of the last printed character. Remember that PRINT without the semicolon causes a carriage return, which can sometimes mess up your intended output by causing the screen to scroll.

In addition to enhancing text, text graphics can be used to draw pictures. The missing ingredient is found in Appendix 2 of the text; turn to it now and take a look. You can use most of the characters listed there anytime in your output; you need only refer to them using their ASCII code and the CHR$ function (see Section 1.5). However, some of the ASCII codes correspond to "nonprinting" characters—for example, CHR$(7) makes the computer beep and CHR$(12) clears the screen. Figure 9.1 shows a few of the many codes that do correspond to printing characters.

Code	Output
CHR$(1)	☺
CHR$(3)	♥
CHR$(14)	♫
CHR$(186)	║
CHR$(187)	╗
CHR$(188)	╝
CHR$(200)	╚
CHR$(201)	╔
CHR$(205)	═
CHR$(219)	█

FIGURE 9.1

Some ASCII Characters

EXAMPLE 3

Let's use some of these characters. To start with, let's rewrite the "Hi Mom!" program by putting a double-lined box around both messages

("Hi Mom!!" and "Love, Junior"). We can use the characters 186, 187, 188, 200, 201, and 205 in the table above. Since we want to enclose *both* messages, this is a perfect time to use a *subprogram*, called, say, DrawBox. DrawBox should have four parameters: the row for its upper left-hand corner; the column for its upper left-hand corner; its height; and its length. An algorithm for drawing this box is shown below.

ALGORITHM FOR SUBPROGRAM DRAWBOX

Parameters: *ulrow, ulcol, height, length*

1. Locate at *ulrow, ulcol,* and draw the upper left-hand corner
2. Draw across the top
3. Draw the upper right-hand corner
4. Draw down the right-hand side
5. Draw the lower right-hand corner
6. Locate back at the upper left-hand corner
7. Draw down the left-hand side
8. Draw the lower left-hand corner
9. Draw across the bottom

Below is our fancier "Hi Mom!!" program, with the DrawBox subprogram. Run it to see that it really works; it's saved as C09EX03.BAS on your SAMPLES disk.

```
DECLARE SUB DrawBox (ulrow!, ulcol!, height!, length!)
'----------------------------------------------------------------
'   Program Title: C09EX03.BAS
'   Author:        A. Jolson
'   Date:          November 23, 1991

'   Uses text graphics to print a message to Mom, including a
'   subprogram that will draw a box around any message.
'----------------------------------------------------------------

'Define the color variables.

    LET yellow = 14
    LET blue = 1
    LET black = 0
    LET lightRed = 12
    LET blink = 16

'Print the message.

    COLOR yellow, blue, black
    CLS
    CALL DrawBox(8, 31, 5, 15)
    COLOR yellow + blink
```

```
    LOCATE 10, 35
    PRINT "Hi Mom!!";
    COLOR lightRed
    CALL DrawBox(15, 29, 5, 20)
    LOCATE 17, 33
    PRINT "Love, Junior";

END

SUB DrawBox (ulrow, ulcol, height, length)
'Draws a double-lined box of given length and height with the upper
'left-hand corner at ulrow, ulcol.

'Print upper left-hand corner

    LOCATE ulrow, ulcol
    PRINT CHR$(201);

'Print top of box

    FOR col = 1 TO length - 2
        PRINT CHR$(205);
    NEXT col

'Print upper right-hand corner

    PRINT CHR$(187);

'Print right side

    FOR row = 1 TO height - 2
        LOCATE ulrow + row, ulcol + length - 1
        PRINT CHR$(186);
    NEXT row

'Print lower right-hand corner

    LOCATE ulrow + height - 1, ulcol + length - 1
    PRINT CHR$(188);

'Print left side

    FOR row = 1 TO height - 2
        LOCATE ulrow + row, ulcol
        PRINT CHR$(186);
    NEXT row

'Print lower left-hand corner

    LOCATE ulrow + height - 1, ulcol
    PRINT CHR$(200);
```

```
'Print bottom

    FOR col = 1 TO length - 2
        PRINT CHR$(205);
    NEXT col

END SUB
```

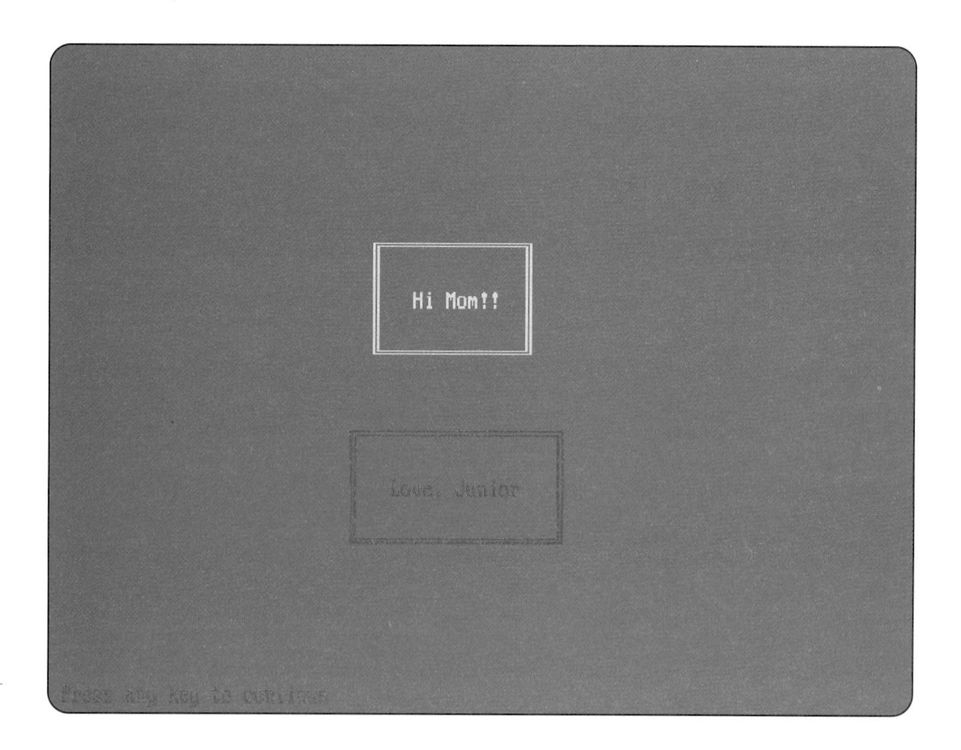

FIGURE 9.2

Output of C09EX03.BAS

Figure 9.2 shows the output—though it looks better on the color monitor with the message flashing. Try it out!

EXAMPLE 4

A very handy character is CHR$(219) (see Figure 9.1); it simply fills up the printing area for one character with the foreground color. We make use of this character and the star ("*") to draw an American flag in the following program (C09EX04.BAS on your SAMPLES disk); notice, again, that it is very convenient to use subprograms (Stripe and Stars):

```

DECLARE SUB Stripe (n!, colr!)
DECLARE SUB Stars (n!)
'---------------------------------------------------------------
'   Program Title:  C09EX04.BAS
'   Author:         B. Ross
'   Date:           July 4, 1776

'Uses text graphics to draw an American flag.
'---------------------------------------------------------------
```

```
'Set white background.

    COLOR 7, 7, 7
    CLS
    LOCATE 5, 13

'Draw the first 8 rows of stars and stripes.

    COLOR 15, 1
    FOR i = 1 TO 4
        PRINT " ";
        CALL Stars(5)
        PRINT "* ";
        CALL Stripe(30, 4)
        LOCATE 5 + 2 * i - 1, 13
        COLOR 15, 1
        PRINT "  ";
        CALL Stars(5)
        CALL Stripe(30, 15)
        LOCATE 5 + 2 * i, 13
    NEXT i

'Draw the ninth row.

    PRINT " ";
    CALL Stars(5)
    PRINT "* ";
    CALL Stripe(30, 4)

'Draw the last 6 rows of stripes.

    LOCATE 14, 13
    FOR i = 1 TO 3
        CALL Stripe(53, 15)
        LOCATE 14 + 2 * i - 1, 13
        CALL Stripe(53, 4)
        LOCATE 14 + 2 * i, 13
    NEXT i
    COLOR 1, 7

END

SUB Stars (n)
'Draws n stars

    FOR i = 1 TO n
        PRINT "*  ";
    NEXT i

END SUB
```

```
SUB Stripe (n, colr)
'Draws a stripe n units long in color colr

    COLOR colr
    FOR i = 1 TO n
        PRINT CHR$(219);
    NEXT i

END SUB
```

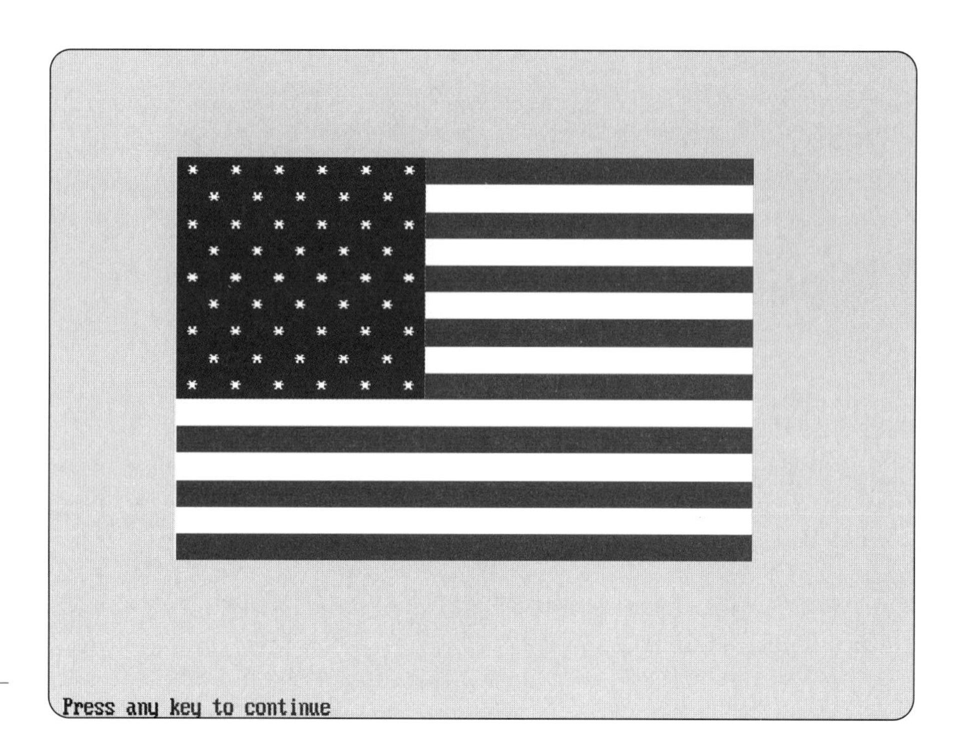
Press any key to continue

FIGURE 9.3

Output of C09EX04.BAS

Figure 9.3 shows the output—though, again, it looks nicer on the color monitor.

In the programming problems at the end of the chapter, you'll see some other "recreational" things that can be done with text graphics. But in the next section, we'll turn our attention to some more "serious" applications of text graphics: enhancing our programs with things like menus and bar graphs.

PRACTICE 9.3

1. For each of the two segments below, figure out exactly what the output is (including colors); then type in the segment to see if you're right. (You will need to consult Appendix 2.)

(a)
```
COLOR 15, 5, 0
CLS
LOCATE 1, 1
PRINT CHR$(14);
LOCATE 25, 1
PRINT CHR$(14);
LOCATE 25, 80
PRINT CHR$(14);
LOCATE 1, 80
PRINT CHR$(14);
LOCATE 13, 40
COLOR 31
PRINT CHR$(15);
```

(b)
```
COLOR 12, 1, 1
CLS
FOR loc = 1 TO 25
    LOCATE loc, loc
    PRINT "X";
    LOCATE loc, 26 - loc
    PRINT "X";
NEXT loc
```

2. Write a program segment that puts 100 yellow stars at random locations on a blue background. Half of them should twinkle, half should not. Hint: You will need a statement like the one below (see Section 3.5).

```
LOCATE INT(25 * RND + 1), INT(80 * RND + 1)
```

9.4 Menus and Bar Graphs

In this section, we'll look at some of the ways to use text graphics to enhance the output of our QuickBASIC programs. To start with, any monitor output is more attractive if we use *colors* rather than the standard white print on black background. We can take *any* program we've written so far and "spice it up" by adding colors to it. As a single example, we can add some color to the Clarence's Clearance program (C09EX02.BAS) in Section 9.2. Look at and run the program C09EX02C.BAS on your SAMPLES disk (C is for "color").

In many interactive programs, the user is given choices of what action is next. It is standard practice to place these choices in a *menu*. We've already written programs with menus in this text; for example, the data analyzer program (C07EX09.BAS) in Section 7.5 gives the user a choice of six different functions to perform on a set of data. Now, we'll examine the use of the COLOR and LOCATE statements to make that program or any program with menus and options more attractive.

Much of the software written today (for example, our own QuickBASIC software!) employs **pull-down menus**. As you know from using QuickBASIC and probably other products, the idea is that the desired menu appears somewhere on the screen when called for and then disappears after it has been used. QuickBASIC allows us to add these to our own programs (with some restrictions), but doing so is somewhat complicated to design. Therefore, we'll stick with an easier application—a single, highlighted menu that appears on a new screen, is used, and then gives way to another screen. Although we've done this all along, we can now make it more attractive.

EXAMPLE 5

Let's enhance the data analyzer program (C07EX09.BAS) from Section 7.5. We want to improve it in the following ways: (1) separate its output into screens, each of which is colored; (2) have user inputs in a different color than the prompts preceding them; and (3) create a "menu box" that displays the six choices.

The first of these is easy; we've already done it a few times. The second is merely a matter of separating the input prompt from the input. For example, the segment

```
COLOR 12, 1
PRINT "How many numbers do you have? ";
COLOR 15
INPUT "", howMany
```

will put the prompt in light red on a blue background but will print the inputted number in high-intensity white. The purpose of the pair of double quotes in the INPUT statement is to avoid the question mark that a "plain" INPUT produces.

The creation of a menu box for the data analyzer program is a little more involved—but, remember, we already created a DrawBox subprogram in the last section (it's part of the final "Hi Mom!!" program—C09EX03.BAS). All we have to do is load DrawBox into our data analyzer program (see Section 6.10 on how to do this). Once it's part of our program, we can call it to create the desired box around the menu. One additional feature would be nice: to have the background inside the box a different color from the screen background. To do this, we simply "fill in" the inside of the box with the desired color. Here is the segment that prints the boxed menu (coming into this segment, the background of the whole screen is blue):

```
CLS
COLOR 14, 4, 0              'Set yellow foreground, red background for box
CALL DrawBox(2, 10, 14, 60)
FOR row = 3 TO 14           'Fill in the inside of the box in red
    LOCATE row, 11
    PRINT SPACE$(58)
NEXT row
LOCATE 4, 17
PRINT "Here are your options for analyzing your data:";
LOCATE 6, 17
PRINT "    A. Find the mean.";
```

```
LOCATE 7, 17
PRINT "     B. Find the standard deviation.";
LOCATE 8, 17
PRINT "     C. Find the range.";
LOCATE 9, 17
PRINT "     D. Sort the data (low to high).";
LOCATE 10, 17
PRINT "     E. Search the data for an item.";
LOCATE 11, 17
PRINT "     F. Find the median.";
LOCATE 13, 17
PRINT "     Your choice? (A-F) ";
COLOR 15
INPUT "", answer$
LET answer$ = UCASE$(LEFT$(answer$, 1))
```

Although this segment is a little more complicated than the old black-and-white version, the result is nicer: on a blue screen, we get a red menu box with yellow border lines and yellow text. The output of this segment is shown in Figure 9.4.

It's time to try the program. Get C09EX05.BAS off your SAMPLES disk, look it over, and run it. You'll probably agree that it's a more pleasant program to use than it was before.

Whenever we deal with data, we want to find ways to make sense out of it. The functions performed by our data analyzer program help to do that, since the mean, the median, and so on *describe* the data to

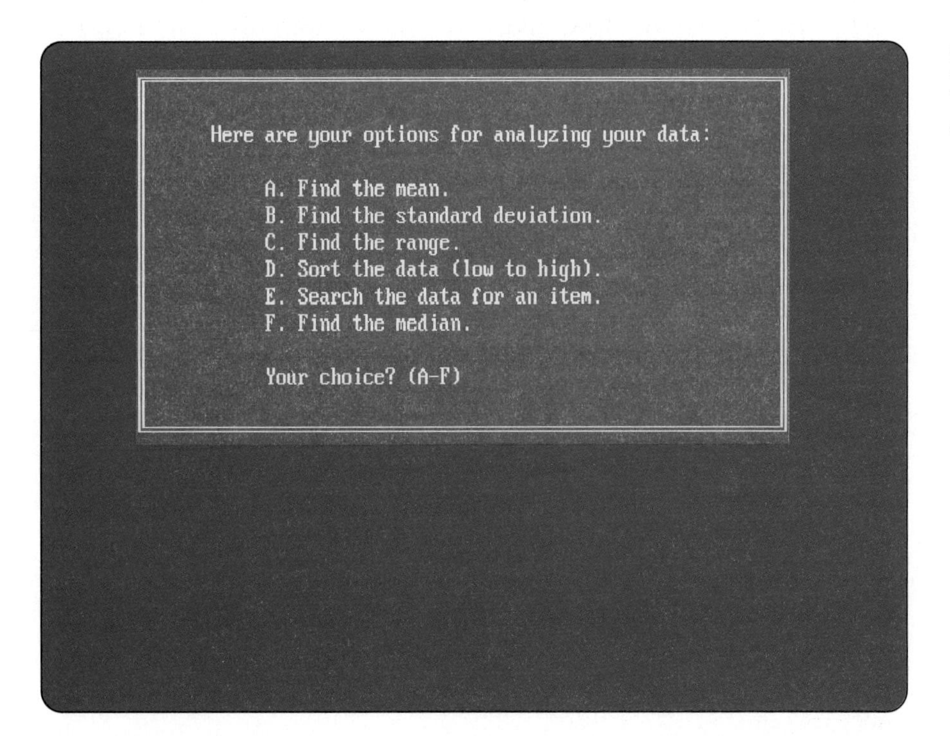

FIGURE 9.4

The Menu of Options in C09EX05.BAS

us in some way. Another way to make sense out of data is to *draw a picture of it*. Depending on the particular situation, there are various ways to do this—but we shall look at just one of them here: the **bar graph**. The basic idea is to put the data into groups and then draw a picture showing the size of each group (usually called the "frequency" of that group). This kind of picture is easy to draw using QuickBASIC text graphics. And the best way to get the idea, as always, is to look at an example.

EXAMPLE 6

At State University, there is always a large section of Sociology 101 (say, between 50 and 100 students), and, each semester, the professor likes to produce and retain a bar graph of the distribution of final averages in the course by "deciles," that is, how many in the 50s, in the 60s, in the 70s, and so on. Let's write a program that takes in all the averages from DATA statements and prints out a colorful bar graph of the results. We'll begin with an algorithm.

LEVEL-1 ALGORITHM

1. Read the grades and keep track of how many are in each decile (we should lump together all grades below 50, say, into one category, and we should put a grade of 100 into the 90s category)
2. Draw the bar graph:
   a. Write the headings
   b. Draw the two axes
   c. Label the axes (it will be easier to make the bars grow from left to right rather than from the bottom up, so let's label it that way)
   d. Draw the bars

Let's consider our variables. We'll need *grade* for each grade as we read it. In addition, it will probably be easiest to store the six frequencies in an array, *frequency( )*, which could be indexed by the tens digit of the group so that, for example, *frequency(7)* is the number of 70s, and so on; *frequency(4)* could include all the grades below 50. It might also be nice to have *semester$* and the *classSize* as variables, since this program is to be used over and over. Let's refine our algorithm.

LEVEL-2 ALGORITHM

1. a. Read *semester$*
   b. Initialize the counters *frequency( )* and *classSize*
   c. Repeat until end of data marker is reached:
      i. Read *grade*
      ii. If *grade* < 50, increase *frequency(4)* by 1
      Otherwise increase *frequency(grade\10)* by 1, where \ is "integer division"
      iii. Increase *classSize* by 1

2. a. Write the headings, including *semester$* and *classSize*
   b. Using CHR$ with 179, 192, and 196, draw the axes down the left-hand side and across the bottom
   c. Label the vertical axis ("90s," and so on), using LOCATE and PRINT; label the horizontal axis (5, 10, and so on, and "FREQUENCY")
   d. For each *index* 4 to 9:
      i. Get a new foreground color
      ii. LOCATE at the left of the correct row
      iii. PRINT CHR$(219) two times *frequency(index)*

Getting this just right takes some work—but it's not *too* hard, and it's fun! Remember, one of the really nice things about computer programs is that they are very easy to change—if you don't get it right the first time, so what!

Here's a program that does the job:

```
'-------------------------------------------------------------
'    Program Title: C09EX06.BAS
'    Author:        C. Babbage
'    Date:          January 10, 1991

'    Groups the final averages in Soc 101 into deciles and draws a
'    bar graph of the results.
'-------------------------------------------------------------

'Read the data and compute the frequencies of each decile. We assume
'that all grades below 50 are lumped into one group and that
'a grade of 100 goes into the 90s group. The array frequency() is
'indexed by the tens digit of the group, e.g., frequency(7) refers
'to the 70s, etc.

    DIM frequency(4 TO 9)

    LET classSize = 0

    READ semester$
    DO
        READ grade
        IF grade < 0 THEN
            EXIT DO
        ELSEIF grade < 50 THEN
            LET frequency(4) = frequency(4) + 1
        ELSEIF grade = 100 THEN
            LET frequency(9) = frequency(9) + 1
        ELSE
            LET index = grade \ 10
            LET frequency(index) = frequency(index) + 1
        END IF
        LET classSize = classSize + 1
    LOOP
```

```
'Now draw the bar graph. We will have the bars starting at the left.
'We assume that no group will contain more than 35 students and scale
'the graph accordingly. First print the headings.

     COLOR 14, 1, 0
     CLS
     LOCATE 3, 25
     PRINT "SOCIOLOGY 101 GRADE DISTRIBUTION";
     LOCATE 5, 25
     PRINT semester$; "     CLASS SIZE -->"; classSize

'Put in the axes.

     COLOR 15
     FOR row = 7 TO 19
         LOCATE row, 8
         PRINT CHR$(179);
     NEXT row
     LOCATE 20, 8
     PRINT CHR$(192);
     FOR col = 9 TO 78
         PRINT CHR$(196);
     NEXT col

'Label the axes.

     LOCATE 8, 3
     PRINT "90s";
     LOCATE 10, 3
     PRINT "80s";
     LOCATE 12, 3
     PRINT "70s";
     LOCATE 14, 3
     PRINT "60s";
     LOCATE 16, 3
     PRINT "50s";
     LOCATE 18, 3
     PRINT "BELOW";
     LOCATE 19, 4
     PRINT "50";
     FOR i = 1 TO 6
         LOCATE 21, 10 * i + 8
         PRINT 5 * i;
     NEXT i
     LOCATE 23, 35
     PRINT "FREQUENCY"

'Now draw the bars in a rainbow of colors.

     FOR index = 4 TO 9
         COLOR 5 + index
         LOCATE 2 * index, 9
```

```
            FOR i = 1 TO frequency(13 - index)
                PRINT CHR$(219); CHR$(219);
            NEXT i
        NEXT index

    'Data Section.

        DATA "FALL 1991"
        DATA 76,81,94,76,85,67,54,74,87,90,68,75,74,83,47
        DATA 84,57,67,74,78,68,78,73,85,82,93,76,80,59,100
        DATA 83,75,87,68,94,87,74,79,63,53,91,89,83,73,46
        DATA 73,85,83,94,72,75,83,71, -1

    END
```

Figure 9.5 shows the output of the program with this data.

We urge you to get C09EX06.BAS off your SAMPLES disk and give it a run. You might like to copy it to your own disk and modify the data several times, confirming that the program really does draw the correct graph.

There are, of course, lots and lots of examples of programs where a bar graph can help make the results clear. See the programming problems at the end of this chapter.

We should mention here that bar graphs can also be drawn using medium- and high-resolution graphics; in those modes, you can also draw other types of graphs (pie charts, line graphs, etc.). These are covered in Chapter 10. But even as you learn how to do medium- and high-resolution graphics, don't forget about the many things you can do fairly easily and very colorfully using text graphics! From now on,

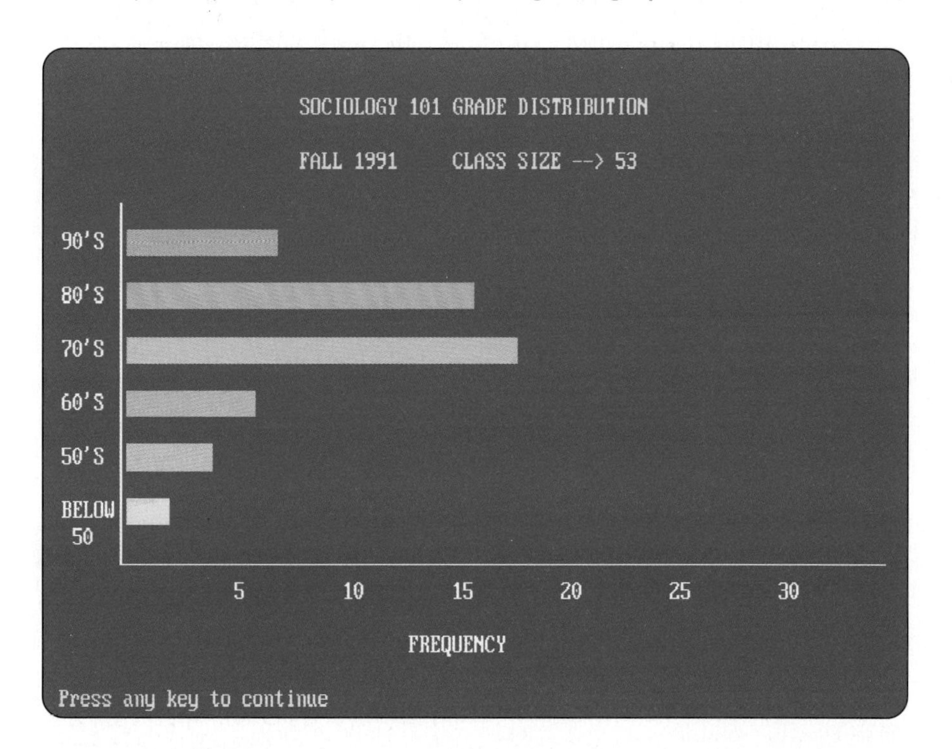

FIGURE 9.5

Sample Output of C09EX06.BAS

you will probably want to include some text graphics in almost every program you write.

PRACTICE 9.4 Take *any* program you've written in QuickBASIC and use the COLOR and LOCATE statements to "fancy up" your output.

Chapter Summary

In this chapter, we've concentrated on ways to make the output of our QuickBASIC programs better looking and more readable. The two new tools we introduced for this task are the PRINT USING statement and text graphics.

The PRINT USING statement allows you to put a single data item or a whole line of output in exactly the format you desire. This is especially helpful when your output is in table form: each line of the table conforms to your chosen format, so that everything lines up the way you want.

Text graphics give you the ability to use up to 16 colors in your output (using the COLOR statement) and to place the cursor wherever you wish on the output screen (using the LOCATE statement). By making use of the many ASCII characters available to you (Appendix 2) and the CHR$ function, you can even draw pictures in this mode.

As examples, the output of many programs can be enhanced by having attractive *menus* of choices for the user or by having the results summarized in a *bar graph*. Both of these can be created using text graphics.

Review Questions

1. Explain each term briefly and give an example:
   (a) **PRINT USING**
   (b) formatting string
   (c) text graphics
   (d) **COLOR**
   (e) **LOCATE**
   (f) ASCII characters

2. Make up an example (different from the ones in the text) where the output is in table form; write a formatting string and PRINT USING statement that would make this table come out well.

3. Being specific, describe two things you can now do in the output of your programs by using text graphics that you could not do before.

Programming Problems

1. Do (or redo) Programming Problem 6 of Chapter 1 using the PRINT USING statement to make the table.

2. Do (or redo) Programming Problem 2 of Chapter 4 using the PRINT USING statement to make the table.

3. Write an end-of-the-month bank statement program. The DATA statements contain, first, the month; second, the opening balance; and then each transaction date followed by the amount of the transaction with a positive entry indicating a deposit and a negative entry a withdrawal. The output should be a table with four columns: date, withdrawal, deposit, and balance. Use the PRINT USING statement, but notice that since each line of the table will have a blank column, you will need (at least) two different formatting strings.

   You should test your program with the following data:

```
DATA July
DATA 1256.73
DATA 2, -125, 3, -43.75, 5, -280.50, 6, 100, 9, -34.82
DATA 9, -65, 12, -120, 15, 880.65, 15, -78.98, 18, -12.45
DATA 21, -160, 22, -56.45, 24, 150, 26, -36.78, 29, -74
DATA 30, -209.98
```

   For your convenience, this data is stored under the name C09PB03.BAS on your SAMPLES disk.

4. Use text graphics to jazz up the automated teller program (Programming Problem 8 in Chapter 5). Try to make your output screen look, as much as possible, like a real automated teller's screen. In particular, do not allow any scrolling.

5. Any game program can be greatly enhanced using graphics (and sound, of course; see Chapter 10). As an example, copy the dart-throwing game (C03EX10.BAS) from your SAMPLES disk and make the output "pretty" using text graphics (e.g., have a different screen for each of the three possible outcomes).

6. (a) Write a program that uses random integers to simulate the roll of two dice; then use text graphics to show a *picture* of the two dice rolled.
   (b) If you want, expand this program into some sort of "Craps" game where the user rolls a pair of dice and, depending on the outcome, either wins, loses, or rolls again. Each time there's a roll, show the picture of what came up.

7. Write a program that simulates the card game Blackjack or 21 (or redo Programming Problem 10 or 11 of Chapter 5). When the player receives his or her two cards, use text graphics to actually show the cards.

8. Use text graphics to draw a colorful picture of a house, a car, a boat, or whatever you wish.

9. One hundred male students at State University were weighed and their weights were recorded in the DATA statements below (which are on your SAMPLES disk under the name C09PB09.BAS).

```
DATA 145,187,175,156,134,158,187,191,125,165,173,143,117,156
DATA 201,187,165,154,168,135,169,198,206,125,173,147,166,118
DATA 157,165,162,175,182,124,169,190,145,167,159,177,145,128
DATA 157,185,145,132,179,171,180,192,143,167,210,167,183,145
DATA 143,168,182,167,192,145,156,151,160,173,187,135,221,128
DATA 156,186,159,163,157,184,193,156,176,182,134,191,156,167
DATA 165,124,176,183,197,156,152,167,161,137,181,159,164,129
DATA 137,167
```

Write a program that groups these weights into the following categories and then draws a bar graph of the results like the one in Example 6 of this chapter: under 120 pounds, 120–139 pounds, 140–159 pounds, 160–179 pounds, 180–199 pounds, 200 and over.

10. Write a program that simulates tossing a coin 400 times and records the number of "heads" obtained (see Example 9 in Section 3.6). Now expand that program so that it does this experiment (i.e., 400 tosses) 100 times, saving the number of heads obtained each time in an array (so the array *numHeads( )* might contain the data 210, 195, 198, 204, etc.). Finally, have your program draw a bar graph of the results, grouping the 100 numbers into the following categories: less than 180 heads, 180–184 heads, 185–189 heads, 190–194 heads, 195–199 heads, 200–204 heads, 205–209 heads, 210–214 heads, 215–219 heads, and 220 or more heads.

CHAPTER

10

GRAPHICS AND SOUND

CHAPTER PREVIEW In this chapter, we'll learn how to write graphics programs that draw pictures, using lines, boxes, and circles, and even how to do simple *animation*, that is, pictures that move! We'll also learn how to add sound and music to our programs.

10.1 Introduction

In Chapter 9, we saw how to add color to text output and how to use the PRINT and LOCATE statements to "draw" a variety of interesting pictures. Most computer languages, including QuickBASIC, provide a collection of special-purpose statements that facilitate the drawing of more sophisticated pictures. In relation to computers and programming languages, the word **graphics** refers to the task of drawing pictures involving shapes made out of lines, circles, ellipses, and so on, and the use of colors in these pictures. The ability to do graphics depends on both hardware (i.e., the characteristics of the particular machine) and software (i.e., the particular language or graphics program being used). In this chapter, we'll learn how to access the graphics capabilities provided by QuickBASIC; we'll also learn how to add *sound* to our BASIC programs (see Section 10.7).

The graphics capabilities of the IBM PC, IBM PS2, and compatible machines depend both on the particular monitor (screen) and the particular computer. Obviously, you can't do *color* graphics without a color screen. Another factor affecting graphics capabilities is the **resolution** of the screen, that is, the number of dots (also called *pixels*) per square inch; the higher the resolution, the better the picture. As discussed below, the computer also imposes restrictions on the resolution.

In addition to the limitations posed by the screen, the computer must be equipped with special circuitry to allow the use of graphics commands. This circuitry is usually mounted on a board that is plugged into the computer—you don't see it because it's inside the machine casing. For the IBM PC and PS2 series, there are five main kinds of *graphics boards*. Listed in approximate order of increasing graphics capability, they are:

Monochrome display adapter	(MDA)
Color/graphics adapter	(CGA)
Enhanced graphics adapter	(EGA)
Multicolor graphics array adapter	(MCGA)
Video graphics array adapter	(VGA)

As its name suggests, the MDA board cannot produce color displays, only monochrome; it is also unable to implement advanced graphics commands—it can display only *text output*, that is, the kind of output produced by a PRINT statement. At the other extreme is the VGA board, which permits the implementation of graphics commands at very high resolution and with a large selection of colors.

The CGA board is what you'll find on many IBM PCs and compatible machines. The newer IBM PS2s generally have either the MCGA or VGA board. Here, we'll discuss *CGA graphics* in detail, and then we'll also say a little about *VGA graphics*. If you have access to a machine with one of the better color graphics boards (EGA, MCGA, or VGA), it will also do CGA graphics; if you want to use the full graphics capabilities of your machine, you can read the QuickBASIC documentation to learn how. For now, let's concentrate on CGA graphics.

The graphics boards listed above all provide one or more *graphics modes* for displaying output. The modes differ from one another in the screen resolution (number of dots per square inch) and number of colors that may be used. The MDA board, for example, has only 1 mode (regular text), whereas the VGA board has 10 different modes. The CGA board provides three graphics modes for displaying output.

Mode 0 *Regular text* mode, which we've been using throughout this book. You cannot execute graphics commands in mode 0. However, as we saw in Chapter 9, you do have a large choice of colors (16, to be exact) for foreground (i.e., the printed characters), background, and border (the border of the screen).

Mode 1 *Medium-resolution graphics* mode. The screen resolution is 320 by 200 pixels (320 columns, 200 rows). In addition, graphics commands can be executed using up to 4 colors.

Mode 2 *High-resolution graphics* mode. The screen resolution is 640 by 200—twice as many pixels as in medium resolution—but the graphics commands can only be executed in monochrome.

From these descriptions, it's clear that you must use modes 1 or 2 for most graphics commands. If color is your main concern, use mode 1; if high resolution counts most, use mode 2. Also remember that while color graphics are best on a color monitor (big surprise!), most monochrome monitors will try to differentiate between colors by shades of gray, just as black-and-white TV does. But try a color monitor if you have the chance, because they're *fun*!

Before we begin to study the BASIC commands that let us do graphics, we need to say a word about *printing* graphics output. So far, we've used *Shift-PrtSc* to print output—but if you try this with output from programs that use graphics modes 1 or 2, nothing will happen. That's because, when you turn on the machine, the default setting is for printed text output only. You can change this easily, at the operating system level, by typing the following command, which should be on your DOS disk (if you get an error message, ask your instructor for help):

```
> GRAPHICS
```

This changes the internal settings so that both text and graphics output will be sent to the printer. If you're already in QuickBASIC and remember that you haven't typed the **GRAPHICS** command to set up the printer, choose the *DOS Shell* option from the File Menu (using Full Menus). This puts you temporarily into the operating system—you can type the DOS command **GRAPHICS** and then return to QuickBASIC by typing **EXIT**.

One final word about printing graphics: Do *not* use a laser printer to print graphics! Most laser printers require special auxiliary software to print graphics output correctly, so stick with *dot-matrix* printers (ask your instructor if you're not sure which you have).

10.2 Set-Up Statements for Graphics Modes 1 and 2

There are quite a few graphics statements in QuickBASIC. We'll begin by covering the statements that put you into graphics mode and get you set up for executing drawing statements. Throughout, it's assumed you're equipped with a CGA board and may or may not have a color monitor. The available colors are the same as for text graphics. For convenience, in Table 10.1 we've reproduced the table from Chapter 9 that lists the colors.

There are three *set-up* statements for graphics: SCREEN, WINDOW, and COLOR. Let's look at each in turn.

SCREEN n For CGA graphics, *n* is 0, 1, or 2. This statement chooses a display mode: 0 for text, 1 for medium-resolution graphics, 2 for high-resolution graphics. You *must* have this statement with n = 1 or 2 to enter CGA graphics mode.

Once you enter graphics mode 1 or 2, points on the screen are labelled using two *coordinates*. The first coordinate (x-coordinate) represents left-right position (column) and the second (y-coordinate) represents up-down position (row). QuickBASIC provides a *default* labelling that labels the upper left-hand corner (0, 0) and the lower right-hand corner either (319, 199) or (639, 199), depending on whether you're in medium- or high-resolution. See Figure 10.1 for a diagram of the medium-resolution screen with default labelling.

It's fairly inconvenient to use this labelling system because, for instance, you need to remember the specific numbers 319 and 199 (or

TABLE 10.1 Colors in QuickBASIC

Number	Color	Number	Color
0	black	8	gray
1	blue	9	light blue
2	green	10	light green
3	cyan	11	light cyan
4	red	12	light red
5	magenta	13	light magenta
6	brown	14	yellow
7	white	15	high-intensity white

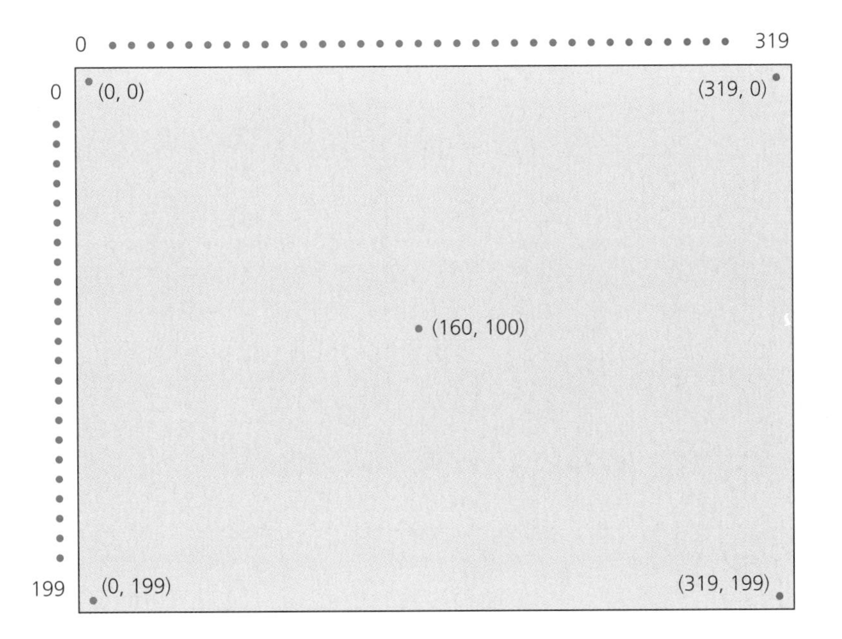

FIGURE 10.1

The Default Coordinates for Graphics Mode 1

639 and 199 in high resolution). However, the *WINDOW* statement lets you choose a different labelling system.

WINDOW (a, b) – (c, d) Sets up a new coordinate system in which the upper left-hand corner has coordinates (a, b) and the lower right-hand corner has coordinates (c, d).

The WINDOW statement requires that the x-coordinate *increase* as you move from left to right, that is, *a* must be less than or equal to c. Similarly, the y-coordinate must increase as you move up the screen, that is, *b* must be greater than or equal to *d*. If this sounds confusing, take heart; if you've ever done graphing in math class, your axes have probably obeyed these rules.

EXAMPLE 1

Suppose we wanted both our x- and y-coordinates to range from −100 to 100. The diagram in Figure 10.2 shows the labelling we have in mind and also shows the coordinates of all the corner points and the center. We've drawn in a pair of x- and y-axes to help you visualize the labelling.

The WINDOW statement to set up this labelling system is:

```
WINDOW (-100, 100) - (100, -100)
```

Note that this labelling puts (0, 0) in the center of the screen; increasing coordinates indicate movement up or right, and decreasing coordinates indicate movement down or left. Also notice that if we use this WINDOW statement, we don't need to worry about which mode we're in, that is, we don't need to memorize the resolutions 320 by

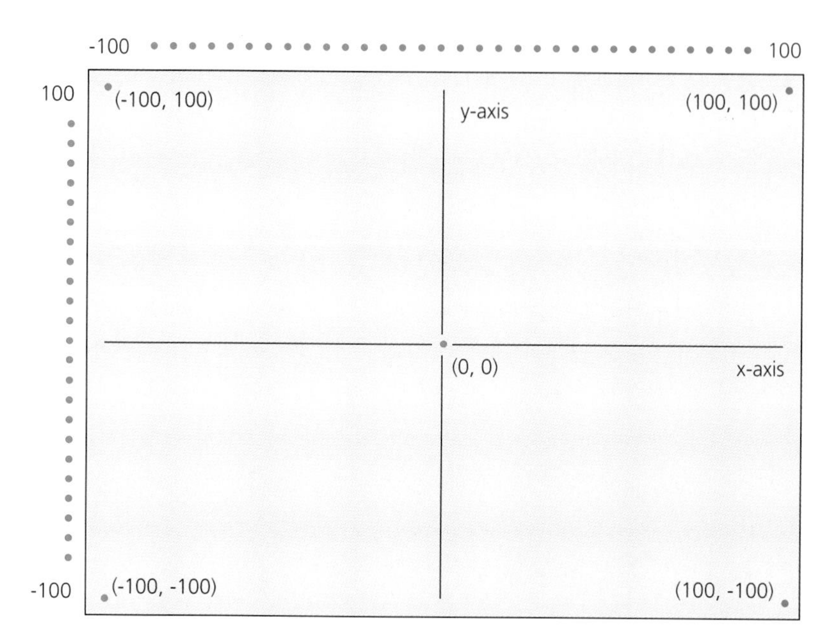

FIGURE 10.2

Coordinates from the Statement "WINDOW (−100, 100)–(100, −100)"

200 and 640 by 200, because we've defined our own coordinate system. For the examples in this text, we'll usually use this labelling for the pixels (although particular examples might be easier with a different WINDOW statement).

COLOR background, palette *For use only in mode 1*; note syntactic differences from mode 0 version. The variables *background* and *palette* are numbers representing the choice of background color (0–15 from Table 10.1) and palette (0 or 1; see below for descriptions).

Each *palette* is a set of 4 colors that may be used as the foreground color. There are two different sets, or palettes, of 4 colors that can be used for foreground colors.

Palette 0	0 = background
	1 = green
	2 = red
	3 = brown[1]
Palette 1	0 = background
	1 = cyan (pale blue)
	2 = magenta (violet)
	3 = high-intensity white

For example, the following program segment puts us into mode 1 (medium-resolution graphics mode), sets the background color to blue, and selects palette 0:

[1] May appear yellow on some monitors.

```
SCREEN 1
COLOR 1, 0
```

This means that we'll use the numbers 0 to 3 to refer to colors when we draw, where 0 = blue, 1 = cyan, 2 = magenta, and 3 = high-intensity white. In medium-resolution graphics, we are limited to a total of four colors at any time.

The default palette is palette 1. The default background color is 0 (black), and the default foreground color is 3 (brown or high-intensity white, depending on the palette). The COLOR statement is optional; if omitted, the background is black (0) and the palette is 1.

PRACTICE 10.2

1. A diagram of a monitor screen is shown in Figure 10.3; five points, labelled P_1 to P_5, are marked. For each of the following WINDOW statements, indicate what the approximate coordinates of these five points would be after executing the statement:
   (a) `WINDOW (-100, 100)-(100, -100)`
   (b) `WINDOW (0, 10)-(20, 0)`
   (c) `WINDOW (-1, 1)-(1, -1)`
2. For each of the following COLOR statements, executed in mode 1, state which colors would be represented, respectively, by the numbers 0, 1, 2, and 3:
   (a) `COLOR 9, 0`
   (b) `COLOR 2, 1`
   (c) `COLOR 0, 1`
   (d) `COLOR 1, 0`

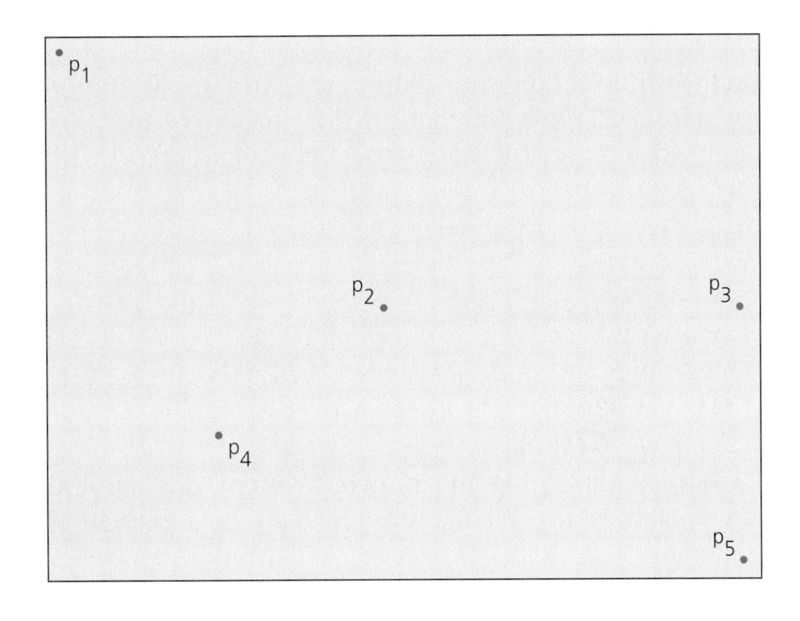

FIGURE 10.3

Diagram for Practice Exercise 1

10.3 Drawing Statements

In addition to the usual PRINT statement, there are special graphics statements to draw a variety of shapes. Below is a list of some of these. (The list is not complete. In particular, it does not include the powerful DRAW statement, which can execute a whole sequence of commands.)

CIRCLE	Draws circles and ellipses
LINE	Draws lines and boxes
PAINT	Fills an entire region with color
PSET	Draws a single point

Throughout the following, it is assumed that we are in a graphics mode and have used the window statement described above:

WINDOW (−100, 100)–(100, −100)

Let's look at the statements listed above, beginning with the simplest, which is PSET.

PSET (x, y), color Draws a point at the specified coordinates (x,y) in the specified color (a number from 0 to 3 in mode 1, a number from 0 to 1 in mode 2).

Color 3 from the current palette (brown or high-intensity white) is the *default* drawing color. In other words, if you omit the *color* argument from the PSET statement, that is, if you have only "PSET (x, y)," then color 3 will be used. This rule also holds for the other drawing statements we'll learn about (LINE, PAINT, and CIRCLE).

EXAMPLE 2

Assuming we're in medium-resolution graphics mode, the program segment below will draw 100 random dots in colors 1 to 3. Note that we have used the variable name *colr* rather than *color*, which is a BASIC reserved word.

```
RANDOMIZE TIMER
FOR i = 1 TO 100
    LET x = INT(201 * RND) - 100      'x and y are random
    LET y = INT(201 * RND) - 100      '#s from -100 to 100.
    LET colr = INT(3 * RND) + 1       'colr is a random
    PSET (x, y), colr                 '# from 1 to 3
NEXT i
```

A program containing the above segment plus another section that illustrates the LINE statement can be found in the file C10EX02.BAS.

The LINE statement is multipurpose: it can be used to draw lines, of course, but it can also be used to draw *boxes* (solid or outlines). Let's begin with the simplest version.

LINE (a, b)–(c, d), color Draws a line from point (a,b) to point (c,d) in the specified color (as with PSET, it is optional to specify the color).

The following two statements draw a giant *X* on the screen in color 2:

```
LINE (-100, 100)-(100, -100), 2
LINE (-100, -100)-(100, 100), 2
```

As mentioned above, the file C10EX02.BAS contains a section that draws random line segments.

To use the LINE statement to draw *boxes*, add the letter *B* or *BF* to the LINE statement as an additional argument after the color.

LINE (a, b)–(c, d), color, B Draws the *outline* of a box with opposite corners (a,b) and (c,d).

LINE (a, b)–(c, d), color, BF Draws a *solid* box (*F* stands for "fill") with opposite corners (a,b) and (c,d).

The following code draws the outline of a box with corners at (0,10) and (50, −50), using color 2:

```
LINE (0, 10)-(50, -50), 2, B
```

If you use *BF* instead of *B*, the box will be a solid color rather than just outlined. The following code draws a filled box, with corners at (−20,−20) and (−5, 2), using the default drawing color (i.e., color 3). Notice the need for an extra comma, so that *BF* wouldn't be mistaken for the *color* argument.

```
LINE (-20, -20)-(-5, 2), , BF
```

PAINT (x, y), color, bordercolor Causes a region of graphics output to be filled in or "painted" with the specified color. The point (*x*,*y*) must be *inside* the region you want to paint—it cannot be on the border of the region. The parameter *bordercolor* indicates the color of the border of the region. Paint will spread out from (*x*,*y*) until the border is reached.

For example, suppose we've drawn, in red, a triangle whose three vertices are at the lower left, lower right, and middle of the screen, that is, at (− 100, − 100), (100, − 100), and (0, 0) respectively, using our coordinate system. Then the point (0, −50) is inside the triangle, and the point (0, 50) is in the region outside the triangle. The following two statements will paint the inside green and the outside brown (all assuming palette 0). Recall that 1 = green, 2 = red, 3 = brown.

```
PAINT (0, -50), 1, 2
PAINT (0, 50), 3, 2
```

***Warning:** If you're not careful, you can paint more than you really want (the whole screen, for example!). For instance, if your border is not completely closed up, the paint will "leak" through and paint the outside of your region, too! In particular, the border of the region you have in mind must be all one color. If, in the above example, two edges of the triangle had different colors, then the triangle edges would not constitute a closed border of a region in any border color.*

At this point, we already have the tools we need to draw some interesting pictures. Designing algorithms for graphics programs requires that we sketch the picture we want to draw on a set of coordinate axes and then outline an algorithm that assembles the picture using the fundamental objects that we can draw in BASIC, namely, dots, lines, and boxes (for now—we'll soon see how to draw circles and ovals).

EXAMPLE 3

Let's design a medium-resolution graphics program that draws a simple house on a grassy lawn with a blue sky behind it. The first step is to sketch a picture on coordinate axes (see Figure 10.4).

Once we have a rough idea of what we want, we can outline an algorithm for drawing the picture, as follows:

1. Set up graphics mode
2. Draw grass (a green box)
3. Draw sky (a blue box)
4. Draw box for house
5. a. Draw lines for roof
   b. Paint roof
6. Draw left window (box) and two lines for windowpanes
7. Draw right window (box) and two lines for windowpanes
8. Draw front door (box) and doorknob (tiny box)

We've limited ourselves to LINE and PAINT statements, but once we learn the CIRCLE statement, we could improve the picture (e.g., making the doorknob round, adding clouds, etc.).

Of course, the first part of any graphics algorithm will be set-up statements for graphics mode (SCREEN, WINDOW, COLOR). In particular, for this program, we must think about what colors we wish to use. We certainly need *blue* for the sky. CGA provides four shades of

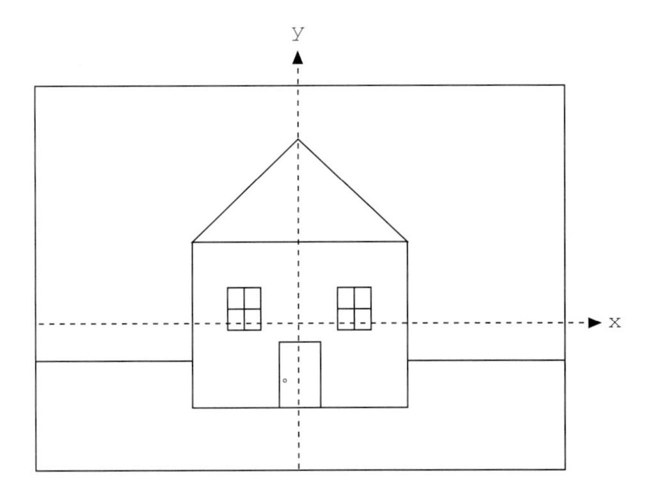

FIGURE 10.4

Rough Sketch of a House

blue (see Table 10.1): blue, light blue, cyan, light cyan. We also need *green* for the grass. The house colors depend on our own taste and the limitations of the two palettes. Let's make the house *white*. Choosing these three colors—blue, green, and white—forces us to use palette 1 with a green background color. Below is a list of possible graphics set-up statements for this program.

```
SCREEN 1
WINDOW (-100, 100)-(100, -100)
COLOR 2, 1


READ green, cyan, magenta, white
DATA   0,     1,      2,        3
```

Notice that, as in Chapter 9, we decided to introduce four variables whose names are colors and whose values match the corresponding colors from our palette. This means we don't have to remember which numbers (0 to 3) represent which colors, and it improves the readability of the rest of the program.

Now, we're ready to translate our rough algorithm into drawing statements. To do this, we will have to make estimates of the coordinates to be used in our LINE and PAINT statements. It's a good idea to pencil these in on the sketch—but remember that we may well decide to adjust them when we try the program and see its output. In fact, we shouldn't wait to test the complete program; instead, we should test it after adding each new object. For example, if we put in all the statements for the house—roof, windows, and door—and then decide the house is too tall, we'll have to adjust all those statements; it's smarter to get the house size right before adding features to it.

Below is our completed program. Remember that the coordinates we used were arrived at by making initial estimates that were adjusted as we examined our output.

```
'-----------------------------------------------------------------------------
    'PROGRAM NAME:   C10EX03.BAS
    'AUTHOR:         Frank Lloyd Wright
    'DATE:           12/6/91

'This program uses medium-resolution graphics to draw a picutre of a house.
'-----------------------------------------------------------------------------

'Set up graphics mode and colors.

    SCREEN 1
    WINDOW (-100, 100)-(100, -100)
    COLOR 2, 1

    READ green, cyan, magenta, white
    DATA   0,    1,     2,       3

'Draw grass and sky.

    LINE (-100, -20)-(100, -100), green, BF
    LINE (-100, 100)-(100, -20), cyan, BF

'Draw box for house and lines for roof; paint roof magenta.

    LINE (-40, 20)-(40, -60), white, BF      'box for house
    LINE (-40, 20)-(0, 60), white            'left roof edge
    LINE (0, 60)-(40, 20), white             'right roof edge
    PAINT (0, 40), magenta, white            'paint roof

'Draw windows and window panes.

    LINE (-30, 10)-(-20, 0), magenta, BF     'left window
    LINE (-25, 0)-(-25, 10), white           'vertical line for pane
    LINE (-30, 5)-(-20, 5), white            'horizontal line for pane

    LINE (30, 10)-(20, 0), magenta, BF       'right window
    LINE (25, 0)-(25, 10), white             'vertical line for pane
    LINE (30, 5)-(20, 5), white              'horizontal line for pane

'Draw front door and doorknob.

    LINE (-10, -60)-(10, -30), magenta, BF  'front door
    LINE (-8, -45)-(-6, -43), white, B      'doorknob

END
```

See Figure 10.5 for the output of this program.

The final drawing statement we'll study here is CIRCLE. Like LINE, CIRCLE can be used in a variety of ways. Depending on the number of

Press any key to continue

FIGURE 10.5

The Output of C10EX03.BAS

parameters and their values, it can draw circles, parts of circles, "pies" or wedges, and ellipses. Let's begin with its simplest version.

CIRCLE (x, y), radius, color Draws a circle, with center (x,y), of the specified radius in the specified color.

For example, to draw a circle with center (0, 0) and radius 25 in color 2, we would write:

```
CIRCLE (0, 0), 25, 2
```

CIRCLE (x, y), radius, color, start, end This variation on the CIRCLE statement draws *part* of a circle. The variables *start* and *end* are numbers that define which part of the circle to draw. They represent *angles in radian measure*, and they must be in the range 0 to 2*pi ≃ 6.28.

Like degrees, *radians* are a unit of measure of angles. A full circle has 2π radians, where π is approximately 3.14 (the symbol π is pronounced "pie"). Since you can't use this symbol in QuickBASIC, we'll use the name "pi" instead; and, in our programs, we'll have a variable named *pi* to which we'll assign the value 3.14. The diagram in Figure 10.6 shows various angles in radian measure.

Once you specify the values for *start* and *end*, the circle will be drawn *counterclockwise* starting at the position given by *start* and ending at the position given by *end*. One detail we must mention is

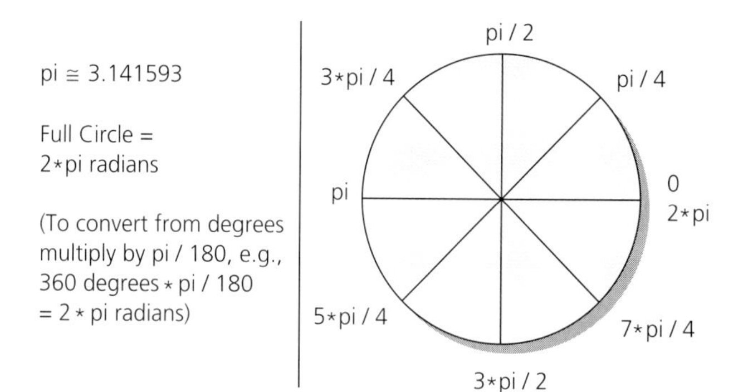

FIGURE 10.6

Angles in Radian Measure

that all angles must be *strictly less than 2*pi*. The actual value of pi is 3.141593 . . . (an infinite, nonrepeating decimal part); but if you use the approximation *3.14* for your variable named *pi* (i.e., only two decimal places), then the corresponding approximation for 2*pi, namely, *6.28*, *will* be strictly less than QuickBASIC's value for 2*pi. The following statements would draw the bottom half of the circle described above:

```
LET pi = 3.14
CIRCLE (0, 0), 25, 2, pi, 2 * pi
```

If we wanted the right half of that circle, we would write:

```
CIRCLE (0, 0), 25, 2, 3*pi/2, pi/2
```

The next variation on the CIRCLE statement lets us draw circle segments with a *radius* drawn at either end of the segment.

CIRCLE (x, y), radius, color, −start, −end If we put a *minus sign* in front of the *start* and/or *end* variables, then a *radius* will be drawn from the center to that point on the circle.

For example, the following statement will draw a pie-shaped wedge from angle pi/4 to angle pi/2:

```
CIRCLE (0, 0), 25, 2, -pi/4, -pi/2
```

One technical detail about drawing radii is that you *cannot* use "−0" to draw a radius at angle 0 (this is because the compiler doesn't distinguish between −0 and 0). The simplest way to get around this is to use a very small angle, e.g., −.0001. Thus, to draw a wedge from angle 0 to angle pi/6, we could write:

```
CIRCLE (0, 0), 25, 2, -.0001, -pi/6
```

EXAMPLE 4

A *pie chart* is a way to display the relative sizes of a list of numbers by dividing a circle into proportionately sized wedges. The following program segment inputs a list of numbers and then uses high-resolution graphics to display a pie chart corresponding to the list. The first number is displayed using a wedge starting at angle 0; this wedge finishes at an angle that is an appropriate fraction of 2*pi. Subsequent wedges begin where the previous wedge stopped, each time adding the appropriate fraction of 2*pi to compute their finish. The complete program can be found in the file C10EX04.BAS.

```
'Intro and get length of list of numbers

    CLS
    PRINT "This program will display a PIE CHART for a list of"
    PRINT "positive numbers."
    PRINT
    PRINT
    INPUT "How many numbers do you have? ", howMany

'Input list into array and compute sum

    CLS
    DIM numList(1 TO howMany)
    LET sum = 0
    FOR count = 1 TO howMany
        PRINT "Enter number #"; count;
        INPUT ": ", numList(count)
        LET sum = sum + numList(count)
    NEXT count

'Initialize high-resolution graphics mode

    SCREEN 2
    WINDOW (-100, 100)-(100, -100)
    LET pi = 3.14

'Draw pie chart one segment at a time

    'Draw first wedge
    LET start = .0001
    LET finish = 2 * pi * numList(1) / sum
    CIRCLE (0, -25), 50, 1, -start, -finish

    'Subsequent wedges begin where the previous wedge left off
    FOR count = 2 TO howMany
        LET start = finish
        LET finish = start + 2 * pi * numList(count) / sum
        CIRCLE (0, -25), 50, 1, -start, -finish
    NEXT count

END
```

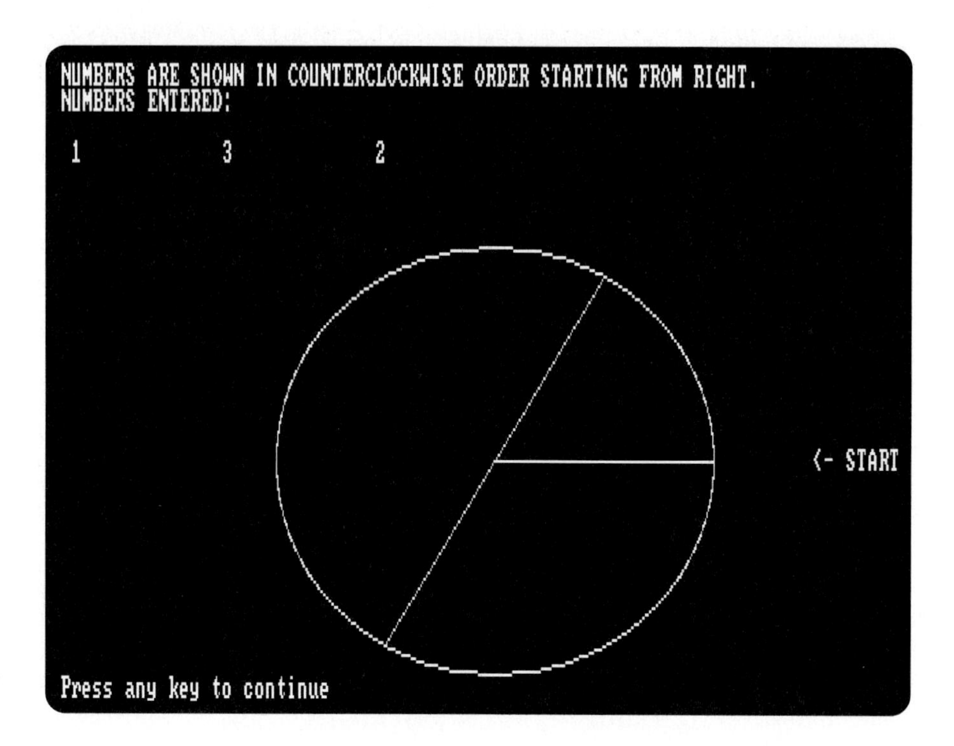

FIGURE 10.7

Sample Output of C10EX04.BAS

If we run this program with the numbers 1, 3, 2, the pie chart looks like that shown in Figure 10.7. Notice that the wedge for 1 is one-sixth of the circle, the wedge for 3 is three-sixths (= one-half) of the circle, and the wedge for 2 is two-sixths (= one-third) of the circle.

Finally, we can stretch either the horizontal or vertical dimension of the circle, making an oval or ellipse, with another variation of the CIRCLE statement.

> **CIRCLE (x, y), radius, color, start, end, aspect** The parameter *aspect* is a positive number that causes the circle (or part of the circle) to be *compressed* vertically or horizontally, producing an *ellipse* or *oval*. If *aspect* < 1, then the circle is compressed vertically; the closer *aspect* gets to 0, the more extreme the vertical compression. If *aspect* > 1, the circle is compressed horizontally; the larger *aspect* gets, the more extreme the horizontal compression.

If you omit the parameter *aspect*, QuickBASIC chooses a value for it that will make the circle appear round on the screen; this value depends on the screen resolution (interestingly, the value 1 does not give a round circle on the screen in either mode 1 or 2, because the *x*-units and *y*-units on the screen have unequal size). The following statements draw two ellipses in foreground color 1, with the first ellipse wide and the second tall:

```
CIRCLE (0, 0), 25, 1, , , 0.3
CIRCLE (0, 0), 25, 1, , , 3
```

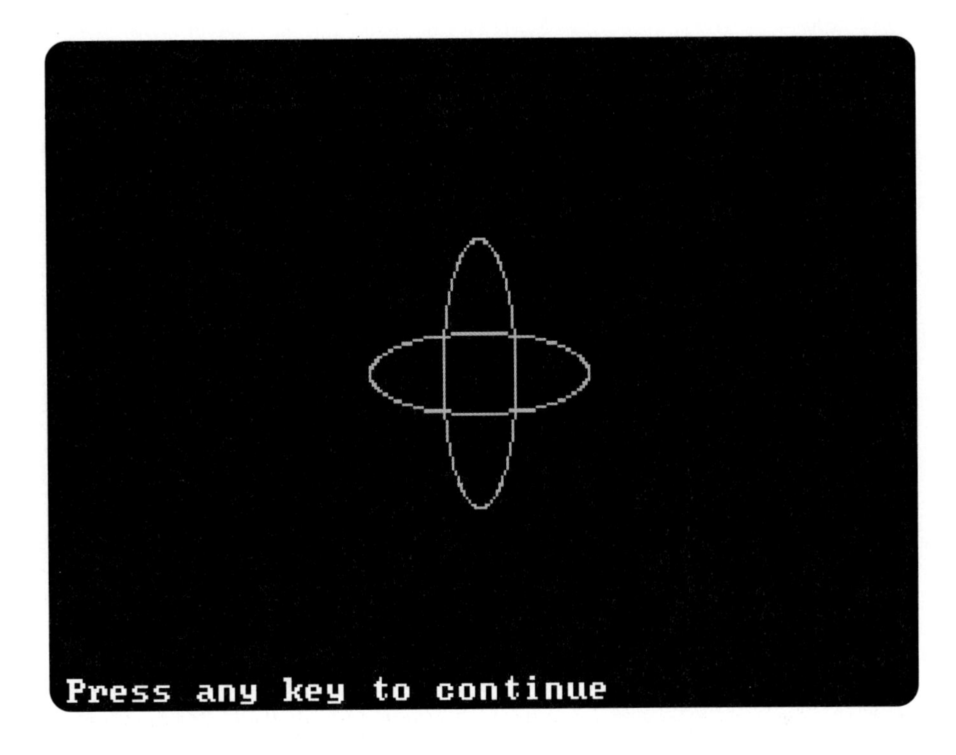
Press any key to continue

FIGURE 10.8

Two Ovals

Notice the extra commas that we used because we did not want to specify values for *start* and *end*. See Figure 10.8 for the output of the above two statements in medium-resolution mode.

PRACTICE 10.3

For each of the BASIC statements and pairs of statements shown below, describe the shape and color of the object that is drawn and sketch it on a piece of paper. Assume throughout that you have first executed the following graphics set-up statements:

```
SCREEN 1
WINDOW (-100, 100)-(100, -100)
COLOR 1, 0
LET pi = 3.14
```

(a) `PSET (0, 50), 1`
(b) `LINE (-10, 0)-(10, 10), 2`
(c) `LINE (-5, -5)-(8, 8), 3, B`
(d) `LINE (0, 0)-(50, 50), 1, BF`
(e) `LINE (-25, 25)-(0, 0), 2, B`
    `PAINT (-10, 10), 3, 2`
(f) `CIRCLE (20, -30), 15, 1`
(g) `CIRCLE (0, 0), 10, 2, pi/4, 7*pi/4`
(h) `CIRCLE (0, 0), 10, 3, -7*pi/4, pi/4`
(i) `CIRCLE (-50, 50), 50, 1, , , .25`
(j) `CIRCLE (0, 0), 30, 2, 0, pi, 4`

10.4 Mixing Graphics and Text

The way the screen behaves when you do text output (i.e., use PRINT statements) is different from when you do graphics output using the statements described above. One important difference is that, when you do text output, the screen "scrolls," that is, if you've printed something on the bottom line of the screen and then executed another PRINT statement, all the previous lines of output will move up one line to make room—thus, the output seems to be unfolding in the same manner as a scroll. On the other hand, the screen stays put during graphics output; you simply move the cursor to different points on the fixed screen, or you can use the CLS statement to clear the screen and start fresh. Thus, there is a fundamental incompatibility between the styles of text and graphics output. However, it *is* syntactically legal to mix PRINT statements with graphics statements. You just have to be careful that in executing PRINT statements, you don't mess up your graphics output by, for example, inadvertently scrolling your graphics picture.

There are two ways to avoid these kinds of problems and successfully mix graphics and text. One is to learn to use two QuickBASIC statements (VIEW and VIEW PRINT) that allow you to break the screen into two different regions (one for graphics and one for text). If you do this, then, for example, scrolling in the text region will not affect the graphics region. If you are interested in learning to use these statements, use the QuickBASIC Help System (or ask your instructor). We will not cover the VIEW and VIEW PRINT statements here.

The other way to successfully combine text and graphics is to simply be careful to program in such a way that you don't allow the two kinds of output to interfere with each other. One way to do this is to clear the screen (or even change graphics modes) between printed output and graphic output. For example, we could write a program that gets all its input data in mode 0 and then shifts to mode 1 to draw a picture using that data.

We can also print words directly on the graphics screen (for labelling, etc.), as long as we leave room for them and then use the LOCATE statement to print them in the correct place (and for safety, put *semicolons* at the end of PRINT statements to prevent scrolling). To use the LOCATE command successfully in modes 1 and 2, there are two important things to remember:

1. Regardless of the mode, the arguments for the LOCATE statement are always *row* and *column*, and have nothing to do with the coordinate system being used in modes 1 and 2.
2. In mode 2 (high-resolution), there are *25 rows* and *80 columns* for printing characters (this is the same as in text mode). In mode 1 (medium-resolution), there are *25 rows* and *40 columns*, that is, characters are twice as wide as in text mode.

For example, suppose we use the same WINDOW statement that we've been using throughout this chapter, that is,

```
WINDOW (-100, 100)-(100, -100)
```

Then the coordinates of the center of the screen are (0, 0), and those are what we would use in graphics statements such as PSET or CIRCLE to draw a dot or circle (or whatever) in the middle of the screen. However, suppose we want to use a PRINT statement to print the letter *X* exactly in the middle of the screen. Then we need to first use the LOCATE command to select the middle row *for printing* and the middle column *for printing*; what these locations are depends on which graphics mode we're in.

In mode 1 (medium-resolution): **LOCATE 13, 20**
In mode 2 (high-resolution): **LOCATE 13, 40**

As in all graphics programming, you can draw a picture and estimate the appropriate coordinates and/or row and column, and then adjust them after testing the program. If you look at the file C10EX04.BAS, which contains the pie-chart program that we discussed in Example 4, you'll see that we've used PRINT statements to label the pie chart.

We need to make one last comment about mixing text and graphics. As mentioned earlier, you may decide, in a particular program, to clear the screen or to switch modes. If you decide to switch modes, you must realize that modes 0 and 2 have "small characters" (80 columns in each row), whereas mode 1 (medium-resolution) has "big characters" (40 columns in each row). But, if you switch to mode 0 from mode 1 (i.e., have a SCREEN 0 statement that comes after a SCREEN 1 statement), you'll find that the characters stay big! If this is what you want, that's fine (you'll still have the better color selection of mode 0), but if you want *small* characters, you'll need to insert a SCREEN 2 statement between the SCREEN 1 and SCREEN 0 statements. In other words, your program will look as follows:

```
SCREEN 1
.
.
.
(graphics statements)
.
.
.

'You need both of the following statements to
'return to text mode with small print
SCREEN 2
SCREEN 0
.
.
.
(text mode statements)
.
.
.
```

EXAMPLE 5

In the previous chapter, you saw how to draw *bar graphs* using only PRINT statements (see Example 6 in Chapter 9). If you can make do with fewer colors, then it's easier to draw bar graphs in medium- or high-resolution graphics mode because you can draw an entire bar with a single LINE statement. Also, it's easy to orient the bars however you wish, compared to text mode (where it's easier to write a program to draw horizontal bars than vertical bars).

In this example, we design a program that generates random integers in the range 1 to 10 and then draws a bar graph showing the relative frequency of each of the ten numbers (if we generate a lot of random numbers from 1 to 10, they each should occur approximately 10% of the time). The algorithm is as follows:

1. Text mode; do program introduction and let user decide how many random numbers to generate
2. Switch to medium-resolution graphics mode; draw and label axes
3. Generate the random numbers, keeping count of occurrences of each possible value (1 to 10)
4. For each value, calculate its frequency and draw bar

In Step 2, we decided to use the *x*-axis to list the possible values, 1 to 10. On the *y*-axis, we list the possible frequencies, from 0 to 100. We want our axes to extend a bit on each end, say, *x* from −1 to 11 and *y* from −10 to 110, and we want some room in the picture around the axes for printing labels. After some experimentation, we decided on the following WINDOW statement:

```
WINDOW (-3, 130)-(12, -40)
```

We must also remember that, when printing labels, these coordinates are meaningless for the LOCATE statement; when using LOCATE, we need to remember that there are 25 rows and 40 columns.

We used a combination of the colors blue, red, and yellow for the text mode introduction, and we chose palette 1 (cyan, magenta, white) on a gray background for drawing the bar graph. The axes and labels are white, and the bars alternate between cyan and magenta. The counts for each value from 1 to 10 are stored in an array. Here's the final section of the program, which draws the bars, after the axes have been drawn and the numbers have been generated (see C10EX05.BAS for the complete program):

```
'For each value from 1 to 10, calculate percentage and draw bar

LET colr = 1
FOR value = 1 TO 10
    LET percent = 100 * (count(value) / howMany)
```

```
        IF percent > 0 THEN
            LINE (value - .5, percent)-(value + .5, 0), colr, BF
        END IF
        IF colr = 1 THEN
            LET colr = 2
        ELSE
            LET colr = 1
        END IF
    NEXT value
```

If we generate only a few numbers, their frequencies will vary quite a bit; but if we generate many, *all* the frequencies should be around 10%. See Figures 10.9 and 10.10 for two sample outputs, the first using 25 random numbers and the second using 250 random numbers. Notice that we've included this information as part of the labelling of the bar graph.

PRACTICE 10.4

In Exercise 1 of Practice 10.2, we asked you to give the coordinates of five points on a diagram, P_1 to P_5, using different WINDOW statements. Referring back to that diagram, give the approximate *row* and *column* that we would use in a LOCATE statement if we wanted to print the letter *X* at each of those five positions. Do this first for mode 1 and then again for mode 2.

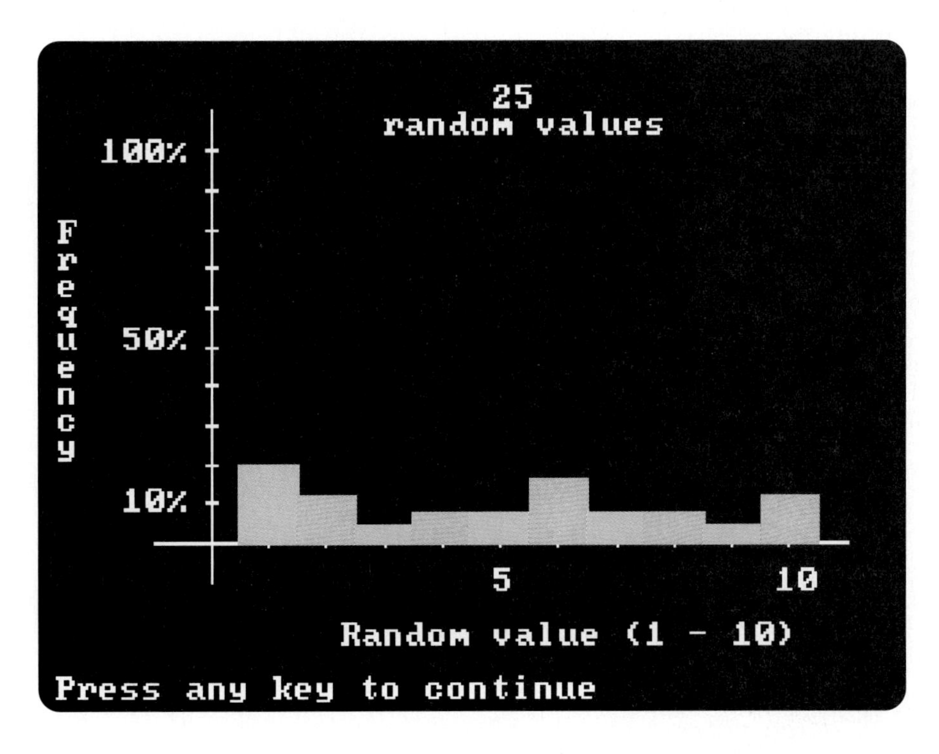

FIGURE 10.9

Sample Output of C10EX05.BAS for 25 Values

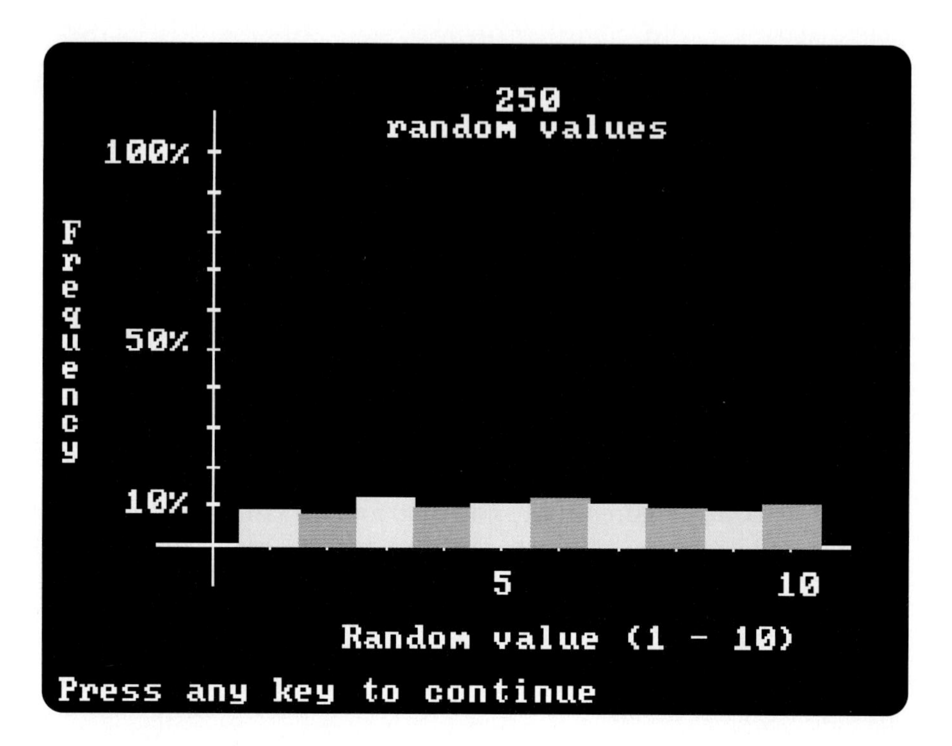

FIGURE 10.10

Sample Output of C10EX05.BAS for 250 Values

10.5 Introduction to Animation

Some of the most exciting computer graphics on TV or in video games involves **animation**, that is, pictures that move. Writing sophisticated animation programs is beyond the scope of this book, but, perhaps surprisingly, it's not too hard to write programs that do simple animation (such as a bouncing ball). Furthermore, the principles that you'll learn in the simple setting still hold for more advanced animation programs.

The basic idea underlying animation is to repeatedly draw an object, slightly changing its position, and each time erasing the drawing in the previous position. Before we describe this process in more detail, let's first notice that we need to refer to the *position* of the object. In medium- or high-resolution graphics mode, we use *coordinates* to describe a position on the screen. For instance, we could describe the position of a circle by using the coordinates of its center; the position of a box might be described by using the coordinates of one corner (say, the upper left-hand corner). Since the position will *change*, it should be represented by a *variable*; in fact, since each position on the screen corresponds to two coordinates, we'll need a variable for each coordinate (e.g., *x* and *y*).

Below is a general algorithm for animating an object on the screen.

BASIC ANIMATION ALGORITHM

1. Choose the initial position (i.e., the initial values for coordinates *x* and *y*) of the object and draw the object in that position

2. Repeat:
    a. Erase the object in its current position
    b. Choose a new position (i.e., new values for *x* and *y*)
    c. Draw the object in its new position

   Until done

Step 1 is fairly straightforward, so let's focus on Step 2. To begin, notice that Step 2 is clearly a loop! Depending on the particular program, it might be FOR...NEXT or DO...LOOP; your program might be "done" when the coordinates reach certain values, or when a certain amount of time has elapsed, or never (i.e., the user presses Ctrl-Break to stop the program)! With the method we'll describe, you'll typically use a DO...LOOP.

To *erase* an object that has been drawn on the screen, we simply draw it again, using the background color (however, if the background is more than one color, erasing is a much more difficult task). Once we've completed Step 2a, we then redraw the object, in its original color, in the new position.

How do we choose the new position? One way to think about it is that we move the current value of *x* a certain amount to the left or right; similarly, we move the current value of *y* a certain amount up or down. These two amounts are sometimes called the **step sizes**. If we use variables for the two step sizes, then we could choose new values for *x* and *y* (Step 2b) as follows:

```
LET x = x + xStep
LET y = y + yStep
```

For instance, if the variables *xStep* and *yStep* both have the value *1*, then the new *x* will be 1 more than the old *x*, and the new *y* will be 1 more than the old *y*. Since larger *x*'s are further to the right and larger *y*'s are further up (assuming we use a WINDOW statement), the new position is above and to the right of the old position. In general, assuming we've used a WINDOW statement,

positive *x* step size	↔	move right
negative *x* step size	↔	move left
positive *y* step size	↔	move up
negative *y* step size	↔	move down

The larger the *magnitudes* of the step sizes, the more the position changes. For instance, suppose we want to move "southeast" (down and to the right). We could make $xStep = 1$ and $yStep = -1$; if, instead, we make $xStep = 2$ and $yStep = -2$, we'll move in the same direction but twice as far. If we do this hundreds of times to achieve the effect of animation, the difference will be one of *speed*: larger step sizes give faster motion. If we make the steps *too* big, though, we'll lose the illusion of *smooth* motion. If, using our usual WINDOW statement, we move 50 units to the right, it will look like a giant leap!

EXAMPLE 6

To experiment with these ideas, let's write a program that draws a moving ball. We'll start the ball at the center of the screen and let the user input the step size so that we can try out motion in different directions. We'll stop the ball when it reaches the edge of the screen. After we've introduced the program, gotten the step sizes from the user, and done our graphics initialization, we'll simply follow the basic algorithm described above. The file C10EX06A.BAS contains a program to do this; the ball is drawn in red on a blue background. Here's the section that draws the moving ball, after the user has chosen the step sizes:

```
'Set up medium-resolution graphics mode

    SCREEN 1
    WINDOW (-100, 100)-(100, -100)
    COLOR 1, 0

    READ blue, green, red, brown
    DATA   0,     1,    2,     3

'Begin animation: get initial x and y and draw ball

    LET x = 0
    LET y = 0
    LET radius = 10 'this makes it easier to adjust ball size
    CIRCLE (x,y), radius, red

'Animation loop: repeatedly erase old picture and draw new one

    DO
        'erase old ball
        CIRCLE (x,y), radius, blue

        'get new values for x and y
        LET x = x + xStep
        LET y = y + yStep

        'draw ball in new position
        CIRCLE (x, y), radius, red

LOOP UNTIL (ABS(x) >= 100 - radius) OR (ABS(y) >= 100 - radius)
```

The condition in our DO...LOOP makes the ball stop when its edge reaches the edge of the screen. For instance, if the radius is 10, the ball is at the left edge when $x = -90$ and at the right edge when $x = 90$. More generally, the ball has reached the left or right edge if

ABS(x) ≥ 100 − radius; similarly, it has reached the top or bottom edge if ABS(y) ≥ 100 − radius.

Another option is to make the ball *bounce* off the edge! If the ball hits the *right* edge, we'll make it turn *left*; if it hits the *left* edge, we'll make it turn *right*. Similarly, if it hits the *top* edge, we'll make it turn *down*, and if it hits the *bottom* edge, we'll make it turn *up*. To reverse direction, we need to change the *sign* of the appropriate step size. Here's how we can modify the basic algorithm. After we've finished Step 2c (drawn the circle in its new position), we'll add the following steps inside the loop:

d. Check if x-position is at edge; if so, reverse x-direction

e. Check if y-position is at edge; if so, reverse y-direction

Since we no longer want to stop the ball when it reaches an edge, we need a new condition in our loop (or *no* condition if we want it to bounce forever!). One option is to use the TIMER function. Recall that this function's value is the number of seconds past midnight on the computer's clock (see Table 1.2 in Section 1.4). Here's a modification of the previous segment that will show a bouncing ball for 30 seconds:

```
LET startTime = TIMER

DO
    'erase old ball
    CIRCLE (x,y), radius, blue
    'get new values for x and y
    LET x = x + xStep
    LET y = y + yStep

    'draw ball in new position
    CIRCLE (x,y), radius, red

    'reverse x-direction if x is at edge
    IF ABS(x) >= 100 - radius THEN
        LET xStep = -xStep
    END IF

    'reverse y-direction if y is at edge
    IF ABS(y) >= 100 - radius THEN
        LET yStep = -yStep
    END IF

LOOP UNTIL TIMER - startTime >= 30
```

One small but important observation is to use ">=" in the loop condition: if exactly 30 seconds is reached while we're in the middle of the loop, equality will never be achieved and the loop will go on forever! To try this program, load the file C10EX06B.BAS.

Below, we've listed a few of the many variations we could use with this program to change the look of its output.

1. We could leave a **trail**, instead of erasing the ball (or whatever object). In Step 2a, redraw the object in a *third* color (e.g., green in this example).
2. We could draw a solid-color object. To draw a solid circle, add an appropriate PAINT statement after each CIRCLE statement. For example, in this program, we would draw the new circle with the following *pair* of statements:

```
CIRCLE (x, y), radius, red
PAINT (x, y), red, red
```

   To erase the circle, we'd replace "red" with "blue" in the above statements. Unfortunately, using PAINT gives the effect of "blinking." You might prefer to use a *solid box*, which can be drawn with a single LINE statement (and which exhibits less noticeable blinking).
3. We could use an object with a more complex shape. As long as you pick a reference point on the object (its center, its upper left-hand corner, etc.), you can use the basic algorithm, although QuickBASIC also provides some more sophisticated animation statements (GET and PUT) to use with more complex animation.
4. For bouncing, you could change the magnitudes of the step sizes (e.g., randomly) when you reverse their directions.
5. Use your imagination!!!

We've incorporated some of these ideas into yet another modification of Example 6; you'll find it in the file named C10EX06C.BAS. This program draws a bouncing box in solid red on a blue background; instead of erasing the old box, we leave a trail by drawing a green border around the old box. This produces fascinating output with a three-dimensional appearance. See Figure 10.11 for what the output looks like when the *x*-step is 2.3 and the *y*-step is −3.2. Try it yourself with different step sizes to see the variety of patterns that are produced (you may also want to change the program so that it runs longer than the 60 seconds that we chose).

For our last graphics example, we'll design a program that draws a curve representing the graph of a function. If you're not familiar with graphing functions, don't worry; you'll still be able to get the basic idea. (The reason this example appears in the section on animation is because you see the curve being drawn when you run the program.)

EXAMPLE 7

We can see a "picture" of a mathematical function $f(x)$ (e.g., $f(x) = \sin(x)$, $f(x) = \log(x)$, $f(x) = 3x^2 - 4$, etc.) by drawing a pair of x- and

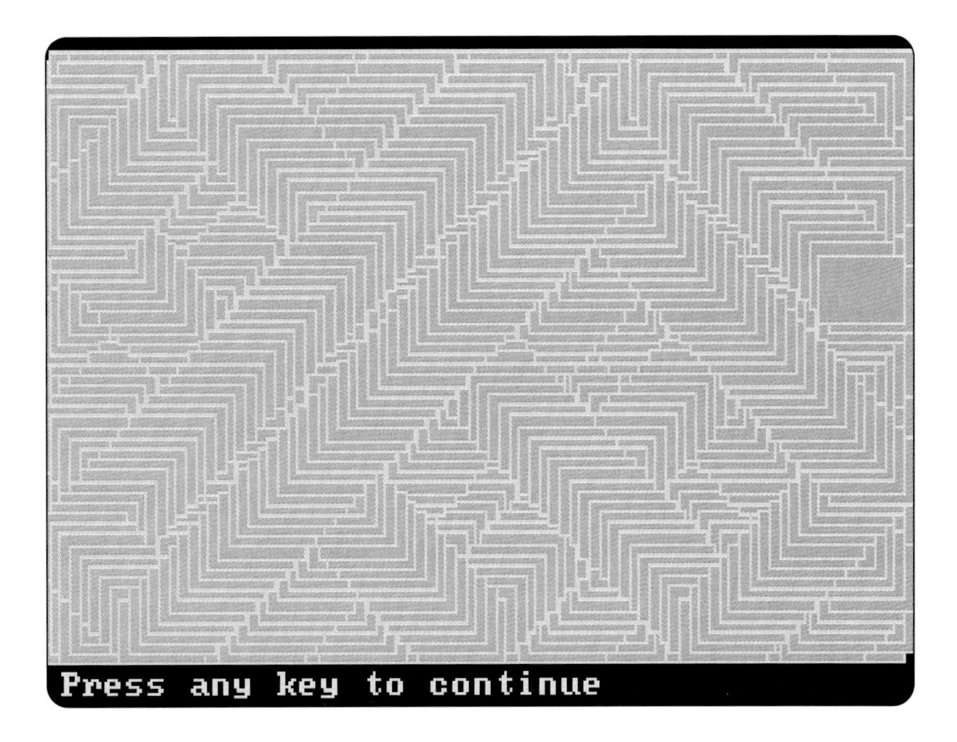
Press any key to continue

FIGURE 10.11

Sample Output of C10EX06C.BAS

y-axes and plotting all the points of the form $(x,f(x))$, that is, all points (x,y) where $y = f(x)$. For this example, we chose the following trigonometric function:

$$a \sin(bx) + c \cos(dx)$$

The graph of this function is a pretty curve that depends on the values chosen for a, b, c, and d. We'll use trigonometric formulas (that you can ignore if you wish!) to choose the lengths of our axes. Then we'll decide how many points to plot and, finally, plot all the points using the PSET function in a loop. Our level-1 algorithm for this problem is:

1. Introduce program, get values for a, b, c, and d, and let user decide how many points to plot
2. Determine how tall and wide we want our axes to be (using trigonometry)
3. Set up graphics mode; use a WINDOW statement that makes coordinates appropriate for the axes
4. From lowest to highest value of x, compute $y = f(x)$, and use PSET to plot the point (x,y)

We decided to use a QuickBASIC user-defined function for calculating the mathematical function $a \sin(bx) + c \cos(dx)$:

```
FUNCTION SinPlusCos (a, b, c, d, x)
'Returns value: a sin(bx) + c cos(dx)

    LET SinPlusCos = a * SIN(b * x) + c * COS(d * x)

END FUNCTION
```

The *period* of this function is the x-interval it needs to complete a cycle; we decided to graph it from x = −period to x = period (an interval of length two times the period). Here is the program segment that actually plots the points (the complete program is in the file C10EX07.BAS):

```
'Draw graph

    LET stepSize = 2 * period / numPoints

    FOR x = -period TO period STEP stepSize
        LET y = SinPlusCos(a, b, c, d, x)
        PSET (x, y), cyan
    NEXT x
```

See Figure 10.12 for sample output using the values $a = 1$, $b = 2.5$, $c = -3$, and $d = 5$, and plotting 2,000 points. If you want to see why this example is in the section on animation, run the program!

PRACTICE 10.5

In each part that follows, we give a pair of numbers representing, respectively, the x-step size and the y-step size. For each pair of step sizes, describe the direction of motion (assume we have executed the usual WINDOW statement).

(a) 3, 3
(b) −3, 3
(c) 3, −3
(d) −3, −3
(e) 4, 0
(f) 0, −2
(g) 0, 0

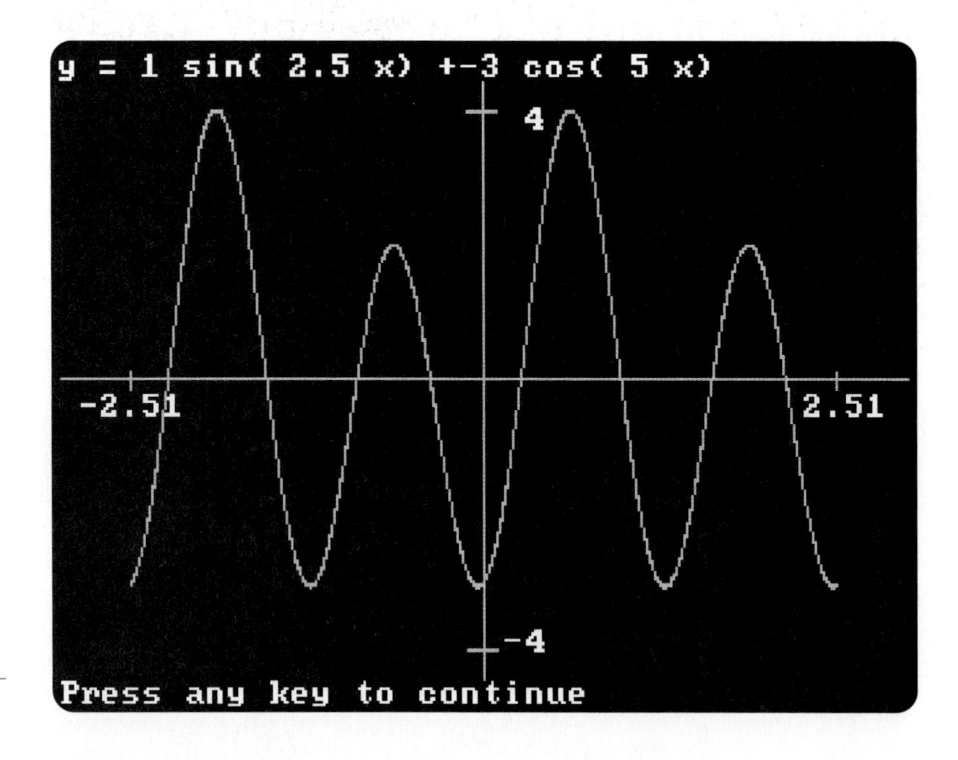

FIGURE 10.12

Sample Output of C10EX07.BAS

10.6 VGA Graphics and Other QuickBASIC Graphics Statements

At the present time, most colleges and universities have computers with CGA graphics boards, but many are beginning to upgrade to IBM PS2s with VGA graphics boards. These boards offer additional screen modes with greatly enhanced color and resolution. In this section, we'll give a brief introduction to VGA graphics.

In addition to the three CGA modes (0–2), VGA has seven additional graphics modes, numbered 7 to 13, that offer a variety of screen resolutions and colors. Descriptions of these modes are shown in Table 10.2.

TABLE 10.2 VGA Graphics Modes

Mode	Colors	Graphics Resolution	Text Rows and Columns
1	4	320 × 200	25 × 40
2	2	640 × 200	25 × 80
7	16	320 × 200	25 × 40
8	16	640 × 200	25 × 80
9	16	640 × 350	25 × 80
10	4	640 × 350	25 × 80
11	2	640 × 480	30 × 80
12	16	640 × 480	30 × 80
13	256	320 × 200	25 × 40

Notice that modes 1 and 2 are the CGA modes we've already discussed. Perhaps the most interesting VGA modes are 12 and 13: mode 12 lets you use 16 colors simultaneously, yet it has more than twice the resolution of CGA's high-resolution mode 2; mode 13 lets you use 256 colors at the same time with resolution equal to that of mode 1! Mode 10 is for use only with a *monochrome* monitor, and its four available colors are actually shades of gray. We'll focus on VGA modes 12 and 13 in this section, but experiment with all of them if you like.

To invoke one of these modes, we simply use the SCREEN statement with the appropriate mode number, as we did for modes 0 to 2. If we also use a WINDOW statement, as we did before, then we don't have to remember the default coordinates (which depend upon the resolution). For instance, the following statements select mode 12 with our usual coordinate system:

```
SCREEN 12
WINDOW (-100, 100)-(100, -100)
```

Using colors in mode 12 is actually easier than in mode 1. The 16 colors available are those listed in Table 10.1, with the corresponding numbers, 0 to 15. To use the colors, we just put the appropriate color number in our drawing statement (PSET, LINE, CIRCLE, or PAINT). For example, the segment below sets up mode 12 with the usual coordinates and then draws green and yellow circles.

```
SCREEN 12
WINDOW (-100, 100)-(100, -100)
CIRCLE (-50, 0), 25, 2    'a green circle
CIRCLE (50, 0), 25, 14    'a yellow circle
```

Notice that we didn't use a COLOR statement; we simply referred directly to colors by their number—much simpler than CGA color graphics! In fact, the COLOR statement is not permitted in modes 2 and 11, and its syntax is different in modes 0, 1, 7 to 10, and 12 to 13! If you want to know more, use the QuickBASIC Help system or the reference manual.

In mode 13, the 256 colors are numbered 0 to 255. As in mode 12, the numbers 0 to 15 correspond to the colors shown in Table 10.1; the remaining numbers in mode 13 correspond to additional colors with a wide variety of hues and intensities (as we'll see in Example 8). Note that the trade-off for having so many colors is that the resolution is not as good as in mode 12.

EXAMPLE 8

The program below displays the range of colors available in modes 12 and 13. To do this, it uses *three* different modes: mode 0 for its introductory output, then a screen showing colors in mode 12, and, finally, a screen showing colors in mode 13. Notice that we have chosen coordinates in each mode that make it easy to fill the screen with one vertical bar in each color. Also, look back at Table 10.2 and observe the different numbers of rows and columns of *text* that can be displayed in each mode and notice how this affects our LOCATE statements.

```

'-----------------------------------------------------------------------------
'   PROGRAM NAME:    C10EX08.BAS
'   AUTHOR:          P. Picasso
'   DATE:            July 31, 1991

'This program shows the colors available in VGA modes 12 and 13 by
'displaying a vertical bar of each color.
'-----------------------------------------------------------------------------

'Program intro

    COLOR 14, 10
    CLS
    LOCATE 8
    LET indent$ = SPACE$(15)    'amount to indent intro text
    PRINT indent$; "This program shows the range of colors available in"
    PRINT indent$; "VGA modes 12 and 13."
    PRINT
    PRINT
```

```
    PRINT indent$; "You can use 16 colors simultaneously in mode 12; the"
    PRINT indent$; "colors are numbered 0 to 15.   In mode 13, there are 256"
    PRINT indent$; "colors, numbered 0 to 255."

'User prompt for next screen

    LOCATE 25, 1
    COLOR 15
    INPUT "Press <Enter> to see a display of mode 12 colors...", a$

'Mode 12 color display

    SCREEN 12
    WINDOW (0, 16)-(16, 0)
    FOR colorNum = 0 TO 15
        LINE (colorNum, 16)-(colorNum + 1, 0), colorNum, BF
    NEXT colorNum

'Heading for mode 12 display

    LOCATE 1, 30
    PRINT "MODE 12 COLORS (0 - 15)"

'Prompt user for next display

    LOCATE 30, 1
    PRINT SPACE$(80);    'this makes bottom line solid black
    LOCATE 30, 1
    INPUT "Press <Enter> to see mode 13 colors...", a$

'Mode 13 color display

    SCREEN 13
    WINDOW (0, 256)-(256, 0)
    FOR colorNum = 0 TO 255
        LINE (colorNum, 256)-(colorNum + 1, 0), colorNum, BF
    NEXT colorNum

'Heading for mode 13 display

    LOCATE 1, 8
    PRINT "MODE 13 COLORS (0 - 255)"

END
```

See Figures 10.13, 10.14, and 10.15 for the three screens of output from this program.

There is much more to learn about graphics in general and VGA graphics in particular. For example, through the use of the PALETTE statement (which we won't cover here), you can actually choose from

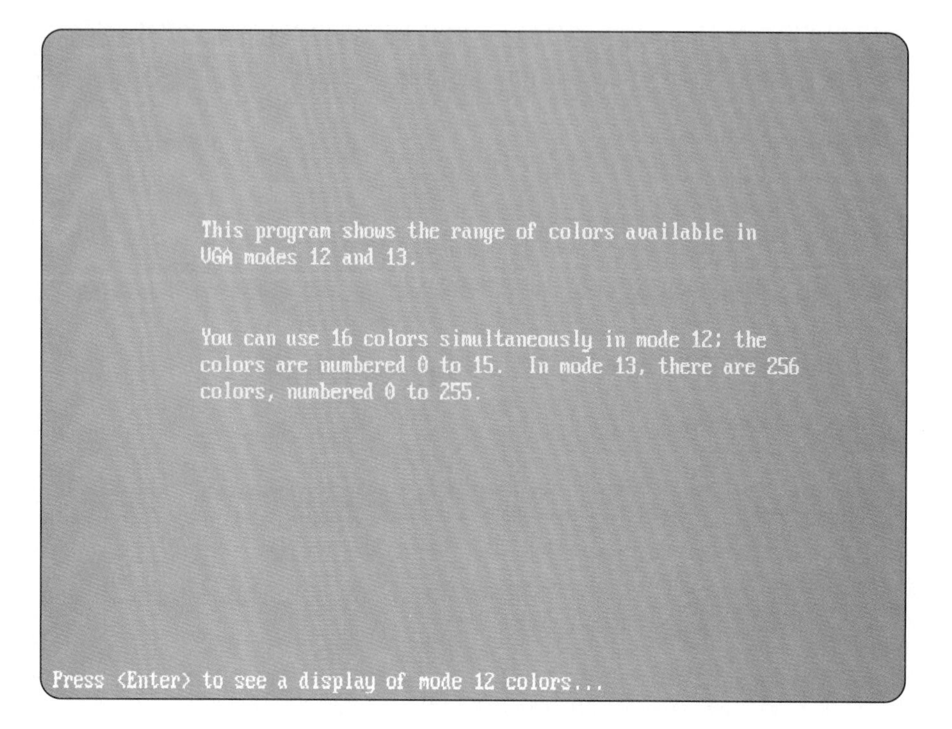

FIGURE 10.13

First Output Screen of C10EX08.BAS

about *260 thousand* colors in screens 11 to 13 (although the total number that appear on screen at the same time is as listed in Table 10.2).

Independent of your particular graphics board, there are several other graphics statements that allow you to do more sophisticated

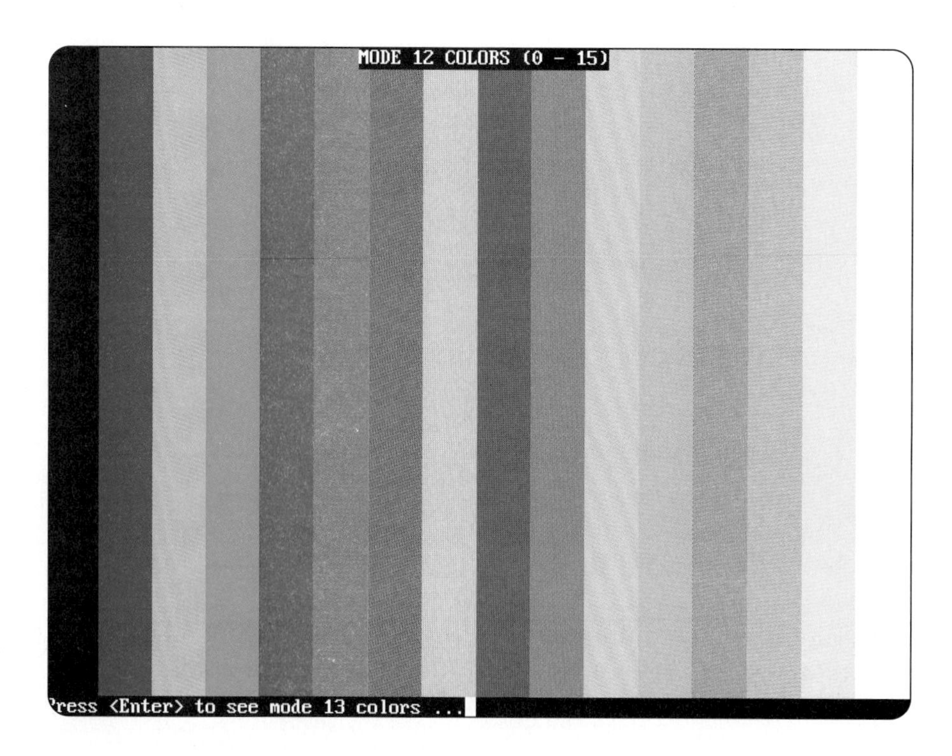

FIGURE 10.14

Second Output Screen of C10EX08.BAS

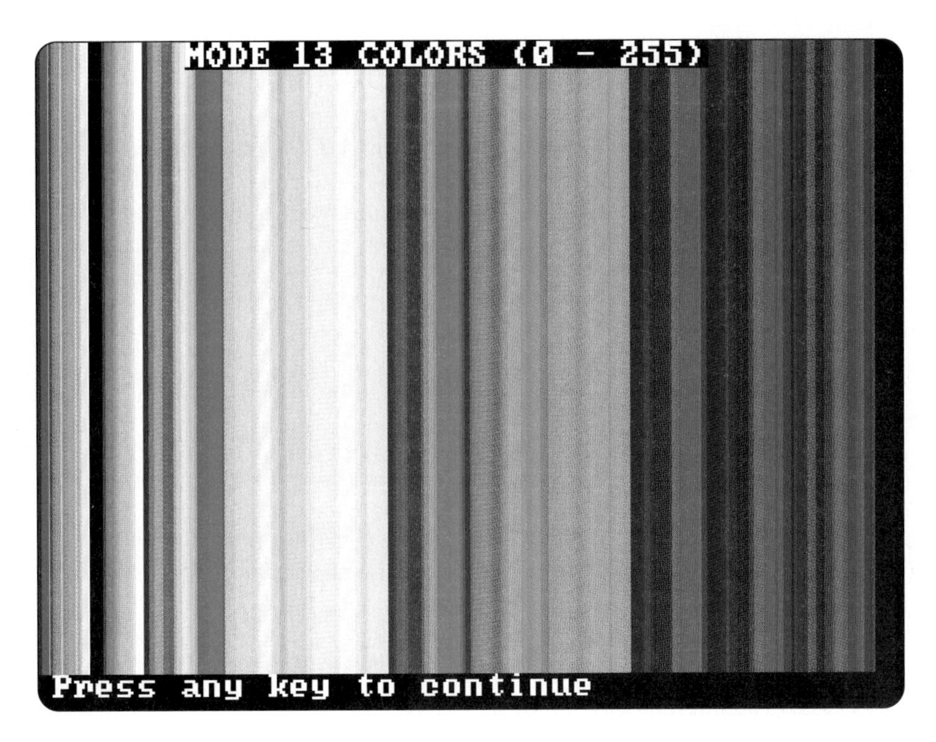

FIGURE 10.15

Third Output Screen of C10EX08.BAS

graphics programs. For example, the DRAW statement lets you specify, by using a character string, a complicated series of graphics commands; thus, you can draw a fairly complex picture using a single line of BASIC code. Second, as mentioned in the previous section, there are statements (GET and PUT) that are useful for writing more sophisticated animation programs. If you are interested in learning about these or other topics that we haven't covered here, talk to your instructor about where to look in the QuickBASIC manual.

PRACTICE 10.6

Suppose we are in mode 12 with our usual coordinates. Describe the output of each of the following segments:

(a)
```
LINE (-100, 0)-(100, 0), 1
LINE (0, 100)-(0, -100), 4
```
(b)
```
LINE (-50, 50)-(50, -50), 13, BF
LINE (-25, 25)-(25, -25), 11, BF
```
(c)
```
CIRCLE (0, 0), 30, 15
PAINT (0, 0), 3, 15
PAINT (50, 0), 6, 15
```

10.7 Sound and Music in QuickBASIC

Now that you've learned to draw pictures on the screen, a natural next step is to add sound. In this section, we'll learn about two statements in QuickBASIC that cause the computer to produce sounds: SOUND and PLAY.

The syntax of the simpler of the two statements to use, the SOUND statement, is described below.

SOUND frequency, duration The numeric parameters *frequency* and *duration* describe, respectively, the pitch of the sound (high vs. low) and the length of time it will last. The *frequency* is a number from 37 to 32,767; the higher the number, the higher the sound. The *duration* represents the length of time in *computer clock ticks*, which occur 18.2 times per second.

Below is a subjective description of the kinds of sounds associated with different frequencies.

Frequency Range	Sounds in That Range
Less than 100	Low but audible
100 to 500	Medium to medium-high human singing voice
500 to 1,000	Medium-high to high human singing voice
1,000 to 3,000	Flute to whistle
3,000 to 5,000	Whistle to barely audible
5,000 to 15,000	Barely audible
Above 15,000	Inaudible

The following program segment would produce sounds, each lasting two seconds, in each of the ranges listed above:

```
DATA 50, 300, 700, 2000, 4000, 10000, 20000

FOR count = 1 TO 7
    READ freq
    SOUND freq, 36.4
NEXT count
```

By varying the frequency and duration in small amounts, you can produce lots of interesting sound effects—so experiment! Of course, you can also use simple sounds to make more effective input prompts, sounds to announce the beginning or end of a program, and so on.

EXAMPLE 9

For this example, we modified the bouncing ball animation program, adding sound effects at the beginning and end, "beeps" to accompany input prompts, and sounds when the ball hits the edge of the screen. Here's the segment that handles the ball's bouncing off the edge:

```
'reverse x-direction if x is at edge
IF ABS(x) >= 100 - radius THEN
    SOUND x + y + 300, 2
    LET xStep = -xStep
END IF

'reverse y-direction if y is at edge
IF ABS(y) >= 100 - radius THEN
    SOUND x + y + 300, 2
    LET yStep = -yStep
END IF
```

We wanted the sounds to get higher as the ball moved further to the right or further up the screen; that made us think of using the numeric expression $x + y$, because it has that property. Unfortunately, though, since x and y range from -100 to 100, the sum ranges from -200 to 200, which is not good for frequencies. Therefore, we decided to *add* something to the sum $x + y$; adding *300*, as we did, brings the new sum into the range 100 to 500, that is, from low to medium-high human voice. The complete program is in the file C10EX09.BAS; try it out!

The second statement we'll study is PLAY, which interprets musical notation transcribed from sheet music into a BASIC string constant. As you'd expect, it's more difficult to use than the SOUND statement; in particular, you need to know how to read musical notation to use it effectively. Its syntax is below.

PLAY music string The "music string" is a string constant whose characters are interpreted according to a set of rules, which correspond roughly to standard rules of musical notation.

Below are the rules for interpreting the characters in a music string.

Character(s)	Meaning
A to **G**	Play the note indicated by that letter.
A to **G**, followed by **#** or **—**	Make the indicated note *sharp* (#) or *flat* (—).
Any note, followed by **.**	Make the note play 1½ times as long.
O0, O1, . . . , O6	Play notes in C-major octaves 0, 1, . . . , 6.
> and <	Greater than (>) means move *up* into the next higher C-octave; less than (<) means move *down* into the next lower C-octave. (Note: Octaves must stay in range 0 to 6.)
Ln	Play the notes that follow for an interval of 1/*n* each, where *n* is in the range 1 to 64, that is, L1 = whole note, L2 = half note, L4 = quarter note, and so on.
Pn	Pause for an interval of 1/*n*.
Tn	Set the tempo, that is, the number of quarter notes per minute. The range for *n* is 32 to 255; the default is 120.
ML, MN, MS	Set music *legato, normal,* or *staccato*. In music normal, the note sounds for 7/8 of its allotted time; in music staccato, for 3/4 of its time; in music legato, for all of its time. Notes in music staccato sound short and choppy, whereas notes in music legato flow together, without any separation.
MF	Music foreground. Program execution pauses while the music is being played.
MB	Music background. Program execution continues while the music is being played.

The following program segment plays the C-major scale six times, from octave 0 up to octave 5:

```
LET scale$ = "L4 C D E F G A B > C"
PLAY "O0"                  'Start in octave 0
FOR octave = 0 TO 5        'Play the C-scale in each octave
    CLS
    LOCATE 12, 36
    PRINT "OCTAVE"; octave
    PLAY scale$
    PLAY "P2"              'Pause after each scale
NEXT octave
```

Notice that the last full scale starts in octave 5 and finishes in octave 6.

The spaces between the characters in music strings are optional, and letters can be upper or lowercase. Music-string arguments in the PLAY statement can also be *concatenations* of string constants or of string variables, but there is one technicality: they may *not* be concatenations of both variables and constants in the same line, for example,

`PLAY scale$ + scale$` is legal, and

`PLAY "C D E" + "E D F"` is legal, but

`PLAY scale$ + "C D E"` is *not legal!*

One legal way to PLAY the last string is the following:

```
LET music$ = scale$ + "C D E"
PLAY music$
```

EXAMPLE 10

The chorus of the song "Oh, Susanna!", by Stephen Foster, is shown in Figure 10.16.[2] The file C10EX10.BAS contains a program that prints the words as the music is being played, one bar at a time.

In order that the music not play before the appropriate words are displayed, it was important that we PLAY a music string containing the characters MF (that line has been highlighted). Try changing MF to MB to see its effect. Be sure to run this program to see (and hear!) its output. The program itself is listed below.

[2] From the *Fireside Book of Folk Ballads*, Margaret Bradford Boni, Editor. Copyright © 1947 by Simon & Schuster, Inc. Copyright renewed in 1981 by Simon & Schuster and Artists and Writers Guild. Reprinted with permission of Simon & Schuster, Inc.

FIGURE 10.16

Chorus of "Oh, Susanna!"

```
'Data section: Each pair of data items consists of the words for one
'bar of music, followed by the music string for that bar. End of data
'is indicated by the data item EOD.

    DATA "Oh, Su -", "L4 G G", "- san-na! Oh,", "L8 B L4 B L8 B"
    DATA "don't you cry for", "L8 A A F# D", "me, For I", "L4 E. L16 D E"
    DATA "come from A - la -", "L8 F# A A. L16 B"
    DATA "- ba - ma with my", "L8 A F# D. L16 E"
    DATA "ban - jo on my", "L8 F# F# E E", "knee.", "L4 D."
    DATA EOD

Make screen yellow on red background with large print

    SCREEN 1
    SCREEN 0
    COLOR 14, 4, 4
    CLS

'Print heading and pause

    LOCATE 10, 16
    PRINT "OH, SUSANNA!"
    LOCATE 12, 13
    PRINT "by STEPHEN FOSTER"
    LET startTime = TIMER
    DO
    LOOP UNTIL TIMER - startTime >= 5
```

```
'Play song as words are being printed

    PLAY "T90 O3 MF"
    DO
        READ words$
        IF words$ = "EOD" THEN
            EXIT DO
        END IF
        READ music$
        CLS
        LOCATE 12, 15
        PRINT words$
        PLAY music$
    LOOP

END
```

EXAMPLE 11

For the last example in this section, we wrote a program that uses text graphics to draw a Christmas tree and uses the PLAY statement to play "We Wish You a Merry Christmas." It's in the file C10EX11.BAS—try it out for fun!

PRACTICE 10.7

1. In each part below, describe the pitch and duration (in seconds) of the sound produced by the given SOUND statement; remember that there are 18.2 clock ticks per second (you could use 20 for thumbnail approximations).

   (a) `SOUND 300, 20` (c) `SOUND 100, 1200`
   (b) `SOUND 2000, 10` (d) `SOUND 4000, 2`

FIGURE 10.17

Chorus of "Clementine"

2. In Figure 10.17, we've reproduced the music for the chorus of the folk song "Clementine."[3] Write one or more PLAY statements to play this music.

Chapter Summary 

In this chapter, we've learned to write BASIC programs that draw pictures in medium- and high-resolution CGA graphics; to do animation; to use VGA graphics; and to add sound and music to our BASIC programs.

The graphics capabilities of your machine depend both on the monitor and on the computer itself. At the time this book was written, the most advanced graphics circuitry commonly available for PCs and PS2s was the *VGA graphics board*. Most machines have at least a *CGA graphics board*, which permits us to do color graphics, although the number of available colors and the screen resolution (i.e., number of *pixels*) is not as good as VGA. In this chapter, we focused on CGA graphics and looked briefly at VGA graphics.

CGA graphics has three modes, which are activated by using the SCREEN statement. *Mode 0* is regular text mode; here, you have the widest color selection, but you cannot use special graphics statements. *Mode 1* is medium-resolution graphics; here, you can use graphics statements, but you have a limited choice of four colors and the screen resolution is 320 by 200. *Mode 2* is high-resolution graphics; as in mode 1, you can use graphics statements, and the screen resolution is even better, 640 by 200—but all drawing is monochrome, that is, white on a black background.

In addition to the CGA modes, VGA graphics provides seven more modes that offer even higher resolution and many colors. *Mode 12* has 16 colors and its resolution is 640 by 480; *mode 13* has resolution 320 by 200 (like mode 1) but has 256 colors!

To *print* the output of graphics programs, your computer should be connected to a dot-matrix (not laser) printer, and you should type the *DOS command* GRAPHICS before starting QuickBASIC.

Once in graphics mode, you can choose your own coordinate system by using the WINDOW statement. If you're in mode 1, you can select one of two *color palettes*, each of which consists of three fixed colors, plus a fourth "background" color, by using the COLOR statement. In subsequent drawing statements, you use the numbers 0 to 3 to refer to the four colors you've chosen.

[3] From the *Fireside Book of Folk Ballads*, Margaret Bradford Boni, Editor. Copyright © 1947 by Simon & Schuster, Inc. Copyright renewed in 1981 by Simon & Schuster and Artists and Writers Guild. Reprinted with permission of Simon & Schuster, Inc.

We learned about four main graphics drawing statements:

CIRCLE (x, y), radius, color, start, end, aspect
Depending on its arguments, this statement is used to draw circles, ovals, parts of circles or ovals, and wedges.

LINE (a, b)—(c, d), color, BF
This statement is used to draw line segments, outlines of boxes, and solid boxes.

PAINT (x, y), color, border
This statement is used to "paint" a region, that is, fill it with the specified color. The paint stops when it reaches the specified border color.

PSET (x, y), color
This statement draws a single dot at the specified position, in the specified color.

We can use PRINT statements in graphics programs to add titles and so on—but we must be careful. First, to position our printed output, we use a LOCATE statement, which requires us to specify *row* and *column* rather than coordinates. In medium-resolution CGA mode there are 25 rows and 40 columns; in high-resolution CGA mode (as in text mode), there are 25 rows and 80 columns. Second, we must be careful not to print so much that the screen *scrolls*, which would ruin the positioning of subsequent graphics statements.

We saw that we can write programs to do *simple animation*; the basic algorithm is to simply draw and redraw the object repeatedly, each time erasing it in the old position before drawing it in the new position. By varying the sign and magnitude of the *step sizes*, we change the direction and speed of motion.

Finally, we learned how to write programs that make sounds, by using the SOUND and PLAY statements. The SOUND statement is a little simpler and requires that we specify the frequency and duration of the sound. The PLAY statement is more sophisticated; by using PLAY with a music string representing musical notation, we are able to transcribe musical notation into a BASIC program.

Appendix 3 is a quick guide to the graphics statements covered in this chapter and in Chapter 9.

? Review Questions

1. Compare modes 0, 1, and 2 with respect to each of the following criteria:

(a) number of colors
(b) screen resolution
(c) number of graphics statements

2. Write the correct BASIC statements needed to accomplish each of the following (all parts refer to CGA graphics):
   (a) Enter high-resolution mode and set up x and y coordinates, each of which range from 0 to 10.
   (b) Enter medium-resolution mode, and choose the following colors for drawing: light blue, green, red, and brown.
   (c) Enter medium-resolution mode, set up x coordinates ranging from −1 to 1, y coordinates ranging from −5 to 5, and draw the coordinate axes.
   (d) Enter high-resolution mode with the coordinates we've used in the chapter, paint the screen white, and then draw a black circle of radius 50 in the middle of the screen.
   (e) Enter medium-resolution mode with the usual coordinates and draw the picture of Pac-Man shown in Figure 10.18, using a circle of radius 25 with center (0,0).

3. For VGA graphics, compare modes 1, 12, and 13 with respect to each of the following:
   (a) number of colors
   (b) screen resolution
   (c) number of rows and columns for text characters

4. Write the correct BASIC statements needed to accomplish each of the following:
   (a) Make a whistlelike sound that lasts 30 seconds.
   (b) Make a sequence of sounds, starting at frequency 100 and ending at frequency 1,000, and increasing in steps of size 50, each of which lasts one-tenth of a second.
   (c) Play the C-major scale *in reverse*, starting in octave 4.

Press any key to continue

FIGURE 10.18

Sample Output for Review Question 2e

Programming Problems

1. Write a program, in medium-resolution CGA graphics, that draws five *nested* boxes (boxes that are inside one another). After you've got the boxes looking the way you want, modify your program so that the regions formed will alternate in color. (This can be done in at least two different ways: using the PAINT statement, or adding the BF modifier to the existing LINE statements.)

2. Modify the program C10EX03.BAS of Example 3, which draws a picture of a house, by adding a sun with rays and a chimney with smoke.

3. Write a program that draws a simple picture of a face.

4. Write a program that tells a brief story accompanied by simple pictures for illustration.

5. In Example 10 and Programming Problem 13 of Chapter 3, we looked at a simulation of dart throwing; now we have the statements we need to make a *visual* simulation. Write a program that draws the dart board pictured in that example; then have the program generate 100 random tosses and draw them using the PSET statement. When the tosses are all done, have the program print the associated approximation for pi. Note: Because the width and height of the screen are unequal, the LINE and CIRCLE statements that draw the dart board will not work properly if the x- and y-coordinates are the same size (try it and see). Instead, try using the WINDOW statement shown below, in mode 1 (medium-resolution). With this statement, your dart board should come out correctly (and room is left for printing).

```
WINDOW (-2, 1.48)-(2, -1.48)
```

6. (a) The numbers below represent the monthly sales revenues for last year, in thousands of dollars, for the Acme Widget Company.

   12, 5, 8, 14.4, 20, 21.5, 21.5, 18, 24, 6, 11.5, 15

   Write a program that draws a *line graph* representing this data. Use the x-coordinate for the months (from 1 to 12) and the y-coordinate for the revenues. Thus, your program should draw line segments that connect the points (1, 12), (2, 5), (3, 8), . . . , (11, 11.5), (12, 15). It should also have axes and titles.

   (b) Write a more general program that lets the user input a list of numbers and then draws a line graph representing that list. For instance, if the user inputs the list 150, 200, 180, 250, 125, then the program should draw appropriate axes and draw line segments connecting the points (1, 150), (2, 200), (3, 180), and so on. Notice that your WINDOW statement will depend on what the user inputs.

7. Modify the program in the file C10EX06B.BAS, which draws a bouncing ball, in the ways listed below.

   (a) Leave a trail by redrawing the old ball in green instead of blue.
   (b) When the ball hits the left or right edge, *halve* the size of *xStep* (as well as reversing direction).
   (c) When the ball hits the top or bottom edge, increase the size of *yStep* by one (as well as reversing direction).

8. (a) The basic animation algorithm discussed in this chapter can be modified by changing the *shape* of an object rather than its position. Use this idea to write a program that draws a "pulsing circle," by changing its *aspect* instead of its center. Try these values: using a circle of radius 30 (with the usual WINDOW statement), let the aspect start at .2 and grow to 2.5 in steps of size .05. The output should show a circle that starts out flat and changes shape repeatedly, ending up tall.

(b) Modify the program of part (a) by adding a segment that makes the circle's shape change in the opposite manner, that is, from tall back to flat.

(c) Use a DO...LOOP to make the program of part (b) repeat, so that the circle continuously oscillates between flat and tall for, say, 30 seconds.

FIGURE 10.19

"She'll Be Comin' Round the Mountain"

9. Write a program that draws a book cover design for a book of your choice. Your output should include the title and author plus some artwork. Write the program using one of the color graphics modes (e.g., CGA mode 1 or VGA mode 12 or 13) and use all the available colors in the mode you choose (e.g., 4 in mode 1, 16 in mode 12, 256 in mode 13).

10. Using VGA graphics, in each of the following, write a program that draws a rainbow with the specified characteristics:
(a) with 16 colors (mode 12)
(b) with 256 colors (mode 13)

11. Write a program that lets users experiment with the SOUND statement. The program should let them input a frequency and a length of time (let users input the time in *seconds;* your program can then convert to the equivalent number of clock ticks); then the program should execute the corresponding SOUND statement. Put the whole process in a loop so that users can try as many sounds as they want.

12. Take any interactive program you've written that involves several inputs and add SOUND statements to give the user an audible input prompt.

13. The music for the folk song "She'll Be Comin' Round the Mountain" is shown in Figure 10.19.[4] Write a BASIC program that uses the PLAY statement to play the melody.

14. Write a program that plays a version of the game Name That Tune. Find sheet music for a song and transcribe it into a music string. Store the characters in DATA statements so that each complete note is a separate data item. Then let two players take turns hearing one note, then two notes, then three, and so on, each time giving them a chance to guess the title of the song. Once you get the simple version working, you can think about ways to have the program choose from more than one song; otherwise, no one would want to play more than once!

---

[4] From the *Fireside Book of Folk Ballads,* Margaret Bradford Boni, Editor. Copyright © 1947 by Simon & Schuster, Inc. Copyright renewed in 1981 by Simon & Schuster and Artists and Writers Guild. Reprinted with permission of Simon & Schuster, Inc.

APPENDICES

BASIC RESERVED WORDS

The following is a list of Microsoft BASIC reserved words:

ABS	COMMAND$	EOF	IOCTL
ACCESS	COMMON	EQV	IOCTL$
ALIAS	CONST	ERASE	IS
AND	COS	ERDEV	KEY
ANY	CSNG	ERDEV$	KILL
APPEND	CSRLIN	ERL	LBOUND
AS	CVD	ERR	LCASE$
ASC	CVDMBF	ERROR	LEFT$
ATN	CVI	EXIT	LEN
BASE	CVL	EXP	LET
BEEP	CVS	FIELD	LINE
BINARY	CVSMBF	FILEATTR	LIST
BLOAD	DATA	FILES	LOC
BSAVE	DATE$	FIX	LOCAL
BYVAL	DECLARE	FOR	LOCATE
CALL	DEF	FRE	LOCK
CALLS	DEFDBL	FREEFILE	LOF
CASE	DEFINT	FUNCTION	LOG
CDBL	DEFLNG	GET	LONG
CDECL	DEFSNG	GOSUB	LOOP
CHAIN	DEFSTR	GOTO	LPOS
CHDIR	DIM	HEX$	LPRINT
CHR$	DO	IF	LSET
CINT	DOUBLE	IMP	LTRIM$
CIRCLE	DRAW	INKEY$	MID$
CLEAR	ELSE	INP	MKD$
CLNG	ELSEIF	INPUT	MKDIR
CLOSE	END	INPUT$	MKDMBF$
CLS	ENDIF	INSTR	MKI$
COLOR	ENVIRON	INT	MKL$
COM	ENVIRON$	INTEGER	MKS$

MKSMBF$
MOD
NAME
NEXT
NOT
OCT$
OFF
ON
OPEN
OPTION
OR
OUT
OUTPUT
PAINT
PALETTE
PCOPY
PEEK
PEN
PLAY
PMAP
POINT
POKE
POS
PRESET
PRINT
PSET
PUT
RANDOM
RANDOMIZE
READ
REDIM
REM
RESET
RESTORE
RESUME
RETURN
RIGHT$
RMDIR
RND
RSET
RTRIM$
RUN
SADD
SCREEN
SEEK
SEG
SELECT
SETMEM
SGN
SHARED
SHELL
SIGNAL
SIN
SINGLE
SLEEP
SOUND
SPACE$
SPC
SQR
STATIC
STEP
STICK
STOP
STR$
STRIG
STRING
STRING$
SUB
SWAP
SYSTEM
TAB
TAN
THEN
TIME$
TIMER
TO
TROFF
TRON
TYPE
UBOUND
UCASE$
UNLOCK
UNTIL
USING
VAL
VARPTR
VARPTR$
VARSEG
VIEW
WAIT
WEND
WHILE
WIDTH
WINDOW
WRITE
XOR

APPENDIX II

ASCII CHARACTER CODES

ASCII CODE	CHARACTER	ASCII CODE	CHARACTER	ASCII CODE	CHARACTER	ASCII CODE	CHARACTER
0		25	↓	50	2	75	K
1	☺	26	→	51	3	76	L
2	☻	27	←	52	4	77	M
3	♥	28	∟	53	5	78	N
4	♦	29	↔	54	6	79	O
5	♣	30	▲	55	7	80	P
6	♠	31	▼	56	8	81	Q
7	•	32		57	9	82	R
8	◘	33	!	58	:	83	S
9	○	34	"	59	;	84	T
10	◙	35	#	60	<	85	U
11	♂	36	$	61	=	86	V
12	♀	37	%	62	>	87	W
13	♪	38	&	63	?	88	X
14	♫	39	’	64	@	89	Y
15	☼	40	(	65	A	90	Z
16	►	41	)	66	B	91	[
17	◄	42	*	67	C	92	\
18	↕	43	+	68	D	93	]
19	‼	44	,	69	E	94	^
20	¶	45	-	70	F	95	_
21	§	46	.	71	G	96	‘
22	■	47	/	72	H	97	a
23	↨	48	0	73	I	98	b
24	↑	49	1	74	J	99	c

ASCII CODE	CHARACTER	ASCII CODE	CHARACTER	ASCII CODE	CHARACTER	ASCII CODE	CHARACTER
100	d	139	ï	178	▓	217	┘
101	e	140	î	179	│	218	┌
102	f	141	ì	180	┤	219	█
103	g	142	Ä	181	╡	220	▄
104	h	143	Å	182	╢	221	▌
105	i	144	É	183	╖	222	▐
106	j	145	æ	184	╕	223	▀
107	k	146	Æ	185	╣	224	α
108	l	147	ô	186	║	225	β
109	m	148	ö	187	╗	226	Γ
110	n	149	ò	188	╝	227	π
111	o	150	û	189	╜	228	Σ
112	p	151	ù	190	╛	229	σ
113	q	152	ÿ	191	┐	230	μ
114	r	153	Ö	192	└	231	τ
115	s	154	Ü	193	┴	232	Φ
116	t	155	¢	194	┬	233	θ
117	u	156	£	195	├	234	Ω
118	v	157	¥	196	─	235	δ
119	w	158	Pt	197	┼	236	∞
120	x	159	ƒ	198	╞	237	Ø
121	y	160	á	199	╟	238	$\in$
122	z	161	í	200	╚	239	$\cap$
123	{	162	ó	201	╔	240	$\equiv$
124	¦	163	ú	202	╩	241	$\pm$
125	}	164	ñ	203	╦	242	$\geq$
126	~	165	Ñ	204	╠	243	$\leq$
127	⌂†	166	ª	205	═	244	⌠
128	Ç	167	º	206	╬	245	⌡
129	ü	168	¿	207	╧	246	$\div$
130	é	169	⌐	208	╨	247	$\approx$
131	â	170	¬	209	╤	248	°
132	ä	171	½	210	╥	249	•
133	à	172	¼	211	╙	250	·
134	å	173	¡	212	╘	251	$\sqrt{}$
135	ç	174	«	213	╒	252	^{n}
136	ê	175	»	214	╓	253	^{2}
137	ë	176	░	215	╫	254	■
138	è	177	▒	216	╪	255	

† ASCII code 127 has the code DEL. Under DOS, this code has the same effect as ASCII 8 (BS). The DEL code can be generated by the CTRL + BKSP key combination.

A QUICK GUIDE TO GRAPHICS COMMANDS

Printing Graphics Output

If you plan to print your medium or high resolution graphics output, you must type the word **GRAPHICS**—*at the operating system level*—before starting QuickBASIC. You can then print graphics output by using **Shift-PrtSc**. Note: Laser printers will not print graphics output. Also, some text graphics characters that can be seen on the screen do not print out properly.

Colors

Number	Color	Number	Color	Number	Color	Number	Color
0	black	4	red	8	gray	12	light red
1	blue	5	magneta	9	light blue	13	light magneta
2	green	6	brown	10	light green	14	yellow
3	cyan	7	white	11	light cyan	15	high-intensity white

NOTE: Add 16 to make color *blink*!

Text Mode Statements (Mode 0)

SCREEN 0 To enter mode 0. Note that this is the default screen mode.

COLOR foreground, background, border To choose colors; foreground 0–31, background 0–7, border 0–15 (no border appears on IBM PS2 computers).

CLS To change background after COLOR statement.

LOCATE row, col To choose printing position; rows 1–25, columns 1–80 (rows 24–25 are used by QuickBASIC for "Press any key to continue" message at end of program execution).

PRINT CHR$(219) To print solid box. See ASCII table (Appendix 2) for other shapes.

Note: LOCATE and PRINT can also be used in graphics modes.

Set-Up Statements for Graphics

SCREEN n To enter graphics mode *n*; the table below describes the available screen modes.

Mode	Colors	Graphics Resolution	Text Rows and Columns	Required Graphics Adapter
1	4	320 × 200	25 × 40	CGA, EGA, MCGA, or VGA
2	2	640 × 200	25 × 80	CGA, EGA, MCGA, or VGA
7	16	320 × 200	25 × 40	EGA or VGA
8	16	640 × 200	25 × 80	EGA or VGA
9	16	640 × 350	25 × 80	EGA or VGA
10	4	640 × 350	25 × 80	EGA or VGA
11	2	640 × 480	30 × 80	MCGA or VGA
12	16	640 × 480	30 × 80	VGA
13	256	320 × 200	25 × 40	MCGA or VGA

COLOR background, palette To choose drawing colors (screen mode 1 only); background 0–15, palette 0 or 1 as shown below (defaults are background 0 and palette 1).

Palette 0 1 = green
2 = red
3 = brown

Palette 1 1 = cyan
2 = magenta
3 = high-intensity white

The COLOR statement is illegal in screen mode 2; in modes 7–9 and 12, colors can be referred to by using the numbers 0–15, as in the table at the beginning of this appendix. To use the COLOR statement in screen modes 7–10 and 12–13, see a reference manual or the QuickBASIC Help system.

WINDOW (x1, y1) – (x2, y2) To choose a coordinate system (x is left-right, *y* is up-down), for example:

```
WINDOW (-100, 100) - (100, -100)
```

Drawing Statements for Use in Modes 1 and 2

PSET (x, y), color To draw point at (x, *y*) in specified color.

LINE (a, b) – (c, d), color To draw line from (a, b) to (c, d) in specified color.

LINE (a, b) – (c, d), color, B To draw outline of box with opposite corners (a, b) and (c, d).

LINE (a, b) – (c, d), color, BF To draw filled box with opposite corners (a, b) and (c, d).

PAINT (x, y), color, bordercolor To paint region in color, starting at (x, *y*), until *bordercolor* is reached.

CIRCLE (x, y), radius, color To draw circle with center (x, *y*).

CIRCLE (x, y), radius, color, start, end To draw part of a circle. The arguments *start* and *end* are angles in radians (0 to pi ≈ 3.14). Putting a *minus sign* in front of *start* and/or *end* will cause a radius to be drawn.

CIRCLE (x, y), radius, color, start, end, aspect To draw an oval. If 0 < aspect < 1, then circle is stretched horizontally; if aspect > 1 then circle is stretched vertically.

USING SUBDIRECTORIES IN DOS

In Workshop 1, we introduced you to microcomputers and *DOS*, the IBM Disk Operating System. We saw that there are a variety of DOS commands that are used to manipulate *files* (for a quick reminder, look at the inside front cover of this book). As you continue to use a microcomputer, you may accumulate many such files; for instance, the SAMPLES disk has over 80 files containing examples from the 2 workshops and 10 chapters of this book. In this appendix, you'll learn some additional DOS commands that will help you organize large numbers of files into several smaller groups of files.

If you have a four-drawer filing cabinet, you probably use the drawers to help you store your file folders in groups according to topic, date, or some other feature. For instance, you might use one drawer apiece for each of the last four years. Furthermore, within each drawer, you might group your files according to topics such as Computer Science Class, English Class, Political Science Class, German Class, Work, and Personal. DOS lets you organize the files on a disk in much the same way; any group of files can be broken up into subgroups, each of which is given a name. Let's see how this is done.

Each group of files on a disk is called a **directory**; when you first format a disk there is only one directory, called the **root directory**. The reason for the word *root* is that, as you successively divide directories into **subdirectories**, the organization of all the subdirectories has a "treelike" structure, with all the other subdirectories "branching" off the root directory. To illustrate this, let's use a disk to store files for two classes, CS 103 (Computer Programming in BASIC) and EN 346 (Shakespeare's Tragedies). The files for CS 103 are to be grouped according to text chapters numbered from 1 to 10, and the files for EN 346 are to be grouped according to each Shakespearean tragedy that is covered. We can use DOS to organize our disk into groups of files as shown in the figure at the top of the next page.

You should now be able to see what we mean by the treelike organization of subdirectories (except that the root of this tree is at the

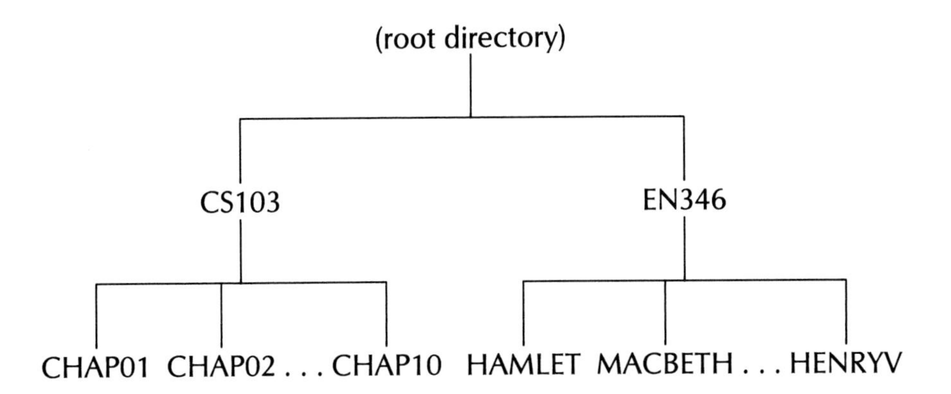

top!). Each one of these directories can contain ordinary files as well as subdirectories. For instance, in addition to containing the ten subdirectories named CHAP01 to CHAP10, the subdirectory CS103 might itself contain several files, for example, INFO.TXT (a file containing general course information) and REVIEW.TXT (a file containing a study guide for the final exam). If this were the case, then a directory listing for CS103 would look like this:

```
Volume in drive A has no label
Directory of A:\CS103

.            <DIR>        5-29-90   11:02a
..           <DIR>        5-29-90   11:02a
INFO     TXT       5120   1-18-90   11:45a
REVIEW   TXT       6470   4-25-90   10:43a
CHAP01       <DIR>        5-29-90   11:04a
CHAP02       <DIR>        5-29-90   11:04a
CHAP03       <DIR>        5-29-90   11:05a
CHAP04       <DIR>        5-29-90   11:05a
CHAP05       <DIR>        5-29-90   11:05a
CHAP06       <DIR>        5-29-90   11:05a
CHAP07       <DIR>        5-29-90   11:05a
CHAP08       <DIR>        5-29-90   11:05a
CHAP09       <DIR>        5-29-90   11:05a
CHAP10       <DIR>        5-29-90   11:05a
      14 File(s)    704512 bytes free
```

This listing shows that the directory named "A:\CS103" contains two files, ten subdirectories labelled CHAP01 to CHAP10, plus two more DIR entries whose names are, respectively, one and two dots. Before we explain the "dot" entries, let's look at the other entries. Rules for naming subdirectories are the same as those for naming files, that is, up to eight characters followed by an optional extension using up to three characters. Notice that each name on the list is a legal file name.

Now, different subdirectories are permitted to contain files of the same name, so the subdirectory EN346 may also contain a file named INFO.TXT. To distinguish between names of files in different subdirectories, we use a complete **path name** that gives not only the file name but the disk and subdirectory where that file is located. Thus, the file INFO.TXT shown above has the path name

```
A:\CS103\INFO.TXT
```

whereas the INFO.TXT file in the EN346 subdirectory would have the path name

```
A:\EN346\INFO.TXT
```

To give the complete path name of a file, you begin with the drive name, then you list the sequence of subdirectories, starting with the root, until you reach the subdirectory containing the file, and finally you list the file name. Each name in the list is separated by the **backslash** symbol; the key for this is probably located either just above the Enter key (PS/2-style keyboards) or right next to the left Shift key (PC-style keyboards). Thus, the complete path name of a file named CH01EX01.BAS, in the CHAP01 subdirectory of CS103, would be (if the disk is in the A-drive):

```
A:\CS103\CHAP01\CH01EX01.BAS
```

To learn how to create and use subdirectories, let's have a hands-on session at the computer.

MACHINES WITH HARD DISKS

Equipment needed: The SAMPLES disk. We'll create subdirectories on the C-drive, and we'll copy files into them from the SAMPLES disk.

MACHINES WITHOUT HARD DISKS

Equipment needed: The SAMPLES disk and a data disk, preferably newly formatted. We'll create subdirectories on the data disk, and we'll copy files into them from the SAMPLES disk.

Step 1. See below for instructions on creating a subdirectory.

MACHINES WITH HARD DISKS

Let's create a subdirectory on the C-drive named BASIC. To do this, make the C-drive the *default* drive and then type the following DOS command:

```
C> MD BASIC
```

MD is short for "make directory." After entering this command, use the DIR command; you should see that a subdirectory named BASIC has been created on the hard drive.

MACHINES WITHOUT HARD DISKS

Let's create a subdirectory on the B-drive named BASIC. To do this, put the data disk in the B-drive and then make the B-drive the *default* drive. Next, type the following DOS command:

```
B> MD BASIC
```

MD is short for "make directory." After entering this command, use the DIR command; you should see that a subdirectory named BASIC has been created on the disk in the B-drive.

Step 2. Now, just as you are always assigned a *default drive* (which you can change by typing the new drive name), you are also assigned a **default (or current) directory** on each drive. Initially, the default directory on each drive is the root directory, but you can change the default directory on a given drive by using the DOS command **CD**, which is short for "change directory." Let's make the BASIC directory we just created the new default directory by typing the following DOS command:

```
> CD BASIC
```

Step 3. Now, if your *DOS prompt* shows only the drive name, you may not be able to tell if the CD command has accomplished anything. One way to check is to use the DIR command, which will show you the path name of the current directory and list any files it contains (the BASIC directory should be empty at this point). *Enter the DIR command.*

Step 4. Another way to keep track of the current directory is to make it be part of the DOS prompt. If your DOS prompt shows only the drive name, enter the following command to make it show the current drive (if the DOS prompt already shows the directory name, just skip this step):

```
> PROMPT $P$G
```

An explanation of "PG" would not be very illuminating, so let's just treat this command as a "magic incantation." If the incantation has worked, your DOS prompt should now display the full path name of the current drive.

MACHINES WITH HARD DISKS

If you created BASIC as a subdirectory of the root directory, your DOS prompt should now be:

```
C:\BASIC>
```

If your prompt is different, it's because your system has been set up in a special way; for the rest of this section, we'll assume that BASIC is a subdirectory of the root directory.

MACHINES WITHOUT HARD DISKS

If you created BASIC as a subdirectory of the root directory, your DOS prompt should now be:

```
B:\BASIC>
```

If your prompt is different, it's because your system has been set up in a special way; for the rest of this section, we'll assume that BASIC is a subdirectory of the root directory.

Step 5: Now, let's move back to the **parent directory**, that is, the directory of which this is a subdirectory (in this case, the parent happens to be the root directory). The parent directory is also called the directory **above** the current directory. To do this, we can use the CD command again, either with the full path name of the parent directory or with the following shorthand way of referring to the parent directory. Give it a try:

```
> CD ..
```

This command gives a clue to the "dot" entries in the subdirectory listing shown above. The **".."** entry refers to the *parent* of the current directory; the **"."** entry refers to the *current* directory itself. Thus, the command "CD ." means "change to the current direcory," that is, do nothing! Try it out if you like.

Step 6. See instructions below for returning to the BASIC directory.

MACHINES WITH HARD DISKS

Your DOS prompt should now indicate that your current directory is the parent of the BASIC directory, which should in fact be the root directory. Your DOS prompt should be:

```
C:\>
```

The symbol "\" by itself can be viewed as a name for the root directory, just as BASIC is the name of a subdirectory. Move *back* to the BASIC directory now by typing **CD BASIC**.

MACHINES WITHOUT HARD DISKS

Your DOS prompt should now indicate that your current directory is the parent of the BASIC directory, which should in fact be the root directory. Your DOS prompt should be:

```
B:\>
```

The symbol "\" by itself can be viewed as a name for the root directory, just as BASIC is the name of a subdirectory. Move *back* to the BASIC directory now by typing **CD BASIC**.

Step 7. Now, let's create two more directories, this time subdirectories of BASIC, to hold sample files for Workshops 1 and 2 of the text. *Enter the following three DOS commands*, being sure to do so *only* from the BASIC subdirectory:

```
> MD WORK01
> MD WORK02
> DIR
```

The directory listing should now show that two new subdirectories of the BASIC subdirectory have been created, namely, WORK01 and WORK02. The figure at the top of the next page shows a tree diagram of the subdirectories we've created so far.

Let's pause now to notice a few things about path names. A *complete* path name lists a drive name followed by a full sequence of parent subdirectories. Thus, no matter what our current drive and/or directory, the following command would give us a directory listing for the subdirectory CHILD of the directory PARENT, which is in turn a subdirectory of the root directory of a disk in the A-drive:

```
> DIR A:\PARENT\CHILD
```

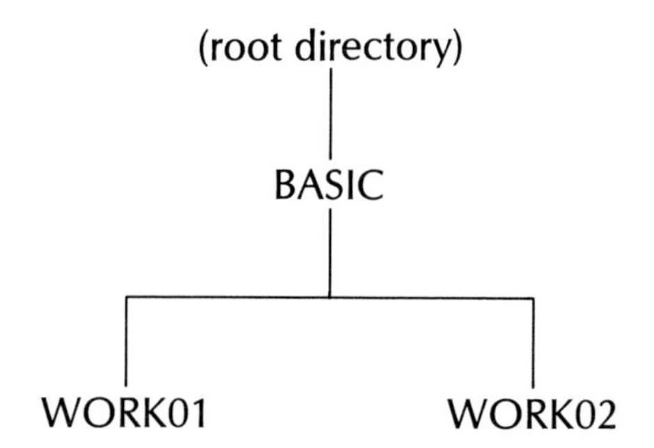

DOS also permits us to use *partial* path names, that is, path names that assume we are referring to subdirectories of the *current* drive or *current* directory. For instance, if our current drive was the A-drive and our current directory was A:\PARENT, we could type the following command to achieve the same effect as the previous one:

```
> DIR CHILD
```

Similarly, if we simply typed DIR with *no* path name, DOS would assume we were referring to the current directory. Using partial path names is a real convenience, but if you get an error message, it may be that your current directory and/or drive are not what you think they are.

Let's return now to the directories we've created, namely, a subdirectory of the root, named BASIC, and two subdirectories of that, named WORK01 and WORK02. In the next few steps, we'll copy appropriate files from the SAMPLES disk into these two subdirectories. Your current directory should be BASIC.

Step 8. With the SAMPLES disk in the A-drive, type:

```
> DIR A:
```

The list of 80 or so files should flash by on the screen. From Workshop 1, we know several ways to handle this problem. In this case, we're only interested in *some* of the files, namely, those in Workshop 1 and Workshop 2. Here's a way we can get the DIR command to give us exactly what we want:

```
> DIR A:\W*.*
```

You should get a listing of only those files whose names begin with *W*. The two asterisks (i.e., "*") in the above command are called *wild cards,* in the sense that they can stand for any string of characters. Thus, this command says to list those files (and subdirectories) that begin with *W*, and the rest of the name and its suffix can be anything at all.

We've tried to take advantage of the asterisk wild card in naming all the files on the SAMPLES disk: all the Workshop 1 files begin with W01, all the Workshop 2 files with W02, all the Chapter 1 files with C01, and so on. Now, list only the Workshop 1 files by typing:

```
> DIR A:\W01*.*
```

Step 9. See instructions below for copying files to a subdirectory.

MACHINES WITH HARD DISKS

With C:\BASIC still our current directory, let's copy all the Workshop 1 files into the WORK01 subdirectory. Here's one way to do it:

```
> COPY A:\W01*.* WORK01
```

This command says to copy all the files in the root directory of the A-drive that begin with W01 to the subdirectory WORK01 of the current drive and directory (i.e., C:\BASIC). To check whether the files were copied correctly, get a directory listing of the WORK01 subdirectory. Here are two different ways to do that, one using full path names, the other using partial path names:

```
> DIR C:\BASIC\WORK01

> DIR WORK01
```

Now, try typing **DIR** only; notice that the names of the subdirectories, WORK01 and WORK02, are listed, but their contents are *not*.

MACHINES WITHOUT HARD DISKS

With B:\BASIC still our current directory, let's copy all the Workshop 1 files into the WORK01 subdirectory. Here's one way to do it:

```
> COPY A:\W01*.* WORK01
```

This command says to copy all the files in the root directory of the A-drive that begin with W01 to the subdirectory WORK01 of the current drive and directory (i.e., B:\BASIC). To check whether the files were copied correctly, get a directory listing of the WORK01 subdirectory. Here are two different ways to do that, one using full path names, the other using partial path names:

```
> DIR B:\BASIC\WORK01

> DIR WORK01
```

Now, try typing **DIR** only; notice that the names of the subdirectories, WORK01 and WORK02, are listed, but their contents are *not*.

Step 10. See below for instructions on another way to copy files to a subdirectory.

MACHINES WITH HARD DISKS

Now, let's copy the Workshop 2 files to our WORK02 directory; but let's do it by first moving into that directory. With C:\BASIC the current directory, type

```
> CD WORK02
```

Your prompt should indicate that the new current directory is C:\BASIC\WORK02. If you type DIR, there shouldn't be any files there. Now, we can copy

MACHINES WITHOUT HARD DISKS

Now, let's copy the Workshop 2 files to our WORK02 directory; but let's do it by first moving into that directory. With B:\BASIC the current directory, type

```
> CD WORK02
```

Your prompt should indicate that the new current directory is B:\BASIC\WORK02. If you type DIR, there shouldn't be any files there. Now, we can copy the

the appropriate files from the SAMPLES disk by typing:

```
> COPY A:\W02*.*
```

We can leave the destination part of the COPY command blank since the destination is the current directory. Type **DIR** to be sure that the files have been copied correctly.

appropriate files from the SAMPLES disk by typing:

```
> COPY A:\W02*.*
```

We can leave the destination part of the COPY command blank since the destination is the current directory. Type **DIR** to be sure that the files have been copied correctly.

We now know how to create subdirectories and how to copy files from one directory to another. Just as we occasionally wish to delete a file, so we may sometimes wish to delete a subdirectory. There are two conditions that must hold in order to delete a subdirectory: first, the subdirectory to be deleted *cannot* be the *current* directory (this makes sense if you think about it—after all, where would you be if you deleted the current directory?); second, the subdirectory to be deleted *must* be *empty*, that is, it should not contain any files or subdirectories of its own. The second condition is there to protect you from accidentally deleting many files in one fell swoop.

Step 11. Let's prepare to delete the WORK02 directory (the current directory). First, we move *out* of this directory, say, to its parent:

```
> CD ..
```

Next, we delete all the files in the WORK02 subdirectory (of course, the order of these two actions could be reversed—we could first delete the files, then move out of the directory). We can use wild cards to delete all the files with one command:

```
> DEL WORK02\*.*
```

Whenever you try to delete *all* the files in a subdirectory, DOS will give you a chance to change your mind. Be sure to double check before you type *Y*; files that are deleted are gone forever!

Step 12. Once you've deleted all the files in the WORK02 subdirectory of the BASIC directory, use the DIR command to check that the subdirectory is empty:

```
> DIR WORK02
```

MACHINES WITH HARD DISKS

We're now ready to delete the WORK02 subdirectory. The command that deletes an empty directory is **RD**, which is short for "remove directory." To

MACHINES WITHOUT HARD DISKS

We're now ready to delete the WORK02 subdirectory. The command that deletes an empty directory is **RD**, which is short for "remove directory." To remove the (empty) WORK02 subdirectory, we can type

```
> RD WORK02
```

if the current directory is its parent, or

```
> RD C:\BASIC\WORK02
```

no matter what the current drive and directory is.

remove the (empty) WORK02 subdirectory, we can type

```
> RD WORK02
```

if the current directory is its parent, or

```
> RD B:\BASIC\WORK02
```

no matter what the current drive and directory is.

If you use the DIR command now, you should see that the WORK01 subdirectory still exists, but the WORK02 subdirectory should be gone.

For more practice working with subdirectories, begin by repeating Step 10 to recreate the WORK02 subdirectory; then, if you like, create one subdirectory of the BASIC directory for each of Chapters 1 through 10 (named, say, CHAP01, CHAP02, . . . , CHAP10) and copy into them the appropriate files from the SAMPLES disk. Below is a summary of the commands you'll need to work with subdirectories.

SUMMARY OF DOS COMMANDS USED WITH SUBDIRECTORIES

MD <*directory name*>: "Make directory," that is, create a directory with the specified name. The name must adhere to rules for file names and path names. If the name is a simple file name, the new directory will be a subdirectory of the current directory; path names can be used to create subdirectories of directories other than the current directory.

CD <*directory name*>: "Change directory," that is, make the specified directory be the new default directory. Type **CD ** to change to the *root* directory of the current drive; type **CD ..** to change to the *parent* directory of the current directory.

RD <*directory name*>: "Remove directory," that is, delete the specified directory. The directory to be removed must be *empty* (it may not contain any files or subdirectories), and it must not be the current directory.

PROMPT PG: Change the DOS prompt so that it shows the full path name of the current directory. The PROMPT command can actually be used to create a "customized" DOS prompt, containing a specified greeting, the time and date, and so on. If you'd like to learn how to do this, ask your teacher for a copy of the DOS reference manual.

ADDITIONAL FEATURES OF THE QuickBASIC SYSTEM

Introduction

As you begin to write longer and longer programs in QuickBASIC, you may find it handy to learn some other features of the system that make it easier to edit what you write; permit you to create "executable" versions of your programs that can be run at the DOS level; and allow you to use the QuickBASIC system as a simple word processor. In this appendix, we'll look briefly at all these features.[1]

Block Editing Techniques

So far, the only way we know to "edit" the text of our programs, that is, to change what we've already typed in, is to use the Delete or Backspace keys to erase characters one at a time and then type in the new text. It is actually possible to edit whole **blocks** of text at one time; for instance, it's quite simple to *mark* several lines of text, delete the marked section, and then reinsert it somewhere else in the program. To help you learn how to edit blocks of text, we'll use the hands-on style of Workshops 1 and 2 and Appendix 4.

Step 1 (getting started). To work through these steps, you'll need the QuickBASIC system and the SAMPLES disk. Start up QuickBASIC and open the program A05EX01.BAS on the SAMPLES disk; this is a simple little program that we'll use to illustrate block editing techniques. Read through the program and run it once or twice so that you know what it does.

Step 2 (marking text). Notice that, when we're editing a program, the cursor is always on a *single* character; if we use the directional keys (arrows, Home, End, etc.) we can move the cursor onto other (single) characters. Now, try moving the cursor right and left while pressing the **Shift** key; you'll see that you can highlight or "mark" a whole *block* of characters.

---

[1] We'll focus on features of the *Easy Menus;* with the aid of the QuickBASIC Help system, you can explore additional features of the *Full Menus* on your own.

Still holding the **Shift** key, press the **down arrow** several times; you should discover that this makes a block of *lines*. If you *release* the Shift key now, the block of lines should remain marked; to *unmark* the block, simply press an (unshifted) **arrow** key to move the cursor back onto a single character.

Step 3 (deleting blocks). Move the cursor onto the first quotation mark of the first PRINT statement; now mark all three characters after the word PRINT (i.e., the characters *"A"*) by holding down the **Shift** key and pressing the **right arrow** three times. *Release* the Shift key, leaving the block of three characters marked, and press the **Delete** key; this should delete the entire block of characters. Now, type the three characters back in (i.e., type **"A"**), so that the program will be back to its original form.

Step 4 (cutting blocks). When you use the Delete key to delete text (either a single character or a block), it's *gone forever*, so be careful! There is an alternative to deletion, called **cutting**, which removes text from the screen but *saves* it in an area of memory that is called a **buffer** or **clipboard**. Unlike deleted text, text that is cut can be retrieved and reinserted, or **pasted**, anywhere in the program. To cut rather than delete a section of text, we hold the **Shift** key while pressing **Delete**.

Move the cursor onto the first quote of the *second* PRINT statement; now, mark the whole string constant (including quotes); press **Shift-Delete** (i.e., hold the Shift key while pressing Delete). The effect looks just like regular deletion, but actually the text has been saved in the clipboard.

Step 5 (pasting text from the clipboard). If we wish to reinsert text that has been cut and saved in the clipboard, we simply move the cursor where we want to reinsert the text and press **Shift-Insert** (i.e., hold the Shift key while pressing the Insert key); press **Shift-Insert** *now* to reinsert the text in the position from which it was cut.

The contents of the clipboard remain the same until we cut some other segment of text (which will then replace it); thus, we can reinsert this text more than once and in more than one position, by repeatedly moving the cursor and then pressing **Shift-Insert**. *Move* the cursor to the end of the first PRINT statement (*PRINT "A"*) and press **Shift-Insert**. The text we cut from the second PRINT statement should be duplicated there. Notice that this first PRINT statement is now syntactically incorrect, because the two string constants should be separated by a semicolon or comma; if we move the cursor *off* the line containing the first PRINT statement, QuickBASIC's *Smart Editor* will make the correction by inserting a semicolon. Before moving on to the next step, delete the text you just inserted so that the program will be back to its original form.

Step 6 (cutting and pasting lines of text). Move the cursor to the *beginning* of the line that forms a border below the program heading (i.e., '-----------------------); while holding the **Shift** key, press the **down arrow** once to mark the entire line. Since most of our programs have this kind of border below *and* above the program heading, let's use cutting and pasting to enhance our program style. *Now,* press **Shift-Delete**; this will erase the line and save it in the clipboard. *Next,* without moving the cursor, press **Shift-Insert** to put the line back in its original position. *Finally,* move the cursor to the beginning of the very first line of the program and press **Shift-Insert** again to put a border at the top of our program heading.

There is actually a single keystroke (*Ctrl-Insert*) that will save a block to the clipboard *without* erasing it on the screen, but you may find it easier to remember the two keystrokes *Shift-Delete* (to cut) and *Shift-Insert* (to paste). You can also use the *Edit Menu* to cut and paste.

Let's pause for a moment to summarize what we've learned. To move blocks of text from one place to another is basically a three-step process: **mark**, **cut**, **paste**. To do this process in QuickBASIC, the moral of the story is *hold the Shift key!!* Namely,

Mark a block: *Shift* + *direction* keys
Cut a block: *Shift* + *Delete* key
Paste a block: *Shift* + *Insert* key

Of course, you may sometimes wish to simply delete a block rather than cut it, in which case you would use the unshifted Delete key. By the way, pressing the *unshifted Insert* key has an effect that you'll discover if you ever press it inadvertently. It acts as a toggle between two *editing modes,* called *Insert Mode* and *Overtype Mode.* In **Insert Mode**, if you place the cursor in the midst of some text and begin typing, the characters already there will be moved over to make room for the new characters you type; this is the default mode when you start up QuickBASIC. In **Overtype Mode**, new characters will simply wipe out any characters that were there previously. Remember that, if you accidentally get into Overtype Mode when you don't want it, pressing the Insert key will take you back to Insert Mode.

Indenting a whole block of lines at once is another block editing technique that can be useful. This comes in handy, for example, if you've written a segment of code and then decide to enclose the whole thing in a FOR...NEXT loop. To do it, you simply mark the lines and then press the Tab key. Let's try it.

Step 7 (block indenting). With the program A05EX01.BAS back in its original form, let's put a FOR...NEXT loop around the five PRINT statements (but *not* the CLS statement), so that the diagonal letters are printed *three times* on the same screen. To begin, use the **shifted arrow** keys to mark the five lines of PRINT statements (and then release the Shift key); these lines need to be indented one tab setting as the body of our FOR...NEXT loop. To do the indenting, simply press the **(unshifted) Tab** key: the entire block of lines should be indented. *With the five lines still marked,* try pressing the **shifted Tab** key; you should discover that this "outdents" the block, that is, moves it back to the previous tab position. Try a few Tabs and Shift-Tabs to see how they move the block back and forth, but be sure to finish with the block indented one tab setting in from its original position.

Now, we need to add the FOR line and the NEXT line. Move the cursor (unshifted) to the end of the CLS statement and press **<Enter>**; now, type in the line "**FOR count = 1 TO 3**." Then, move the cursor to the end of the *last* PRINT statement and press **<ENTER>**. Before typing the line "**NEXT count**," you should press **Backspace** to move the cursor to the previous tab position (or alternatively, type the line first and then outdent it by pressing **Shift-Tab**). When you're all done, the segment should look as follows. Be sure to *test* it to see that it works!

```
CLS
FOR count = 1 TO 3
    PRINT "A"
    PRINT "  B"
    PRINT "    C"
    PRINT "      D"
    PRINT "        E"
NEXT count
```

The very last thing we'll mention in this section on block editing is a single keystroke that lets you cut a whole line. The keystroke is **Ctrl-Y** (i.e., hold the **Ctrl** key while pressing **Y**), and it will cut (delete and copy to the clipboard) the line on which the cursor is resting. With the cursor on any line of the program, try pressing **Ctrl-Y** to cut the line and then **Shift-Insert** to put it back. This keystroke can be a handy shortcut when you have several lines to cut or delete; but *remember* that, as you begin to use these block editing techniques, *only* the *last* block that was cut is saved in the clipboard.

Keep the program A05EX01.BAS loaded, because we'll continue to work with it in the three brief sections that follow.

Searching for and Changing Text

The **Search Menu** in QuickBASIC provides tools for *finding* specified strings of text and for *replacing* one string with another. The option **Find...** in the Search Menu lets you type in a string; when you press <Enter>, QuickBASIC brings you to the *next* occurrence it finds of that string.

Step 8 (finding text). With the cursor anywhere you like, select the *Find...* option from the Search Menu and type the word **print** (upper or lowercase) in the box that appears; then press **<Enter>**. QuickBASIC will highlight the next appearance of the string *print* that it finds *below* the cursor position (it wraps around to the beginning if it doesn't find it below the cursor). This search is done without regard to upper and lowercase unless you select that option in the Find dialog box before pressing <Enter> (there is also an option that will only search for *whole word* occurrences, e.g., not highlighting *printing* when you search for *print* as a whole word).

You can repeat the search for *print* by selecting the Find option again, but the function key **F3** is a shortcut. Try pressing **F3** several times to see what we mean.

Step 9 (replacing text). To replace one string of text with another, you select the **Change...** option from the Search Menu. Let's try using it to put two commas after the word *PRINT* in each of the five PRINT statements (this will indent the diagonal output). Again, with the cursor anywhere, select the *Change* option from the Search Menu. This time, you'll have to type two strings: the string you want to change *and* the new string to replace it with. In the first field (labelled *Find What:*), type the word **print**; then use the **TAB** key to move to the second field (labelled *Change To:*) and type **print , ,** (the word *print* followed by two commas); finally, press **<Enter>.** QuickBASIC will take you to *every* occurrence of the string *print*, one by one, and give you the opportunity to change each one to *print , ,*. To make the change you press **C** (for "change," or you can press **<Enter>**); to leave an occurrence as is, you press **S** (for "skip"); to cancel the whole process, press **Esc** (as you would to cancel any menu option). The program has *seven* occurrences of the string *print*, two in comments (so they shouldn't be changed) and five in PRINT statements (so they should). QuickBASIC will tell you when the change is complete; when it is, be sure to *run* the program to see the effect of the change.

Making Executable Files

We hope that you'll write many programs in QuickBASIC that you'll find useful and enjoyable. If there is a program that you would like to be able to run from DOS, without having to start up the QuickBASIC system, you can create a file, called an **executable** file, containing the compiled version of your program (i.e., its translation into machine language). These files can be run from the DOS level by simply typing the file name as a DOS command. Let's try it.

Step 10 (getting ready). Before making an executable file, always be sure that your program is syntactically and logically *correct* by thoroughly *testing* it (see Chapter 4). Once you're satisfied with your program, you must *save* it (if you forget to do this, QuickBASIC will insist that you do it when you try to compile your program). So to begin, you should test and then save the file A05EX01.BAS (you can save it on one of your data disks). Since we've changed the original program (it now has a loop), let's save it under a different name, say, DIAGONAL.BAS. Once you've done this, you're ready to make an executable version.

Step 11 (making an executable file). To make an executable file from your program, you simply select the option *Make EXE File* from the Run Menu. When you do this, you'll see that a dialog box appears with a suggested name for your executable file, which is the same as the original file name except that the *.BAS* suffix has been replaced by *.EXE* (if you wish, you can type in a different name, but be sure to use the *.EXE* suffix); press **<Enter>** to *create* the executable file.[2] You'll see some information printed on the DOS screen while your program is being compiled; when the process is finished, you press any key to return to the QuickBASIC screen.

Step 12 (using an executable file). If your program was compiled successfully, a file named DIAGONAL.EXE should have been created. This file will be located on the drive (and subdirectory; see Appendix 4) from which you started QuickBASIC; you can use the DOS command COPY if you want to have the file copied somewhere else.

To try out DIAGONAL.EXE, you must be at the *DOS level*, so you should now *quit* QuickBASIC.[3] After doing this, check that the executable file has been created by typing the following (at the DOS level):

```
> DIR D*.*
```

This will list *all* files whose names begin with *D*; among them should be the following two files: DIAGONAL.EXE and DIAGONAL.OBJ. The second file, with the suffix *.OBJ* is an auxiliary file, which you can delete if you wish. To try out DIAGONAL.EXE, you simply type the main part of its name, DIAGONAL, as a DOS command (you can type the full name, including the *.EXE* suffix, but you don't have to):

```
> DIAGONAL
```

You should see the output of the program, followed by the DOS prompt.

Document Files

Now that you've learned most of QuickBASIC's convenient editing features, you may wish to occasionally use the system as a simple *word processor* to write letters or short papers, which you store as **text** (or **document**) files (a true word processor contains additional features like margin and paragraph formatting and the ability to change the look of characters by underlining, italicizing, etc.). The one complication here is QuickBASIC's *Smart Editor*, which is great if you're writing a BASIC program, because it automatically checks and corrects syntax (among other things). However, the odds of a letter to your parents being a syntactically correct BASIC program are very poor!

In Section 8.4, we talked about using the QuickBASIC editor to create sequential input files; since these are simply text files, the same procedures can also be used to create text files that *aren't* going to be used as input to programs. If you want to try this, you can use the

---

[2] If you're using QuickBASIC Version 4.0 or Full Menus in Version 4.5, you should select the option *Stand-Alone EXE File* before pressing <Enter>; this is the better choice for programs that are not very long.

[3] If you're using Full Menus, you could also choose the *DOS Shell* option from the File Menu.

five-step procedure outlined in that section (but ignore Step 3, which describes the way data files have to look). You may recall that the basic idea there is to *create* or *load* (but *not* open) a file as a *document*; these are options on the *File Menu* (using Full Menus in QuickBASIC Version 4.5).

SUMMARY OF ADDITIONAL QuickBASIC FEATURES

Block editing

Mark a block of text	*Shift* + *direction* keys
Cut a block (delete, but save in clipboard)	*Shift* + *Delete* (or *Cut* option on Edit Menu)
Paste a block (reinsert text from clipboard)	*Shift* + *Insert (or Paste* option on Edit Menu)
Indent/outdent a block	*Tab/Shift* + *Tab*

Searching and changing text (Search Menu)

Search for string	*Find...* option
Change one string to another	*Change...* option

Making executable files (Run Menu)

Create an executable file	*Make EXE File* option

SOLUTIONS TO THE PRACTICE EXERCISES

PRACTICE 1.1

1. (a) (new screen)
```
abracadabra
```
(new screen)

(b) (new screen)
```
1 + 2 + 3 + 4 =

10
```

(c)
```
ALABAMA
ARIZONA
```

(d)
```
CALIFORNIA
COLORADO
```

2.
```
'List of favorite movies
CLS
PRINT "Casablanca"
PRINT "Star Wars"
PRINT "Godfather Part 1"
END
```

PRACTICE 1.2

1. (a) valid numeric variable
   (b) valid numeric variable
   (c) not valid (it does not start with a letter)
   (d) valid string variable
   (e) not valid (it is a BASIC reserved word)
   (f) valid string variable
   (g) not valid (it is a BASIC reserved word)
   (h) not valid (it does not start with a letter)
2. Output:

(new screen)
```
This program computes your exam average.

Enter your last name: Quayle
Enter your first name: Dan

Enter three exam grades, separated by commas.
? 60,50,40

NAME: Dan Quayle
AVERAGE: 50
```

Variable values:

last$	Quayle
first$	Dan
exam1	60
exam2	50
exam3	40
average	50

PRACTICE 1.3

(a) 8.2
(b) 9
(c) HappySad
(d) 5.1
(e) 20
(f) 3
(g) Sad and Happy

PRACTICE 1.4

1. (a) 11.48
   (b) 8
   (c) 7
   (d) −9
   (e) −10
   (f) 9
   (g) 0
   (h) 1
   (i) 123.5
2. The formula's result for each value is, respectively, 4, 4, 3, 3, −2, −2, −2. It rounds *up*.

PRACTICE 1.5

1. (a) Goo (string)
   (b) Kirk (string)
   (c) yeM (string)
   (d) a1b2c3d4 (string)
2.
```
INPUT "Type in a word: ", word$
PRINT "Its first letter is "; UCASE$(LEFT$(word$, 1))
```

PRACTICE 2.2

1. (a)
```
Hello
Hello
Hello
Hello
```
   (b)
```
HelloHelloHelloHello
```
   (c)
```
0
2
4
6
8
10
```

2. (a)
```
FOR num = 3 TO 7
    PRINT num
NEXT num
```

(b)
```
FOR count = 1 TO 3
    PRINT "Fun!"
NEXT count
```

(c)
```
FOR num = 1 TO 6
    PRINT 5 * num;
NEXT num
```

PRACTICE 2.3

1.

`For i = 6 TO 10`	6, 7, 8, 9, 10
`FOR i = 1 TO 12 STEP 2`	1, 3, 5, 7, 9, 11
`FOR i = 4 TO 0`	none
`FOR i = 4 TO 0 STEP -1`	4, 3, 2, 1, 0
`FOR i = .2 TO 1.5 STEP .3`	.2, .5, .8, 1.1, 1.4

2. (a)
```
0
4
16
36
64
```

(b)
```
1 2 2 3 4
```

PRACTICE 2.4

1. (a) `20`

(b) `35`

(c) `81`

2.
```
LET sum = 0
FOR num = 1 TO 100
    LET sum = sum + num
NEXT num
PRINT sum
```

PRACTICE 2.5

1. (a)
```
1    1    1
2    2    2
3    3    3
4    4    4
```

(b)
```
1
2    2
3    3    3
4    4    4    4
```

(c)
```
0    0    0    0
0    1    2    3
0    2    4    6
```

2. (a)
```
FOR row = 1 TO 4
    FOR col = 1 TO 10
        PRINT "#";
    NEXT col
    PRINT
NEXT row
```

(b)
```
FOR row = 1 TO 4
    FOR col = 1 TO row
        PRINT "*";
    NEXT col
    PRINT
NEXT row
```

(c)
```
FOR row = 1 TO 4
    FOR col = 1 TO 5 - row
        PRINT "**";
    NEXT col
    PRINT
NEXT row
```

PRACTICE 2.6

1. (a)
```
 7
 3
-1
 2
```

(b) `BASIC`

(c) `60`

2.
```
READ numberOfWords
FOR count = 1 TO numberOfWords - 1
    READ word$
    PRINT word$; " ";
NEXT count
READ word$          'This is the last word.
PRINT word$; "."
```

PRACTICE 3.1

1. (a) `high`

(b) `1`

(c) `1  2  3  4  5  6  7  8  9  10  9  8  7  6  5  4  3  2  1`

2.
```
INPUT "Type in a number: ", num
PRINT "Your number is ";
IF num > 0 THEN
    PRINT "positive."
ELSEIF num = 0 THEN
    PRINT "zero."
ELSE
    PRINT "negative."
END IF
```

PRACTICE 3.2

1. (a) `maybe so` (c) `no`
   (b) `yes` (d) `no info`

2.
```
INPUT "What was your gross income? ", gross
IF gross <= 10000 THEN
    LET rate = 0
ELSEIF gross <= 25000 THEN
    LET rate = .15
ELSE
    LET rate = .24
END IF
LET tax = gross * rate
PRINT "Your tax this year is $"; tax
```

PRACTICE 3.3

1. (a) T (e) T
   (b) T (f) T
   (c) F (g) T
   (d) T

2.
```
LET sum = 0
FOR count = 1 TO 12
    INPUT num
    IF (num >= 0) AND (num <= 100) THEN
        LET sum = sum + num
    END IF
NEXT count
PRINT "The sum is"; sum
```

3.
```
INPUT "What is your favorite flavor of ice cream? ", answer$
IF (answer$ = "chocolate") OR (answer$ = "strawberry") THEN
    PRINT "I love that, too!"
ELSE
    PRINT "I'm not crazy about that."
END IF
```

PRACTICE 3.4

1. `This sure is fun!`

2.
```
INPUT "Type in a number from 2 to 20: ", number
PRINT "This number is ";
SELECT CASE number
    CASE 2
        PRINT "even and prime."
    CASE 4,6,8,10,12,14,16,18,20
        PRINT "even but not prime."
```

```
    CASE 3,5,7,11,13,17,19
        PRINT "odd and prime."
    CASE 9,15
        PRINT "odd but not prime."
    CASE ELSE
        PRINT "not in the specified range."
END SELECT
```

PRACTICE 3.5

1. Letting x be the number generated:
   (a) $17 \leq x < 22$ (any numbers)
   (b) $0 \leq x \leq 100$ (integers)
   (c) $-8 \leq x < 12$ (any numbers)
   (d) $-10 \leq x \leq 10$ (integers)
   (e) $0 \leq x < 1$ (any numbers)
   (f) $x = 0$ (integer)
2. (a) `100 * RND`
   (b) `INT(48 * RND + 18)`
   (c) `RND - .5`
   (d) `INT(46 * RND - 15)`

PRACTICE 3.6

1. flipping four coins
2.
```
RANDOMIZE TIMER
LET die1 = INT(6 * RND + 1)
LET die2 = INT(6 * RND + 1)
PRINT "You rolled"; die1; "and"; die2; "."
```

PRACTICE 4.4

1.
```
CLS
INPUT "Type in a number: ", num
IF num >= 0 AND num <= 10 THEN
LET num = num + 3
ELSE
    PRINT "Out of range!"
END IF
PRINT num
```
2.
```
LET product = 1
INPUT howMany
For k = 1 TO howMany
    INPUT num
    LET product = product * num
NEXT k
PRINT product
```

PRACTICE 4.5

1. The third line of the FOR...NEXT loop should be:

```
    LET headCounter = headCounter + 1
```

PRACTICE 5.1

1. (a)
```
3
4
5
6
7
```
(b)
```
3
4
5
6
```

2. (a)
```
Testing
```
(b)
```
Testing
Testing
Testing
   .
   .
   .
```
(infinite loop)

(c) no output

3.
```
DO
   INPUT "Type in a word: ", word$
   LET first$ = LEFT$(word$, 1)
LOOP UNTIL first$ = "n"
```

PRACTICE 5.2

1.
```
5.2
4.8
4.4
End.
```

2. It always results in an infinite loop.

3.
```
LET x = 1
DO WHILE x <= 10
    PRINT x;
    LET x = x + 1
LOOP
```
```
LET x = 1
DO UNTIL x = 11
    PRINT x;
    LET x = x + 1
LOOP
```
```
LET x = 1
DO
    PRINT x;
    LET x = x + 1
LOOP WHILE x <= 10
```
```
LET x = 1
DO
    PRINT x;
    LET x = x + 1
LOOP UNTIL x = 11
```
```
LET x = 1
DO
    PRINT x;
    LET x = x + 1
    IF x = 11 THEN
        EXIT DO
    END IF
LOOP
```
```
FOR x = 1 TO 10
    PRINT x;
NEXT x
```

PRACTICE 5.3

1. (a) `120` (b) `NBA`

2.
```
READ number             'Read the first number
LET big = number        'Use it to initialize big
DO                      'Now loop through the remaining data
    READ number
    IF number = -111 THEN
        EXIT DO
    ELSEIF number > big THEN
        LET big = number
    END IF
LOOP
PRINT "The biggest number in the list is"; big; "."
```

PRACTICE 5.4

1. (a) NO, no, no way, naboo
   (b) no, no way, nope, not a chance
2. Any noninteger (like 5.3, 4.72, etc.) is being trapped.
3.
```
PRINT "Type in 10 words starting with 't': "
FOR count = 1 TO 10
    DO
        PRINT "Word #"; count;
        INPUT word$
        IF UCASE$(LEFT$(word$, 1)) = "T" THEN
            EXIT DO
        ELSE
            PRINT "Try again: ";
        END IF
    LOOP
NEXT count
```

PRACTICE 6.3

(d)
```
SUB ExplainOperatingSystem

    PRINT "An operating system is a collection of programs"
    PRINT "that coordinate the various functions"
    PRINT "of a computer."

END SUB
```

PRACTICE 6.4

1. (a)
```
5    3
3    5
```

   (b) Parameters: *num1, num2*
   Arguments: *x, y*

   (c) It swaps the values of *num1* and *num2*.

2. (a)
```
Gr s
ae
Gog uh
```

(b) Parameters: *word$, num*
Arguments: *name$, 3, "abcde", x, name$, x − 2*

(c) It picks out and prints every "numth" character in *word$*, starting at the first character (e.g., if *num* is 3, it picks off the first, fourth, seventh, etc.).

PRACTICE 6.5

1. The arguments *x* and *y* are both passed by reference.
2. The arguments *names$* (twice) and *x* are passed by reference; *3, "abcde"*, and *x − 2* are passed by value.

PRACTICE 6.6

1. The variable *temp* is local to MysterySub.
2. The variable *i* is local to SecretSub.

PRACTICE 6.7

(a)
```
4
5
```

(b) It rounds *up*.

(c) Parameters: *num*
Arguments: *3.2, x* (also, −*num* is an argument of the INT function)
Local variables: none

(d) The argument *3.2* is passed by value; *x* is passed by reference.

PRACTICE 6.10

1. Changes in main program:

```
:
SELECT CASE termNum
    CASE 1
        CALL ExplainOperatingSystem
    CASE 2
        CALL ExplainSoftware
    CASE 3
        CALL ExplainProgrammingLanguage
END SELECT
:
```

New subprogram:

```
SUB ExplainProgrammingLanguage

    PRINT "A programming language is, like a 'natural' language,"
    PRINT "a set of words composed of symbols from some alphabet,"
    PRINT "together with rules of grammar and meaning. The difference"
    PRINT "between a programming language and a natural language (such"
    PRINT "as English) is that the 'sentences' in a programming language"
    PRINT "represent instructions to be carried out by a computer. Most"
    PRINT "programming languages must be translated into a language, called"
    PRINT "machine language, that can be understood by the computer."

END SUB
```

Change in subprogram ListTerms:

```
SUB ListTerms
    .
    .
    .
    PRINT
    PRINT " 1. Operating system"
    PRINT " 2. Software"
    PRINT " 3. Programming language"
    PRINT
    PRINT

END SUB
```

2. (a) Main program:

```
CLS
CALL PrintBye
END
```

Subprogram:

```
SUB PrintBye

  PRINT "Bye"

END SUB
```

(b) Main program:

```
CLS
CALL PrintHi
END
```

Subprogram:

```
SUB PrintHi

  PRINT "Hi"

END SUB
```

(c) Final main program:

```
CLS
CALL PrintHi
CALL PrintBye
END
```

PRACTICE 7.2

1. (a) Sets aside 25 memory locations labelled *price(1), price(2), . . . , price(25)* to hold numeric data and initializes each to 0.

   (b) Sets aside 1,000 memory locations labelled *lastName$(1), lastName$(2), . . . , lastName$(1000)* to hold string data and initializes each to the empty string.

   (c) Sets aside 201 memory locations labelled *num(−100), num(−99), . . . , num(100)* to hold numeric data and initializes each to 0.

2. `auto 4 sale`

3.
```
DIM num(1 TO 20)
FOR count = 1 TO 20
    INPUT num(count)
NEXT count
FOR count = 20 TO 1 STEP -2
    PRINT num(count)
NEXT count
```

PRACTICE 7.3

2. Selection Sort

34	23	56	7	24	13	21	37
7	23	56	34	24	13	21	37
7	13	56	34	24	23	21	37
7	13	21	34	24	23	56	37
7	13	21	23	24	34	56	37
7	13	21	23	24	34	37	56

Bubble Sort

34	23	56	7	24	13	21	37
23	34	56	7	24	13	21	37
23	34	7	56	24	13	21	37
23	34	7	24	56	13	21	37
23	34	7	24	13	56	21	37
23	34	7	24	13	21	56	37
23	34	7	24	13	21	37	56

23	7	34	24	13	21	37	56
23	7	24	34	13	21	37	56
23	7	24	13	34	21	37	56
23	7	24	13	21	34	37	56

```
7  23  24  13  21  34  37  56
7  23  13  24  21  34  37  56
7  23  13  21  24  34  37  56

7  13  23  21  24  34  37  56
7  13  21  23  24  34  37  56   Whew!
```

PRACTICE 7.4

1. (a) It sets aside 150 numeric variables named

```
num(1,1),   num(1,2), . . . , num(1,15),
num(2,1),   num(2,2), . . . , num(2,15),
:
num(10,1), num(10,2), . . . , num(10,15)
```

and initializes them all to 0.

(b) It sets aside 140 string variables named *item$(1,1,1)*, *item$(1,1,2)*, and so on up to *item$(4,7,5)*, and initializes them all to the empty string.

2. For answer to parts (a) and (b), see the following figure.

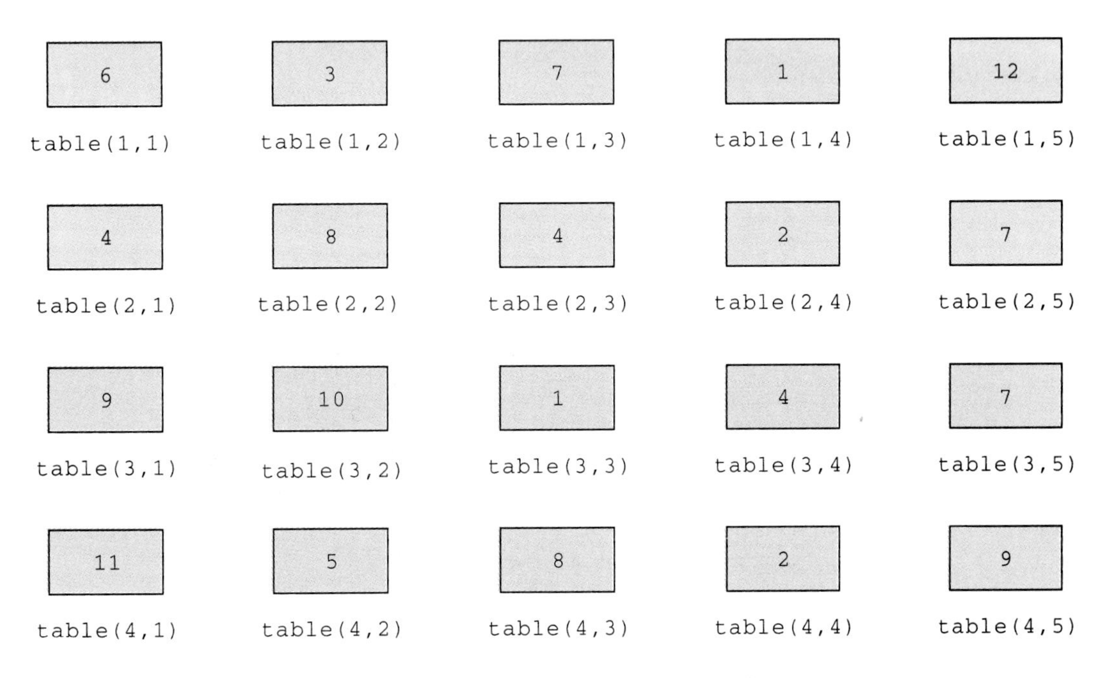

(c) The value is 17. (It adds up the "diagonal" values 6, 8, 1, and 2.)

PRACTICE 7.5

The value is 12. (The subprogram Rev reverses the order of the elements in the array *list*. Hence, after the subprogram executes, the new value of *list(4)* is the value fourth from the *end* of the data.)

PRACTICE 8.2

(a)
```
HELLO      33.5     GOODBYE
```

(b)
```
HELLO      33.5     GOODBYE
TODAY     -1243     TOMORROW
```

(c)
```
HELLO      33.5     GOODBYE
TODAY     -1243     TOMORROW
"HELLO",33.5,"GOODBYE"
```

(d)
```
"TODAY",-1243,"TOMORROW"
```

PRACTICE 8.3

1.
```
Hello Goodbye   13
Today           5
Tomorrow        8
```

A fourth time through the loop would produce an "Out of DATA" error.

2. (a) New data file:
```
4
Hello,Goodbye
Today,Tomorrow
```

New program:
```
OPEN "WORDS1.DAT" FOR INPUT AS #1
INPUT #1, howMany
FOR count = 1 TO howMany
    INPUT #1, word$
    PRINT word$
NEXT count
CLOSE #1
```

(b) New data file:
```
Hello,Goodbye
Today,Tomorrow
EOD
```

New program:
```
OPEN "WORDS1.DAT" FOR INPUT AS #1
DO
    INPUT #1, word$
    IF word$ = "EOD" THEN
        EXIT DO
    END IF
    PRINT word$
LOOP
CLOSE #1
```

(c) Data file:
```
Hello,Goodbye
Today,Tomorrow
```

New program:
```
OPEN "WORDS1.DAT" FOR INPUT AS #1
DO UNTIL EOF(1)
    INPUT #1, word$
    PRINT word$
LOOP
CLOSE #1
```

PRACTICE 8.5

(a) SINGLE
(b) STRING*15
(c) LONG
(d) SINGLE
(e) DOUBLE

PRACTICE 8.6

1.
```
TYPE CerealType
    brand AS STRING * 20
    cost AS INTEGER
    rating AS INTEGER
    calories AS INTEGER
END TYPE
```

Note: We cannot use *name* for the brand-name field because it is a BASIC reserved word.

2.
```
DIM cereal AS CerealType
```

3.
```
INPUT "What is the cereal's name? ", cereal.brand
INPUT "Cost (in cents per ounce)? ", cereal.cost
INPUT "Fiber content rating (1 - 5)? ", cereal.rating
INPUT "Calories per ounce? ", cereal.calories
```

4.
```
SELECT CASE cereal.rating
    CASE 5
        LET descrip$ = "excellent"
    CASE 4
        LET descrip$ = "good"
    CASE 3
        LET descrip$ = "fair"
    CASE 2
        LET descrip$ = "poor"
    CASE 1
        LET descrip$ = "bad"
END SELECT
PRINT RTRIM$(cereal.brand); " has "; descrip$;
PRINT " fiber content."
```

PRACTICE 8.7

1.
```
OPEN "CEREAL.DAT" FOR RANDOM AS #1 LEN = LEN(cereal)
```

2.
```
PUT #1, , cereal
```

3.
```
LET lastPos = LOF(1) / LEN(cereal)
```

4.
```
PRINT "Select a number from 1 to", lastPos;
INPUT ": ", pos
GET #1, pos, cereal
SELECT CASE cereal.rating
```

(and so on as in Practice 8.6, Exercise 4)

PRACTICE 8.8

1. `DIM SHARED cereal AS CerealType`
2.

```
SUB FindGood
'Prints out cereals in "CEREAL.DAT" with good or excellent
'fiber content.

    PRINT "The following cereals have good or excellent"
    PRINT "fiber content:"
    PRINT
    LET lastPos = LOF(1) / LEN(cereal)
    FOR pos = 1 TO lastPos
        GET #1, pos, cereal
        IF cereal.rating >= 4 THEN
            PRINT cereal.brand
        END IF
    NEXT pos

END SUB
```

PRACTICE 9.2

1. (a) `588` (d) `   $78.00`
   (b) `43.3` (e) `2,654,784.9`
   (c) `$   78.00` (f) `this i`
2.

```
LET f$ = "#####    \                \    $##.##    ##.#    $###.##"
PRINT USING f$; idNum, name$, wage, hours, wage * hours
```

PRACTICE 9.3

1. (a) It puts high-intensity white musical notes in each corner of a magenta-colored screen and then adds a blinking, high-intensity white star in the middle.
   (b) It draws a large, light-red *X*, using the character *X*, on a blue background on the left third of the screen.
2.

```
COLOR 14, 1, 1
CLS
RANDOMIZE TIMER
FOR twinkle = 0 TO 1
    COLOR 14 + 16 * twinkle
    FOR star = 1 TO 50
        LOCATE INT(25 * RND + 1), INT(80 * RND + 1)
        PRINT "*";
    NEXT star
NEXT twinkle
```

PRACTICE 10.2

1. (a) $P_1 = (-100,100)$ $P_2 = (0,0)$ $P_3 = (100,0)$
   $P_4 = (-50,-50)$ $P_5 = (100,-100)$

(b) $P_1 = (0,10)$ $P_2 = (10,5)$ $P_3 = (20,5)$
$P_4 = (5,5)$ $P_5 = (20,0)$

(c) $P_1 = (-1,1)$ $P_2 = (0,0)$ $P_3 = (1,0)$
$P_4 = (-.5,-.5)$ $P_5 = (1,-1)$

2. (a) 0 = light blue 1 = green 2 = red 3 = brown
(b) 0 = green 1 = cyan 2 = magneta 3 = high-intensity white
(c) 0 = black 1 = cyan 2 = magneta 3 = high-intensity white
(d) 0 = blue 1 = green 2 = red 3 = brown

PRACTICE 10.3

Every figure appears on a blue background.

(a) A single green dot located on the upper middle of the screen.
(b) A short red line starting just left of the center of the screen and extending upward and to the right.
(c) The outline of a small rectangle drawn in brown near the middle of the screen.
(d) A solid-green rectangle in the upper-right quarter of the screen.
(e) A small, solid-brown rectangle outlined in red in the upper-left quarter of the screen.
(f) A green circle of radius 15 centered at (20,−30) in the lower-right quarter of the screen.
(g) A section of a small, red circle, centered at the middle of the screen, starting in the upper-right quarter and circling counter-clockwise to the lower-right quarter of the screen.
(h) The segment of the circle that was left out in part (g), drawn in brown and with a radius drawn from the center to the lower edge of the segment.
(i) A green oval, vertically compressed, in the upper-left quarter of the screen.
(j) The upper half of a red oval, horizontally compressed, located in the center of the screen.

PRACTICE 10.4

Mode 1 (40 columns)

	Row	Column
P_1	1	1
P_2	13	20
P_3	13	40
P_4	19	10
P_5	25	40

Mode 2 (80 columns)

	Row	Column
P_1	1	1
P_2	13	40
P_3	13	80
P_4	19	20
P_5	25	80

PRACTICE 10.5

1. (a) to the right and up
   (b) to the left and up
   (c) to the right and down
   (d) to the left and down
   (e) right
   (f) down
   (g) no motion

PRACTICE 10.6

(a) A horizontal line drawn in blue across the middle of the screen, crossed by a vertical line drawn in red down the middle of the screen.

(b) A solid box in light cyan inside a solid box in light magenta, in the center of the screen.

(c) A circle of radius 30, drawn in high-intensity white, centered at the middle of the screen, with the inside region painted cyan and the outside region painted brown.

PRACTICE 10.7

1. (a) medium singing voice for just over one second
   (b) flute sound for just over half a second
   (c) low singing voice for just over one minute
   (d) whistle sound for just over a tenth of a second

2.
```
PLAY "o3 L8 F. L16 F L4 F C L8 A. L16 A L4 A F L8 F A >"
PLAY "L4 C. L8 C < B- A L2 G L8 G. L16 A L4 B- B- L8 A. L16 G"
PLAY "L4 A F L8 F. L16 A L4 G C L8 E. L16 G L2 F"
```

INDEX

Elements of Structured BASIC

Statements and Structures	Purpose	Section
' (single quote)	Remark	1.1
CALL <subprogram name>	Call named subprogram	6.2
CIRCLE (<x>, <y>), <radius>, <color>, <start>, <end>, <aspect>	Graphics: Draw circle or ellipse	10.3
CLOSE # <number>	Close data file	8.2
CLS	Clear the output screen	1.1
COLOR <foreground>, <background>, <border>	Text: Set output colors	9.3
COLOR <background>, <palette>	Graphics: Set output colors	10.2
DATA <list of constants>	List data for READ statement	2.6
DECLARE <name> (<parameter list>)	Declare subprogram or function	6.2
DIM <array name> (<first> **TO** <last>)	Declare an array	7.2
DIM <name> **AS** <type name>	Declare user-defined variable	8.6
DIM SHARED <name> **AS** <type name>	Declare global variable	8.8
DO...LOOP	Conditional loop	5.2
END	Indicate end of main program	1.1
EXIT DO	Leave a DO...LOOP	5.2
FOR...NEXT	Unconditional loop	2.2
FUNCTION <name>**...END FUNCTION**	Define function	6.7
GET # <file number>, <record number>, <variable>	Input from random-access file	8.7
IF...END IF	Decision structure	3.2
INPUT <list of variables>	Accept data from keyboard	1.2
INPUT # <file number>, <list of variables>	Input from sequential data file	8.3
LET <variable> = <expression>	Assign value to variable	1.2
LINE (<a>, <b>)-(<c>, <d>), <color>, <**B** or **BF**>	Graphics: draw line or box	10.3
LOCATE <row>, <col>	Move cursor to specified position	9.3
OPEN "<file name>" **FOR INPUT AS #**<file number>	Open sequential input file	8.3
OPEN "<file name>" **FOR** <**OUTPUT** or **APPEND**> **AS #**<file number>	Open sequential output file	8.2
OPEN "<file name>" **FOR RANDOM AS #**<number> **LEN = LEN(**<record variable>**)**	Open random-access file	8.7
PAINT (<x>, <y>), <color>, <border color>	Graphics: Paint region	10.3
PLAY <music string>	Play specified music	10.7
PRINT <list of values>	Print output on screen	1.1
PRINT #<file number>, <list of values>	Print to data file	8.2
PRINT USING "<format string>"; <values>	Print with given format	9.2
PSET (<x>, <y>), <color>	Graphics: draw point at (x,y)	10.3
PUT #<file number>, <record number>, <variable>	Output to random-access file	8.7
RANDOMIZE TIMER	Change start value of RND	3.5
READ <list of variables>	Accept data from DATA statement	2.6
RESTORE	Reset DATA to first item	2.6
SCREEN <mode number>	Select graphics mode	10.2, 10.6
SELECT...END SELECT	Decision structure	3.4
SOUND <frequency>, <duration>	Make specified sound	10.7
SUB <name> (parameter list)**...END SUB**	Define subprogram	6.2, 6.4
SWAP <variable>, <variable>	Swap values of two variables	8.8
TYPE...END TYPE	Define data type	8.6
WINDOW (<x1>, <y1>)-(<x2>, <y2>)	Set coordinate ranges for graphics	10.2
WRITE #<file number>, <list of values>	Write values to sequential file	8.2

Arithmetic Operators (Section 1.3)	+, -, *, /, ^ (exponentiate), \ (integer quotient), **MOD** (integer remainder)
String Operators (Section 1.3)	+ (concatenation)
Built-in Numeric Functions (Section 1.4)	**ABS, ATN, CINT, COS, EXP, FIX, INT, LOG, RND, SGN, SIN, SQR, TAN, TIMER**
Built-in String Functions (Sections 1.5, 8.6, 9.2)	**ASC, CHR$, LCASE$, LEFT$, LEN, LTRIM$, MID$, RIGHT$, SPACE$, RTRIM$, STRING$, TAB, UCASE$**
Built-in File Functions (Sections 8.3, 8.7)	**EOF, LOF**